Diversity Ideologies in Organizations

Since the increased attention toward diversity in the workplace, the concepts of "diversity initiatives" and "diversity management" have become commonplace in many conversations among academics and practitioners alike. The diversity movement in the workplace originated from the increased advocacy for equal treatment of minority groups due to the dynamic composition of the modern workforce. Many organizations were forced to face these changes and the dilemma of how to respond to group differences to maintain and/or increase organization effectiveness and productivity. This volume will present new research on the colorblindness versus multiculturalism debate, assist in broadening the diversity ideology conversation, share this conversation across social science domains including industrial/organizational psychology, social psychology, and law and public policy, and highlight how the nature of diversity ideology may be fluid and therefore differ depending on the diversity dimension discussed.

Kecia M. Thomas is Professor of Industrial/Organizational (I/O) Psychology at the University of Georgia and the founding director of the Center for Research and Engagement in Diversity (RED). She also serves as the Interim Associate Dean and the Senior Advisor to the Dean of the Franklin College of Arts and Sciences at the University of Georgia on matters related to inclusion and diversity leadership.

Victoria C. Plaut, a social and cultural psychologist, is Professor of Law and Social Science at UC Berkeley School of Law and a Faculty Affiliate in the psychology department at Berkeley.

Ny Mia Tran is currently a doctoral student in the Industrial/Organizational Psychology program at the University of Georgia. She received her B.S. in Psychology and Business Management from Georgia Southern University in 2007 and her M.S. from the University of Georgia in I/O Psychology in 2010.

SERIES IN APPLIED PSYCHOLOGY

Jeanette N. Cleveland, Colorado State University
Kevin R. Murphy, Landy Litigation and Colorado State University
Series Editors

Edwin A. Fleishmann, Founding series editor (1987–2010)

Winfred Arthur, Jr., Eric Day, Winston Bennett, Jr., and Antoinette Portrey
Individual and Team Skill Decay: The Science and Implications for Practice

Gregory Bedny and David Meister
The Russian Theory of Activity: Current Applications to Design and Learning

Winston Bennett, David Woehr, and Charles Lance
Performance Measurement: Current Perspectives and Future Challenges

Michael T. Brannick, Eduardo Salas, and Carolyn Prince
Team Performance Assessment and Measurement: Theory, Research, and Applications

Neil D. Christiansen and Robert P. Tett
Handbook of Personality at Work

Jeanette N. Cleveland, Margaret Stockdale, and Kevin R. Murphy
Women and Men in Organizations: Sex and Gender Issues at Work

Aaron Cohen
Multiple Commitments in the Workplace: An Integrative Approach

Russell Cropanzano
Justice in the Workplace: Approaching Fairness in Human Resource Management, Volume 1

Russell Cropanzano
Justice in the Workplace: From Theory to Practice, Volume 2

David V. Day, Stephen Zaccaro, and Stanley M. Halpin
Leader Development for Transforming Organizations: Growing Leaders for Tomorrow's Teams and Organizations

Diversity Ideologies in Organizations

Edited by

Kecia M. Thomas

Victoria C. Plaut

Ny Mia Tran

Routledge
Taylor & Francis Group

NEW YORK AND LONDON

First published 2014
by Routledge
711 Third Avenue, New York, NY 10017

and by Routledge
27 Church Road, Hove, East Sussex BN3 2FA

Routledge is an imprint of the Taylor & Francis Group, an informa business

Library of Congress Cataloging in Publication Data
Diversity ideologies in organizations/[edited by] Kecia M. Thomas,
Victoria Plaut, Ny Tran.
  pages cm
  1. Diversity in the workplace. 2. Organizational behavior.
  I. Thomas, Kecia M.
  HF5549.5.M5D568 2014
  331.13′3—dc23
  2013030286

ISBN: 978-1-84872-965-0 (hbk)
ISBN: 978-1-84872-966-7 (pbk)
ISBN: 978-1-315-85218-8 (ebk)

Typeset in Minion by
Florence Production Ltd, Stoodleigh, Devon, UK

Printed and bound in the United States of America by Sheridan Books, Inc. (a Sheridan Group Company).

Contents

Series Foreword

Jeanette N. Cleveland
Colorado State University

Kevin R. Murphy
Landy Litigation and Colorado State University
Series Editors

The goal of the Applied Psychology Series is to create books that bring together research, scholarly insight, and practice to address issues that are of concern to both psychologists and to the broader society. The volumes in this series offer publications that emphasize state-of-the-art research and its application to important issues of human behavior in a variety of societal settings. The objective is to bridge both academic and applied interests.

In this volume, *Diversity Ideologies in Organizations*, Kecia Thomas, Victoria Plaut and Ny Mia Tran, bring together a collection of scholars to examine the underlying assumptions and (perhaps) unintended consequences or correlates of two implicit models of diversity management, colorblindness and multiculturalism. The colorblind diversity model suggests that race or skin color should be hidden or not noticed. However, as documented among the chapters, by ignoring race or color and thus ignoring differences, the colorblindness model may enhance more covert discrimination in organizations. The second model that is explored throughout this volume is multiculturalism, which seeks to identify, explain and recognize difference. One goal of the volume is to understand how these two ideologies in organizations may either undermine or enhance interracial interactions. In addition, this volume attempts to identify parameters that may be used to assess ideology effectiveness.

Kecia Thomas—editor of previous Applied Psychology Series volume *Diversity Resistance in Organizations*—and her coeditors have brought together other leaders and innovators in the field of diversity management. In Chapters 1–7 of this volume, key issues associated with employee experiences within largely colorblind and multicultural organizations are presented. Using both existing theoretical frameworks (e.g., Attraction–Selection–Attrition) and multiple levels of analysis, the chapters deal with minority member experiences within either a colorblind or multicultural organization, racial denial among dominant group members, and color minimization and color cognizance. In addition, diversity ideology is explored within the context of how individuals and organizations deal with past injustices (e.g., slavery) as well as through the lens of discrimination based on gender and sexual orientation. Chapters 8–10 focus on the evolving diversity ideologies and subsequent practices within the US military, impact of diversity ideology on worker feelings of inclusion and trust, and how the social psychological literature can be applied to integrate both unity and diversity at the same time. The book concludes with three chapters (11–13) that identify ways to evaluate the effectiveness of these diversity ideologies as well as the generalizability of the discussion to other countries including the UK, Germany, and South Africa.

Special features of this edited volume are the inclusion of chapters that address the different levels of analysis reflected in diversity ideologies in organizations (e.g., interpersonal relationship, group interactions, and organizational effects) as well as lessons gleaned from multiple sub-disciplines of psychology. The book provides a balanced treatment of practical and scientific issues and concludes with the extension of such ideologies to other dimensions of diversity including gender and sexual orientation as well as to other work environments such as the military and internationally. This book will apply to social scientists and students, but it is also highly relevant to managers and executives in organizations. We regard this book as a highly significant publication in a critically important area of industrial/organizational psychology. It should be required reading for researchers in this area and for practitioners who oversee human resource practices in organizations. We are extremely happy to add *Diversity Ideologies in Organizations* to the Applied Psychology Series.

Preface and Acknowledgments

The article, "Is multiculturalism or colorblindness better for minorities?" (Plaut, Thomas, & Goren, 2009), began the editors' journey into delving more deeply into the issue of diversity ideologies in organizations. In that short piece published in *Psychological Science*, we used field data to investigate the implications of Whites' beliefs around diversity for the ethnic minorities in their workgroups. We found that beliefs were important for others' outcomes. Whites' beliefs in minimizing race were linked to lower minority co-worker engagement. In contrast, Whites' beliefs in attending to and supporting diversity showed the opposite relationship, more engagement. In fact, minorities in these workgroups sensed less bias, which helped explain their greater engagement.

This research brief received a lot of attention. Several large media outlets covered this research and the *Chicago Tribune* even created a special interactive blog focused on this research. Plaut and Thomas did a number of interviews, even an extensive radio session on Diversity Matters. Clearly we had struck a chord. Our community of diversity scholars and the public at large wanted to discuss, debate, and learn more about diversity ideologies. Many people thanked us for bringing these issues to light. Perhaps most important in this evolving discussion have been the revelations that there are many different diversity ideologies and most come from a desire to do what is right, to be fair.

In the spring of 2010 Tran and Thomas chaired a symposium on diversity ideologies at the annual meeting of the Society for Industrial Organizational Psychology (SIOP). The standing room only audience was deeply engaged in our conversation as different teams of researchers presented their work on diversity ideologies, color minimization, racial denial, and negotiating space in work environments that some considered "post-racial." The enthusiasm for the session was not easily contained. In fact, for most of the diversity sessions held for the remainder of the conference, the topic of diversity ideologies and our symposium again emerged. It was there that the collaborators became editors and decided that there was much more to discuss and that an edited volume was warranted.

This volume presents research that was presented in that 2010 symposium as well as other research and ideas from colleagues across disciplines, industries, and the world. Our goal for *Diversity Ideologies in Organizations* is not to have the final word on how ideologies promote or resist organizational diversity. Instead we hope to stimulate more thought and consideration of how ideologies and belief systems, often well meaning, can create opportunities for diversity to flourish and subsequently improve organizational functioning and personal outcomes or how beliefs might restrict and stigmatize diversity in ways that impair organizational effectiveness and individual growth. We also hope the audience will consider the nuances of diversity ideologies across various dimensions of diversity such as race, gender, sexual orientation, and other identity dimensions. As a society we have implicit beliefs about different groups that shape not only our attitudes, but reactions, practices, and policies too. The acceptability of various ideologies likely also depends upon the environments in which they are employed. Therefore, by discussing diversity beliefs across organizational types we also hope to encourage more consideration of how "place" matters.

We are indebted to the authors who have shared their hard work and insights with us in the production of this volume. Not only did each author team submit their work for inclusion in this volume, but they also took time to provide substantive reviews of other chapters in the volume. Their hard work and persistence in this task is greatly appreciated. Likewise, our external reviewers were equally instrumental in providing constructive feedback. Therefore, we would like to thank Vernon Andrews, Leslie Ashburn-Nardo, Donna Chrobot Mason, Richard Crisp, Barbara Gutek, Lt. Col. Shirley Raguindin, Robert Sleight, and Sabrina Volpone-Kouns, for their time and thoughtful reviews. Students involved in the Center for Research and Engagement (RED) at the University of Georgia and the Culture, Diversity, and Intergroup Relations Lab at the University of California, Berkeley provided useful dialogue and critique of our ideas as they began forming. Finally, we are extremely grateful for the Routledge team, including Anne Duffy, editor, and Elizabeth Lotto for their consistent support and encouragement without which this volume may not have been completed.

REFERENCES

Plaut, V. C., Thomas, K. M., & Goren, M. J. (2009). Is multiculturalism or color blindness better for minorities? *Psychological Science, 20*(4), 444–446.

About the Editors

Kecia M. Thomas is Professor of Industrial/Organizational (I/O) Psychology at the University of Georgia and the founding director of the Center for Research and Engagement in Diversity (RED). She also serves as Interim Associate Dean and the Senior Advisor to the Dean of the Franklin College of Arts and Sciences at the University of Georgia on matters related to inclusion and diversity leadership. Her work focuses on understanding systems of privilege and resistance that limit the career development of women, people of color, and gay and lesbian workers, as well as the learning and effectiveness of the institutions in which they are employed. She is author of *Diversity Dynamics* (Wadsworth-Thomson)—the first I/O psychology textbook on workplace diversity—and numerous book chapters, and peer reviewed articles in diverse outlets such as the *Journal of Applied Social Psychology*, *Journal of Applied Psychology*, and *Psychological Science*. She also served as the editor of *Diversity Resistance in the Workplace* (LEA–Taylor & Francis) and a special issue of the *Journal of Career Development* on Black Women as Organizational Outsiders Within. She is an elected Fellow of both the Society for Industrial & Organizational Psychology and the American Psychological Association. Dr. Thomas holds undergraduate degrees in psychology and Spanish from Bucknell and her M.S. and Ph.D. from The Pennsylvania State University.

Victoria C. Plaut, a social and cultural psychologist, is Professor of Law and Social Science at Berkeley School of Law, where she directs the Culture, Diversity, and Intergroup Relations Lab and teaches courses on the psychology of diversity and discrimination. She is also a faculty affiliate in the psychology department at Berkeley. Her research on diversity, culture, and inclusion addresses the challenges and opportunities of working, living, and learning in diverse environments. Recent projects include studies related to diversity climate, diversity resistance, perceptions of inclusion, colorblind vs. multicultural models of diversity, gender diversity and recruitment, and models of deafness and disability, among others. She has contributed her social psychological expertise on diversity in amicus briefs to the U.S. Supreme Court and has consulted on diversity issues for a wide range of clients including school districts, universities, corporations, law firms, and health-care organizations. She earned her B.A. in Psychology from Harvard University, M.Sc. in Social Psychology from the London School of Economics, and Ph.D. in Psychology from Stanford University.

Ny Mia Tran is a doctoral candidate in the Industrial/Organizational Psychology program at the University of Georgia. She received her B.S. in Psychology and Business Management from Georgia Southern University in 2007 and her M.S. from the University of Georgia in I/O Psychology in 2010. Her research interests broadly focus on diversity in the workplace. Her most recent research includes professional women of color, diversity ideology in organizational settings, and diversity training/teaching. She also teaches an undergraduate course on cultural diversity and served as a doctoral research intern at the American Institute for Managing Diversity (AIMD) and Fors Marsh Group LLC.

Contributors

Laura G. Barron holds a Ph.D. in I/O Psychology from Rice University, where her research focused on the efficacy of employment anti-discrimination laws. Currently a Personnel Research Psychologist with the U.S. Air Force, Dr. Barron is responsible for development and validation of selection and classification assessments, including cognitive and non-cognitive measures for the Air Force Officer Qualifying Test (AFOQT) and Test of Basic Aviation Skills (TBAS). Previously an Assistant Professor of Psychology in the University of Wisconsin system, she has published widely on workplace diversity issues in the *Journal of Applied Social Psychology, Industrial and Organizational Science: Perspectives on Science and Practice, Rehabilitation Psychology, Journal of Workplace Rights, Psychology, Public Policy, and Law*, and *Human Performance*.

Cori M. Bazemore is a Ph.D. student in the University of Georgia Industrial–Organizational Psychology Program. She hails from the Seneca Nation of Indians and has extensive experience in the recruitment and retention of Native American college students. Her current research focuses on tokenism and the ethnic minority experience in the workplace. She plans to work in an applied setting helping organizations with diversity and other group issues as well as with tribal organizations.

Tamara R. Buckley earned an M.A. in organizational psychology and a Ph.D. in counseling psychology from Columbia University, Teachers College. Before returning to graduate school, Dr. Buckley worked in investment banking and consulting, having earned a B.S. in business administration from U.C. Berkeley. She is a New York State Licensed Psychologist. Dr. Buckley teaches both clinical and didactic courses in the graduate counseling program. As a professor, she focuses on helping students to integrate theoretical and self-knowledge with multicultural factors. Dr. Buckley has taught the following courses: theories of counseling, foundations of school counseling, clinical supervision, counseling skills, and multicultural aspects of counseling. Dr. Buckley's research program focuses on building knowledge and awareness of racial/cultural factors in health and health promotion and diversity in organizations. Dr. Buckley has received numerous awards for her research including an in-residence Visiting Scholars Fellowship at the Russell Sage Foundation (2007–2008) and the Carolyn Payton Early Career Psychology Award, from APA, Division 35, Psychology of Black Women. Her research has been funded by the National Institutes of Health and the City University of New York: PSC-CUNY, Faculty Fellowship Publications Program, Junior Faculty Development Award, and George N. Shuster Faculty Fellowship. Her publications include peer-reviewed articles in counseling and health psychology and management, and various chapters in edited volumes. Dr. Buckley also has three web-based publications based on research funded by the Ford Foundation's Leadership for a Changing World initiative.

Christina Stevens Carbone is completing her Ph.D. in the Jurisprudence and Social Policy Program at the University of California, Berkeley. She also holds a J.D. from Berkeley Law and a B.A. in psychology from Berkeley. Her research interests lie at the intersection of psychology and the law, focusing particularly on judgment and decision making, implicit and explicit bias, diversity, discrimination, and organizations. Some of her recent work examines the effect of diversity ideologies on hiring decisions and institutional strategies to attenuate the influence of cognitive biases in decision processes.

Ruth K. Ditlmann is a Postdoctoral Fellow at the WZB Social Research Center Berlin, Germany. Her research focuses on the role of cultural and historical narratives and how they affect intergroup dynamics, particularly across cultures and subcultures. Her research also examines how implicit motives affect communication strategies in interracial and interethnic dialogues about past injustice. Dr. Ditlmann received her Ph.D. in Social Psychology from Yale University in 2012 and Diploma in Psychology from the University of Constance, Germany in 2007.

Erica Gabrielle Foldy is an Associate Professor of Public and Nonprofit Management at the Wagner Graduate School of Public Service at New York University. She is affiliated faculty with the Research Center for Leadership in Action, based at Wagner, and with the Center for Gender in Organizations at the Simmons School of Management in Boston. Professor Foldy's research addresses the question: What enables and inhibits working and learning together across potential divisions such as race and gender? She is interested in how cognitive processes, such as framing and sense-making, affect our ability to connect with others, and how leaders act as "sensegivers" to affect their constituents' capacity for joint work. Professor Foldy has roughly two dozen publications, including articles in *Academy of Management Learning and Education, Leadership Quarterly,* and *Journal of Public Administration Research and Theory,* among other journals, and a variety of book chapters. She also co-edited the *Reader in Gender, Work and Organization.* She holds a B.A. from Harvard College and a Ph.D. from Boston College, and was a Post Doctoral Fellow at Harvard Business School in 2002–2003. During the 2007–2008 academic year, she was a Visiting Scholar at the Russell Sage Foundation.

Heather Foster is an Atlanta native and she holds a degree in Education and Social Policy from Northwestern University. She has served for years as a local and national catalyst for faith-based, nonprofit, and government collaboration to improve schools and revitalize communities.

Kerrin E. George is a 2013 graduate of the Industrial–Organizational Psychology program at the University of Georgia. She received her B.A. in Psychology from the University of Connecticut in 2008 and her M.S. from the University of Georgia in 2011. Her research has focused primarily on organizational diversity management and its implications for minority inclusion in the workplace. Currently, she is examining the implications of transformational leadership behaviors for shaping organizational diversity management ideologies. She has also worked as an organizational consultant for both non-profit and Fortune 100 organizations. Dr. George currently works at the corporate headquarters of Home Depot.

Matt J. Goren is a Ph.D. candidate in the Social–Personality Psychology Program at the University of California, Berkeley. His research addresses issues related to organizational and inter-personal diversity, using theory and research to answer practical questions. More specifically, he studies how colorblindness, multiculturalism, and White racial identity can affect attitudes about diversity, interracial cooperation, and interracial relationships. He also studies ways in which organizations can encourage and best manage diversity, such as diversity training, climate for diversity, and diversity policies and initiatives. He has published his research in

Psychological Science, Self and Identity, and presented it at national social and industrial/organization conferences. He also has a strong background in statistics and research methodology and has consulted with various organizations including the Food and Drug Administration. Mentoring and teaching are also important to Mr. Goren. He has taught statistics and methodology in psychology, mentored dozens of undergraduate research assistants, and has helped many to begin their own graduate careers. As an undergraduate, Mr. Goren majored in psychology with minors in history and statistics at the University of Florida, where he received his bachelor's degree, summa cum laude.

Adam Hahn is currently a post-doctoral fellow in Bertram Gawronski's Social Cognition Lab at the University of Western Ontario in London, Ontario, Canada. Adam received his *Diplom* (German M.A. level degree) from *Freie Universität Berlin* in Germany in 2007, receiving part of his training at Yale University. He subsequently joined the University of Colorado Ph.D. Program in social psychology, and received his M.A. in 2009, and his doctorate in 2012. Adam continues collaboration with all of these institutions today. He is a member of, and his training and research have been funded by, the German national academic foundation and the German Academic Exchange Services DAAD. His research focuses on the social-cognitive roots of intergroup relations. Adam's works has focused on introspection and awareness of implicit evaluations people may hold towards social groups, the meaning of social categories, and the meaning of national identities and values for intergroup relations.

Holly A. Haynes is an Associate Professor of Behavioral Sciences at Truett-McConnell College. She completed her bachelor's degree in history and science at Harvard College and went on to complete her master's and doctoral degrees at Harvard University in human development and psychology, respectively. During the completion of these degrees, she was involved in research on mother–child relationships and early childhood trauma with Boston's Children's Hospital, The California Endowment, and the Harvard Graduate School of Education.

Michelle R. ("Mikki") Hebl is a Full Professor in the Industrial–Organizational Psychology program at Rice University. She graduated with her B.A. from Smith College and her Ph.D. at Dartmouth College, and joined the faculty at Rice University in 1998. As an applied psychologist, Mikki's research focuses on workplace discrimination and the barriers stigmatizing individuals, as well as the ways both individuals and organizations might remediate discrimination. Mikki has more than 85 publications to her credit, but simultaneously stresses her passion and commitment to teaching. She has been the recipient of 13 teaching awards and currently serves as the Society for Industrial Organizational Psychology's (SIOP) Educating and Training Chair.

Andrea Holyfield is the Director of Career Services at Georgia Perimeter College. She is primarily responsible for the Center's internal functions, managing the experiential education program. She sits on the board of the Georgia Career Development Association and is active in a variety of other professional organizations. She has a bachelor's in journalism and mass communications from Kent State University and a master's in professional counseling from Georgia State University.

C. Douglas Johnson is a Professor of Leadership and Management at Georgia Gwinnett College. He received his B.S. in accounting from Clemson University, an MBA in human resources from the University of Connecticut, and a M.S. and Ph.D. in industrial/organizational psychology from the University of Georgia. During his academic career, he has published and/or presented over 100 papers. His research focuses on social capital, careers, diversity, and the experiences of organizational outsiders within (individuals who have been marginalized, harassed, or discriminated against). He has published in outlets such as the *Academy of Management Learning and Education, Journal of Vocational Behavior,* and *Educational and Psychological Measurement.* He is editor of the book *Social Capital: Theory, Measurement, and Outcomes,* and co-editor of the forthcoming book, *Intersectionality and Student-Centered Learning.* He is a past Associate Editor and editorial board member for the *Business Journal of Hispanic Research,* and has served in various leadership capacities within the Academy of Management, Kappa Alpha Psi Fraternity, and the community. He is committed to personal and professional development through mentoring activities, and has received awards for his teaching, student engagement, scholarship and creative activities, service, and professional achievements.

Karsten Jonsen is a Research Fellow in Organizational Behaviour at IMD, Switzerland. He earned his M.Sc. in Economics from CBS in Copenhagen,

MBA from ESCP–EAP in Paris, France and a Ph.D. from the University of Geneva. His research interests include team performance, virtual teams, stereotyping, research methodology, career mobility, cross-cultural communication, gender and workforce diversity: published in journals such as *Journal of International Business Strategy*, *Human Relations* and *British Journal of Management*. Dr. Jonsen has served as advisor to large corporations in the field of workforce diversity and he is the winner of the Carolyn Dexter Award for best international research paper at the Academy of Management 2010.

Charles M. Judd is College Professor of Distinction in the Department of Psychology and Neuroscience at the University of Colorado at Boulder. He was previously on the faculty at Harvard University and the University of California, Berkeley. He has published extensively both in social psychology and also in quantitative methods in psychology. He is the past editor of the *Journal of Experimental Social Psychology* and is currently the editor of the *Journal of Personality and Social Psychology: Attitudes and Social Cognition*.

Eden B. King joined the faculty of the I/O Psychology program at George Mason University after earning her Ph.D. from Rice University in 2006. Eden pursues research that seeks to guide the equitable and effective management of diverse organizations. Eden has published over 50 books, chapters, and articles that integrate organizational and social psychological theories in conceptualizing social stigma and the work–life interface. This research addresses three primary themes: 1) current manifestations of discrimination and barriers to work–life balance in organizations, 2) consequences of such challenges for its targets and their workplaces, and 3) individual and organizational strategies for reducing discrimination and increasing support for families. In addition to her academic positions, Dr. King has consulted on applied projects related to climate initiatives, selection systems, diversity training programs, and has worked as a trial consultant. She is currently an Associate Editor of both the *Journal of Management* and the *Journal of Business and Psychology*.

Eric D. Knowles is an Assistant Professor of Psychology at New York University. He received his Ph.D. in Psychology from the University of California, Berkeley. His research examines how people perceive and react to the fact that some groups in society have more than others. He is especially interested in how different types of motivations—e.g., to bolster the hierarchy, to see oneself as a good and deserving person—lead people to deny the existence of inequity, dis-identify with their ingroup, or form attitudes likely to reduce intergroup disparities.

Daniel P. McDonald is the Director of Research for the Defense Equal Opportunity Management Institute (DEOMI) located on Patrick Air Force Base. During his tenure, DEOMI's research mission has expanded not only to include traditional equal opportunity topics, but also to encompass vital work in the areas of cross-cultural competence, diversity management, strategic planning, and consultation DoD wide. Dr. McDonald has worked as a research psychologist and consultant for the DoD since 1993, with tenure at the U.S. Army Research Institute, U.S. NavalAviation Enterprise, and lastly the Navy's Human Performance Center before coming to DEOMI. Throughout his career he has focused on improving individual and organizational performance through human-centered methodologies and applied research. He has managed large acquisition R&D projects in support of the development of simulation and training systems and human systems integration. His previous work also focused on development of measurement methodology, implementing human factors design and engineering, applying organizational development strategies, conducting evaluations/experimentation, and providing workshops and consultation on measurement and teamwork for a variety of DoD and non-DoD agencies. Dr. McDonald was also an adjunct professor at the University of Central Florida teaching research and statistical methods in psychology.

Larry R. Martinez is a 2012 graduate of the I/O Psychology Ph.D. program at Rice University. He graduated with his B.A. from Rice University and earned his master's degree from Rice University in 2010. Larry's research focuses on interpersonal stigmatization that minority group members experience such as women in academia and adult employees who have survived childhood cancer. Larry also has a passionate interest in examining the workplace experiences of GLBT employees. Dr. Martinez is currently an assistant professor in the School of Hospitality Management at Penn State.

Elena Wright Mayville received her bachelor's degree from Stanford University and is a Ph.D. candidate in clinical psychology at Yale University who is researching emotion regulation and interpersonal interactions. She is currently completing her pre-doctoral clinical internship at the New York–Presbyterian/Weill Cornell Medical Center.

Joel T. Nadler (Ph.D., 2010, Applied Psychology, Southern Illinois University Carbondale) is an Assistant Professor in the I/O psychology program at Southern Illinois University Edwardsville. His research focuses on social cognition, stereotypes, and social roles and he is interested in explicit and implicit gender bias in selection and performance appraisal, sexual harassment, organizational attractiveness, adverse impact (EEO law), and assessing inclusive diversity practices. Additionally, Dr. Nadler has expertise in advanced measurement, design and statistical techniques. His research has been published in journals such as *Industrial Organizational Psychology: Perspectives on Science and Practice, Sex Roles, Social Issues and Policy Review, Journal of Applied Social Psychology, American Journal of Evaluation,* and *Journal of Leadership and Organizational Studies.* Dr. Nadler is a member of the SIOP, and The Society for the Psychological Study of Social Issues (SPSSI). Dr. Nadler teaches I/O Psychology, Personnel Selection, Employee Development, Test and Measures, graduate and undergraduate Research Design and Statistics, Social Psychology, and Psychology of Gender.

Stella M. Nkomo is a Professor in the Department of Human Resource Management at the University of Pretoria, South Africa. Her internationally recognized work on race and gender and managing diversity appears in numerous journals and edited volumes and she is listed in the International Who's Who in the Management Sciences. She is co-author with Professor Ella L. J. Bell of the critically acclaimed Harvard Business School Press book, *Our Separate Ways: Black and White Women and the Struggle for Professional Identity.* In 2009, she received the Sage Scholarly Contributions Award (Academy of Management) for her contributions to gender and diversity research in organizations. She is an Associate Editor of the *British Journal of Management.* Her current research projects include a study of gender representation and company performance in South Africa and how multicultural women become authentic leaders.

Ana P. Nunes is a post-doctoral fellow at the Institute of Social Sciences of the University of Lisbon, Portugal. Dr. Nunes received her doctorate in social psychology at the University of Colorado Boulder.

Her research interests focus on person perception processes and the effect of diversity mandates on judgments and behavior, especially in high-stake decision contexts such as hiring. She formerly directed testing studies of housing discrimination for Project Sentinel in Palo Alto, CA, and employment discrimination studies for the Discrimination Research Center in Berkeley, CA.

Mustafa Özbilgin is a Professor of Organisational Behaviour and Human Resource Management at Brunel University London. He also holds chairs at Université Paris-Dauphine, and Koç University in Istanbul. His research is on equality, diversity and inclusion at work. He is the editor in chief of the *British Journal of Management*. He has published in *Academy of Management Review, Human Resource Management, Human Relations, Journal of Vocational Behavior,* and *Social Science and Medicine,* among others. He has authored and edited 11 books. His research is supported by grants from national and international agencies, professional bodies, and government departments.

Bernadette Park is Professor of Psychology and Neuroscience at the University of Colorado at Boulder. She received her doctorate at North-western University in 1985, and has been a faculty member at the University of Colorado for the past 25 years. She is a Fellow of the American Psychological Association, as well as a fellow of Division 8 (The Society for Personality and Social Psychology) and Division 9 (The Society for the Psychological Study of Social Issues) of the APA. She is also a member of The Society of Experimental Social Psychology. Professor Park has served as both the Editor (Jan. 2003–Dec. 2005), and as an Associate Editor (1990–1994) for the *Journal of Experimental Social Psychology*. She is currently serving as an Associate Editor for *Personality and Social Psychology Review*. Her research has appeared in the top Social Psychology outlets, including the *Journal of Personality and Social Psychology,* the *Journal of Experimental Social Psychology, Personality and Social Psychology Bulletin,* and *Personality and Social Psychology Review*. She has also published in *Psychological Review*. She was the 2009 recipient of the Donald W. Fiske Distinguished Lecturer Award, and the 2001 Thomas M. Ostrom Person Memory Interest Group Award. Her research has been continuously funded by the National Science Foundation and/or the National Institutes for Health. Prof. Park's areas of expertise include work on stereotype and intergroup relations, strategies for prejudice reduction, understanding the role of the self in managing work–family conflicts, and person perception and impression formation.

Kizzy M. Parks was recently recognized by *Profiles in Diversity Journal* as a Women Worth Watching®. Dr. Parks is President of K. Parks Consulting, Inc. (KPC), a rapidly growing, SBA 8(a) certified, minority woman-owned small business, headquartered in Melbourne, FL with satellite locations in Orlando, FL and DC. Founded in 2005, KPC specializes in diversity and inclusion, analytics and metrics services, training and development, and workforce consulting to help organizations reach higher results. The firm brings both consulting experiences and research-based problem-solving to assist in developing solutions for diverse organizations. Dr. Parks is also heavily involved in research focusing in diversity and inclusion management, work–life balance, and organizational wellness and effectiveness. Her published work includes an active blog with *Diversity Executive Magazine*, recent articles in the *Journal of Occupational Health Psychology* and the *Business Journal of Hispanic Research*. She has an edited book titled *Managing Diversity in the Military: The Value of Inclusion in a Culture of Uniformity*.

Valerie Purdie-Vaughns is an Assistant Professor of Psychology at Columbia University and Director of the Intergroup Relations and Diversity (IRDL) Lab. She holds positions as core faculty for the Robert Wood Johnson Health & Society Scholars and fellow for the Institute for Research on African American Studies (IRAAS) at Columbia. Her research focuses on the role of identity in academic and workplace settings and how threats to one's group undermine the achievement of under-represented groups. Her most recent work examines how stigma affects biological stress systems that undermine long-term health and designs interventions to mitigate the negative effects of identity-based stress.

Jeanine L. Skorinko is an Associate Professor of Psychology at Worcester Polytechnic Institute in the Department of Social Science and Policy Studies. She received her Ph.D. in Social Psychology at the University of Virginia. Her research program attempts to understand how factors in our social environment, especially those factors we are unaware of, influence decisions and interpersonal interactions. She investigates how different types of external and internal influences (e.g., social tuning, stereotypes/ stigmas, the ability to perspective take, cultural orientation) affect attitudes, decisions, and interactions. She is particularly interested in how these factors influence decisions and relationships within the legal and organizational domains. Ultimately, she aims to promote and enhance equality, diversity, and cultural understanding. She also enjoys teaching and mentoring students. Dr. Skorinko's work has appeared in *Journal of Applied Social Psychology*, *Journal of Experimental Social Psychology*, and *Psychology and Marketing*, among many others.

Margaret (Peggy) S. Stockdale (Ph.D., 1990, Industrial and Organizational Psychology, Kansas State University) is a Fellow of the American Psychological Association, Professor, and Chair of Psychology at Indiana University–Purdue University Indianapolis. Her primary research concerns gender issues in the workplace, primarily sexual harassment. Her research articles have appeared in *Psychology, Public Policy and the Law, Law and Human Behavior, Psychology of Women Quarterly, Journal of Vocational Behavior, Basic and Applied Social Psychology, Psychology of Men and Masculinity*, among others. In addition, she is co-author/editor of five books. Peggy is also an active applied psychology consultant, having conducted training programs for major corporations, local agencies, and businesses, and serving as an expert witness for sex discrimination in employment cases.

Ahu Tatli is a senior lecturer in the School of Business and Management at Queen Mary University of London, UK. The focus of her research is equality and diversity at work. Her empirical research explores strategies of the key equality actors, intersectionality of disadvantage and privilege in organizational settings, diversity management, agency and change in organizations, and inequality and discrimination in recruitment and employment. She has widely published in edited collections, practitioner and policy outlets, and international peer-reviewed journals such as *Academy of Management Review, British Journal of Management, Canadian Journal of Administrative Sciences, European Journal of Industrial Relations, Entrepreneurship and Regional Development, International Business Review, Human Relations*, and *International Journal of Management Reviews*.

Miguel M. Unzueta is an Associate Professor of Management & Organizations at the UCLA Anderson School of Management. He received his

Ph.D. in Organizational Behavior from the Stanford Graduate School of Business. His research explores how people understand their position within social and interpersonal hierarchies and the impact this understanding has on their perceptions of self, others, and group-based inequality. His latest research explores the manner in which members of majority and minority racial groups define the concept of diversity.

Joana Vassilopoulou is a Lecturer in Organisational Behaviour and Human Resource Management at the School of Business, Management and Economics, University of Sussex. She received her Ph.D. degree from Norwich Business School, University of East Anglia on the organizational habitus of managing ethnic diversity in Germany. Her research interests include the management of ethnic diversity, discrimination at work, race and racism, immigration and integration in Europe, gender and race inequalities at work, talent management, global diversity management and social and organizational change. She has published in edited collections and journals such as the *European Journal of Industrial Relations*, *International Business Review* and the *International Journal of Human Resource Management*.

1

Diversity Ideologies in Organizations

An Introduction

Victoria C. Plaut, Kecia M. Thomas,
Ny Mia Tran, and Cori M. Bazemore

As diversity researchers and practitioners, we have come across many implicit models, philosophies, and worldviews of how diversity *should be* managed in organizations. These models of thinking and subsequently addressing and managing diversity are all around us—in our laws, in our organizations' mission statements, websites, advertisements, college and university hiring and admissions guidelines, and even in the daily interactions that make up our work environments. For example, when discussing increasing interest in recruiting a more racially diverse student body, a supportive colleague at one of our institutions mentioned that the role of diversity in higher education is to teach "them" to be more like "us." This fleeting and even well-intentioned comment was very informative in sharing that person's belief that a more racially diverse student body would need to be altered or somehow fixed in order to become more like the ingroup—a change likely perceived as desirable.

On another occasion, a doctoral student who was interning at the headquarters of a major company with a bold official stance on diversity complained that she did not "fit" in her new workplace. As a highly educated woman of color she was used to having conversations with peers about a wide range of topics, some of them dealing with issues such as race, gender, or sexuality. However, in her new work environment those topics were off limits. Even discussing the issue of school rezoning in their urban area and its potential impact upon the education of minority youth was not allowed during informal lunchtime conversation. The company sent the message that some things should not be discussed, even

1

when another institution is the focus. Issues around diversity and equity simply were silenced despite the organization's aggressive diversity mission statement.

Both of these incidents reflect implicit models of diversity that silence differences, and in fact in the second example, may actually make the mere thought about the reality of differences taboo (Schofield, 1986; D. A. Thomas, 1989). Taboos can be particularly pernicious because they inherently involve covert agreements to not consider or think about an issue, and therefore subsequently to not *do* anything about the issue.

This book seeks to document ways in which diversity models and ideologies operate in organizations and create particular challenges and opportunities for the pursuit of equality and inclusion. Implicit diversity models and ideologies are not new; however, in the past couple of decades social scientists have directed renewed attention to this area to better understand the conditions under which diversity in organizations—and even integration in a larger societal sense—are most effectively supported. For example, frequently U.S. ideologies around diversity have worked to silence conversations around difference and have actually worked to downplay and minimalize differences. Thomas, Mack, and Montagliani (2004) discuss three U.S. ideologies that on the surface seem to support diversity but at their foundation promote diversity resistance (K. M. Thomas, 2008).

For example, the (myth of) meritocracy ideology suggests that *everyone* has an equal opportunity to succeed and accomplish the American dream if they simply work hard enough. What the myth of meritocracy actually does is to hide the systemic ways in which historic legacies of slavery, Jim Crow laws, segregation, and legalized discrimination have created generational barriers to "making it" that are frequently ignored. The explicit message of equal opportunity and the implicit silencing of the reality in which marginalized groups struggle for upward mobility create the illusion that all is well and that the few marginalized group members who succeed are the "good ones," while those who do not are simply not good enough.

Another mixed-message diversity ideology portrays the United States as a melting pot. Like the meritocracy ideal, the melting pot is also a myth. At its core, portraying the United States as a melting pot would mean that everyone who immigrated to the US, voluntarily or involuntarily, equally gave up and contributed their own culture in order to create a *new* American identity. Yet the reality is more the expectation of immigrant assimilation. Today the pressure to assimilate is most clearly seen in immigration debates, English-only language policies, and a recent spate of restrictive state legislation and local ordinances throughout the nation. The pressure to assimilate (and often the mistaken impression that a group is not integrating) comes down particularly hard on the least valued and most marginalized ethnic groups (Chavez, 2008).

Colorblindness is the final American ideology discussed by Thomas and colleagues (2004), and this particular ideology speaks most directly to the theme of this volume. The colorblind ideal explicitly stipulates that as Americans we should not notice skin color. The message is that to notice differences would be bad and make one vulnerable to prejudiced thoughts and/or discriminatory behavior. As Supreme Court Justice O'Connor put it:

> [Racial] classifications of any sort pose the risk of lasting harm to much of our society. They reinforce the belief, held by too many for too much of our history that individuals should be judged by the color of their skin.
>
> (Shaw v. Reno, 1993)

The result, however, has been to diminish recognition of color (and inherently differences in general) while simultaneously normalizing and privileging whiteness as the cultural default (Jones, 2001). Of course, as stated earlier, our concern is that dismissing differences becomes a process by which those differences also become a taboo as well as a source of stigma.

Another concern that arises is that it is simply impossible to *not* notice skin color, yet the colorblind ideal allows individuals to use skin color in making evaluations and decisions, while perpetuating the perception that they are not. For example, a robust literature in implicit social cognition suggests that individuals hold automatic and often unconscious biases that can result in discriminatory behavior (see Jost et al., 2009). Additionally, aversive forms of contemporary racism that rely upon attribution ambiguity and actors' lack of self awareness, are likely fueled—or at least left undetected—by this colorblind ideal (see Pearson, Dovidio, & Gaertner, 2009). Ultimately, colorblindness may create the conditions under which covert modern subtle forms of discrimination can flourish.

More recent conversations in the social science literature, especially in psychology, have positioned colorblindness against another ideological stance, multiculturalism (e.g., Wolsko, Park, Judd, & Wittenbrink, 2000;

for reviews see Plaut, 2010; Plaut, Cheryan, & Stevens, in press; Rattan & Ambady, 2013). Whereas colorblindness seeks to silence and hide differences, multiculturalism seeks to identify, articulate, and use differences. O'Brien and Gilbert (2013) discuss diversity ideologies as either hierarchy enhancing or hierarchy attenuating. This language seems to fit the colorblind–multiculturalism distinction well (but see Levin et al., 2012 who define both as hierarchy attenuating; and Knowles, Lowery, Hogan, & Chow, 2009, who suggest both hierarchy-enhancing and attenuating uses of colorblindness). Colorblindness is hierarchy enhancing in that it avoids challenging the status quo and thus maintains historic and social systems that foster social dominance inside and outside organizations. In contrast, multiculturalism seeks to question these social dominance hierarchies and instead disrupts this process by seeking to understand the strengths and hidden talents within our differences. One of our goals for this volume is to understand how ideologies in organizations, especially workplaces, undermine diversity through hierarchy enhancing belief systems and system justifying actions (or perhaps the lack of action), as well as identifying the hierarchy attenuating practices that may exist.

In this book we and other authors use diversity ideologies, models, and other similar terms relatively interchangeably. For example, Wolsko et al. (2000) used the term interethnic ideologies (e.g., colorblindness and multiculturalism), which formed two sides of the ideological debate over how to "achieve the peaceful and mutually satisfactory coexistence of diversity cultural and ethnic groups" (p. 635). Building in part on historian George Fredrickson's (1999) work on models of U.S. ethnic relations, Plaut (2002) defined models of diversity as "shared understandings and practices of how groups come together or should come together, relate to one another, and include and accommodate one another in light of the differences associated with group identity" (p. 368). Plaut highlighted four models—sameness, common identity creation, value-added, and mutual accommodation—the former focusing on minimizing difference and the latter two acknowledging difference. Jones (1998) wrote about models and strategies that collide in the "New American Dilemma," characterized by a conflict between the principle of equality without regard to race (race neutrality) and the belief that taking race into account is necessary in order to bring about racial equality (race consciousness).

Focusing more on what is being communicated to employers and students, others have used terms such as diversity philosophies (Purdie-

Vaughns, Steele, Davies, Ditlmann, & Crosby, 2008) and messages (Apfelbaum, Pauker, Sommers, & Ambady, 2010). And working more specifically within organizational behavior, others have used terms such as paradigms (Thomas & Ely, 1996). While these terms may vary in their level of analysis (e.g., individual, organizational, societal) or their relative emphasis on cultural beliefs and ideas, power structures, and policies and practices, all of them highlight beliefs about how diversity *should* operate.

SOCIAL PSYCHOLOGY OF DIVERSITY IDEOLOGIES

In one of the earliest social psychological investigations of colorblindness, Schofield (1986) conducted an ethnography in a racially integrated school. Through interviews, observation, and experiments, she revealed many ways in which teachers, administrators, and students claimed that they did not notice race or act on the basis of race. Yet, Schofield also observed in classrooms, hallways, the cafeteria, and on the playground, that race actually mattered quite a bit in interactions, disciplinary practices, and other behaviors. She concluded that not only did the colorblind perspective make it easier for discrimination to occur, but it also worked against the creation of opportunities to provide students of color with an effective education.

Social psychologists have also used a variety of procedures to study diversity ideologies in laboratory experiments. For example, they have used essay prompts (Wolsko et al., 2000) or survey items (Morrison, Plaut, & Ybarra, 2010) to expose people to colorblind versus multicultural ideologies. Individuals in these studies subsequently complete a variety of tasks, ranging from implicit and explicit stereotyping and prejudice measures (Richeson & Nussbaum 2004; Ryan, Hunt, Weible, Peterson, & Casas 2007; Wolsko et al., 2000), to rating how much they like an outgroup member who does or does not conform to group stereotypes (e.g., a Black student who enjoyed country dancing and surfing; Gutiérrez & Unzueta, 2010), to interacting with a peer of a different race (Vorauer, Gagnon, & Sasaki, 2009), to making a judgment about how universities should allocate their budget to underrepresented student organizations (Morrison et al., 2010). In many (but not all) of these studies, colorblindness contributes to more support for inequality.

In another study (Apfelbaum et al., 2010), researchers showed elementary schoolchildren a video in which a teacher advocated for racial equality by focusing on sameness and the unimportance of race (the colorblindness frame) or difference and the value of difference (the value diversity frame). They then had them report the presence of racial discrimination in scenarios involving varying degrees of ambiguity. Children exposed to colorblindness were subsequently less likely to perceive discrimination than children exposed to the value diversity frame, even when the incident was *explicitly* racial.

Some studies in this area have investigated the implications of diversity ideologies for employees or students of color. For example, Plaut, Thomas, and Goren (2009) examined the relationship between White employees' endorsement of colorblindness and multiculturalism and the psychological engagement of their co-workers of color. This work suggested that when working in departments where Whites were more inclined toward racial colorblindness, employees of color detected more bias and felt less committed to their work and organization; the reverse was found in departments where Whites supported diversity. Holoien and Shelton (2012) followed up this work in the laboratory, finding that Black and Asian college students who interacted with a White partner who had been exposed to a colorblind message (by reading an editorial) experienced more cognitive depletion than their counterparts who had interacted with a White partner who had been exposed to multiculturalism. In other words, for students of color, interacting with a White peer who was at least temporarily in a colorblind mindset was more mentally taxing than interacting with a White peer in a multicultural mindset.

The interracial interaction studies that focus on Whites' (or dominant group members') behavior have also, on balance, found detrimental effects of colorblindness (e.g., Apfelbaum, Sommers, & Norton, 2008; Holoien & Shelton, 2012; Vorauer et al., 2009). For example, in the study described above, Holoien and Shelton found that Whites who had been exposed to a colorblind message were perceived by coders who were students of color to be more prejudiced than Whites exposed to a multicultural message. In another study (Vorauer et al., 2009), Whites exposed to a colorblind message behaved more negatively toward their outgroup interaction partner, in part because they were trying to prevent the exchange from going badly! Those exposed to a multicultural message, in contrast, showed more positive, other-directed behavior toward their outgroup interaction partner.

While the social psychological studies cited above tend to suggest negative effects of a color-minimizing approach for intergroup relations and disadvantaged group outcomes, it is important to note that not all studies have pointed in this direction. For example, Levin et al. (2012) found colorblindness to be related to *lower* individual orientations toward social dominance and support for inequality. Likewise, the research has not shown that we should straightforwardly expect improvements in intergroup relations and disadvantaged group outcomes from a multicultural approach. For example, the positive effects of multiculturalism may diminish or even reverse in circumstances of threat or conflict (Correll, Park, & Smith, 2008; Vorauer & Sasaki, 2011). Moreover, multiculturalism may backfire by provoking resistance in advantaged group members who see multiculturalism as excluding them (e.g., Stevens, Plaut, & Sanchez-Burks, 2008), by unfairly expecting conformity to outgroup stereotypes (Gutiérrez & Unzueta, 2010), or by prompting other ineffective or harmful practices (Purdie-Vaughns & Walton, 2011).

Two other psychological literatures have also made large contributions to the study of different approaches to diversity. For example, cross-cultural psychologists have long studied acculturation attitudes and strategies in among cultural groups in plural societies (e.g., Berry, 1984). Also, counseling psychologists have produced a voluminous literature on multiculturalism and colorblindness. This work has suggested, for example, that people high in colorblind racial attitudes (such as discounting the presence of racism in society), score higher on a number of prejudice measures (Neville et al., 2000) and exhibit more apathy toward racially offensive images (Tynes & Markoe, 2010).

ORGANIZATIONAL DIVERSITY MODELS

Much of the scholarship around diversity models has taken place within workplaces. Diversity is now a legitimate and frequent organizational concern for most organizations not only because of federal affirmative action and equal employment opportunity mandates but also because of the changing nature of both the available labor pool as well as the consumer market. To not pay attention to the diversity of those who do the work and those who consume the goods and services would be threatening to organizational effectiveness and longevity. Yet, as organizations pay attention to diversity, they do so from a particular standpoint or philosophy that subsequently drives both formal management practices as well as the informal structure of the organization, which in turn teaches and informs individual workers of their value and perhaps even their future prospects. Some organizations may present themselves as equitable and inclusive in mission statements and other verbiage, and actually aggressively recruit underrepresented talent, yet practice "blanket" human resource development policies that ignore historic and social legacies and subsequent manifestations of exclusion that demand continuing attention to the development and professional support of those very workers. In some organizations this is a matter of *not* practicing what they preach, but for others it is a matter of good intentions not being fully put into practice (Thomas & Plaut, 2008).

Two of the most well-known theories of organizational diversity come from Cox (1991) and Thomas and Ely (1996). Each describes organizations as pursuing different diversity goals and enacting different practices depending upon the diversity belief system in place. According to Cox (1991), most companies in the United States fall into one of three common categories of cultural identity: monolithic, plural, or multicultural. Similarly, Thomas and Ely (1996) suggest that companies tend to invest in one of three common diversity paradigms: discrimination-and-fairness, access-and-legitimacy, and learning-and-effectiveness.

Monolithic companies have a low cultural identity (Cox, 1991). They are very homogeneous, consisting of mostly White male employees with high levels of occupational segregation, or containing demographic fault-lines (Lau & Murninghan, 1998) in which most female and ethnic minority employees occupy only the lower level positions in the organization. Implicitly, minority employees are expected to assimilate to the cultural norm of the dominant employees and intergroup conflict based on cultural differences is usually high. The organization places little to no value on the resources that ethnic minorities can bring and thus these employees lack feelings of inclusion or engagement with the company (Cox, 1991).

Likewise, the discrimination-and-fairness paradigm also focuses on colorblindness and assimilation. Typically in this type of organization employees are viewed as being exactly the same and differences are to be diminished. Minorities in these organizations are expected to blend in to keep from receiving special or unfair treatment. Employees are discouraged from incorporating their culturally based differences and perspectives, thus limiting their effectiveness, engagement, and personal identification with their work. Using this model "actually undermines the organization's capacity to learn about and improve its own strategies, processes, and practices" (Thomas & Ely, 1996, p. 82), therefore also limiting the organization's full potential.

What is interesting about these organizations in particular is that they are not actively seeking to undermine diversity. In fact, they are often preoccupied with diversity recruitment as the major tactic by which to have a diverse workforce. It is their lack of action once they employ an underrepresented worker and the lack of attention to workers' professional and developmental needs that result in the manifestation of colorblindness. The organization may have the mindset that treating all people the same is fair, and engaging in blanket human resource development, when in actuality that belief system and subsequent work toward treating all people the same is what reinforces the status hierarchy in those workplaces. The lack of attention to access to informal networks, mentors, and developmental opportunities keeps the door closed to these critical developmental tools for underrepresented workers who may need them the most.

The majority of companies are plural and tend to have a low to medium level of cultural identity (Cox, 1991). These companies are more heterogeneous and more embracing of employees' cultural differences than monolithic organizations. Yet, plural organizations can be skewed in terms of job placement faultlines, thus resulting in incomplete integration that results in "diversity pockets" across an organization (Cox, 1991).

These plural companies most likely incorporate the access-and-legitimacy paradigm (Thomas & Ely, 1996), which also focuses on differentiation and celebrates diversity in organizations, but does not fully incorporate that diversity into the core of the company. Organizations utilizing this model work hard to recruit employees who reflect niche markets in their consumer base and use them solely for access to and legitimacy with their respective cultural populations. Leaders in these organizations "are too quick to push staff with niche capabilities into differentiated pigeonholes without trying to understand what those capabilities really are and how they could be integrated into the company's mainstream work" (Thomas & Ely, 1996, p. 83), therefore limiting diverse employees' access to other jobs in the company, including potential upward mobility. These pigeonholed employees may also be the first to go when downsizing occurs as they are considered special, but not essential, components of the company. This leaves many employees feeling tokenized, used, and exploited, while the companies still do not benefit from incorporation of diversity in the rest of the organization (Thomas & Ely, 1996).

Finally, companies that have a high level of cultural identity are multicultural (Cox, 1991). These are the companies who have learned to fully embrace diversity both in their employees and in their everyday practices. They place real value on how diversity can improve the organizational functions and diverse employees feel appreciated and a sense of belonging. Multicultural organizations have equal opportunity for job placement in all levels of the company for women and ethnic minorities. There are only low levels of intergroup conflict as discrimination is not tolerated and the importance of diversity is well established company-wide (Cox, 1991).

Multicultural organizations also are likely to adopt the learning-and-effectiveness paradigm. These companies have learned to tap into the true benefits of diversity by incorporating their diverse "employees' perspectives into the main work of the organization and to enhance work by rethinking primary tasks and redefining markets, products, strategies, missions, business practices, and even cultures" (Thomas & Ely, 1996, p. 85). Such organizations allow their employees the flexibility to integrate their cultural values and norms into their work, which allows for finding new and unique approaches rather than ascribing to a single way of getting work done, therefore giving the company a higher competitive advantage in the marketplace. In this paradigm, all employees can feel a sense of belonging and engagement in their organization (Thomas & Ely, 1996).

Based on its implicit model of diversity management, an organization enacts an environment that determines how diversity issues are considered and incorporated into the workplace. This implicit diversity model is what allows or disallows an organization to identify with and support employees' voice and concerns around multicultural issues. These diversity models determine whether organizational leaders use their power and authority to determine whether matters of diversity are to be valued and integrated or ignored and dissuaded from the mainstream policies and strategies of the business. The employees have only the power to decide whether they will choose to remain with a company or to leave, and naturally the less connection that they feel toward their company, the less likely they are to have any reason to feel connected to their work or to stay with the organization (Chrobot-Mason & Thomas, 2002).

At the foundation of these models of diversity management are larger diversity ideologies that fuel whether and how diversity is addressed in organizations. Both the Cox and Thomas and Ely models discuss organizations that are perhaps the most diversity resistant as promoting colorblindness and assimilation through focusing on recruitment but not the climate of inclusion that is needed to retain a diversity of workers. Organizations that are the most diversity-ready, in contrast, support inclusion through seeking to understand differences and attempt to use that multicultural information as a strategic advantage.

BOOK OVERVIEW

Our goal in *Diversity Ideologies in Organizations* is not only to closely examine multiple sides of two prominent diversity ideologies, color-blindness and multiculturalism, but also to leave room for the possibility that there are other, overlapping ideologies. In fact, while the research has focused on these two ideologies, we do not assume that they are either fixed (Knowles et al., 2009) or the only options (Purdie-Vaughns & Walton, 2011). We also hope to discover the contingencies involved in deeming an ideology effective. Clearly this particular question may in large part be in the eyes of the beholder. For example, the empirical literature has generally demonstrated dominant group members perceive colorblindness as preferable, whereas marginalized groups are more likely to be proponents of multiculturalism (e.g., Ryan et al., 2007). However, just because group members express a preference for an ideology does not mean it is effective or optimal.

We also wondered about how these ideologies play out for other dimensions of difference besides race. Much of the conversation around diversity ideologies in organizations has revolved around race and the extent to which each supports racial diversity. Yet at the foundation of these ideologies is the issue of how differences are managed. Therefore, the colorblindness and multiculturalism ideologies have implications for other socially significant differences such as gender and sexuality as well as race, ethnicity, and culture. Appropriate questions from this line of research are, therefore, how does downplaying differences versus acknowledging them support the inclusion of women in organizations or hamper the upward mobility of sexual minorities?

There is also the issue of context. How does context, such as industry, impact the effectiveness of a particular ideology? Actually, even prior to this discussion we must ask how does one assess ideological effectiveness? Is it through the eyes of the organization with an emphasis on bottom line outcomes, or perhaps specifically the Human Resource function of a workplace concerned with financial, as well as the time, and talent loss that stem from diversity resistance (K. M. Thomas, 2008)? The priorities of an organization change over time, given institutional age and environmental threats as well. There is already evidence that racial diversity benefits organizations' bottom line indicators, but most specifically when the company's strategic posture is toward growth (Richard, 2000). Employees are concerned with their own issues such as the opportunity to have voice, to develop, and to ascend professionally.

Our discussion begins with Chapter 2 by Johnson, Haynes, Holyfield, and Foster who focus on the experience of minority members of organizations who exist in organizations in which multiculturalism or colorblindness predominates. These authors contend that if we embrace theories that focus on similarity-attraction (Byrne, 1971) models, such as Schneider's (1987) Attraction-Selection-Attrition (ASA) model, then minorities who are attracted to colorblind organizations versus those that are more multicultural likely have very different experiences and enact different coping mechanisms while in those institutions.

In some ways Chapter 3, by Goren and Plaut, also focuses on coping. Their chapter focuses on the practice of racial denial among dominant group members in diverse organizations. Through an examination of White identity, privilege, and colorblindness, these authors expand our understanding of diversity resistance but also use these dynamics to provide recommendations for organizations on how to embrace diversity and inclusion through training and leadership development for greater effectiveness.

In Chapter 4, Foldy and Buckley describe color minimization as a potential alternative to either ignoring or highlighting difference in the workplace. In contrast to our discussion thus far, they turn their attention to issues of colorblindness and color cognizance (rather than multiculturalism). In essence color minimization supports the acknowledgement of differences and subsequently downplays their importance. They summarize their research on the effectiveness of these ideologies in child protective services, an environment in which concern and conversation around race and ethnicity are supported and workers are charged with being culturally competent.

Whereas Foldy and Buckley examine current day workplaces to discern the effectiveness color minimization, the authors of Chapter 5, Ditlmann, Mayville, and Purdie-Vaughns, examine how individuals and organizations use different diversity ideological approaches to deal with past injustices, most noticeably slavery. These authors examine both individual responses to the sensitive topic of slavery as well as how organizations whose foundations were in part built upon slavery have chosen to engage in a conversation about race and slavery or avoid it.

Stockdale and Nadler (Chapter 6) likewise examine the issue of diversity ideology from a more macro point of view. Rather than dealing with race, they turn our attention toward gender, and deal with the role of diversity ideology in men's and women's employment patterns. These patterns have implications for where men and women work of course, but also subsequently impact developmental opportunities and gender inequity in pay.

Similarly, Hebl and colleagues (Chapter 7) address diversity ideologies through the lens of identity blind or conscious management practices that impact the workplace experiences of Lesbian, Gay, Bisexual, and Transgendered (LGBT) employees. They argue that identity blind or conscious management practices signal to LGBT workers whether and how they might disclose all aspects of their own individual identities at work.

The next set of chapters focus on the evolution of diversity ideologies, the impact of diversity ideology on employee outcomes, and recommendations for embracing similarity and differences simultaneously in a diverse workplace. Carbone, Parks, and McDonald (Chapter 8) cover the U.S. military's evolving diversity ideologies and subsequent practices. The evolution of these ideologies and subsequent military practices has impacted racial minorities, women, as well as LGBT service people. The military is also broad, therefore this evolution has played out differently depending upon whether one is focused on the Air Force, Navy, or Army etc. Those in the service who are members of marginalized groups and who are also in different branches of the U.S. service therefore may have very different work experiences around diversity.

Tran, Thomas, and George (Chapter 9) consider how diversity ideology affects workers' feelings of inclusion and trust. Yet they move beyond the aforementioned finding that minority group members express more preference for multiculturalism while majority group members prefer colorblindness, by suggesting an interactive model that takes into account *both* individual diversity ideology and organizational diversity ideology. These authors extend this discussion further by proposing these demographic differences may be a reflection of these employee outcomes.

Hahn, Nunes, Park, and Judd (Chapter 10) conclude this section of the volume by offering recommendations from the social psychology literature that supports diverse workplaces in embracing both unity and diversity at the same time. In particular, they synthesize and glean lessons from research on common ingroup identity, multiculturalism and colorblindness, and ingroup projection in order to suggest strategies for managing conflict and diversity.

The volume concludes with three targeted chapters that encourage the reader to reflect on the foundation upon which these diversity ideologies are in some ways evaluated as effective and the generalizability of this discussion around the world. Chapter 11 by Unzueta and Knowles critiques the business case for diversity that may underlie the discussion of whether colorblindness or multiculturalism is best. Vassilopoulou, Jonsen, Özbilgin and Tatli consider the discussion of colorblindness and multiculturalism within the United Kingdom and Germany (Chapter 12), and Nkomo in South Africa (Chapter 13).

The authors cover significant ground in adding to the academic discussion of colorblindness and multiculturalism. Their work helps us to better understand the negotiation of race and ethnicity for those who hold dominant as well as marginalized identities. Furthermore, we've been able to extend the discussion to other dimensions of diversity such as gender and sexuality while also considering environment, such as the military and the broader international context.

There are always other questions and work to be done. For researchers and academics, there are issues to consider such as the conceptualization and measurement of these constructs. Another research question involves the intersectionality of individuals' identities in how one responds to these ideologies, especially if one aspect of one's identity affords one privilege and another does not. We hope to stimulate more reflection by organizational practitioners whose practice is focused on diversity as a strategic opportunity for the companies they serve. Specifically, those working in government may more closely examine how diversity rhetoric matches or conflicts with the laws and decisions made by courts and lawmakers. This volume could also help to highlight the frequent lack of congruence between diversity beliefs and/or policies and actual behavior surrounding diversity. Ultimately, we hope that this volume's examination of diversity ideologies, which affect many aspects of organizational life and employee outcomes in the United States and all over the world, will provide important lessons for individuals and organizations.

REFERENCES

Apfelbaum, E. P., Pauker, K., Sommers, S. R., & Ambady, N. (2010). In blind pursuit of racial equality? *Psychological Science, 21*(11), 1587–1592.

Apfelbaum, E. P., Sommers, S. R., & Norton, M. I. (2008). Seeing race and seeming racist? Evaluating strategic colorblindness in social interaction. *Journal of Personality and Social Psychology, 95*(4), 918–932.

Berry, J. W. (1984). Cultural relations in plural societies: Alternatives to segregation and their socio-psychological implications. In M. B. Brewer, & N. Miller (Eds.), *Groups in contact* (pp. 11–17). New York: Academic Press.

Byrne, D. E. (1971). *The Attraction Paradigm* (Vol. 11). New York: Academic Press.

Chavez, L. R. (2008). *The Latino Threat: Constructing immigrants, citizens, and the nation.* Stanford, CA: Stanford University Press.

Chrobot-Mason, D. L., & Thomas, K. M. (2002). Minority employees in majority organizations: The intersection of individual and organizational racial identity in the workplace. *Human Resource Development Review, 1*(3), 323–344.

Correll, J., Park, B., & Smith, J. A. (2008). Colorblind and multicultural prejudice reduction strategies in high-conflict situations. *Group Processes and Intergroup Relations, 11*(4), 471–491.

Cox, T. A. (1991). The multicultural organization. *The Executive, 5*(2), 34–47.

Fredrickson, G. M. (1999). Models of American ethnic relations: A historical perspective. In D. Prentice, & D. Miller (Eds.), *Cultural divides: Understanding and overcoming group conflict* (pp. 23–34). New York: Russell Sage.

Gutiérrez, A. S., & Unzueta, M. M. (2010). The effect of interethnic ideologies on the likability of stereotypic vs. counterstereotypic minority targets. *Journal of Experimental Social Psychology, 46*(5), 775–784.

Holoien, D. S., & Shelton, N. J. (2012). You deplete me: The cognitive costs of colorblindness on ethnic minorities. *Journal of Experimental Social Psychology, 48*(2), 562–565.

Jones, J. M. (1998). Psychological knowledge and the new American dilemma of race. *Journal of Social Issues, 54*(4), 641–662.

Jones, M. (2001). *The social psychology of prejudice.* New York: Pearson.

Jost, J. T., Rudman, L. A., Blair, I. V., Carney, D. R., Dasgupta, N., Glaser, J., & Hardin, C. D. (2009). The existence of implicit bias is beyond reasonable doubt: A refutation of ideological and methodological objections and executive summary of ten studies that no manager should ignore. *Research in Organizational Behavior, 29,* 39–69.

Knowles, E. D., Lowery, B. S., Hogan, C. M., & Chow, R. M. (2009). On the malleability of ideology: Motivated construals of color blindness. *Journal of Personality and Social Psychology, 96*(4), 857–869.

Lau, D. C., & Murninghan, J. K. (1998). Demographic diversity and faultlines: The compositional dynamics of organizational groups. *Academy of Management Review, 23*(2), 325–340.

Levin, S., Matthews, M., Guimond, S., Sidanius, J., Pratto, F., Kteily, N., Pitpitan, E. V., & Dover, T. (2012). Assimilation, multiculturalism, and colorblindness: Mediated and moderated relationships between social dominance order and prejudice. *Journal of Experimental Social Psychology, 48*(1), 207–212.

Morrison, K. R., Plaut, V. C., & Ybarra, O. (2010). Predicting whether multiculturalism positively or negatively influences White Americans' intergroup attitudes: The role of ethnic identification. *Personality and Social Psychology Bulletin, 36*(12), 1648–1661.

Neville, H. A., Lilly, R. L., Duran, G., Lee, R. M., & Browne, L. (2000). Construction and initial validation of the Color-Blind Racial Attitudes Scale (CoBRAS). *Journal of Counseling Psychology, 47,* 59–70.

O'Brien, L. T., & Gilbert, P. N. (2013). Ideology: An invisible yet potent dimension of diversity. In Q. M. Robersons (Ed.), *The Oxford handbook of diversity and work* (pp. 132–156). New York: Oxford University Press.

Pearson, A. R., Dovidio, J. F., & Gaertner, S. L. (2009). The nature of contemporary prejudice: Insights from aversive racism. *Social and Personality Psychology Compass, 3*(3), 314–338.

Plaut, V. C. (2002). Cultural models of diversity: The psychology of difference and inclusion. In R. Shweder, M. Minow, & H. R. Markus (Eds.), *Engaging cultural differences: The multicultural challenge in liberal democracies* (pp. 365–395). New York: Russell Sage.

Plaut, V. C. (2010). Diversity science: Why and how difference makes a difference. *Psychological Inquiry, 21,* 77–99.

Plaut, V. C., Cheryan, S., & Stevens, F. G. (in press). New frontiers in diversity research: Conceptions of diversity and their theoretical and practical implications. To appear in P. Shaver, & M. Mikulincer (Eds.) *Handbook of personality and social psychology,* E. Borgida & J. Bargh (Vol. Eds.), Vol. 1, *Attitudes and Social Cognition,* Washington DC: American Psychological Association.

Plaut, V. C., Thomas, K. M., & Goren, M. J. (2009). Is multiculturalism or color blindness better for minorities? *Psychological Science, 20*(4), 444–446.

Purdie-Vaughns, V., Steele, C. M., Davies, P. G., Ditlmann, R., & Crosby, J. R. (2008). Social identity contingencies: How diversity cues signal threat or safety for African Americans in mainstream institutions. *Journal of Personality and Social Psychology, 94*(4), 615–630.

Purdie-Vaughns, V., & Walton, G. (2011). Is multiculturalism bad for Black Americans? In R. Mallett, & L. Tropp (Eds.), *Beyond prejudice reduction: Pathways to positive intergroup relations* (pp. 159–177). Washington, DC: American Psychological Association.

Rattan, A., & Ambady, N. (2013). Diversity ideologies and intergroup relations: An examination of colorblindness and multiculturalism. *European Journal of Social Psychology, 43*(1), 12–21.

Richard, O. C. (2000). Racial diversity, business strategy, and firm performance: A resource-based view. *Academy of Management Journal, 43*(2), 164–177.

Richeson, J. A., & Nussbaum, R. J. (2004). The impact of multiculturalism versus color-blindness on racial bias. *Journal of Experimental Social Psychology, 40*(3), 417–423.

Ryan, C. S., Hunt, J. S., Weible, J. A., Peterson, C. R., & Casas, J. F. (2007). Multicultural and colorblind ideology, stereotypes, and ethnocentricism among Black and White Americans. *Group Processes and Intergroup Relations, 10*(4), 617–637.

Schneider, B. (1987). The people make the place. *Personnel Psychology, 40*(3), 437–453.

Schofield, J. W. (1986). Black–White contact in desegregated schools. In M. Hewstone, & R. Brown (Eds.), *Social psychology and society* (pp. 79–92). Cambridge, MA: Basil Blackwell.

Shaw v. Reno, 509 U.S. 630 (1993).

Stevens, F. G., Plaut, V. C., & Sanchez-Burks, J. (2008). Unlocking the benefits of diversity: All-inclusive multiculturalism and positive organizational change. *Journal of Applied Behavioral Science, 44*(1), 116–133.

Thomas, D. A. (1989). Mentoring and irrationality: The role of racial taboos. *Human Resource Management, 28*, 279–290.

Thomas, D. A., & Ely, R. J. (1996). Making differences matter: A new paradigm for managing diversity. *Harvard Business Review, Sept.–Oct.*, 79–90.

Thomas, K. M. (2008). *Diversity resistance in organizations.* New York: LEA–Taylor & Francis.

Thomas, K. M., & Plaut, V. C. (2008). The many faces of diversity resistance in the workplace. In K. M. Thomas (Ed.), *Diversity resistance in organizations* (pp. 1–22). New York: Taylor & Francis.

Thomas, K. M., Mack, D. A., & Montagliani, A. (2004). Challenging diversity myths: A critical analysis of backlash. In P. Stockdale, & F. Crosby (Eds.), *The psychology and management of diversity in organizations* (pp. 31–51). Malden, MA: Blackwell Publishers.

Tynes, B. M., & Markoe, S. L. (2010). The role of color-blind racial attitudes in reactions to racial discrimination on social network sites. *Journal of Diversity in Higher Education, 3*(1), 1–13.

Vorauer, J. D., Gagnon, A., & Sasaki, S. J. (2009). Salient intergroup ideology and intergroup interaction. *Psychological Science, 20*(7), 838–845.

Vorauer, J. D., & Sasaki, S. J. (2011). In the worst rather than the best of times: Effects of salient intergroup ideology in threatening intergroup interactions. *Journal of Personality and Social Psychology, 101*(2), 307–320.

Wolsko, C., Park, B., Judd, C. M., & Wittenbrink, B. (2000). Framing interethnic ideology: Effects of multicultural and color-blind perspectives on judgments of groups and individuals. *Journal of Personality and Social Psychology, 78*(4), 635–654.

2

Negotiating Space, Finding Your Place

Reconciling Identity Management and Coping Strategies with Diversity Ideology

C. Douglas Johnson, Holly A. Haynes, Andrea Holyfield, and Heather Foster

A prevailing notion in the organizational management literature is the Attraction–Selection–Attrition (ASA: Schneider, 1987) model, which suggests that organizational members are *attracted* to an organization based on variables/factors deemed important to the individual, are *selected* based on the employer's perceived fit with the organizational values, culture and position requirements, and ultimately will remain or *attrite* based on the actual fit or ability to effectively manage impressions regarding fit. As organizations became increasingly diverse (e.g., age, gender, race) and some employees sought to maintain their identities, an interesting diversity paradox emerged: how do we embrace heterogeneity while achieving a sense of community (fit)? Can individuals maintain individuality while developing a sense of belongingness and cohesion? Organizations have typically responded by adopting either a colorblind or multicultural ideology (e.g., Kandaswamy, 2007; Plaut, Thomas, & Goren, 2009). While other intergroup ideologies exist, this chapter will focus primarily on these two as the prevailing diversity ideologies on which the others spawn.

The ASA model corresponds with the increasingly popular colorblind diversity management ideology; however, some organizations subscribe to the multicultural ideology where holistic employees are valued and encouraged to maintain their identities (e.g., Norton, Vandello, Biga, & Darley, 2008; Plaut et al., 2009). While the goal of the two ideologies is theoretically the same, the manifestation of each in organizational settings varies in significant ways and has differing effects based on an individual's status within the firm. For the organizational outsider within (i.e., those who operate on the margins or periphery of an organization based on distinguishable group membership, or are marginalized: Proudford & Thomas, 1999), they develop coping strategies in an effort to negotiate their organizational space with members of the dominant culture, as well as fellow outsiders. While those in the dominant culture (group) may view the work rules as fair and equitable, "those who view themselves as outsiders have had to learn to navigate the dominant culture in order to be successful" (Novogratz, 2009, p. 154).

The purpose of this chapter is to propose a conceptual–theoretical description of the dynamic reconciliation process of identity management and coping strategies with diversity ideology for persons of color. The chapter is not exhaustive in terms of including all individual differences and organizational factors, but representative and serves as a point of departure for better understanding the complex, continuous process that many persons of color engage in as they attempt to negotiate space, or find their place, in organizations based on the enacted and/or espoused diversity ideology. We highlight the extant literature of these competing diversity management ideologies (i.e., multiculturalism and colorblindness), and underscore complementary theoretical perspectives that could enhance our understanding of the complexities organizational outsiders within (OOW) contend with as they attempt to negotiate their organizational space. Further, we present various identity management and coping strategies OOWs could employ as they negotiate organizational space.

Similar to Kanter's (1986) *A Tale of "O,"* the coping strategies posited in this chapter can be applied broadly (e.g., gender, age, disability); we focus primarily on the issue of race/ethnicity, specifically on African Americans and Caucasians within the United States. Why? In part because we seek to simplify a complex topic, but also as Thomas (2001) and West (1994) put it, race [still] matters. The evidence abounds in the scholarly literature and popular press that African Americans still lag in many employment and personal outcomes as compared with their White counterparts (e.g., underemployment, unemployment, organizational level, subjective and objective career success, leadership opportunities, mentors) (Bell & Nkomo, 2001; Burrell, 2010; Johnson & Eby, 2011; Johnson & Pegues, 2013; Thomas, 2001; Thomas & Gabarro, 1999). We acknowledge that strides have been made with regards to the number of racioethnic minorities present in the workforce; the issue of the color line still exists and affects organizational life for many (Johnson & Pegues, 2013), and often times race/ethnicity is excluded as a variable of interest in scholarly pursuits relative to organizations (e.g., Dawson, Johnson, & Ferdman, 2013; Nkomo, 1992). As noted by Kanter (1986), the O is always under the microscope, receiving extra attention and/or scrutiny, which can affect both their attitude and performance, but also that of the dominant group who may envy the attention given to the O. As such, additional attention is needed with the hopes of continuing to propel the workforce forward where *all* employees maximize their contribution.

COMPETING DIVERSITY MANAGEMENT IDEOLOGIES

Spurred by the publication of *Workforce 2000* (Johnston & Packer, 1987), much has been written in the scholarly and popular press about the importance of diversity management and the business case for diversity (e.g., O'Leary & Weathington, 2006; Rios, 2007; Stockdale & Crosby, 2004). In assessing the business case for diversity, studies show that positive relationships exist between diversity and productivity (Richard, 2000), creativity (e.g., Jackson & Schuler, 2002; McLeod, Lobel, & Cox,1992), and other desirable organizational outcomes. Others recognize the importance of effectively managing diversity, given the shifting demographics and the ongoing need to attract and retain the most talented workforce possible in order to attain and/or sustain a competitive advantage (e.g., Avery & McKay, 2006; McKay, Avery, Tonidandel, Morris, Hernandez, & Hebl, 2007). As such, organizations must decide which diversity management strategy, if any, to employ. Two competing ideologies that have been promulgated in organizations and appear in the diversity literature are colorblindness and multiculturalism, each with its advocates and opponents.

In essence, proponents of the colorblind ideology are subscribing to the ideals of Ockham's Razor, where plurality is avoided while simplicity is embraced. In an effort to reduce complexities, some individuals (often those of the dominant culture) prefer to reduce things to its simplest form;

however, this, in effect, robs the person of their "complex personhood" (Gordon, 2004), yet makes things simpler for the dominant group. Color-blindness gives everyone the same identity (i.e., employee of Company X), although not everyone wants to "check their identity at the door" (Wagner, 2006), given it would require a change in cultural worldview embedded in every aspect of the person's being. Further, proponents of this ideology argue that given the election of President Barack Obama, race is no longer a salient factor affecting a person's ability to achieve career success (e.g., Lum, 2009; McKenzie, 2009).

This mindset typically follows the social justification beliefs (Kaiser, Dyrenforth, & Hagiwara, 2006) and systems justification theory (see Jost, Banaji, & Nosek, 2004), which posits that America is a meritocracy where anyone can pull him/herself up by their bootstraps through hard work. It is also rationalized by those who are high on social dominance orientation (see Sidanius, Pratto, van Laar, & Levin, 2004), seeking to maintain the current hierarchy where the dominant group sustains their privilege of Whiteness (Harris, 1993; Maier, 1997; McIntosh, 1990, 1993). Further, it supports the "white [dominant] is right" perspective (Welcome, 2004), where the White experience becomes the social template that OOWs are expected to conform to and adjust their beliefs to fit within that frame. However, separating their identity and becoming "raceless" is a difficult task for some African Americans, given the historic past of the United States and the lingering attitudes of racial inferiority. Dixson and Rousseau (2005 as cited in Ward, 2011) note that the colorblind approach, which is possibly rooted in good intentions, is counterproductive and perpetuates the myth of meritocracy, undermines the interest of OOWs, and supports White privilege.

Separating identity and becoming "raceless" is a difficult task for people of color in America because of the historic racist past of the United States and the lingering attitudes of racial superiority and inferiority (Burrell, 2010). This inability to separate self into multiple identities or negate parts of one's identity can be explained through the concept of intersectionality. The term intersectionality was first coined by Crenshaw (1989), but has been expanded upon primarily by feminist authors of color (e.g., Collins, 1986, Crenshaw, 1994). If intersectionality is applied from a racial perspective, it can be stated that it is difficult for people of color to divorce themselves from the meaning attached to their cultural or racial background. Perspectives, behaviors, and ideologies can possibly be influenced by culture and are attached to a person's identity. Culture and race/ethnicity have become an integral part of a person's sense of self (Dawson et al., 2013). Unfortunately, many who maintain the privilege of a) not thinking about racial identity and b) not having negative stereotypes attached to racial identity have difficulty comprehending integral selves (Helms, 1984, 1990). Often, it is not until a person faces discrimination related to the maintenance of an outsider identity (e.g., racial/ethnic minorities, religious minority or gender minority: Proudford & Thomas, 1999) that they begin to recognize the complexity of one's identity and the impact of that intricate identity on one's behaviors. Therefore, the colorblind ideology does not appeal to everyone.

Given that the colorblind ideology does not speak to the lived experiences of all people (see Andrews, 2003; Caver & Livers, 2002; Ward, 2011; Welcome, 2004), some prefer multiculturalism, a pluralistic diversity ideology. Multiculturalism celebrates similarities and differences, and encourages employees to maintain their individuality for the benefit of the organization. Several studies have assessed the relationship between multiculturalism and racial bias, and found lower bias associated with multiculturalism (e.g., Wolsko, Park, & Judd, 2006). Further, scholars have argued that organizations should recognize the dual imperative associated with diversity management: a business imperative and an ethical imperative (see O'Leary & Weathington, 2006). Moving beyond representation of persons of color, to fully integrating all employees into the organizational mainstream is not only the right thing to do from the perspective of the bottom line, but is also the ethical thing to do in terms of treating people with respect and creating a just workplace.

In some of the seminal work on multicultural organizations, Cox (1993) took a multidimensional, multilayered approach to the topic of diversity in organizations which more closely captured the complexities associated with this topic and offered a model to assist with the understanding of the issues such that action items could be appropriately derived. Cox states that "more organizations are coming to realize that the potential creativity and problem-solving advantages of a culturally diverse workforce is a resource that remains grossly underutilized in most of the world" (p. ix). Organizations applying the multicultural diversity ideology seek to capitalize on this and provide an environment where their employees have a stronger possibility of maximizing their potential and impacting the organization's performance. In his interactional model of cultural diversity,

Cox seeks to explicate those factors within the organization's diversity climate that have the potential to affect individual career outcomes and the organization's overall effectiveness. He posits that those organizations who embrace diversity can gain and sustain a competitive advantage by engaging a greater proportion of its workforce.

Given that many organizations have begun to make diversity and inclusion an organizational priority and have expended resources to ensure diverse workforces realize their full potential, scholars have questioned whether such investments are prudent. Roberson and Park (2007) assessed the effects of diversity reputation and leader racial diversity on firm financial performance, and found that there are economic benefits to placing an emphasis on diversity management, as well as a complex relationship relative to racial minority representation in leadership and performance. Specifically, they found that financial performance declines as representation of diverse leaders increases to a certain point, and then organizations see an increase. These findings highlight the importance of adopting a long-term orientation and commitment to diversity and inclusion.

Negotiating Space: Strategies for Coping in the Organizational Setting

In an effort to understand the impact of these two diversity management strategies on OOW, it is imperative to apply critical theory and look through the lenses of race, gender, and class (as well as other salient identities), to otherwise shatter the complete identity of the individual. These salient dimensions often affect a person's behavior in an organizational setting. The notion we put forth is that the OOW (as defined by racioethnicity, gender, or religious affiliation) uses a variety of coping mechanisms to function in their settings. However, the strength of their coping strategies often depends on the strength and malleability of their identity.

The malleability of identity allows for the preservation of self, and the OOW develops and uses a set of coping strategies to sustain relationships within an organization while also maintaining one's integrity. Terms such as "code switching" and putting on "masques" were used by hooks (2001) to describe strategies used by OOW in an effort to maintain a healthy self. Bell (1990) talked about biculturalism, and how the person transitions between two cultures (work and home). Collectively, these can be described as "negotiating space" where the individual seeks to understand the environment and behave in a manner that supports personal success in that environment (Haynes, 2009). There are many individual differences that affect the development of such coping strategies, which are also influenced by the diversity climate or ideology of the organization.

A large body of work exists relating to workplace identity, both from the perspective of the individual and the organization. Research by Avery and McKay (2006), for example, highlights the different tactics organizations employ in an effort to present themselves favorably to potential diverse employees. The tenets of impression management can be applied to either the organization or the individual, which can have significant implications that must be dealt with if either is not being authentic. Chrobot-Mason and Thomas (2002), extending work by Helms (1984), draw upon research from various psychological domains (counseling, developmental, social, and Black psychology) and other fields to propose four different types of employee–employer relationships that develop based upon the racial identity levels of both the organization and the minority employee. This aligns with our chapter in that the suggested strategies are dependent upon the individual and diversity ideology chosen by the organization.

Other authors have even begun to delineate ways OOWs can successfully navigate their workspace to promote change (Myerson, 2001). Roberts (2005) forwards this notion in her discussion of "impression management." According to Roberts, those who work in diverse organizations must be aware of and learn to manage their professional image in order to succeed in the organization. While her model applies well to those invested in diverse organizations, it does not address organizational outsiders or the interplay between being culturally different from the majority of the people in the organization. What the literature has solidly established is that people shift their actions based on their "impressions" of their workspace and themselves. Roberts suggests that what is missing from the ongoing dialogue is the specifics of the coping strategies that are used for what she calls, "impression management." Negotiating space differs from impression management in that negotiating space allows for the OOW the preservation of an authentic self and the maintenance of identity. Impression management assumes conformity to the dominant, or corporate, standard. The OOW is constantly pursuing a positive presentation of self and is at the mercy of the employer. Negotiating space allows for more self-efficacy and a certain amount of personal freedom (Bandura, 1992). We posture that it is not just the managing of perceptions and the desire to fit into an organizational structure, but the behaviors of the OOWs are guided by 1) their self-identification and 2) their potential for changing those identities as situations in the organization shift. As noted by Pinkett and Robinson (2011), as OOWs learn the rules of organizational life, the rules change and continually shift without notification.

We depart slightly from a sole reliance on social/organizational psychological literature to include developmental psychological and intersectionality theories in order to understand the individual who sees himself outside the group, and in doing so, strategizes to conflict, coexist, or cooperate with the dominant group (Collins, 1986). The strategies will differ and are usually viewed in the literature on measures of success (e.g., paths to promotion, job advancement, acceptance). However, there is the possibility for personal success to be obtained for the highly conflicted/ resistant, marginalized employee if they see themselves as using that conflict to bring about organizational change. We will explore what we term, "*negotiating space*" because we feel that the challenge to OOWs is constant and enigmatic. As such, "impression management" and identity maintenance become part of that negotiation, but the underlying strategies of engagement give us insight into how the OOW adapts to their environment. As Wasserman, Gallegos, and Ferdman (2008) note, it is essential to understand the constant movement involved in this dance between individuals and organizations.

Defining "Negotiating Space" and Offering Coping Strategies

"Negotiating space" refers to the coping strategies used by OOWs to understand, navigate, and change their organizations. The premise of negotiating space is that the person assesses their environment and seeks to present self in the most beneficial way. Roberts (2005) considers this managing the professional image. The strategies of negotiating space for the OOWs allow for the maintenance of the professional image for those working in large corporations. Yet, there is more to impression management than maintaining a consistency with the dominant group by acting like, dressing like, and speaking like the dominant group. Negotiating space becomes an active process of self-awareness and mindfulness that leads to strategically positioning oneself for perceived organizational "power" and mobility. For this chapter, we will focus on five identified strategies of "negotiating space": code switching, developing allies, creatively connecting, constructing support systems, and becoming superhuman.

Code Switching. Originally coined by Blom and Gumperz (1972), code switching is a term from sociolinguistics that represented the social implications of language and how members of dominant and subdominant cultures switch language codes to blend in with a particular culture. Stemming from the Sapir-Whorf hypothesis (Hoijer, 1954), which considers language and culture to be entwined, code switching is a way to deem oneself an insider to a particular culture. If we relate code switching to negotiating space, we find that the OOW who successfully "negotiates space" will be able to speak the language of the company (i.e., talk the talk), while also maintaining the language of their own personal identity. Specifically, we can use the example of an African American male executive who is able to speak in Standard English in the boardroom, but may also sit on the board of a local community organization or mentoring youth while playing basketball at the inner city recreational center where he must employ African American Vernacular English (AAVE) from time to time. However, code switching is more than just spoken language as language includes both verbal and nonverbal cues.

Within an organization, an OOW may also employ the nonverbal cues from his member groups as well as the dominant group. Again, we can employ the example of the African American male employee of a predominantly White male organization. To further the scenario, the African American male is from an inner city family occupying the lower class. Anderson (1999) suggests that there is a "code of the streets" for those who live in lower income urban areas, which embodies language, dress, attitudes, and behaviors. Similar to Bell's (1990) biculturalism, Martin (2010) labels this phenomenon strategic assimilation, where the OOW works (and sometimes lives) alongside the dominant group members while maintaining social ties with their racial group. Andrews (2003) argues that Blacks (OOWs) must assimilate to an extent in order to achieve progress in a racially conscious society. Our African American male executive who holds degrees from prestigious institutions has lived life in multiple worlds and has probably learned the code of the middle and upper classes as well as being versed in the code of the streets. Code-switching behaviors for this individual may include changes in posture at meetings, changes to outward appearance, and changes in attitude. In urban areas, especially those with higher rates of violence, men often posture themselves to appear aggressive. Recently, rap artists (whose lyrics often compose the code of the streets) have dubbed this "swagger." The term "swagger" has recently been mainstreamed, but the appearance of swagger in the boardroom is that of cool confidence. It resembles that of the street, but it must be toned down in corporate environments.

A specific case of this comes in the story of Dwayne Graham. Dwayne is the son of middle class immigrant parents. While Dwayne was a child, his parents lived in Decatur, Georgia. Decatur is a densely populated city just outside of Atlanta, Georgia. Dwayne grew up in the equivalent of a lower-middle class neighborhood. The code of his childhood neighborhood was similar to that of the code described in many urban neighborhoods. As Dwayne grew up, he learned the language of his parents as well as their customs and traditions, but he was mostly influenced by the code of the streets of Decatur. Young Black men in Decatur had to develop strong characters, and manhood was the "hard" masculinity often seen in inner city urban areas. Dwayne was educated at a good state institution, and was then hired by a Fortune 100 company where he was able to quickly move into middle management. Although his ascent in the company is filled with examples of the ability to code switch, a recent career setback is also a representation of the difficulty of "negotiating space" through code-switching. Dwayne was interviewed for an advanced position at another company. He was denied the job because he was "too corporate; too refined." Ironically, his interpretation of the situation was that he had to switch his quiet demeanor for the interview to that of a more aggressive approach that demonstrated that he was knowledgeable and educated, easily speaking the language of the corporation. However, what the company sought was someone affable and "down-to-earth" who could switch to the language of the client. The client in mind was the complete opposite of the cultures that Dwayne was fluent in, so, the coping mechanism that had brought him success within his organization was useless in this new setting because he could not translate it. So, while he was perceived as competent, the underlying, nonverbal codes needed to successfully obtain the position were not a part of his identity.

Dwayne works for a company that promotes itself as one that embraces multiculturalism. However, Dwayne notes that multiculturalism is promoted at a surface level. He describes diversity trainings and the company's declared interest in hiring and promoting a racially diverse workforce. However, Dwayne asserts that the strategies that he used to attain his management position forced him to shed the code of the streets of his childhood as they were not acceptable in this very diverse corporation. Even though he was denied the position, he felt he further needed to learn the code of the corporation rather than integrating the codes of his upbringing. He was still code switching in his attempt to conform to the preferred identity of the organization. The deeper ideology of the company was that you were first and foremost an employee of their company, and as such, for upward mobility within the corporation, learning the code of the organization was most heavily rewarded. So, for OOWs, not only must they be able to switch from their code of origin to the dominant culture's code, they must also develop the ability to code switch into the code of the corporation in both colorblind and multicultural organizations. The negotiation for the OOW is based on an understanding of how and when to switch code and is embedded in the OOW's knowledge of the culture of the company. If the OOW had a mentor(s), then he could have been provided additional information/insights to assist with effectively navigating cross-race differences; however, access to mentors in positions of influence is limited.

Developing Allies. In addition to code switching, there are other coping mechanisms that involve the retention/preservation of identity for OOWs. One such strategy is what we have termed, "developing allies." Developing allies involves seeking out and partnering with people across the organization. It is similar to the concept of networking, but rather than focusing on allying with people of equal or higher status, those who develop allies do so at every level of the organization. Often, the one who uses developing allies as a way of negotiating space is able to utilize relationships with others for both personal and organizational gain. Myerson (2001) discusses how change can take place in an organization through passive resistance; however, in order to effect this change, one needs to connect with others to forge that change. As a coping strategy, developing allies is effective because it serves to give the OOW perceived power in the organization. The ability to connect with various employees broadens the network of the OOW, but it also allows that person to leverage the ideas, positions, and identities of various people in the organization. Unfortunately, as posited by Johnson and Pegues (2013), not everyone is viewed as adding value to a person's social network and therefore may not be able to develop allies as readily as others. Despite this, OOWs still should seek to identify those within the organization who share their values or are potentially kindred spirits.

An example of developing allies can be found in the following case. Katherine Parsons is a successful attorney who recently joined a new firm. As she negotiates the spaces in this organization, she reaches out to various people at different levels in the organization. For example, she gets to know the janitors at the organization, and she knows the head of the mailroom. She also develops relationships with attorneys at various levels. The relationships that are created allow her to leverage power across the organization. Some of the relationships allow her to gain access to professional mentoring that will help her rise in position. Similar to mentors/sponsors (Thomas, 1990), allies who are at higher levels can provide the OOW access to information that will help them navigate the internal operations of the organization. Alliances with those in lower status can also serve to give the OOW a perception of power within the organization. As we are reminded of Roberts' (2005) "impression management," we can think of these alliances as the underlying mechanism of the management of perceptions. Connections to "lower status" individuals allow for the individual to be perceived as "likable." Likeability can then lead to two advantages: a) people perceive you as a good co-worker or good manager and b) people desire to connect with you to accomplish a goal. Hence, your ability to organize/galvanize people for organizational change is greatly increased. Those who can easily connect and make allies are perceived as leaders. In the negotiation of organizational space, making allies allows for a person to develop positive impressions of self with a variety of people.

If we explore alliances in the context of multicultural versus colorblind organizations, it appears that what may differentiate the types of alliances is the diversity of the alliance. For those in colorblind organizations, one may choose to seek out alliances with those who are perceived as having more knowledge of organizational culture. One might feel more comfortable beginning with alliances across employment levels of people of the same culture. Hence, the notion of "fictive kinship" may supersede an alliance per se. Because there is a general culture and adherence to that culture is valued, a new OOW may seek out and bond with a seasoned OOW whom they perceive shares the same background, ideologies, and struggles. Returning to Roberts, the new OOW becomes an apprentice of sorts to the seasoned OOW and learns how to develop an identity that is consistent with that of the corporate identity. Positive impressions can be developed and maintained. In a strong alliance, the seasoned OOW can aid the newcomer by painting a favorable impression of that new employee. Both help each other by allowing for moments of code switching at appropriate times and by working together to help each other maintain cultural identity without losing corporate identity.

A multicultural corporation seeks to promote diversity and, as such, multicultural organizations may promote more diverse alliances. Because culture and diversity are promoted, there is a certain level of freedom in retaining an intersectional self. Alliances may be formed around a variety of issues not related to race or ethnicity. For example, people may ally around common philosophies rather than around race. A new OOW may seek out people of different racial and cultural backgrounds whom they perceive as successful. There may be no need for the fictive kinship found in colorblind organizations. By celebrating diversity, the OOW may feel more comfortable with his integrated self and seek to make alliances with those perceived as understanding the broader goals of the corporation, regardless of cultural background. We could also extend the argument to suggest that it may be that in the multicultural organization the de-emphasis on one corporate culture may give rise to the formation of not just alliances but also the destruction of competition to create an environment where more are working toward a common goal. The meaning of forming alliances may then change from Morgan–Roberts self-promoting and self-preserving alliance to commitment to the strategic goals of the corporation.

Creatively Connecting. "Creatively connecting" involves adding language, customs, and other aspects of dominant culture to your daily practice to connect with others in your organization. In recent developmental studies of high school peer groups, researchers have found that there are some children who belong to particular low and high status groups. Their identity in those groups is fixed, and they rely on others to determine their membership in those groups. However, there is an emergent group of students who do not belong to any one group. In fact, they travel between groups of people and are extremely well liked by peers of varying social cliques. The person who negotiates their organizational space by "creatively connecting" uses the strategies of this latter group of high schoolers. They are extremely popular and are able to make connections across groups of people. They have knowledge about a variety of subjects and are willing to move to the level of the person they are interacting with to put the person at ease.

But, how are they able to connect so easily within an organization? There are many types of people within an organization, and as Roberts (2005) analyzes, the organization is a set of groups. Some of the connectors are the simple, non-work related discussions that people engage in on a daily basis. For the most part, topics of discussion that connect people on a day-to-day basis often are impacted by race and gender. A simple example can be found in daily discussions about last night's football game or a recent *Desperate Housewives* episode. Although many men enjoy Monday Night Football, some do not. Some have never really had an interest in the game or may be from a culture where football refers to what we, in America, term soccer. Rather than continuing on amiss to the mailroom and boardroom discussions of Peyton Manning's prowess as a quarterback in last night's thrilling double-overtime game, the negotiator of space learns to watch the game of football in an effort to connect with the men at the office. This strategy works across culture and gender. This is an easy strategy that allows an OOW to break down the barriers of perceived difference. People begin to think, "We have something in common." This eases some tension and prejudice. Once again, the OOW preserves their own identity, but incorporates the knowledge of the outside group to develop relationships across the organization.

If we assess this strategy in light of the nature of the organization (colorblind or multicultural), we find that this strategy is nearly the same in both types of organizations. However, the OOW in a colorblind organization may find herself taking deliberate steps to integrate components of the dominant culture into her lifestyle outside of work, whereas the OOW in a colorblind organization may take the opportunity to share her culture's perception of a broader cultural artifact with her co-workers. A specific example can be found in religious practice. In the Southeast, the Bible Belt, one may find that many attend Christian religious services on Sunday. The church permeates much of the lives, thoughts, and beliefs of people regardless of cultural or racial background. It is a shared cultural element. However, church is also one of the most segregated settings. On Monday morning when colleagues come together, those in a colorblind organization may seek to talk about elements of their religious service they feel may be common to all religious services.

They may focus on the message. Some may choose to attend a church where they then become the OOW to better relate to their colleagues. They may even go on the suggestion of their colleagues. In the Southeast, where churches have served as an integral part of culture, the ability to discuss and share one's experience is important to many. But, the OOW at the colorblind organization makes a deliberate attempt to reduce the differences in religious practice in favor of maintaining a connectedness with others in the organization.

On the other hand, OOWs in a multicultural organization may feel that they have more ability and freedom to share their whole experience as connecting. So, rather than making a deliberate effort to demonstrate the similarities of their churchgoing experience, they may be more comfortable describing the differences. They still make a connection with their co-workers, but they are not pressed to make their experiences conform to the dominant worldview of church. Moving away from the church illustration, the central idea of connecting in multicultural organizations is not organized around similarity of experience but across the differences. Even though the experience of going to a religious service may be shared, a Muslim co-worker may be more prone to share breaking fast during Ramadan with their Christian co-worker because the environment celebrates that freedom. This is not to say that colorblind organizations do not promote differential engagement; we are merely suggesting that for the OOW, they may feel more pressure to conform in order to connect in colorblind organizations than in multicultural ones.

Constructing Support Systems. Perhaps one of the most important coping mechanisms and negotiation strategies is the one that serves to preserve the mental health of the OOW. Although all of the strategies serve to make the task of work easier, the OOW is often at work figuring out which strategy to employ to alleviate the pressures of being the organizational outsider. In clinical psychology, it is noted that those who alleviate stress effectively often have sound support systems. Herman (1997) notes in *Trauma and Recovery* that the support networks we maintain often mediate our responses to traumatic events. In many ways, working in an environment where you may be marginalized or where your identity severely clashes with the dominant culture of the organization can be traumatizing. But, for an event to be completely traumatizing, a person will not have any coping strategies at their command. Forming systems of support prevents a person from falling into an abyss of depression about or sustained anger with their institution.

The support networks formed usually consist of people the OOW shares something with—race, gender, religion, or ideology. It may be the fact that you found the only single parent of six in the organization. The two of you can share stories, ease stress, bear burdens, possibly even share a demanding workload. The support system allows the OOW to be completely authentic. There is no need to employ the other coping strategies with this person as this person shares in the various issues generated, but also serves as an aide in negotiating the organization. In the diversity literature, Lau and Murninghan (1998) describe these natural, dividing lines as "diversity faultlines" (p. 328), which are based on a salient demographic characteristic(s) where the individuals have an affinity. These faultlines become important as they also relate to relative power and status within the organization associated with the organizational level and/or role and status shared by the OOWs.

It is common for the OOW to be their real self within their support system. There are no facades. There is no desire to impress or give an impression to those in the support network. Some in the support network may be allies, but many times these are not strategic alliances. These are probably the true friendships that exist among colleagues. In chaotic or difficult environments, the support networks exist to help the OOW maintain a sense of perspective or give a dose of reality. An OOW who negotiates space well in both colorblind and multicultural environments will seek out a group that can give wise counsel about the organization. The most difficult setting for an OOW is to be the only OOW. Someone may feel that there is nowhere to turn in an organization for support. A poor negotiator may look to someone who is similar to themselves ethnically or racially for support but may find that the person does not share the same ideologies or may see themselves in competition with the one who sought him out. Many OOWs possess feelings of loneliness and fail to trust others around them. However, those with good support networks learn to navigate their organization with more confidence.

Becoming Superhuman. OOWs often want to resist being the "necessary hire," and avoid the "affirmative action stigma" (Heilman, Block, & Stathatos, 1997) associated with such. Therefore, to demonstrate competence in the workplace, they often perform at a level higher than any of the other people at their level. If we relate this to race, many people of Latino and African American heritage seek perfection in their daily work because they do not want a label of being ineffective or incompetent in their performance. They want to resist stereotypes that might prevail in the office. Additionally, they want to deter any unjust treatment as a result of job performance. It is important to note that sometimes this level of achievement may lead to unintended consequences, such as being seen as overly productive or threatening to those not performing at that level of excellence, or viewed as a non-team player outshining everyone else. Kanter (1986) identifies these types as overachievers or "Super Os."

Becoming superhuman is a negotiation strategy if the OOW can manage performing consistently at a high pace. In order to reduce ridicule and increase praise, the OOW may become superhuman in a number of ways. First, the OOW may just seek to perform tasks to perfection. Assignments given will always be completed beyond expectations. Second, the OOW may take several tasks (while still performing impeccably at standard tasks). The OOW then maintains power in that they become the most valuable player in the organization. They are able to negotiate change in the organization because they are either involved in a variety of tasks *or* appear to hold the knowledge about a given task in the institution.

Again, we can relate this to Roberts' (2005) concept of impression management. Regardless of the knowledge base of OOWs, they will work hard to ensure that no one can question their merit. They seek to maintain the impression that they are knowledgeable and valuable employees. In many ways, this may seem to be the goal of all employees or those that are considered type A. However, if we employ the concept that one's cultural identity is critical to one's overall identity then what seems to take place is that the OOW seeks to erase any negative stereotype of that racial or cultural identity in an effort to present their work and commitment to the organization in the best possible light. The concept of impression management is often linked to constructing a positive identity that may or may not be one's true identity. One attempts to be perceived in the best possible light to attain success. Often the OOW is not concerned with advancement; he is concerned with maintenance. He wants to maintain his job. He wants to open doors for those of the same racial group that may be potential hires. He carries the weight of cultural perception on his shoulders in attempting to erase stereotypes.

This strategy is effective in negotiating space because it allows for the OOW to stake out territory, to maintain a positive work identity. Often, it also allows the OOW to present themself in a positive light while also allowing them to maintain their authentic identity. The OOW is associated with hard work and competence. For the person negotiating space, it is a tool that will help them move upward in an organization without compromising core values and principles, but again, the goal may be just to ensure that they challenge stereotypes.

Much like the strategy of developing support groups, it is possible that this stereotype is guided by the impression of the OOW of the organizational culture regardless of the organization's structure as colorblind or multicultural. Often this strategy is rooted in our broader culture's marginalization and stereotypes of the culture of the OOW. Often times, regardless of a company's commitment to inclusiveness, OOWs feel the pressure of being the Atlas of their culture, holding the world's perception of their culture on their shoulders. So, what looks like a highly productive, highly competent worker is merely an employee trying to reconstruct perceptions of a culture. This strategy comes with high stress and pressure for the OOW. The stronger the support network inside and outside of the organization, the better the OOW's ability to produce at a superhuman level.

COPING WITH THE COPING: EXIT STRATEGIES

What happens when we do not effectively negotiate space? There are three general possibilities. First, we assess that the environment is too difficult to effectively work. The ideology is that even if one were to use the coping strategies described above, maintaining one's sense of identity and authenticity would be compromised in a negative way. Second, one might shut down completely and withdraw from extra duties and responsibilities. One might have difficulties completing basic tasks. This is dangerous as it could lead to termination from the job and justify what many might think is an "affirmative action" hire of a lower skilled person for a high skilled job. The third reaction is to become a minimalist. Minimalists take a less extreme approach from leaving or "retiring on the job." A minimalist continues to perform their duties well, but does not invest extra time in the organization. Their motivation may turn to family. If we look at this through the lens of intersectionality, the minimalist detaches the job from their persona. It is not part of their identity. It does not define who they are, but is just a product. This does not mean that the minimalist does not continue to do a superior job on given tasks; it merely means that the job is just that—a job.

Closing

How one should navigate his or her way within a given organizational context is quite complex, potentially for all employees. This may be further complicated for those who find themselves, in reality or perceptually, operating on the periphery of the organization. As such, these OOWs must attempt to understand what the espoused, but more so enacted, diversity ideology is within that organization in order to determine how that aligns with their personal values and beliefs such that they can maximize satisfaction and performance. With the prevailing diversity ideologies of multiculturalism and colorblindness, the OOW must consider their own personal identity and desires to impression manage in deciding which coping strategy to employ. They should recognize that there are consequences associated with those decisions and attempt to minimize any dissonance that may occur when resistance persists to their presence in the environment, regardless of diversity ideology or coping strategy selected. As noted by Thomas and Plaut (2008), diversity resistance has shifted from being overt to covert, yet still can adversely affect organizations and individuals. Given that diversity is likely to persist in organizations in the future, it is important that effective strategies be adapted such that individual and organizational success can be attained. Research is needed to assess the effectiveness of the aforementioned strategies. Further, other coping mechanisms should be explored. One possible concept to apply, especially in organizations where norms of conformity are strongest, is Hewlin's facades of conformity (2003; 2009), which describes how individuals may attempt to appear as if they buy into the organizational culture, when the organizational values are really opposite of their core values. This may be another strategy that could be effective for certain OOWs, and is akin to self-monitoring that some dominant group members have been able to successfully employ. Further, given the role of racial identity (Helms, 1990), future research should also investigate the effectiveness of "acting White" as noted by Ogbu (2004). Some might see this coping mechanism as appropriate for the colorblind ideology, yet it may have some unintended consequences associated with it. In the end, OOWs must decide how they will navigate their employment situation in their quest for success and well-being.

REFERENCES

Anderson, E. (1999). *Code of the street.* New York: W. W. Norton.

Andrews, V. L. (2003). Self-reflection and the reflected self: African American double consciousness and the social (psychological) mirror. *Journal of African American Studies, 7*(3), 59–79.

Avery, D. R., & McKay, P. F. (2006). Target practice: An organizational impression management approach to attracting minority and female job applicants. *Personnel Psychology, 59*, 157–187.

Bandura, A. (1992). Exercise of personal agency through the self-efficacy mechanism. In R. Schwarzer (Ed.), *Self-efficacy: Thought control of action* (pp. 3–38). Washington, DC: Hemisphere.

Bell, E. L. (1990). The bicultural life experience of career-oriented Black women. *Journal of Organizational Behavior, 11*, 459–477.

Bell, E. L., & Nkomo, S. M. (2001). *Our separate ways: Black and White women and the struggle for professional identity.* Boston, MA: Harvard Business School Press.

Blom, J-P., & Gumperz, J. J. (1972). Social meaning in linguistic structure: Code-switching in Norway. In J. J. Gumperz, and D. Hymes (Eds.), *Directions in sociolinguistics: The ethnography of communication* (pp. 407–434). Oxford: Basil Blackwell.

Burrell, T. (2010). *Brainwashed: Challenging the myth of Black inferiority.* New York: SmileyBooks.

Caver, K. A., & Livers, A. B. (2002). Dear White boss . *Harvard Business Review, November*, 76–81.

Chrobot-Mason, D., & Thomas, K. M. (2002). Minority employees in majority organizations: The intersection of individual and organizational racial identity in the workplace. *Human Resource Development Review, 1*, 323–344.

Collins, P. H. (1986). Learning from the outsider within: The sociological significance of Black feminist thought. *Social Problems, 33*, 14–32.

Cox, T., Jr. (1993). *Cultural diversity in organizations: Theory, research, and practice.* San Francisco, CA: Berrett-Koehler.

Crenshaw, K. (1989). Demarginalizing the intersection of race and sex: A Black feminist critique of antidiscrimination doctrine, feminist theory, and antiracist politics. *University of Chicago Legal Forum*, 139–167.

Crenshaw, K. (1994). Mapping the margins: Intersectionality, identity politics, and violence against women of color. In M. A. Fineman, & R. Mykitiuk (Eds.), *The public nature of private violence* (pp. 93–118). New York: Routledge.

Dawson, B. L., Johnson, C. D., & Ferdman, B. M. (2013). Organizational psychology. In F. T. L. Leong (Ed.), *APA handbook of multicultural psychology* (vol. 1, pp. 471–487. Washington, DC: American Psychological Association.

Dixson, A. D., & Rousseau, C. K. (2005). And we are still not saved: Critical race theory in education ten years later. *Race, Ethnicity and Education, 8*(1), 7–27.

Gordon, A. (2004). Theory and justice. In A. Gordon (Ed.), *Keeping good time: Reflections on knowledge, power, and people* (pp. 99–105). Boulder, CO: Paradigm.

Harris, C. (1993). Whiteness as property. *Harvard Law Review, 106,* 1707–1791.

Haynes, H. A. (2009). Masquing well-being: "Negotiating space" and the self-concept of poor, Black women. *Journal of the Association for Research in Mothering, 11*(1), 95–109.

Heilman, M. E., Block, C. J., & Stathatos, P. (1997). The affirmative action stigma of incompetence: Effects of performance ambiguity. *Academy of Management Journal, 40,* 603–625.

Helms, J. E. (1984). Toward a theoretical explanation of the effects of race on counseling: A Black and White model. *The Counseling Psychologist, 12,* 153–164.

Helms, J. E. (1990). *Black and White racial identity.* New York: Greenwood.

Herman, J. (1997). *Trauma and recovery.* New York: Basic Books.

Hewlin, P. F. (2003). And the award for best actor goes to . . .: Facades of conformity in organizational settings. *Academy of Management Review, 28,* 633–642.

Hewlin, P. F. (2009). Wearing the cloak: Antecedents and consequences of creating facades of conformity. *Journal of Applied Psychology, 94,* 727–741.

Hoijer, H. (Ed.) (1954). *Language in culture: Conference on the interrelations of language and other aspects of culture.* Chicago, IL: University of Chicago Press.

hooks, b[sic] (2001). *All about love: New visions.* New York: HarperCollins.

Jackson, S. E., & Schuler, R. S. (2002). Managing individual performance: A strategic perspective. In S. Sonnentag (Ed.), *Psychological management of individual performance* (pp. 372–390). Chichester: John Wiley & Sons.

Johnson, C. D., & Eby, L. T. (2011). Evaluating career success of African American males: It's what you know and who you are that matters. *Journal of Vocational Behavior, 79,* 699–709.

Johnson, C. D., & Pegues, D. A. (2013). The role of "who" in social capital formation: Linking "who you are" and "who you know". In C. D. Johnson (Ed.), *Social capital: Theory, measurement, and outcomes* (pp. 21–64). Hauppauge, NY: Nova Science Publishers.

Johnston, W. B., & Packer, A. H. (1987). *Workforce 2000.* Indianapolis, IN: Hudson Institute.

Jost, J. T., Banaji, M. R., & Nosek, B. A. (2004). A decade of social justification theory: Accumulated evidence of conscious and unconscious bolstering of the status quo. *Political Psychology, 25,* 881–919.

Kaiser, C. R., Dyrenforth, P. S., & Hagiwara, N. (2006). Why are attributions to discrimination interpersonally costly? A test of system- and group-justifying motivations. *Personality and Social Psychology Bulletin, 32,* 1523–1536.

Kandaswamy, P. (2007). Beyond colorblindness and multiculturalism: Rethinking anti-racist pedagogy in the university classroom. *Radical Teacher, 80,* 6–11.

Kanter, R. M. (1986). *The tale of O: On being different in an organization.* New York: HarperCollins.

Lau, D., & Murninghan, J. K. (1998). Demographic diversity and faultlines: The compositional dynamics of organizational groups. *Academy of Management Review, 23,* 325–340.

Lum, L. (2009, February 5). The Obama era: A post-racial society? *Diverse Education,* 14–16.

McIntosh, P. (1990). White privilege: Unpacking the invisible knapsack. *Independent School*, 31–36.

McIntosh, P. (1993). White privilege and male privilege: A personal account of coming to see correspondence through work in women's studies. In A. Minas (Ed.), *Gender basics: Feminist perspectives on women and men* (pp. 30–38). Belmont, CA: Wadsworth.

McKay, P. F., Avery, D. R., Tonidandel, S., Morris, M. A., Hernandez, M., & Hebl, M. R. (2007). Racial differences in employee retention: Are diversity climate perceptions the key? *Personnel Psychology, 60*, 35–62.

McKenzie, W. (2009, January 20). Inaugural begins a discussion about post-racial society. *McClatchy–Tribune Business News.*

McLeod, P. L., Lobel, S. A., & Cox, T. H. (1996). Ethnic diversity and creativity in small groups. *Small Group Research, 27*, 248–264.

Maier, M. (1997). Invisible privilege: What White men don't see. *The Diversity Factor, Summer*, 28–33.

Martin, L. L. (2010). Strategic assimilation or creation of symbolic Blackness: Middle-class Blacks in suburban contexts. *Journal of African American Studies, 14*, 234–246.

Myerson, D. E. (2001). Radical change, the quiet way. *Harvard Business Review, October*, 92–100.

Nkomo, S. M. (1992). The emperor has no clothes: Rewriting "race in organizations." *Academy of Management Review, 17*, 487–513.

Norton, M. I., Vandello, J. A., Biga, A., & Darley, J. M. (2008). Colorblindness and diversity: Conflicting goals in decisions influenced by race. *Social Cognition, 26*, 102–111.

Novogratz, J. (2009). *The blue sweater: Bridging the gap between rich and poor in an interconnected world*. New York: Rodale.

Ogbu, J. U. (2004). Collective identity and the burden of "acting White" in Black history, community, and education. *The Urban Review, 36*(1), 1–35.

O'Leary, B. J., & Weathington, B. L. (2006). Beyond the business case for diversity in organizations. *Employee Responsibilities and Rights Journal, 18*, 283–292.

Pinkett, R., & Robinson, J. (2011). *Black faces in white places: 10 game-changing strategies to achieve success and find greatness*. New York: AMACOM.

Plaut, V. C., Thomas, K. M., & Goren, M. J. (2009). Is multiculturalism or color blindness better for minorities? *Psychological Science, 20*, 444–446.

Proudford, K. L., & Thomas, K. M. (1999). The organizational outsider within. *Journal of Career Development, 26*, 3–5.

Richard, O. C. (2000). Racial diversity, business strategy, and firm performance: A resource-based view. *Academy of Management Journal, 43*, 164–77.

Rios, R. (2007). Embracing a diversity twenty-first century workforce. *American Waterworks Association (AWWA) Journal, January*, 38–41.

Roberson, Q. M., & Park, H. J. (2007). Examining the link between diversity and firm performance: The effects of diversity reputation and leader racial diversity. *Group & Organization Management, 32*, 548–568.

Roberts, L. M. (2005). Changing faces: Professional image construction in diverse organizational settings. *Academy of Management Review, 30*, 685–711.

Schneider, B. (1987). The people make the place. *Personnel Psychology, 40*, 437–453.

Sidanius, J., Pratto, F., van Laar, C., & Levin, S. (2004). Social dominance theory: Its agenda and method. *Political Psychology, 25*, 845–880.

Stockdale, M. S., & Crosby, F. J. (Eds.) (2004). *The psychology and management of workplace diversity*. Malden, MA: Blackwell.

Thomas, D. A. (1990). The impact of race on managers' experiences of developmental relationships (mentoring and sponsorship): An inter-organizational study. *Journal of Organizational Behavior, 11,* 479–492.

Thomas, D. A. (2001). Truth about mentoring minorities: Race matters. *Harvard Business Review, 79,* 99–107.

Thomas, D. A., & Gabarro, J. J. (1999). *Breaking through: The making of minority executives in corporate America.* Boston, MA: Harvard Business School Press.

Thomas, K. M., & Plaut, V. C. (2008). The many faces of diversity resistance in the workplace. In K. M. Thomas (Ed.), *Diversity resistance in organizations* (pp. 1–22). Mahwah, NJ: Lawrence Erlbaum Associates.

Wagner, V. (2006). *Do we check it at the door?* Retrieved from www.maynardije.org/news/features/020829_checkit on September 20, 2006.

Ward, C. J. (2011). Purgatory's place in the South: A Black woman's journey to the promised land. Unpublished dissertation.

Wasserman, I. C., Gallegos, P. V., & Ferdman, B. M. (2008). Dancing with resistance: Leadership challenges in fostering a culture of inclusion. In K. M. Thomas (Ed.), *Diversity resistance in organizations* (pp. 175–200). Mahwah, NJ: Lawrence Erlbaum Associates.

Welcome, H. A. (2004). "White is right": The utilization of an improper ontological perspective in analyses of Black experiences. *Journal of African American Studies, 8*(1 & 2), 59–73.

West, C. (1994). *Race matters.* New York: Vintage.

Wolsko, C., Park, B., & Judd, C. M. (2006). Considering the tower of Babel: Correlates of assimilation and multiculturalism among ethnic minority and majority groups in the United States. *Social Justice Research, 19,* 277–306.

3

Racial Identity Denial and its Discontents

Implications for Individuals and Organizations

Matt J. Goren and Victoria C. Plaut

How do Whites think about their racial identity? Do they embrace it, consider it important or relevant to who they are, or reject the notion altogether? What consequences flow from denial of one's race and racial identity, especially if one belongs to a dominant social group? A growing body of research in social, counseling, and organizational psychology addresses these questions. In this chapter, we review this literature and argue that Whites' *racial identity denial*—the motivated denial of one's own race and racial identity—has significant and often negative interpersonal and organizational repercussions.

In particular, we develop our conception of racial identity denial by highlighting research on three related constructs: White racial identity, the belief in White privilege, and racial colorblindness. Through this literature and some of our preliminary empirical findings, we explore the implications of racial identity denial for diversity climate, which predicts greater job satisfaction and engagement, retention, and group cohesion for both Whites and people of color (McKay et al., 2007; Plaut, Thomas, & Goren, 2009; Walsh, Matthews, Tuller, Parks, & McDonald, 2010). We then suggest how these lessons can inform diversity training, leadership, and organizational effectiveness. Ultimately we hope that understanding and addressing racial identity denial, and its attendant resistance to diversity, will help foster more inclusive workplaces (Stevens, Plaut, & Sanchez-Burks, 2008; Thomas, 2008).

RELATED CONSTRUCTS: WHITE IDENTITY, WHITE PRIVILEGE, AND COLORBLINDNESS

In this section, we examine literature on phenomena related to racial identity denial: White identity, White privilege, and colorblindness. These three constructs form an important basis for understanding racial identity denial as each implicates the recognition of race and racism. We describe each construct, its implications for diversity climate, and how it informs an understanding of racial identity denial.

Racial Identity Denial and White Identity. In contrast to most racial minorities, most White people in Europe and its former colonies report that their race is not an important part of their self-definition (e.g., Phinney, Cantu, & Kurtz, 1997). We speculate that racial identity denial precipitates these low self-reports for some Whites. In this section, we contrast racial identity denial with another cause of Whites' low self-reported racial identity, *racial naïveté*. We then present evidence suggesting that multiple racial identity concerns motivate racial identity denial among Whites.

One starting point for thinking about racial identity denial and White identity is to consider that in North American and European societies, Whiteness appears universal, especially to Whites. Most White Americans do not live, work, or go to school with many people from different ethnic backgrounds—despite growing diversity, racial segregation is actually increasing (Orfield, Kucsera, & Siegel-Hawley, 2012). Segregation extends to the media, where depictions of racial minorities are rare and tend to perpetuate negative stereotypes (Orbe & Harris, 2006). Given the perception of White universality, it is not surprising that many Whites fail to even see their race as a viable social category (e.g., Perry, 2007). Patricia Williams (1997) has proposed, "Whiteness is unnamed, suppressed, beyond the realm of race" and, accordingly, Whites have the "majoritarian privilege of never noticing themselves" (p. 7). We argue that Whites' failure to see their race can be related in some cases to racial naïveté and in others to motivated denial.

White Identity and Racial Naïveté. According to White racial identity development theorists, low White racial identity stems from racial naïveté—a benign ignorance of the importance race has in shaping the self and society. Every White racial identity development model includes a weakly identified, racially naïve identity form (see Goren & Plaut, 2012), typically associated with little exposure to diversity (Helms, 1990; Knowles & Peng, 2005; Perry, 2001). For example, in Helms' (1990) model, Whites in the "Contact" status have "ignorance, naïveté, or obliviousness to the socio-political implications of race as it is defined in this country" (p. 241). According to Phinney (1990), racially naïve Whites do not engage in either identity exploration (the active process of exploring about how one's ethnicity affects the self-definition) or identity commitment (the belief that one's ethnicity is an important part of their self-definition). As they experience more interracial contact (Helms, 1990), identity exploration (Phinney, 1990), or diversity training (e.g., Brown, Parham, & Yonker, 1996), however, their understanding of racial issues and their racial identification increases.

Racially naïve Whites tend to endorse relatively benign, if not positive, attitudes toward racial and ethnic diversity. For example, they use fewer negative racial stereotypes (Gushue & Carter, 2000) and exhibit less prejudice (Goren & Plaut, 2012). Whites with weak racial identities are also less likely to perceive or respond negatively to interracial threats (for review, see Ellemers, Spears, & Doosje, 2002). Moreover, when racially naïve White counselors engage in interracial therapeutic relationships, both counselor and client tend to like one another (Burkard, Juarez-Huffaker, & Ajmere, 2003; Carter, 1995), even though racial naïveté seems detrimental to actual therapeutic outcomes (Carter, 1995; Vinson & Neimeyer, 2003).

White Identity and Racial Identity Denial. For some Whites, racial identity coincides with a heightened perception of inter-group competition and threats toward the ingroup (Verkuyten & Zaremba, 2005; Helms, 1990). For these people, success in this imagined racial competition means maintaining and justifying the racial status quo (Quist & Resendez, 2002) and endorsing symbolic or modern racism (Kinder & Sears, 1981; McConahay, Hardee, & Batts, 1981). Another way Whites can maintain the racial status quo is to deny their place in it, that is, to engage in racial identity denial. Consequently, it may be greatest among anti-egalitarian Whites (Block & Carter, 1996; Perry, 2001) and when the White ingroup is economically or symbolically threatened (Knowles, Lowery, Hogan, & Chow, 2009).

The possibility of being seen as prejudiced may also motivate Whites to engage in racial identity denial (Goff, Steele, & Davies, 2008). The perceived seriousness of this threat is not without merit. Prejudiced Whites are disliked even by other Whites (e.g., Greenberg, Schimel, Martens, Solomon,

& Pyszcznyski, 2001). Social scientists have suggested that racists suffer from undesirable personality types (e.g., authoritarianism, Adorno, Frenkel-Brunswik, Levinson, & Sanford, 1950; or social-dominance orientation, Sidanius & Pratto, 1999), poor psychosocial health (Hightower, 1997), and even existential terror (Greenberg et al., 2001). Notably, the most visible racist outlaws—Neo-Nazi groups—are also the greatest champions of White racial identification and pride (Young & Craig, 1997). Given this racial backdrop, White people may distance themselves from racism by shifting their conception of racism (Sommers & Norton, 2006) or shifting their own association with Whiteness. If they believe that identifying as White is synonymous with being prejudiced, they may be hesitant to publically identify as White or to feel that Whiteness is central to their self-concept (Katz & Ivey, 1977).

We propose that people engage in racial identity denial when they recognize their racial membership, perceive threats to the self or ingroup, and attempt to subvert these threats by downplaying or denying their racial identity. A person who engages in racial identity denial thus experiences a qualitatively different racial identity than people who are racially naïve. Identity form theorists such as Helms (1990) have long noted this discrepancy. Helms and her colleagues contrast racially naïve Whites to Whites who intellectualize race, label "other" cultures as dysfunctional, and blame racial others, but not Whites, for continued racism (Block & Carter, 1996). Unlike racially naïve Whites, Whites who engage in racial identity denial do not fail to recognize their race; rather, they deflect blame and guilt for racial injustice away from their racial ingroup, and by extension, their self.

Supporting the hypothesis that they "should know better," research suggests that Whites who engage in racial identity denial have more interracial contact than Whites who are racially naïve (Perry, 2001). Perry (2001) reported that some White students in a diverse high school were quick to deny that their race had any meaning or affected their attitudes or behavior. Yet simultaneously, they assigned considerable meaning to others' races. For example, these students blamed *others'* "ethnic" music and dance for White students' avoidance of pep rallies and extracurricular events and it was *others'* fixation on race and ethnicity that prevented racial harmony both at the school and in society generally.

This pattern of results suggests that Whites who engage in racial identity denial have a negational identity, that is, they know who they are by what they are not. People who have negational identities tend to see members of other groups as dissimilar to themselves and also engage in more outgroup derogation (Zhong, Phillips, Leonardelli, & Galinsky, 2008). In short, a negational racial identity allows Whites to mark race as a property of non-Whites and to rationalize the exclusion of racialized others.

Whites can also project Whiteness onto superordinate national ethnic identities, for example, Dutch (Meeus, Duriez, Vanbeselaere, & Boen, 2010) or American (Devos & Banaji, 2005). This "ingroup projection" among Whites seems pronounced in Western Europe, where discussion of the White race is particularly taboo (Goldberg, 2006). In some cases, ingroup projection seems to be a cognitive bias; however, people are particularly motivated to engage in ingroup projection under conditions of threat (Rosa & Waldzus, 2012). Most work on ingroup projection investigates how citizens of various European Union member states think about their common European identity (for a review, see Wenzel, Mummendey, & Waldzus, 2007); for example, Germans and Portuguese tend to report that the typical European is essentially German or Portuguese, respectively. People who engage in ingroup projection tend to be prejudiced against fellow superordinate group members who do not fit their superordinate group prototype—in other words, Germans who believe Europeans act like Germans tend to dislike Portuguese who do not act very German (Waldzus, Mummendey, & Wenzel, 2005). Similarly, Whites who project Whiteness onto superordinate national identities tend to be more racially prejudiced (Meeus et al., 2005; Reijerse, Van Acker, Vanbeselaere, Phalet, & Duriez, in press).

In sum, theories of racial identity suggest that White universalism and racial segregation cause many White people to be unaware of the importance of race (i.e., to be racially naïve). More racially aware Whites tend to have experienced interracial contact or received multicultural education. For some White people, however, these experiences are threatening. We suggest that perceived interracial threats can invoke racial identity denial. Research from a variety of fields suggests that it predicts more prejudice and system-justifying beliefs.

Racial Identity Denial and White Privilege. Recognizing White privilege is difficult or threatening for most White people (Lowery, Knowles, & Unzueta, 2007; Neville, Worthington, & Spanierman, 2001), let alone those who actively engage in racial identity denial. As McIntosh (1990, p. 31) notes in her seminal piece on the "invisible knapsack" of White privilege:

As a white person, I realized I had been taught about racism as something that puts others at a disadvantage, but had been taught not to see one of its corollary aspects, white privilege, which puts me at an advantage.

Anti-racism activist Tim Wise (2008) also recognizes the invisibility of White privilege, comically noting its implied absence in most dictionaries:

Type in overprivileged. And watch how fast that little red line pops up. That line that says, "nope, you're an idiot, making up words that don't exist; try again and get back to us." But if there is an underprivileged, there must be an overprivileged. Why don't we talk about it?

In this section, we discuss the relationship between racial identity denial and the belief in White privilege and also how the White privilege lesson itself may increase racial identity denial for some Whites.

The "White privilege lesson" in which White students learn about the myriad ways in which Whites benefit from their place atop the Western racial hierarchy has important implications for race relations. Collectively, Whites' failure to recognize White privilege helps to perpetuate racism (Sue, 2003). According to many diversity trainers (e.g., Ramsey, 1996), helping White trainees recognize their racial privileges is an essential step in the training process. Identity development theorists (Helms, 1990; Knowles & Peng, 2005) also predict that privilege-cognizant Whites are the most likely to hold pro-diversity attitudes. Empirical work supports this prediction. Among Whites, the belief in White privilege predicts less ingroup bias, greater support for affirmative action, and stronger behavioral intentions to report workplace discrimination (Case, 2007; Chrobot-Mason & Hepworth, 2005; Eichstedt, 2001; Powell, Branscombe, & Schmitt, 2005; Swim & Miller, 1999). Notably, the belief in White privilege has also been linked to more positive doctor–patient relationships (Paez, Allen, Beach, Carson, & Cooper, 2009). Racially naïve Whites, not surprisingly, are unlikely to be privilege-cognizant (Hays, Chang, & Havice, 2008). But Whites who engage in racial identity denial do not simply fail to recognize their own White privilege; they actively deny their Whiteness.

Depending on how the White privilege lesson is conveyed (c.f., Doosje, Branscombe, Spears, & Manstead, 1998; Lowery et al., 2007; Ramsey, 1996), it may trigger White guilt—a sense of guilt among Whites derived from past and present racist transgressions against racial minorities. On the one hand, Swim and Miller (1999) suggest that after receiving the White privilege lesson, "these feelings of guilt may in turn cause White Americans to look more favorably on policies, such as affirmative action programs, that are intended to ameliorate the impact of White privilege" (p. 500). White guilt has empirically predicted prejudice reduction and support for pro-diversity policies in both laboratory studies (Powell et al., 2005; Swim & Miller, 1999) and actual diversity training (Case, 2007). On the other hand, others have found that White guilt is unlikely to produce pro-diversity attitudes or behavioral change. For example, White guilt is a poor predictor of support for most equal opportunity policies (Iyer, Leach, & Crosby, 2003), particularly among the highly prejudiced or racially identified (Doosje et al., 1998). Cornelius Golightly (1947) wrote that Whites were most likely to reduce their collective guilt by justifying racism, endorsing negative stereotypes of racial minorities, and offering trinket, paternalistic philanthropy. Shelby Steele (1990) blames White guilt for ineffectual efforts toward egalitarianism that "deliver the look of innocence to society and its institutions but that do very little actually to uplift blacks" (p. 498).

In other words, under some circumstances at least, the White privilege lesson may ironically cause White racial identity denial or disidentification (Chow, Lowery, & Knowles 2008; Knowles & Marshburn, 2010), possibly through its infliction of White guilt. White guilt is by its nature directed toward the self and the ingroup and may make Whites question their own morality and goodness (for review, Branscombe, 2004; Iyer et al., 2003). When endorsing pro-diversity policies is a simple and immediately available guilt reduction strategy, White guilt tends to predict pro-diversity attitudes (Batson, 1998). But generally speaking, people who feel guilty are motivated to eliminate their guilt quickly, even in ways that don't logically resolve the initial source of the guilt (Batson, 1998; Branscombe, 2004; Golightly, 1947; Steele, 1990). For many Whites, the quickest way to alleviate this guilt is *not* to become anti-racism activists or to thoroughly question their own prejudices and biases. For many Whites, engaging in racial identity denial is a considerably easier method of reducing White guilt.

In sum, recognizing White privilege appears to be an important component of anti-racism. Whites who engage in racial identity denial are by definition unwilling to recognize their racial privilege. The White privilege lesson has been found to reduce prejudice, but it may backfire and unintentionally increase racial identity denial.

Racial identity denial and colorblindness. Colorblindness is a diversity ideology that stresses that race should not matter and that people should be treated as individuals. While colorblindness sounds desirable, it does not reflect current reality (Williams, 1997) and may lead to greater racial bias (e.g., Richeson & Nussbaum, 2004) and strained interracial interactions (e.g., Apfelbaum, Sommers, & Norton, 2008; Holoein & Shelton, 2012). Like colorblindness, racial identity denial emphasizes that race does not matter; but unlike colorblindness, this premise is applied to one's own identity. That is, Whites high in racial identity denial believe their own race is irrelevant to who they are. Therefore, we would expect to see overlap between colorblindness and racial identity denial, such that Whites who endorse colorblindness may also be particularly likely to adopt a strategy of racial identity denial. In this section, we first explore motivations for racial identity denial that map on to those in the colorblindness literature. We then suggest that, like colorblindness, racial identity denial may have negative intergroup consequences.

The denial of race as relevant to one's self may have roots similar to those of colorblindness. One factor that could motivate racial identity denial is the desire to protect the status quo. According to Bonilla-Silva (2003), colorblindness has developed and has been wielded by Whites in order to justify inequality. Indeed, previous research has found that, especially when threatened, Whites high in social dominance orientation adopt colorblindness to safeguard the social hierarchy (Knowles et al., 2009a). Likewise, Whites high in social dominance employ post-racialism—the idea that race no longer matters—to justify support for inequality (Knowles, Lowery, & Schaumberg, 2009b). Similarly, especially in the face of threats to the social hierarchy (e.g., diversity initiatives that are perceived to disfavor Whites), Whites who engage in racial identity denial may be strategically adopting a colorblind or post-racial stance (i.e., that race either should not or does not matter) regarding their own racial identity in order to justify a system that rejects racially based remediation of inequities.

Another factor that could motivate racial identity denial is the threat of being seen as a prejudiced person, as we note above. Previous research on colorblindness in interracial interactions suggests that Whites adopt a colorblind stance in an effort to appear unprejudiced (Apfelbaum et al. 2008). In fact this work links colorblindness to external, but not internal, motivation to control prejudice. For White Americans, not identifying or self-categorizing with a race could be one of the simplest ways to dodge the threat of *appearing* racially prejudiced. As with colorblindness, many Whites who engage in racial identity denial may do so because of an external, but not internal, motivation to control prejudice. Furthermore, research grounded in Self-Determination Theory (Deci & Ryan, 2002) has demonstrated that Whites with an external, rather than internal, motivation to control prejudice may harbor implicit and explicit prejudice against racial outgroups (Devine, Plant, Amodio, Harmon-Jones, & Vance, 2002; Legault, Green-Demers, Grant, & Chung, 2007).

Therefore, paradoxically, instead of scaffolding a more positive climate for diversity, colorblindness—and by association, racial identity denial—may foster a more *negative* one. For example, colorblind racial attitudes predict belief in a just world and modern racism (Neville et al., 2001), and exposing Whites to a colorblind message increases implicit and explicit racial bias (e.g., Richeson & Nussbaum, 2004; but see Levin, et al. 2012). Moreover, Whites' attempts to disregard race lead to more strained intergroup interactions (e.g., Apfelbaum et al., 2008; Holoien & Shelton, 2012). Further, rather than provoking more positive workplace outcomes, White employees' endorsement of colorblindness predicts lower psychological engagement among minority employees (Plaut et al., 2009).

In sum, if racial identity denial resembles colorblindness turned inward, then we can expect it to stem from motivations ranging from protection of the social hierarchy to avoidance of being seen as prejudiced. Moreover, we can expect that racial identity denial also predicts anti-diversity attitudes and contributes to a negative climate for diversity.

Summary. Most White people live in a racially segregated world, believe that race should be ignored, and are naïve to the role their own race plays in their lives. Interracial contact can be threatening for these people in many ways: they may feel threats to their physical or economic well-being, symbolic threats to their ideals, and the stereotype threat of appearing prejudiced. Research has demonstrated that how Whites manage these threats affects their attitudes toward diversity. Whites who identify as White but also recognize White privilege and adopt an internal motivation to control prejudice tend to endorse relatively positive attitudes toward diversity. In contrast, Whites who resolve these threats by downplaying the importance of race in society (i.e., colorblindness) or to their selves (i.e., racial identity denial) tend to endorse anti-diversity attitudes and foster negative climates for diversity.

PRELIMINARY EMPIRICAL WORK

Preliminary evidence from two studies we conducted in organizational contexts (Goren, Plaut, & Thomas, 2013) sheds some light on how racial identity denial relates to White identity, White privilege, colorblindness, and diversity attitudes more generally. We measured racial identity denial with items such as "The notion of race doesn't really apply to me" and "I don't feel like I belong to any racial/ethnic category." Across two studies conducted with a professional association and a large health-care organization, we generally found that for White employees racial identity denial correlated moderately negatively with racial identity, negatively with the recognition of White privilege, and positively with colorblindness, indicating that racial identity denial is a related but distinct construct. Moreover, racial identity denial predicted more anti-diversity attitudes (e.g., system justifying beliefs) and fewer positive attitudes toward diversity (e.g., multiculturalism) even when controlling for colorblindness and for racial identity. Additionally, in one study the more Whites engaged in racial identity denial, the less they intended to participate in diversity initiatives.

We also asked White participants in one of the studies to give suggestions for improving the climate for diversity in their organization. We found that Whites who engage in racial identity denial were especially likely to believe that the organization focused too much on diversity and to propose the organization do less (e.g., "stop pushing the idea [of diversity] so much"). They also suggested the organization did too little on similarities. For example, some Whites who engaged in racial identity denial rejected the very idea of racial diversity. One wrote "there is only 1 group . . . people. Some are lighter or darker than others."

Other responses from White employees who engaged in racial identity denial were more insidious. Dozens equated organizational diversity with misguided efforts to appease minorities. One noted that the organization was "hiring unqualified" people of color "just to have that ethnic group represented" while another said the organization should "hire skilled employees rather than diverse employees." A third employee made a thoughtful suggestion to reestablish the balance of power: "Please do not make MLK a Mandatary [sic] Holiday, if you do please allow staff to work or take off US Presidents Day." Others noted that "majorities" are "purposefully excluded" by the "goal of becoming more diverse." These types of responses indicate that "others" benefit from pro-diversity policies while "normal people" suffer. Tellingly, White employees who most engaged in racial identity denial avoided words such as "Whites," "Caucasians," or similar derivatives altogether.

In sum, Goren et al. (2013) found that Whites' racial identity denial was related to racial identity, colorblindness, White privilege, and diversity attitudes and fostered a less inclusive diversity climate for racial minorities. Moreover, in other laboratory and field studies, we have psychometrically distinguished between a weak White racial identity and racial identity denial (Goren & Plaut, 2011). Participants in these studies completed questionnaires that include *positively* worded racial identity items such as "I have a clear sense of my ethnic background and what it means to me" as well as *negatively* worded racial identity denial items such as "The notion of race doesn't really apply to me." Although these items seem to be mirror images, further analysis reveals that this is not necessarily the case. Furthermore, racial identity denial appears to have predictive value above and beyond racial identity measures. In other words, identifying with a race is not the psychological opposite of racial identity denial.

Together, these preliminary findings illuminate the potential corollaries and consequences of racial identity denial but leave open the question of whether and how it is motivated. To the extent the racial identity denial is motivated, it is unclear why certain people possess this motivation. Also unclear is the role of threat to the ingroup. Finally, the generalizability of these findings is unknown beyond White, middle-aged professionals, though we speculate about and share some preliminary empirical findings for employees of color in the studies in the proceeding section.

RACIAL IDENTITY DENIAL BY PEOPLE OF COLOR

Before turning to the implications of Whites' racial identity denial, we first briefly suggest its possible causes and consequences among people of color. Because of White universalism (Perry, 2007), the racial identity denial processes described in this chapter may best apply to Whites. Racial and ethnic minorities tend to score much higher than Whites on measures of racial identity (Phinney et al., 1997) and much lower than Whites on our measures of racial identity denial. That said, some people of color do engage in racial identity denial.

As with racial naïvety among Whites, very low racial identity among people of color may be owing to a lack of racial awareness or salience (Sellers, Rowley, Tabbye, Shelton, & Smith, 1997; Worrell, Vandiver, Schaefer, Cross, & Fhagen-Smith, 2006; Zagefka & Brown, 2002). Some people of color may engage in racial identity denial to cope with societal disadvantage for people associated with a low status group (Cross, 1991; Jost & Hunyady, 2005; Major, Quinton, & Schmader, 2003; Phinney, 1990). People of color who believe the status quo is just tend to have low self-esteem, poor psychological functioning, and dislike their own racial ingroup (Jost & Hunyady, 2005)—but only if they are strongly identified with this ingroup (Major et al., 2003; O'Brien & Major, 2005). People of color who believe in a just world may therefore endorse racial identity denial to avoid these negative psychological outcomes.

In our preliminary empirical research (Goren et al., 2013), we examined the correlates of racial identity denial for Black Americans. Consistent with the reasoning above, Blacks' racial identity denial predicted more system justifying beliefs, more colorblindness, and less multiculturalism. In addition, Blacks high in racial identity denial reported receiving racial privileges (i.e., getting more opportunities and advantages due to their race) and perceived a positive organizational diversity climate (e.g., a sense that the organization supports diversity). We also examined these relationships for Asians and Latinos, finding only significant relationships for Asians between racial identity denial and more colorblindness and less multiculturalism. This lack of effects may be due to low statistical power.

IMPLICATIONS OF RACIAL IDENTITY DENIAL FOR PRACTICE

The study of racial identity denial has numerous practical implications for individuals and organizations. We discuss implications for cross-race interpersonal relations, diversity training, leadership, and organizational effectiveness.

Implications for Cross-Race Interpersonal Relations. Racial identity denial can be a substantial barrier to effective cross-racial communication. In a series of studies, Saguy and her colleagues (see Saguy, Pratto, Dovidio, & Nadler, 2009) investigated the intergroup communication preferences of dominant and minority groups. Across a variety of real-world and artificial groups, they found that members of dominant groups preferred to avoid discussion of differences and group identities. By directing the conversation away from these topics, members of dominant groups are able to help maintain the status quo. Whites who engage in racial identity denial seem to be especially likely to avoid discussing differences. By avoiding the topics that members of racial minority groups want to discuss, Whites who engage in racial identity denial may create more awkward or hostile interactions.

Trust, empathy, and perspective taking are vital for relationships (Batson, 1998). Whites who engage in racial identity denial may struggle to gain the trust of people of color or establish empathy and perspective taking. Racial identity denial may be particularly problematic for relationships in which a White person occupies a position of power, such as in mentoring (Chrobot-Mason, 2004; Thomas, 1998) or counseling (Mindrup, Spray, & Lamberghini-West, 2011). When Whites in these settings fail to identify with their race or recognize their unearned racial privileges, they are worse mentors and therapists, demonstrate low cultural competency, and cause their charges to disengage. In part in recognition of this problem, all accredited counseling programs (American Psychological Association, 2008) and most businesses (Esen, 2005) have implemented diversity training.

Implications for Diversity Training. Diversity training tends to reduce racial identity denial among Whites (Brown et al., 1996; Neville, Heppner, Louie, Thompson, Brooks, & Baker, 1996; cf., Chrobot-Mason, 2004). That said, the type of diversity training used as well as the specific audience play important moderating roles. The quickness of some Whites to brush off the reality of racial privilege and even their own race is a special problem for teachers of the White privilege lesson. Yet this problem is exacerbated when trainers confront and blame White students themselves for racial inequalities (e.g., Ramsey, 1996). These methods are likely to cause "backlash" from Whites, especially White men, that can derail the training session (e.g., Boatright-Horowitz & Soeung, 2009; Goldstein, 2001) and even lead to more negative interracial attitudes (Branscombe, Schmitt, & Schiffhauer, 2007) and interactions (Holladay & Quiñones, 2008).

One way to avoid backlash is to increase racial self-awareness in non-threatening environments (Holladay, Knight, Paige, & Quiñones, 2003; Pendry, Driscoll, & Field, 2007). A common recommendation is to discuss the most threatening aspects of training in racially homogeneous class-rooms (e.g., Roberson, Kulik, & Pepper, 2001). In racially mixed classes, initial activities should "break the ice" (Fowler, 1994) or raise awareness through fun, non-threatening activities such as sharing interesting cultural artifacts (Chavez & Poirier, 2007). Once rapport is established, trainers can broach the White privilege lesson (e.g., Pendry et al., 2007). The non-threatening approach to raising racial awareness has created positive outcomes in many domains, including business (e.g., Holladay et al., 2003) and medicine (e.g., Griswald, Zayas, Kernan, & Wagnar, 2007).

Alternatively, contact theorists suggest that White people can understand White privilege from positive interracial contact (e.g., from team sports; Butryn, 2002). If White people learn the White privilege lesson in a non-threatening way from their trusted friends and peers, they are less likely to feel paralyzing White guilt or defensively engage in racial identity denial. Intergroup contact also increases empathy toward racial others (Pettigrew, 1998). Empathy is a far better predictor of pro-social behavior than guilt (Batson, 1998). Moreover, Whites who both believe in White privilege and feel empathy toward racial minorities seem to endorse the most pro-diversity attitudes (e.g., Eichstedt, 2001).

Implications for Leadership and Organizational Effectiveness. According to Ely and Thomas (2001), most organizations adopt one of three diversity management perspectives: discrimination-and-fairness, access-and-legitimacy, or integration-and-learning. In this section, we discuss how these perspectives might influence the experiences and behaviors of White managers and employees who engage in racial identity denial.

Organizations that adopt the discrimination-and-fairness perspective avoid illegal discriminatory policies and implement mandated Affirmative Action programs but also pigeon-hole "diversity hires," fail to embrace diversity "in any fundamental way" (Ely & Thomas, 2001, p. 246), and perpetuate a colorblind, hostile climate for diversity. In these organizations, White employees who engage in racial identity denial would not be required to attend diversity training or multicultural events. They would not need to be racially aware or culturally competent. Such an organization may also attract and retain people of color with low ethnic identity, a group that tends to be relatively tolerant of Whites who engage in racial identity denial (Chrobot-Mason, 2004; Helms, 1990).

The lack of formal support for diversity makes these organizations relatively uncomfortable for most people of color (Ely & Thomas, 2001).

People of color who draw attention to racial discrimination may only confirm the belief of Whites who engage in racial identity denial that *others* are obsessed with race and are trying to subvert the organization's culture. White managers who engage in racial identity denial are unlikely to address these claims or work to improve the climate for diversity (Thomas, 1993). They may further dampen the diversity climate and reduce numerical diversity by ignoring or removing people who "pull the race card." Rare efforts to embrace diversity may be paternalistic. In a misguided attempt to help and protect people of color, White managers who engage in racial identity denial may accept lower qualifications, adopt lower performance evaluation thresholds, and create segregated career paths. These practices would create a shadow organization where people of color are prevented from succeeding and advancing alongside the "regular" (i.e., White) employees. People of color in these workplaces may engage in racial identity denial to fit in and psychologically protect their selves from the negative climate for diversity.

Organizations that adopt the access-and-legitimacy perspective use their diverse workforce to better tap culturally diverse client bases. For example, an international firm based in the United States may hire Chinese ex-pats to expand its presence in the Chinese market. While organizations that adopt this perspective do see increased numerical diversity, management positions and organizational culture are typically dominated by Whites (Ely & Thomas, 2001). The access-and-legitimacy perspective, therefore, may create two very different climates for diversity in a single workplace.

In the "core" office, where diversity is relatively low and the climate for diversity is poor, White employees and managers who engage in racial identity denial are unlikely to be pressured to develop a racial identity or consciousness. They might even embrace increasing diversity in the organizational periphery so long as it does not interfere with the "core mission" or require giving up positions of power to people who are just "diversity hires." In other words, they may rationalize the need for diversity so long as "regular people" continue to hold most positions, and especially the most powerful positions, in the organization. Within the hostile diversity climate of the "core" office, employees of color may engage in racial identity denial to avoid negative social and psychological consequences. White managers who engage in racial identity denial may even use their power to limit advancement opportunities for people who work in the "diversity" office, a practice that would disproportionately impact employees of color. They are unlikely to interpret this behavior as racial discrimination; to them, people in the diversity office are simply not an important part of the *real* organization or its mission.

Within the diversity office itself, where numerical diversity is high and cultural awareness is a necessity, we suspect there would be very few if any Whites who engage in racial identity denial. First, Whites are unlikely to be hired into the diversity offices of organizations that embrace the access-and-legitimacy perspective. Second, Whites who do work in these offices are likely to have high levels of racial self-awareness either by selection (Eichstedt, 2001; Page-Gould, Mendoza-Denton, & Tropp, 2008; Trawalter, Richeson, & Shelton, 2009) or acculturation (Dutton, Singer, & Devlin, 1998; Helms, 1990; McKinney, 2006).

Integration-and-fairness organizations weave the skills, knowledge, and abilities of their diverse workforces into their core. As a consequence, employees from all backgrounds are expected to appreciate diversity and act accordingly. For example, a law partnership that operates in the integration-and-fairness perspective would expect all of its lawyers, and not just the Latinas, to work with Latina clients in a culturally competent manner (Ely & Thomas, 2001). Organizational effectiveness also improves as members of minority groups are no longer assigned to the organizational periphery or to token status (Dawson, 2011).

Whites as well as people of color who engage in racial identity denial would be ill-suited for this type of workplace (Block, Roberson, & Neuger, 1995; Chrobot-Mason, 2004). Success in these organizations requires the consideration of how one's own race and ethnicity affects relationships with co-workers and clients (Thomas, 1998). According to Ely and Thomas (2001), White employees working in the integration-and-learning perspective must "learn to take up, on their own, the issues and concerns that might initially have been raised by their colleagues of color" (p. 243). White employees who engage in racial identity denial may be unwilling or unable to be an advocate for diversity and to work well with a diverse workforce and clientele. Despite the inclusive stance of the integration-and-fairness perspective, these people may also not feel included in the organization's definition of diversity, believing for example that the organization is pushing for an ethnic kaleidoscope to which they cannot contribute as "normal" or "average" people.

In an integration-and-learning organization, racial tensions are unlikely to be suppressed because people are less inclined to mask conflict (Ely &

Thomas, 2001). While this openness tends to promote organizational effectiveness, it makes a poor climate for White managers or employees who engage in racial identity denial. Employees may try to avoid colleagues or even exit the organization; unlike some of their peers, they may be uninterested in learning about their own or their co-workers' cultural identities and perspectives. Managers, in contrast, may use their power to dominate the discourse (Hall, Coats, & LeBeau, 2005) and turn the discussion away from cultural differences (Saguy et al., 2009). These actions may increase burnout for employees of color, derail diversity initiatives, and create an atmosphere generally inconsistent with the organizational pursuit of an integration-and-learning perspective.

Organizations that adopt the integration-and-learning perspective may actually reduce racial identity denial. According to contact theorists (see Pettigrew, 1998), majority group members' interactions with minority outgroup members typically increase empathy while reducing stereotyping and discrimination. Others note, however, that increased minority representation may cause backlash from powerful groups (Holladay & Quiñones, 2008). We argue that Whites who engage in racial identity denial are particularly likely to engage in backlash and resistance because they tend to see diversity as threatening. They are also unlikely to think that people from different racial backgrounds share their values, a belief that moderates the relationship between organizational diversity and effectiveness (e.g., Chatman, Polzer, Barsade, & Neale, 1998).

CONCLUSION

In this chapter, we have introduced the construct of racial identity denial. We have informed our understanding of this construct using theories of White racial identity, White privilege, and racial colorblindness. Racial identity denial appears to be motivated by a desire to mitigate threats to the ingroup or self rather than to a relatively benign lack of racial awareness, as with racial naïveté. Additionally, our preliminary empirical work suggests that racial identity denial is associated with prejudice, system-justification, and more hostile organizational diversity climates. Future research should better incorporate racial identity denial into existing streams of research and also consider how an understanding of racial identity denial can call into question current perspectives on social-organizational issues. Future work must also test our hypotheses regarding the development of racial identity denial.

We believe that racial identity denial has important implications for organizations: it can be a barrier to effective interracial communication and cooperation, particularly when adopted by Whites in leadership positions, and can have negative repercussions for organizational effectiveness and climate, particularly in diverse, integrated organizations. So long as they take care to avoid backlash, organizations may be able to reduce racial identity denial through diversity training and ultimately create more inclusive workplaces.

REFERENCES

Adorno, T. W., Frenkel-Brunswik, E., Levinson, D. J., & Sanford, R. N. (1950). *The authoritarian personality*. New York: Harper.

American Psychological Association (2008). Guidelines and principles for accreditation of programs in professional psychology. Washington, DC: Author.

Apfelbaum, E. P., Sommers, S. R., & Norton, M. I. (2008). Seeing race and seeming racist? Evaluating strategic colorblindness in social interaction. *Journal of Personality and Social Psychology, 95*, 918–932.

Batson, C. D. (1998). Altruism and prosocial behavior. In D. T. Gilbert, & S. T. Fiske (Eds.), *The handbook of social psychology* (Vol. 2, pp. 282–316). Boston, MA: McGraw-Hill.

Block, C. J., & Carter, R. T. (1996). White racial identity attitudes theories: A rose by any other name is still a rose. *The Counseling Psychologist, 24*, 326–334.

Block, C. J., Roberson, L., & Neuger, D. A. (1995). White racial identity theory: A framework for understanding reactions toward interracial situations in organizations. *Journal of Vocational Behavior, 46*, 71–88.

Boatright-Horowitz, S., & Soeung, S. (2009). Teaching White privilege to White students can mean saying good-bye to positive student evaluations. *American Psychologist, 64*, 574–575.

Bonilla-Silva, E. (2003). *Racism without racists: Color-blind racism and the persistence of racial inequality in the United States*. Lanham, MD: Rowman & Littlefield.

Branscombe, N. R. (2004). A social psychological process perspective on collective guilt. In N. R. Brandscombe, & B. Doosje (Eds.), *Collective guilt: International perspectives* (pp. 320–334). Cambridge: Cambridge University Press.

Branscombe, N. R., Schmitt, M. T., & Schiffhauer, K. (2007). Racial attitudes in response to thoughts of White privilege. *European Journal of Social Psychology, 37*, 203–215.

Brown, S. P., Parham, T. A., & Yonker, R. (1996). Influence of a cross-cultural training course on racial identity attitudes of White women and men: Preliminary perspectives. *Journal of Counseling & Development, 74*, 510–516.

Burkard, A. W., Juarez-Huffaker, M., & Ajmere, K. (2003). White racial identity attitudes as a predictor of client perceptions of cross-cultural working alliances. *Multicultural Counseling and Development, 31*, 226–244.

Butryn, T. M. (2002). Critically examining White racial identity and privilege in sport psychology consulting. *The Sport Psychologist, 16*, 316–336.

Carter, R. T. (1995). *The influence of race and racial identity in psychotherapy: Toward a racially inclusive model.* New York: Wiley.

Case, K. A. (2007). Raising White privilege awareness and reducing racial prejudice: Assessing diversity course effectiveness. *Teaching of Psychology, 34*, 231–235.

Chatman, J. A., Polzer, J. T., Barsade, S. G., & Neale, M. A. (1998). Being different yet feeling similar: The influence of demographic composition and organizational culture on work processes and outcomes. *Administrative Science Quarterly, 43*, 749–780.

Chavez, C. I., & Poirier, V. H. (2007). Stimulating cultural appetites: An experiential gourmet approach. *Journal of Management Education, 31*, 505–520.

Chow, R. M., Lowery, B. S., & Knowles, E. D. (2008). The two faces of dominance: The differential effect of ingroup superiority and outgroup inferiority on dominant-group identity and group esteem. *Journal of Experimental Social Psychology, 44*(4), 1073–1081.

Chrobot-Mason, D. (2004). Managing racial differences: The role of majority managers' ethnic identity development on minority employee perceptions of support. *Group Organization Management, 29*, 5–31.

Chrobot-Mason, D., & Hepworth, W. K. (2005). Examining perceptions of ambiguous and unambiguous threats of racial harassment and managerial response strategies. *Journal of Applied Social Psychology, 35*(11), 2215–2261.

Cross, W. E., Jr. (1991). *Shades of black: Diversity in African-American identity.* Philadelphia, PA: Temple University Press.

Dawson, B. L. (2011). An analysis of successors, ethnic identity and inclusive organizations as buffers to stereotype threat. (Unpublished Doctoral Dissertation). Athens, GA: University of Georgia.

Deci, E. L., & Ryan, R. M. (2002). *Handbook of self-determination research.* Rochester, NY: University of Rochester Press.

Devine, P. G., Plant, A. E., Amodio, D. M., Harmon-Jones, & Vance, S. L. (2002). The regulation of explicit and implicit race bias: The role of motivations to respond without prejudice. *Journal of Personality and Social Psychology, 82*, 835–848.

Devos, T., & Banaji, M. R. (2005). American=White? *Journal of Personality and Social Psychology, 88*, 447–466.

Doosje, B., Branscombe, N. R., Spears, R., & Manstead, A. S. R. (1998). Guilty by association: When one's group has a negative history. *Journal of Personality and Social Psychology, 75*, 872–886.

Dutton, S. E., Singer, J. A., & Devlin, A. S. (1998). Racial identity of children in integrated, predominantly White, and Black schools. *The Journal of Social Psychology, 138*, 41–53.

Eichstedt, J. L. (2001). Problematic White identities and a search for racial justice. *Sociological Forum, 16*, 445–471.

Ellemers, N., Spears, R., & Doosje, B. (2002). Self and social identity. *Annual Review of Psychology, 53*, 161–186.

Ely, R. J., & Thomas, D. A. (2001). Cultural diversity at work: The effects of diversity perspectives on work group processes and outcomes. *Administrative Science Quarterly, 46*, 229–273.

Esen, E. (2005). *2005 Workplace Diversity Practices Survey Report*. Alexandria, VA: Society for Human Resource Management.

Fowler, S. M. (1994). Two decades of using simulation games for cross-cultural training. *Simulation and Gaming, 25*, 464–476.

Goff, P. A., Steele, C. M., & Davies, P. G. (2008). The space between us: Stereotype threat and distance in interracial contexts. *Journal of Personality and Social Psychology, 94*, 91–107.

Goldberg, D. T. (2006). Racial Europeanization. *Ethnic and Racial Studies, 29*(2), 331–364.

Goldstein, T. (2001). "I'm not White": Anti-racist teacher education for white early childhood educators. *Contemporary Issues in Early Childhood, 2*(1), 3–13.

Golightly, C. L. (1947). Race, values, and guilt. *Social Forces, 26*(2), 125–139.

Goren, M. J., & Plaut, V. C. (2011, January). *"I don't have a race": Individual and organizational implications of racial denial*. Paper presented at the annual meeting of the Society for Personality and Social Psychology, San Antonio, TX.

Goren, M. J., & Plaut, V. C. (2012). Identity form matters: White racial identity and attitudes toward diversity. *Self and Identity, 11*, 237–254.

Goren, M. J., Plaut, V. C., & Thomas, K. M. (2013). "I don't have a race": Individual and organizational implications of racial denial. Unpublished manuscript, Berkeley, CA: University of California.

Greenberg, J., Schimel, J., Martens, A., Solomon, S., & Pyszczynski, T. (2001). Sympathy for the Devil: Evidence that reminding Whites of their mortality promotes more favorable reactions to White racists. *Motivation and Emotion, 25*(2), 113–133.

Griswald, K., Zayas, L. E., Kernan, J. B., & Wagnar, C. M. (2007). Cultural awareness through medical student and refugee patient encounters. *Journal of Immigrant Health, 9*, 55–60.

Gushue, G. V., & Carter, R. T. (2000). Remembering race: White racial identity attitudes and two aspects of social memory. *Journal of Counseling Psychology, 47*, 199–210.

Hall, J. A., Coats, E. J., & LeBeau, L. S. (2005). Nonverbal behavior and the vertical dimension of social relations: A meta-analysis. *Psychological Bulletin, 131*, 898–924.

Hays, D. G., Chang, C. Y., & Havice, P. (2008). White racial identity statuses as predictors of White privilege awareness. *Humanistic counseling, education, and development, 47*, 234–246.

Helms, J. E. (1990). *Black and White racial identity*. New York: Greenwood.

Hightower, E. (1997). Psychosocial characteristics of subtle and blatant racists as compared to tolerant individuals. *Journal of Clinical Psychology, 53*(4), 369–374.

Holladay, C. L., Knight, J. L., Paige, D. L., & Quiñones, M. A. (2003). The influence of framing on attitudes toward diversity training. *Human Resource Development Quarterly, 14*, 245–263.

Holladay, C. L., & Quiñones, M. A. (2008). The influence of training focus and trainer characteristics on diversity training effectiveness. *Academy of Management Learning and Education, 7*(3), 343–354.

Holoien, D. S., & Shelton, J. (2012). You deplete me: The cognitive costs of colorblindness on ethnic minorities. *Journal of Experimental Social Psychology, 48*, 562–565.

Iyer, A., Leach, C. W., & Crosby, F. J. (2003). White guilt and racial compensation: The benefits and limits of self-focus. *Personality and Social Psychology Bulletin, 29*, 117–129.

Jost, J. T., & Hunyady, O. (2005). Antecedents and consequences of system-justifying ideologies. *Current Directions in Psychological Science, 14*(5), 260–265.

Katz, J. H., & Ivey, I. (1977). White awareness: The frontier of racism awareness training. *Personnel and Guidance Journal, 55*, 485–488.

Kinder, D. R., & Sears, D. O. (1981). Prejudice and politics: Symbolic racism versus racial threats to the good life. *Journal of Personality and Social Psychology, 40*, 414–431.

Knowles, E. D., Lowery, B. S., Hogan, C. M., & Chow, R. M. (2009a). On the malleability of ideology: Motivated construals of color-blindness. *Journal of Personality and Social Psychology, 96*, 857–869.

Knowles, E. D., Lowery, B. S., & Schaumberg, R. L. (2009b). Anti-egalitarians for Obama? Group-dominance motivation and the Obama vote. *Journal of Experimental Social Psychology, 45*(4), 965–969.

Knowles, E. D., & Marshburn, C. K. (2010). Understanding white identity politics will be crucial to diversity science. *Psychological Inquiry, 21*(2), 134–139.

Knowles, E. D., & Peng, K. P. (2005). White selves: Conceptualizing and measuring a dominant-group identity. *Journal of Personality and Social Psychology, 89*, 223–241.

Legault, L., Green-Demers, I., Grant, P., & Chung, J. (2007). On the self-regulation of implicit and explicit prejudice: A Self-Determination Theory perspective. *Personality and Social Psychology Bulletin, 33*, 732–749.

Levin, S., Matthews, M., Guimond, S., Sidanius, J., Pratto, F., Kteily, N., Pitpitan, E. V., & Dover, T. (2012). Assimilation, multiculturalism, and colorblindness: Mediated and moderated relationships between social dominance orientation and prejudice. *Journal of Experimental Social Psychology, 48*, 207–212.

Lowery, B. S., Knowles, E. D., & Unzueta, M. M. (2007). Framing inequality safely: Whites' motivated perceptions of racial privilege. *Personality and Social Psychology Bulletin, 33*, 1237–1250.

Major, B., Quinton, W. J., & Schmader, T. (2003). Attributions to discrimination and self-esteem: Impact of group identification and situational ambiguity. *Journal of Experimental Social Psychology, 39*(3), 220–231.

McConahay, J. B., Hardee, B. B., & Batts, V. (1981). Has racism declined in America? It depends on who is asking and what is asked. *The Journal of Conflict Resolution, 25*, 563–579.

McIntosh, P. (1990). White privilege: Unpacking the invisible knapsack. *Independent School*, 31–36.

McKay, P. F., Avery, D. R., Tonidanel, S., Morris, M. A., Hernandez, M., & Hebl, M. R. (2007). Racial differences in employee retention: Are diversity climate perceptions the key? *Personnel Psychology, 60*, 35–62.

McKinney, K. D. (2006). "I really felt white": Turning points in whiteness through interracial contact. *Social Identities: Journal for the Study of Race, Nation and Culture, 12*(2), 167–185.

Meeus, J., Duriez, B., Vanbeselaere, N., & Boen, F. (2010). The role of national identity representation in the relation between in-group identification and out-group derogation: Ethnic versus civic representation. *British Journal of Social Psychology, 49*, 305–320.

Mindrup, R. M., Spray, B. J., & Lamberghini-West, A. (2011). White privilege and multicultural counseling competence: The influence of field of study, sex, and racial/ethnic exposure. *Journal of Ethnic & Cultural Diversity in Social Work: Innovation in Theory, Research & Practice, 20*, 20–38.

Neville, H. A., Heppner, M. J., Louie, C. E., Thompson, C. E., Brooks, L., & Baker, C. E. (1996). The impact of multicultural training on white racial identity attitudes and therapy competencies. *Professional Psychology: Research and Practice, 27*, 83–89.

Neville, H. A., Worthington, R. L., & Spanierman, L. B. (2001). Race, power, and multicultural counseling psychology: Understanding White privilege and color-blind racial attitudes. In J. Ponterotto, J. M. Casas, L. A. Suzuki, & C. M. Alexander (Eds.), *Handbook of multicultural counseling* (pp. 257–288). Thousand Oaks, CA: Sage.

O'Brien, L. T., & Major, B. (2005). System-justifying beliefs and psychological well-being: The roles of group status and identity. *Personality and Social Psychology Bulletin, 31*, 1718.

Orbe, M. P., & Harris, T. M. (2006). Race/ethnicity, the mass media, and interracial communication. *Interracial communication: Theory into practice.* Stamford, CT: Wadsworth.

Orfield, G., Kucsera, J., & Siegel-Hawley, G. (2012, September). *E Pluribus . . . Separation: Deepening Double Segregation for More Students.* Retrieved from http://civilrights project.ucla.edu/research/k-12-education/integration-and-diversity/mlk-national/e-pluribus. . .separation-deepening-double-segregation-for-more-students/orfield_epluribus_revised_omplete_2012.pdf

Paez, K. A., Allen, J. K., Beach, M. C., Carson, K. A., & Cooper, L. A. (2009). Physician cultural competence and patient ratings of the patient–physician relationship. *Journal of General Internal Medicine, 24*, 495–498.

Page-Gould, E., Mendoza-Denton, R., & Tropp, L. R. (2008). With a little help from my cross-group friend: Reducing anxiety in intergroup contexts through cross-group friendship. *Journal of Personality and Social Psychology, 95*(5), 1080–1094.

Pendry, L. F., Driscoll, D. M., & Field, S. C. T. (2007). Diversity training: Putting theory into practice. *Journal of Occupational and Organizational Psychology, 80*, 27–50.

Perry, P. (2001). White means never having to say you're ethnic: White youth and the construction of "cultureless" identities. *Journal of Contemporary Ethnography, 30*(1), 56–91.

Perry, P. (2007). White universal identity as a "sense of group position." *Symbolic Interaction, 30*(3), 375–393.

Pettigrew, T. F. (1998). Intergroup contact theory. *Annual Review Psychology, 49*, 65–85.

Phinney, J. S. (1990). Ethnic identity in adolescents and adults: Review of research. *Psychology Bulletin, 108*, 499–514.

Phinney, J. S., Cantu, C., & Kurtz, D. (1997). Ethnic and American identity as predictors of self-esteem among African American, Latino, and White adolescents. *Journal of Youth and Adolescence, 26*, 165–185.

Plaut, V. C., Thomas, K. M., & Goren, M. J. (2009). Is multiculturalism or color-blindness better for minorities? *Psychological Science, 20*, 444–446.

Powell, A. A., Branscombe, N. R., & Schmitt, M. T. (2005). Inequality as ingroup privilege or outgroup disadvantage: The impact of group focus on collective guilt and interracial attitudes. *Personality and Social Psychology Bulletin, 31*, 508–521.

Quist, R. M., & Resendez, M. G. (2002). Social dominance threat: Examining social dominance theory's explanation of prejudice as legitimizing myths. *Basic and Applied Social Psychology, 24*, 287–293.

Ramsey, M. (1996). Diversity identity development training: Theory informs practice. *Journal of Multicultural Counseling and Development, 24*, 229–240.

Reijerse, A., Van Acker, K., Vanbeselaere, N., Phalet, K., & Duriez, B. (in press). Beyond the ethnic-civic dichotomy: Cultural citizenship as a new way of excluding immigrants. *Political Psychology.*

Richeson, J. A., & Nussbaum, R. J. (2004). The impact of multiculturalism vs. color-blindness on racial bias. *Journal of Experimental Social Psychology, 40*, 417–423.

Roberson, L., Kulik, C. T., & Pepper, M. B. (2001). Designing effective diversity training: Influence of group composition and trainee experience. *Journal of Organizational Behavior, 22*, 871–885.

Rosa, M., & Waldzus, S. (2012). Efficiency and defense motivated ingroup projection: Sources of prototypicality in intergroup relations. *Journal of Experimental Social Psychology, 48*(3), 669–681.

Saguy, T., Pratto, F., Dovidio, J. F., & Nadler, A. (2009). Talking about power: Group power and the desired content of intergroup interactions. In S. Demoulin, J. Leyens, & J. F. Dovidio (Eds.), *Intergroup misunderstandings: Impact of divergent social realities* (pp. 213–232). New York: Psychology Press.

Sellers, R. M., Rowley, S. A. J., Tabbye, M. C., Shelton, J. N., & Smith, M. A. (1997). Multidimensional Inventory of Black Identity: A preliminary investigation of reliability and construct validity. *Journal of Personality and Social Psychology, 73*, 805–815.

Sidanius, J., & Pratto, F. (2001). *Social dominance: An intergroup theory of social hierarchy and oppression.* New York: Cambridge University Press.

Sommers, S. R. & Norton, M. I. (2006). Lay theories about White racists: What constitutes racism (and what doesn't). *Group Processes and Intergroup Relations, 9*, 117–138.

Steele, S. (1990). White guilt. *The American Scholar, 59*(4), 497–506.

Stevens, F. G., Plaut, V. C., & Sanchez-Burks, J. (2008). Unlocking the benefits of diversity: All-inclusive multiculturalism and positive organizational change. *Journal of Applied Behavioral Science, 44*, 116–133.

Sue, D. W. (2003). *Overcoming our racism: The journey to liberation.* San Francisco, CA: Jossey-Bass.

Swim, J. K., & Miller, D. L. (1999). White guilt: Its antecedents and consequences for attitudes toward affirmative action. *Personality and Social Psychology Bulletin, 25*, 500–514.

Thomas, D. A. (1993). Racial dynamics in cross-race developmental relationships. *Administrative Science Quarterly, 38*, 169–194.

Thomas, K. M. (1998). Psychological readiness for multicultural leadership. *Management Development Forum, 1*, 99–112.

Thomas, K. M. (2008). *Diversity resistance in organizations.* New York: LEA–Taylor & Francis.

Trawalter, S., Richeson, J. A., & Shelton, J. N. (2009). Predicting behavior during interracial interactions: A stress and coping approach. *Personality and Social Psychology Review, 13*, 243–268.

Verkuyten, M., & Zaremba, K. (2005). Interethnic relations in a changing political context. *Social Psychology Quarterly, 68*, 375–386.

Vinson, T. S., & Neimeyer, G. J. (2003). The relationship between racial identity development and multicultural counseling competency: A second look. *Journal of Counseling and Development, 31*, 262–277.

Waldzus, S., Mummendey, A., & Wenzel, M. (2005). When "different" means "worse": In-group prototypicality in changing intergroup contexts. *Journal of Experimental Social Psychology, 41*(1), 76–83.

Walsh, B. M., Matthews, R. A., Tuller, M. D., Parks, K. M., & McDonald, D. P. (2010). A multilevel model of the effects of equal opportunity climate on job satisfaction in the military. *Journal of Occupational Health Psychology, 15*, 191–207.

Wenzel, M., Mummendey, A., & Waldzus, S. (2007). Superordinate identities and intergroup conflict: The ingroup projection model. *European Review of Social Psychology, 18,* 331–372.

Williams, P. J. (1997). *Seeing a color-blind future: The paradox of race.* New York: Noonday Press.

Wise, T. (2008). *Tim Wise on White privilege: Racism, White denial & the costs of inequality* [Film]. Northampton, MA: Media Education Foundation.

Worrell, F. C., Vandiver, B. J., Schaefer, B. A., Cross, W. E., Jr., & Fhagen-Smith, P. E. (2006). Generalizing Nigrescence Profiles: Cluster analyses of Cross Racial Identity Scale (CSIS) Scores in three independent samples. *The Counseling Psychologist, 34,* 519–547.

Young, K., & Craig, L. (1997). Beyond White pride: Identity, meaning, and contradiction in the Canadian skinhead subculture. *Canadian Review of Sociology and Anthropology, 34,* 175–206.

Zagefka, H., & Brown, R. (2002). The relationship between acculturation strategies, relative fit and intergroup relations: Immigrant–majority relations in Germany. *European Journal of Social Psychology, 32,* 171–188.

Zhong, C., Phillips, K. W., Leonardelli, G. J., & Galinsky, A. D. (2008). Negational categorization and intergroup behavior. *Personality and Social Psychology Bulletin, 34,* 793–806.

4

Color Minimization

The Theory and Practice of Addressing Race and Ethnicity at Work

Erica Gabrielle Foldy and Tamara R. Buckley

A growing literature in multiple fields is investigating the impact of colorblindness and its opposite, what we call "color cognizance," in small group and work settings. Taken as a whole, research suggests that color-blindness detracts from interactions in racially diverse dyads or groups while color cognizance enhances such interactions (Ely & Thomas, 2001; Evans, 2007; Richeson & Nussbaum, 2004; van Dick, van Knippenberg, Hagele, Guillaume, & Brodbeck, 2008; Wolsko, Park, Judd, & Wittenbrink, 2000). Though colorblindness has been the dominant approach in the United States (as well as many other Western countries) for decades, color cognizance informs much of the "managing diversity" movement that has swept through today's workplaces (Cox, 1994; Litvin, 1997; Plaut, 2002; Pless & Maak, 2004; Roberson, 2006). Thus far, however, little data documents how workers on the ground make sense of these dueling discourses.

This paper draws on an intensive study of child welfare workers to suggest that one approach that attempts to bridge or harmonize the two perspectives is "color minimization": a perspective that acknowledges, but then downplays, the importance of race and ethnicity.[1] In a sense, color minimization allows the simultaneous endorsement of both colorblind-ness and color cognizance, which ultimately undermines a color conscious approach (cf. Ryan, Hunt, Weible, Peterson, & Casas, 2007). This finding is particularly noteworthy, given that child protection is a context in which race is salient and in which employees are charged to pursue cultural competence. If color cognizance cannot find a foothold in this environment, it suggests there may be significant barriers to establishing it in the majority of work environments where issues of race and culture are less salient, though not necessarily less relevant. Given the accumulating evidence of the positive effects of a color cognizant perspective, our paper has implications for a wide range of workplaces.

We begin by reviewing previous research on colorblindness and color cognizance, focusing on research done in organizational contexts. We then describe our study and its findings, and end with some implications of this work for research and practice.

COLORBLINDNESS AND COLOR COGNIZANCE

A large stream of research in sociology, psychology, and other fields has documented and investigated different ways that Americans make sense of race and ethnicity by examining "models" or "discourses" related to cultural diversity (Berrey, 2005; Neville, Roderick, Duran, Lee, & Browne, 2000; Plaut, 2002; Spencer, 1994). While language can vary, the great majority of this research compares colorblindness, a belief that race and culture are irrelevant because "we are all the same under the skin," with some version "of color cognizance" (this term is adapted from Frankenberg, 1993), sometimes called multiculturalism (Correll, Park, & Smith, 2008; Nemetz & Christensen, 1996; Richeson & Nussbaum, 2004; Spencer, 1994; Wolsko, Park, & Judd, 2006; Wolsko et al., 2000) or color consciousness (Crenshaw, 1989; Ladd, 1997). Color cognizance is the belief in the importance of racial and ethnic differences because of their impact on individuals, groups, communities, and societies. Experimental and lab research with dyads and small groups, from a social psychology perspective, largely shows that some version of color cognizance leads to better outcomes or processes than colorblindness (Apfelbaum, Sommers, & Norton, 2008; Norton, Sommers, Apfelbaum, Pura, & Ariely, 2006; Richeson & Nussbaum, 2004; Wolsko et al., 2006; Wolsko et al., 2000).[2] For example, one study found that multiculturalism was associated with less bias than colorblindness (Richeson & Nussbaum, 2004) while another found that colorblindness led to greater perceived unfriendliness in dyadic encounters (Norton et al., 2006).

Organizational researchers in management and social psychology have also begun similar research, though the inquiry "is still at an embryonic stage" (van Knippenberg & Schippers, 2007, p. 531). Several terms have been used to refer to organizational members' cognitions about diversity. This volume, of course, uses the term "diversity ideologies." Van Knippenberg and Schippers have used both "diversity mind-sets" (van Knippenberg & Schippers, 2007) and "diversity beliefs" (Homan, van Knippenberg, van Kleef, & de Dreu, 2007; van Dick et al., 2008; van Knippenberg, Haslam, & Platow, 2007); Ely and Thomas coined the term "diversity perspectives" (Ely & Thomas, 2001) while Purdie-Vaughns and colleagues use the term "diversity philosophy" (Purdie-Vaughns, Steele, Davies, Ditlmann, & Crosby, 2008). In all cases, however, these cognitions refer to how the individual or group understands the role of diversity in the workplace; in particular, comparing beliefs that support the suppression of diversity or the active engagement of it because it is perceived to have value for group task and processes (cf. Hobman, Bordja, & Gallois, 2004). Research has investigated attitudes toward gender diversity (Homan et al., 2007; van Knippenberg et al., 2007) and racial and ethnic diversity (Ely & Thomas, 2001; Plaut, Thomas, & Goren, 2009; Purdie-Vaughns et al., 2008; van Dick et al., 2008).

In experimental studies, researchers have manipulated diversity beliefs to be either pro-diversity (participants are told that diverse groups typically have stronger performance than homogeneous groups) or pro-similarity (participants are told homogeneous groups typically perform better) or used simple measures to capture participants' existing beliefs. This research has found that, under certain conditions, groups with pro-diversity beliefs out-perform groups with pro-similarity beliefs (Homan et al., 2007) and tend to have higher group identification (van Dick et al., 2008; van Knippenberg et al., 2007). One set of experimental studies compared colorblind and "value-diversity" perspectives, finding that African Americans felt less comfort and trust in a company with a colorblind approach (Purdie-Vaughns et al., 2008).

These studies have made a significant contribution by suggesting that our sensemaking about racial and ethnic diversity matters for group outcomes, but they have two limitations. First, the perspectives they worked with were simple and dichotomous: A person or team was either pro-diversity or pro-similarity (or colorblind.) Field studies in sociology and political science exploring this sensemaking in neighborhoods and schools, however, have found far more complex approaches among their informants (Bell & Hartmann, 2007; Berrey, 2005; Pollack, 2004; Walsh, 2007). In the organizational literature, Ely and Thomas conducted interviews and observed staff meetings in three racially heterogeneous organizations in order to explore their rationale for being diverse (2001). They identified three different diversity perspectives among the workgroups they studied. Two could be considered pro-diversity, but only the perspective that recognized cultural experience as a broad and deep source of work-related expertise and skill led to greater effectiveness. A pro-diversity perspective that valued employee diversity only because of its potential for reaching new customer or client populations did not lead to better results, nor did a colorblind perspective that saw no work-related value to diversity.

Further, given the widespread and ongoing societal debate between colorblindness and color cognizance, many may be legitimately uncertain about what to believe, as others have also pointed out: "[Diversity training] participants may be confused about programs that emphasize racial or gender differences when they had been taught in the past to be *color blind* or *gender neutral*" (Nemetz & Christensen, 1996, p. 453; their italics). Perhaps a general desire to be "politically correct" (Ely, Meyerson, & Davidson, 2006)—though this can mean very different things to different audiences—encourages some to endorse both colorblindness and multi-culturalism at the same time. Other organizational studies show that individuals often hold conflicting ideas about the impact of gender identity at work rather than one consistent belief (Bartunek, Walsh, & Lacey, 2001; Foldy, 2006). As a whole, this work suggests the importance of documenting actual sensemaking in the workplace, sensemaking that is likely to be layered and complex and even contradictory.

Second, these experimental studies did not explore how diversity beliefs affect actual practice. Perhaps people hold espoused beliefs of one kind or another, but do not behave in ways consistent with those beliefs. Such inconsistency has been established regarding other organizational issues (Argyris, Putnam, & Smith, 1985; Argyris & Schon, 1996) and one study did find that while MBA students said that they valued cultural diversity, their study and friendship groups were largely homogeneous (Tomlinson & Egan, 2002). In their field study described above, Ely and Thomas (2001) describe three workgroups, each holding a different perspective, and each with a concordance between belief and behavior. However, their study was not designed to investigate the link between the two.

The study we describe in this paper investigated in depth the sense-making of child welfare workers about the role and impact of racial and ethnic diversity—a critical component of clinical work—as manifested both in their responses to interview questions and in their discussions of their cases. Therefore we can compare their espoused beliefs with their actual approach to their casework. Also, because we asked questions in a variety of ways, we were able to capture the complex thinking of these social workers about the role of race and culture in their work.

METHODS

Research Site

This study was designed to explore how work groups understand the role of race and ethnicity in their work and, in particular, where they stand on the continuum between color cognizance and colorblindness. Since few workplaces explicitly discuss these issues, we took extra care in finding an appropriate context, since we required a setting in which race, ethnicity, and culture were salient enough that they might actually be addressed on some level. The field of child welfare seemed promising: it focuses on dynamics in the home, on intimate details of family life and child rearing that are broadly understood to be culturally informed. It is an environment in which race and culture are often salient and in which professional standards call for cultural competence (National Association of Social Workers, 2007). However, there is a robust debate in the field about the role and impact of race and ethnicity. Some believe that cultural competence is central to effective casework (Cohen, 2003; Courtney et al., 1996; Yan, 2005), while others believe that race has been overemphasized (Bartholet, 1999, 2006). Moreover, research suggests that many workers lack the specific attitudes, knowledge, and behaviors that comprise culturally competent approaches (Maiter, 2004; Pyles & Kim, 2006; Uttal, 2006). In fact, studies show that families of color are often treated differently, and more punitively, than White families (Becker, Jordan, & Larsen, 2007; Roberts, 2002; Rodenborg, 2004). Therefore, child welfare seemed to be a setting in which employees might be engaged in active sensemaking about the role of race and ethnicity in their work.

Our particular site was a state child protection agency. In 2004, it launched a pilot teaming program to explore how a team-based structure could improve social worker morale as well as services to families. The agency was concerned about its front-line employees who worked directly with clients and suffered considerable stress and isolation. It hoped that a team-based model could facilitate better outcomes for workers and clients by bringing together a broader set of perspectives and experiences in thinking about how to work with a given family as well as by providing more emotional support to individual workers.

These front-line workers were the agency employees in the field, going to people's homes to investigate allegations of child abuse or neglect, speaking with teachers, counselors, and other "collaterals" as the agency called them, finding resources (such as counseling or temporary financial support) for families, and making recommendations to their superiors about whether or not a child should be removed from a home. The work involved both clinical expertise, as workers attempted to understand the dynamics of a family and what interventions could create positive change, and administrative tasks, such as identifying agencies who could provide needed services and coordinating a network of family members and caregivers to support a family.

In the traditional set-up, each social worker was a member of a "unit" with a supervisor and four or five workers. Members of these units sat near each other, but each worker had his or her own caseload, and was singly responsible for those cases. (Caseload was officially capped at 18, but often went higher.) In the teaming program, the structure was similar: each worker was a member of a "team" with a supervisor and four or five social workers. However, the form of service delivery was expected to change in that multiple workers would be involved in cases and all team members could be called on for advice and assistance. Further, all teams were expected to meet at least weekly to discuss their cases, their team processes, and administrative issues.

While the teaming program was not explicitly linked to diversity or cultural competence, the agency had recently identified six core practice values, one of which was "committed to cultural diversity/cultural competence." While agencies and social workers vary in their adoption of the field's standards of cultural competence (Rodenborg, 2004; Yan, 2005), the leaders of this agency site sought to send a message that awareness, knowledge, and skills related to race and ethnicity were critical to child welfare practice.

Data Collection

The teaming program involved seven teams in six offices around the state that were all enrolled in the research. Data collection included both interviews and observation. We conducted interviews with each team (meeting as a whole) in three rounds: at the beginning of the teams' work together, as a baseline (2004), after about one year (2005), and after two to two-and-a-half years (2006–07). We also conducted interviews with four team stakeholders or observers for each team, including the team's immediate superior, the director of the office in which the team was located, a teaming consultant working directly with the teams, and the coordinator of the Teaming Initiative. These two latter stakeholders were familiar with all the teams. All told, this chapter draws on 28 interviews.

Data collection also included observation of team meetings approximately every other month, for a total of 47. (These meetings lasted at least an hour and sometimes longer.) We wrote field notes as we observed, as well as taped the meetings. All transcripts were transcribed. We also compared these transcripts with the field notes, since the latter captured things such as non-verbal behavior that the transcripts did not.

The Sample. Overall, the sample consisted of 64 social workers, 78% female. (Because the workers were largely women, we will use "she" to refer to them throughout the paper.) About 70% of the sample was White, with about 30% people of color. (All racial or ethnic identifications were self-reported.) Of the people of color, about half were Latina or Latino and one-third were African American. Two people categorized themselves as Asian and two checked the "other" box. All of the teams had some racial or ethnic diversity; all included at least one bilingual worker; all teams had significant diversity in their caseloads, and all the members of all the teams faced a significant likelihood that they would work with families with backgrounds different from their own.

Gathering Data on Espoused and Enacted Diversity Perspectives. Data were gathered from team members on how they understood the role and impact of race and culture on their work with families in four ways:[3] 1) Asking whether (and why) it was important for the agency to be racially diverse; 2) Providing a brief case scenario related to race and asking for their reactions; 3) Asking members to discuss a recent case in which "race or ethnicity was an issue" (see the exact wording of all three of these questions in the Appendix); and 4) Observing case discussions in team meetings. The first question was designed to elicit their espoused beliefs while questions 2 and 3 were designed to get beyond purely espoused beliefs since they asked participants to think about behavior, both imagined and actual. Finally, observation of case discussions captured enacted perspectives because these discussions were where workers thought together about how to approach a case and, therefore, would be the venue for an exploration of how race or ethnicity might be relevant.

Data Analysis

We are a diverse team, albeit a team with two members. The first author is a professor of management, while the second author is a professor of counseling psychology, a clinical field like social work. Also, the first author is White, while the second author is African American.

We used these different positions as a way to deepen our analysis and check our assumptions throughout the data analysis process. In particular, we tried to use our occasional conflicts to fruitful ends. As an illustration, we initially approached the research assuming we would find individuals holding relatively definitive colorblind or color cognizant beliefs. It was only as we disagreed—when one of us would feel that a particular coded excerpt was basically colorblind while the other felt it was more color aware—that we began to wonder whether simple assessments would actually be accurate. That was the genesis of the "color minimization" approach.

Overview. The goal of our data analysis was to identify how these workers understood the role of race and ethnicity in their work with families, as it was revealed both in the interviews and in their behavior during case discussions. We began with the interview transcripts. From our earliest analyses, it became clear that the workers' thinking was complex and varied. Therefore, our analysis strategy was to document the different lines of thinking that we heard and then look for underlying patterns across the participants. From this analysis emerged the notion of color minimization and several different ways in which it was manifested. Once this construct was clarified, we turned to the data from team meeting observation to see whether and how the teams engaged issues of race or ethnicity in their casework discussions. We did not initially use color minimization as a guide or lens for this analysis; rather we simply identified whether race or ethnicity was mentioned and what kinds of things were discussed. It was only after some months of analyzing these discussions that we realized there might be a mirroring of sensemaking and behavior, with the teams manifesting color minimization in their casework. We then began explicitly making a distinction between espoused and enacted diversity perspectives and ultimately identified a disjuncture between the approach that these workers described when we asked their opinions and the approach that came through when they described or we observed their practice. We elaborate each of these steps below.

Specific Steps. We began with analysis of the interview transcripts, in which team members thought aloud about the role of race and ethnicity in their work with families. Using Atlas.ti, the qualitative analysis software, the first author used general codes, such as "diversity: perspective" and "diversity: casework" to identify all the material in the team interview and team stakeholder transcripts related in any way to team members' diversity perspectives in theory or practice.[4] She then excerpted all this material, took out any identifying codes, and put it in one long document that included material from all the teams.

Both authors independently and systematically analyzed this material, using finer-grained codes including "diversity: type," "diversity: identity and cultural background" and "diversity: intergroup relations." We then each read all the material relating to each code. As we read, we wrote analytic memos to distill the data into more manageable summaries and to identify emerging insights. While early memos were more descriptive, later memos pushed beyond explicit sensemaking to find deeper, more implicit patterns of thought that we saw across the individuals in the study. We were looking as much for the *absence* of discussions of race, or for the absence of particular topics, as we were for their presence. As we relate in the Findings section, our analysis draws as much from things that were not discussed as those that were. These memos, written independently but shared with each other, captured and deepened our understandings.

One memo raised the notion of "color minimization" as an underlying phenomenon. After some discussion and reviewing the data, we agreed that the construct seemed to capture what we were seeing, though we began to notice that responses seemed to differ according to what questions were asked. More specifically, we saw a distinction between questions designed to capture espoused beliefs about the role of race and ethnicity compared with questions designed to elicit their imagined and actual behavior. The first set of questions were more likely to result in color cognizant responses that noted the importance of race and ethnicity; the second set often revealed colorblind patterns of action. We then went back to the data and used memos to systematically distinguish among responses to different questions and to ultimately identify three particular patterns of thought in which color minimization seemed to manifest itself: 1) "Color is a factor to consider, but is not central to a child's needs"; 2) "Color is about language and culture, not race"; and 3) "We need to learn about our clients' cultures, not about our own." We present these at greater length in the next section.

We then turned to the field notes and transcripts from observation of a total of 47 team meetings. We began the process by counting the number of case discussions each team had over the full course of the observation, for a total of 96 case discussions across all teams. Then, we noted whether anyone, at any point in the discussion, in any way mentioned the family's race or ethnicity. Twenty-one of the 96 discussions, or about 21%, included at least a mention of the race or ethnicity of the family, if not additional discussion.[5] We then created a document that included all of the relevant material for all 21 occurrences. Excerpts ranged from a single worker naming or asking a question about the race of the family with no additional discussion to several members having a substantive discussion about the family's race or ethnicity and the implications for casework.

Each of us then independently analyzed these excerpts, looking at the length and substance of the conversation. We initially explored the depth of the discussion, making a distinction between "superficial" and "in-depth" conversations: Superficial incidents involved just one worker stating the racial or ethnic background of the family or making a brief statement or question that did not elicit any responses from other team members. We considered an incident in-depth if it involved at least two team members and they used race or ethnicity diagnostically—that is, using clients' cultural backgrounds to better understand family dynamics and how to intervene. (Please see Table 4.1 for examples.) Ultimately, we coded ten of the conversations as in-depth and 11 as superficial. As we conducted this analysis, however, we saw some preliminary data that suggested the participants might be enacting in their case discussions the three specific color minimizing ways of thinking identified earlier. We then analyzed the meeting transcripts to establish more systematically whether this was the case, and found that it was. The next section provides our findings.

TABLE 4.1

Examples of an In-depth and a Superficial Discussion Related to Race, Ethnicity, or Culture

Illustration of In-depth Discussion	Illustration of Superficial Discussion
A Latina team member asked her team members and a consulting psychologist for feedback to help her think through a disciplinary technique that her Latina client was using: "In Latin culture there is a thing . . . where a kid goes into the corner and they kneel for the time out. I did it when I was little. I'd face the wall [for] ten or fifteen minutes . . . Should I tell her that she can't do that? . . . It's a cultural thing. I haven't said anything." The team discussed it for a few minutes. The psychologist noted that someone could speak with the mother about alternatives, "including cultural alternatives that are considered acceptable." He added that since the family lived in a studio apartment, the mother had few alternatives since the child couldn't be sent to his or her room. [*This discussion involved multiple team members investigating whether or not a disciplinary practice potentially informed by culture could be abusive.*]	The caseworker, after describing a case involving a Dominican grandmother and her grandchildren, said, "I like this family, I don't mind working with them. The risk of abuse and neglect are low. There are parenting concerns, not major concerns . . . but one, it's cultural and two, she has some resentment of her own kids [her children who are the parents of the grandchildren she has responsibility for] and that plays out in [her] parenting." [*In other words, the caseworker notes that, while there are concerns about the grandmother's parenting, she herself believes that her parenting is culturally informed, which makes it less problematic. There was no further discussion.*]

COLOR MINIMIZATION IN THEORY AND PRACTICE

Overall, we found that these workers initially espoused the importance of race and culture, but under deeper probing, and in their behavior, didn't hold on to it.

When simply asked for their opinions about the role of racial and ethnic diversity in their work, participants overwhelmingly gave color cognizant answers, in that they explicitly recognized and valued cultural differences. Some of these statements referred to the importance of cultural matching between a worker and a family—clients like to work with people "with similar faces"—or between the agency and its community—"I think it is important that you really [racially] match the community that you are servicing ..." One person noted, "Somebody coming from that ethnic background might be able to have a better understanding maybe of the needs of the particular family that we are working with or their culture." Another said that employee diversity wasn't just about enhancing work with particular families, but about the broader benefits of racial and ethnic heterogeneity: "I really see our bilingual, bicultural workers training all of us ... That the understanding that they bring ... Sometimes it cuts through things that the rest of us can't cut through."

Other color cognizant statements recognized the presence of racism and discrimination and the difficulty of addressing these issues as part of their work:

> The great thing about having diverse staff is it really gets you to check your ethnocentrism at the door, or try to ... Like the ability to try to see the world through somebody else's eyes. Or understand another way of making sense of a problem.

Others noted the importance of workers being willing to have difficult conversations about tough issues. One person spoke soon after Hurricane Katrina:

> It was very clear from what was happening in New Orleans that there's still in this country a lack of understanding that barriers still exist and people don't want to talk about it ... For me, it's really important to share those differences and to be able to conduct a conversation about it.

And one respondent spoke to professional values about the importance of tough conversations:

> I think of social workers. Our job is so much different than anybody else's job in the world. We have to open ourselves up to difference ... In that there are conversations and you are comfortable with other people talking about that. It's hard to do sometimes.

However, when we asked questions designed to get beyond espoused beliefs, by asking participants to imagine their behavior by presenting them with a scenario and to describe past behavior by asking them to discuss a recent case in which race or ethnicity had been an issue, we found the respondents used, overall, a very different perspective. We also identified this perspective in their case discussions in team meetings. This approach acknowledged the importance of race and culture, while downplaying them in some way. We call this pattern "color minimization" and identified several ways or strategies that the workers used to minimize race. These appeared to be inadvertent strategies, not deliberate ones, but they were repeated multiple times as we looked across the dataset.

The first strategy was *"Color is a factor to consider, but is not central to a child's needs."* These workers continually invoked the notion of "the child's needs" as the touchstone of their decision making. However, they also differentiated these "needs" from race and culture. This came up primarily in discussions about a scenario presented to the team, about a young Black child who needed to be placed in a foster home. The scenario stipulated that both a Black home and a White home were available and added a few more details. The respondents were asked in which home they would place the child and to explain their reasoning (the full scenario is in the Appendix). There was no right answer to this question; we were simply interested in how the workers thought through the issues involved.

The dominant response was to acknowledge race and ethnicity as one of many factors, point to the overriding importance of the child's "needs," and then distinguish between those needs and racial or cultural factors. "It's kind of like what [team member] said about looking at all the kid's needs and discussing that, and then being culturally sensitive," said one team member. Another said, "Race wasn't the first factor that I was thinking of. It was the child's needs and who could address those best for the child." Therefore, respondents didn't see considerations of race or culture as primary to a child's well-being, thereby minimizing the importance of color in their work with families.

If this were borne out in practice, we would expect to see relatively few discussions in which race or ethnicity were raised (though not zero, since that would suggest a fully colorblind practice), and even fewer that explored culture in any depth. And that was what we found: race and ethnicity were raised occasionally as part of their discussions, but often quite briefly. We observed 96 case discussions; race or culture was mentioned in 21 of these, but 11 were very superficial. Therefore, in only ten instances, or roughly 10% of all case discussions, was race or culture discussed in any depth.

(As noted in the Methods section, we considered an incident in-depth if it involved at least two team members and they used race or culture diagnostically to help them better understand what might be happening with a family and how best to intervene. Table 4.1 provides examples of superficial and in-depth discussions.) The relative rarity of these conversations indicates that these concerns appeared to the workers to be tangential to their goal of attending to the child's needs.

A second color minimizing strategy was, "*Color is about language and culture, not race.*" Overall, these workers were far more attentive to issues of cultural diversity when working with immigrant families, rather than native-born White families or families of color. For example, when asked whether the team worked differently with families in which "race or ethnicity plays a role," one respondent said, "I think it is individual to the case. If you have a family that has just recently been here . . . their level of acculturization is certainly different . . . than somebody who has been here six years, fifteen years." This suggests that racial or ethnic issues only arise with immigrant families and particularly with those who arrived more recently.

This strategy also manifested itself when the team was asked to name a case that they had discussed in their team meetings "in which race or ethnicity was an issue." The teams always mentioned an immigrant family, not a native-born one. When pushed to think more broadly, the respondents often went back to issues related to immigrant families, as suggested in this example.

> *Interviewer*: Can you think of a case in which race or ethnicity is an issue?
> *Respondent*: Mostly it would be just around language . . .
> *Interviewer*: So you can't think of any cases where language was not an issue, but race or ethnicity still played a role?
> *Respondent*: Well, if we didn't have a Spanish-speaking worker, I think that would be a huge issue. And there's not enough bilingual workers.

In this case, the respondent went back to issues of language, even when asked to consider cases in which language was not an issue. We consider this strategy to be color minimizing because respondents were much more likely to associate race, ethnicity, and culture with immigrants, rather than families born in this country, and therefore downplayed racial or cultural issues related to the native-born, particularly White or African American families.

If this approach were mirrored in practice, one would assume that the 21 case discussions during which race or ethnicity was raised would be largely those of immigrant families rather than native-born White families or families of color. A review of the 21 discussions indicates that 17 of them were about immigrant families. Perhaps more tellingly, of the ten in-depth case discussions, nine involved immigrant families. Taken together, this suggests that their practice reflected the perspective articulated in their interviews in that the workers were associating racial and ethnic issues with immigrant families rather than native-born families.

The third color-minimizing strategy was *"We need to learn about our clients' cultures, not about our own."* Respondents sometimes noted that it was essential to learn about their clients' cultural backgrounds in order to enhance their work with them, but they never suggested that they might harbor any bias based on their own racial or cultural background. Moreover, they never referred to the importance of learning about their own cultural background and how it might influence their casework. This issue came up most often when discussing the demographic make-up of the agency's employees. While the agency had some racial and ethnic diversity, some respondents noted that it was still disproportionately White given its client population. Most also went on to say that this was less of a problem because workers could learn about a given family's culture from employees of that background. For example, one team member said, "We [team members] just are from different backgrounds . . . Just by having them in my team, it's just like a reference page right next to you," while another noted, "How many times have I said to [Latina team member]: 'You have to explain your Latino culture because you have got to help me understand.'" A third referred to one common issue: "Like disciplining techniques. Some that are common with certain cultures, we might term abusive, but someone on staff can explain that that is culturally acceptable in that culture."

This strategy put the focus entirely on the clients' cultural backgrounds, not the workers'. As one member said, families may raise race as an issue and "we acknowledge and are sensitive to those issues, but also remain focused on why the department is there and not my race or my background or what not." This quote suggests that this worker has nothing to learn about her background and how it affects her work in child protection. Workers seemed to see themselves as neutral learners, blank slates who could straightforwardly absorb information about other cultures, rather than as individuals with prior knowledge, assumptions and biases, all of which could affect whether and what they learned. Therefore, they appeared to dramatically minimize the role of race and culture in their own background and experiences, including disregarding the possibility of their own racism or ethnocentrism.

If this were borne out in practice, we would see conversations in which the team members explored how their clients' cultures might affect their family life and how the workers should intervene, but few to no conversations in which team members reflected on their own racial or ethnic background and how it might affect their work with families. And, as with the other two strategies, this third strategy was reflected in the evidence regarding the workers' theory-in-use. In several of the ten in-depth case discussions enacted a color cognizant perspective by trying to learn about the immigrant families they were working with. One team had a long discussion about a West African[6] family with a 14-year-old son who had to be institutionalized. They debated whether the boy's habit of standing very close and "put[ting] his face in yours," as the caseworker described it, could be informed by cultural norms regarding interpersonal distance. They also wondered whether his sister should work with a female caseworker, given possible cultural norms about interaction between unrelated people of different sexes. Ultimately, they decided that they should hire a consultant to do a cultural audit with the family. In another case, a team discussed a mother from the Dominican Republic who was hearing voices. A psychologist who met regularly with the team and was informally considered a team member said that hearing voices could be considered normal in some cultures. In a third instance, the caseworker noted that in one of her cases, the immigrant Latino parents were reluctant to send their child to kindergarten because they worried that he did not have the appropriate clothing. She wondered if this concern could be culturally informed.

These examples, in which workers note their lack of knowledge and need for learning about their clients' cultures, are illustrations of color cognizant practice. But they are being cognizant only about the families' backgrounds, not about their own. We never saw a team member raise a question or issue related to her own racial or ethnic heritage, whether it might affect how she saw the family, how the family saw her, or how she intervened with the family. To the extent that these workers were learning about race and ethnicity in their work, it was about their families' cultures, not about their own.

DISCUSSION

Two basic approaches to racial and ethnic diversity contend for influence in our workplaces: a color blind approach meant to suppress difference and a color cognizant one that acknowledges and values the impact of difference (Hobman et al., 2004). Research in social psychology and management has demonstrated that color cognizant approaches generally result in better dyadic and group outcomes or processes but little work has investigated how employees on the ground make sense of these dueling models. Our research conducted such an investigation, examining not only participants' sensemaking but their behavior as well, thus contributing to research and practice on diversity in organizations in several ways.

First, it is important to document workers' actual sensemaking about how racial and ethnic diversity affects their work as it comes up in their day-to-day tasks. In particular, we've documented the complexity of their thinking, showing how it goes far beyond simple pro-diversity, pro-similarity or colorblind beliefs. Further, our analysis probes beneath the explicit meaning of our informants' words to identify underlying patterns across informants, patterns that aren't readily apparent, but once surfaced provide a deeper understanding. Research such as ours could inform future studies of diversity perspectives, either in the lab or in the field, since it suggests additions or alternatives to the current roster of potential perspectives.

Second, identifying the particular pattern of color minimizing is valuable because of research in several fields that suggests that color cognizance enhances relationships across difference in groups and organizations (Ely & Thomas, 2001; Evans, 2007; Homan et al., 2007; van Dick et al., 2008; van Knippenberg et al., 2007). Many employees, particularly White ones, may engage in colorblindness because it feels like a safe and egalitarian approach to race, but it can have the opposite effect, actually impeding cross-race relationships (Apfelbaum et al., 2008; Norton et al., 2006). While color minimization acknowledges the importance of race and ethnicity more than colorblindness, it stops far short of the full color cognizance that may be critical for better relational and effectiveness outcomes in dyads or groups.

Further, while this study doesn't shed light on how common color minimization is across workplaces, it may be on the rise. Color minimization may be one potential response to bridging the oppositional models of colorblindness and color cognizance, by superficially acknowledging the importance of race and ethnicity without actually incorporating this understanding into deeper thought and action. Color minimization could be a way of holding both models at once and could emerge from an ambivalence or confusion about how important race really is (Nemetz & Christensen, 1996). Further work could investigate how widespread it actually is, and whether it looks different in different organizational contexts.

Finally, diversity perspectives only get us so far; what matters is how employees behave. Therefore, it is critical to explore whether employees enact what they espouse. In our case, because we asked a variety of questions in interviews while also observing behavior, we were able to identify a misalignment between espoused beliefs and deeper beliefs and actions. Thus our research supports earlier work suggesting that such misalignments are common in organizations (Argyris et al., 1985; Argyris & Schon, 1996), while expanding this literature to include espoused theories and theories-in-use related to race and ethnicity. This previous literature also suggests another possible motivation for color minimization: espoused and enacted beliefs often diverge because it is somehow difficult or unsafe to act out what one might believe. Race and ethnicity are charged, often taboo, topics in organizations, which may have inhibited these teams from exploring them in more depth (Thomas, 1989). However, this taboo itself stems at least in part from the predominance of colorblindness in most work settings, suggesting one possible mechanism for how diversity perspectives actually influence behaviors at work.

Our research also has implications for practice. Getting at employees' diversity perspectives is critical because it can inform organizational interventions such as supervision, training, coaching, and other develop- mental activities. In this agency, which explicitly holds cultural competence and sensitivity to diversity dynamics as a core value, simply holding more trainings that extol the importance of cultural competence or the virtues of diversity may not work. However, naming color minimization as a dominant pattern—and illustrating the various ways in which that pattern manifests itself—would provide employees with real data about their approach. This avenue could enable organizational leaders to ground their work with employees where those workers currently stand as opposed to presuming assumptions that they may not hold. Leaders could work with employees to investigate the pros and cons of their current thinking and its impact on their case practice. This provides a solid platform from which to explore new ways of thinking that could underlie new ways of working with families. While these particular manifestations of color minimization are likely to be context-bound, employees in other workplaces may well hold contradictory beliefs just as these workers did. Therefore an approach such as this that surfaces inconsistent impulses related to race and ethnicity and encourages trainees to explore those contradictions and learn from them could work in a wide variety of workplaces.

Despite these contributions, this research also has limitations that suggest further avenues of research. First, it took place in a child welfare agency, a context in which race and ethnicity are salient and employees are charged to pursue cultural competence. This is uncommon in American workplaces. However, just because race may be less salient doesn't mean that it is less relevant. Employees in many work organizations engage with diverse clients or customers and many participate in culturally diverse workgroups. An individual's or group's diversity beliefs could inform—positively or negatively—both their performance and their interaction processes. As we noted, we think color minimization might be found more broadly, though empirical study is required to prove that. However, the particular color minimizing strategies we identified in this research may be limited to particular contexts, such as social service agencies.

Second, this is an intensive, exploratory study of a small sample. One strength of this kind of work is that it can identify the presence or existence of a phenomenon, such as color minimization, but larger, quantitative studies are necessary to establish the extent of that phenomenon. Further, we used a sample-as-a-whole analysis for this paper, as opposed to looking at teams or individuals. Once we identified the presence and extent of color minimization across the dataset, we felt we had an important story to tell, since we have not seen any work that details this understanding. Also, because of our sample-as-a-whole approach, we don't distinguish between employees of color and White employees, though other research provides ample evidence that, broadly speaking, they differ in their attention to and perspectives on race and ethnicity (Alderfer, Tucker, Morgan, & Drasgow, 1983; Proudford & Smith, 2003; Purdie-Vaughns et al., 2008; Simons, Friedman, Liu, & McLean Parks, 2007; Tsui, Egan, & Xin, 1995). However, we heard color minimizing coming in some respect from all participants, regardless of cultural background. This doesn't mean there may not be individual differences that may be based at least partly on race. Nor can we rule out the possibility that members of color, in the minority on most of the teams, were going along with the dominant view even if they didn't agree with it. However, despite these important caveats, color minimization dominated the dataset, which we believe is important to document in itself. We also believe that more fine-grained analyses would provide additional insight into the phenomenon.

Third, our paper does not link color minimization to effectiveness or other outcomes. Given the quantity of previous research, reviewed earlier in this chapter, which testifies to the positive consequences of color cognizance, we think it is plausible that that would be the case in this agency. But we cannot make that claim based on our data. However, future work could investigate the relationship between color minimization and group outcomes.

Finally, the racial and ethnic background of the researchers can affect what data is gathered, how it is analyzed, and what conclusions are drawn. While we are a biracial research team, we do not claim a purely objective or omniscient standpoint (DeVault, 1990; Harding, 1993). Further work done by larger and more diverse groups of researchers could add new insights into the perspectives held by employees and groups and their impact on practice. We believe, just as a color cognizant lens would suggest, that the wisdom and expertise of people from a wide variety of cultural backgrounds is necessary to fully understand the complex dynamics of race and ethnicity in organizations.

ACKNOWLEDGMENTS

We thank Tien Ung for her research assistance. We also thank Robin Ely, David Thomas, Kecia Thomas, several anonymous reviewers, and the members of Fulton 214 (Pacey Foster, Danna Greenberg, Tammy MacLean, Peter Rivard, Jenny Rudolph, and Steve Taylor) for their feedback. Finally, we are especially appreciative to the employees at our research site, a child welfare agency, for sharing their thoughts and allowing us to observe them at work.

APPENDIX

Questions used to elicit team members' understandings of the role of race and ethnicity in their work with families

Round one:

1. Team members were asked: Is it important for [agency] staff to be racially and culturally diverse? Why? If the client population is racially homogeneous, then should the staff be homogeneous or heterogeneous?
2. Respondents were given a sheet of paper with the following scenario and room to write their reactions:

    Suppose you had a child who needed long-term placement in a foster home. The child is five years old and is African American. An African American foster family is available, but both parents work full-time outside the home. A White home is also available. In this case, while the father works full-time, the mother is at home full-time. In which home would you place the child? Write down your choice and your reasoning.

Round two:

Respondents were given a sheet of paper with the following and asked to record their answers. After that we had a group discussion about why team members had chosen the rank order they did.

Please rank order the importance, in your view, of each of the following reasons for why [this agency] should hire a racially and ethnically diverse workforce. **1 is the most important reason and 5 is the least important reason**. Give one reason a 1, give another a 2, give another a 3, etc.

[This agency] should be committed to hiring a racially and ethnically diverse workforce in order:

_____ (a) To give us legitimacy in the eyes of other care providers.
_____ (b) To draw on the perspectives and insights of one another that come as a result of our experiences in different racial and ethnic groups.

_____ (c) To provide equal opportunities to people from all racial and ethnic groups.
_____ (d) To give us credibility in the eyes of the families we work with.
_____ (e) To give all of us an opportunity to learn about the needs of families from all backgrounds.

Round three:

Team members were asked the following:

Can you think of one case that the team has handled recently in which cultural diversity—race or ethnicity—was an issue?

1. Describe the case and how race or ethnicity played a role
2. Did race/ethnicity affect how you managed the case? How?
   (a) Who worked on the case? Was there more than one worker? How did you divvy up the work?
   (b) (How) did it affect how you worked with the family?
      (i) Did you attempt to get culturally relevant information? How?
      (ii) Did you work with anyone outside the team who had expertise in this area? Access any other resources?
      (iii) Did you discuss this case as a team more than you might have otherwise?
   (c) Overall, did you work with the family as you would have worked with any other family, or did you approach it differently?
3. What, if anything, do you feel you learned from that case? Does the case have lessons for other cases?

NOTES

1. While the concepts of race, ethnicity, culture, and color are analytically distinct and meaningful, in practice they can be hard to distinguish. Indeed, colloquially and academically, they are often used interchangeably. For readability, we often use "race" or "culture" to stand in for the complex of these entwined constructs. However, where relevant, we make distinctions between these terms and use more specific terminology. Further, we use "color" to name our main constructs because of the broad dissemination of the term "colorblind."

2. One exception is Correll et al. (2008), an experimental study that found that in high conflict situations, colorblindness led to less prejudice than multiculturalism. However, after a delay of 20 minutes, colorblind participants showed a rebound effect, evidencing greater prejudice than multicultural participants. The authors conclude that color-blindness only works well in very short-term situations. Given that most work relationships, either dyads or groups, would be considered long term, this study also suggests that multicultural approaches have better outcomes in actual work settings.

3. We focused on work with families rather than the group's teamwork, because the field's professional standards emphasize cultural competence in work with clients, as opposed to with their colleagues.

4. This paper is part of a broader study on how the teams worked and learned together, so only a subset of material was related to sensemaking about race and ethnicity in particular.

5. This analysis prompts the question of whether naming or engaging race or ethnicity in some way is always called for or whether it is really appropriate only for certain kinds of cases or families. In other words, if we use the number of times the team engages race as the numerator, then what should the denominator be? All cases, or just a subset of cases?

   Certainly the level of relevance of race will vary among families. But in this kind of work, race always has the potential of being relevant. The first example most of us might jump to is workers of one race or ethnicity working with families of another race or ethnicity—for example, a white worker working with a Latino family or vice versa. Attention to culture is very important under those circumstances. But it could be important even when workers and families are matched by race or ethnicity. For example, there is great heterogeneity even within racial groups. A White, Jewish social worker could be working with a devoutly Catholic Polish family. An African American social worker could be working with a Haitian immigrant one. Further, even with a close match, issues related to race could still be relevant. For example, a Vietnamese immigrant mother might claim that the agency is targeting her because of her race or ethnicity, but her Vietnamese-American social worker might disagree. Though they are from the same racial and ethnic background, race could still be an important issue. In fact, whether race or ethnicity is relevant to a particular case is usually a subjective determination, not an objective property. And diversity ideology is a driving factor in how a worker assesses relevance—if she is colorblind then she is less likely to see race or culture as relevant; those who are color cognizant are much more likely to see their relevance. Therefore, we believe that questions of race or ethnicity are potentially pertinent in any case and, therefore, do not distinguish among the various cases that are brought up for team discussion.

6. We are deliberately withholding the name of the country in order to camouflage the family's identity.

REFERENCES

Alderfer, C. P., Tucker, R. C., Morgan, D. R., & Drasgow, F. (1983). Black and white cognitions of changing race relations management. *Journal of Occupational Behaviour, 4,* 105–136.

Apfelbaum, E. P., Sommers, S. R., & Norton, M. I. (2008). Seeing race and seeming racist? Evaluating strategic colorblindness in social interaction. *Journal of Personality and Social Psychology, 95*(4), 918–932.

Argyris, C., Putnam, R., & Smith, D. M. (1985). *Action science.* San Francisco, CA: Jossey-Bass.

Argyris, C., & Schon, D. A. (1996). *Organizational learning II: Theory, method and practice.* Reading, MA: Addison-Wesley Publishing.

Bartholet, E. (1999). *Nobody's children: Abuse and neglect, foster drift, and the adoption alternative.* Boston, MA: Beacon Press.

Bartholet, E. (2006). Cultural stereotypes can and do die: It's time to move on with transracial adoption. *Journal of the American Academy of Psychiatry and the Law, 34,* 315–320.

Bartunek, J. M., Walsh, K., & Lacey, C. A. (2001). Dynamics and dilemmas of women leading women. *Organization Science, 11*(6), 589–610.

Becker, M. A., Jordan, N., & Larsen, R. (2007). Predictors of successful permanency planning and length of stay in foster care: The role of race, diagnosis and place of residence. *Children and Youth Services Review, 29,* 1102–1113.

Bell, J. M., & Hartmann, D. (2007). Diversity in everyday discourse: The cultural ambiguities and consequences of "happy talk." *American Sociological Review, 72,* 895–914.

Berrey, E. C. (2005). Divided over diversity: Political discourse in a Chicago neighborhood. *City and Community, 4*(2),143–170.

Cohen, E. P. (2003). Framework for culturally competent decisionmaking in child welfare. *Child Welfare, 82*(2), 143–155.

Correll, J., Park, B., & Smith, J. A. (2008). Colorblind and multicultural prejudice reduction strategies in high-conflict situations. *Group Processes and Intergroup Relations, 11*(4), 471–491.

Courtney, M. E., Barth, R. P., Berrick, J. D., Devon, B., Needell, B., & Park, L. (1996). Race and child welfare services: Past research and future directions. *Child Welfare, 75*(2), 99–137.

Cox, T., Jr. (1994). *Cultural diversity in organizations: Theory, research and practice.* San Francisco, CA: Berrett-Koehler.

Crenshaw, K. W. (1989). Toward a race-conscious pedagogy in legal education. *National Black Law Journal, 11,* 1–14.

DeVault, M. L. (1990). Talking and listening from women's standpoint: Feminist strategies for interviewing and analysis. *Social Problems, 37*(1), 96–116.

Ely, R. J., Meyerson, D. E., & Davidson, M. N. (2006). Rethinking political correctness. *Harvard Business Review, 84*(9), 78–87.

Ely, R. J., & Thomas, D. A. (2001). Cultural diversity at work: The effects of diversity perspectives on work group processes and outcomes. *Administrative Science Quarterly, 46*(2), 229–273.

Evans, A. E. (2007). School leaders and their sensemaking about race and demographic change. *Educational Administration Quarterly, 43*(2), 159–185.

Foldy, E. G. (2006). Dueling schemata: Dialectical sensemaking about gender. *Journal of Applied Behavioral Science, 42*(3), 350–372.

Frankenberg, R. (1993). *White women, race matters: The social construction of whiteness.* Minneapolis, MN: University of Minnesota Press.

Harding, S. (1993). Rethinking standpoint epistemology: What is "strong objectivity"? In L. Alcoff, & E. Potter (Eds.), *Feminist Epistemologies* (pp. 49–82). New York: Routledge.

Hobman, E. V., Bordia, P., & Gallois, C. (2004). Perceived dissimilarity and work group involvement: The moderating effects of group openness to diversity. *Group & Organization Management, 29*(5), 560–588.

Homan, A. C., van Knippenberg, D., van Kleef, A. G., & de Dreu, C. K. W. (2007). Bridging faultlines by valuing diversity: Diversity beliefs, information elaboration, and performance in diverse work groups. *Journal of Applied Psychology, 92*(5), 1189–1199.

Ladd, J. (1997). Philosophical reflections on race and racism. *American Behavioral Scientist, 41*(2), 212–222.

Litvin, D. R. (1997). The discourse of diversity: From biology to management. *Organization, 4*(2), 187–210.

Maiter, S. (2004). Considering context and culture in child protection services to ethnically diverse families: An example from research with parents from the Indian Subcontinent (South Asians). *Journal of Social Work Research and Evaluation, 5*(1), 63–80.

National Association of Social Workers (2007). NASW Standards for Cultural Competence in Social Work Practice. Retrieved from www.socialworkers.org/practice/standards/NASWCulturalStandardsIndicators2006.pdf

Nemetz, P. L. & Christensen, S. L. (1996). The challenge of cultural diversity: Harnessing a diversity of views to understand multiculturalism. *Academy of Management Review, 21*(2), 434–462.

Neville, H. A., Roderick, L. L., Duran, G., Lee, R. M., & Browne, L. (2000). Construction and initial validation of the Color Blind Racial Attitudes Scale (CoBRAS). *Journal of Counseling Psychology, 47,* 59–70.

Norton, M. I., Sommers, S. R., Apfelbaum, E. P., Pura, N., & Ariely, D. (2006). Color blindness and interracial interaction: Playing the political correctness game. *Psychological Science, 17*(11), 949–953.

Plaut, V. C. (2002). Cultural models of diversity in America: The psychology of difference and inclusion. In R. Schweder, M. Minow, & H. R. Markus (Eds.), *Engaging cultural differences: The multicultural challenge in liberal democracies* (pp. 365–395). New York: Russell Sage.

Plaut, V. C., Thomas, K., & Goren, M. (2009). Is multiculturalism or color blindness better for minorities? *Psychological Science, 20*(4), 444–446.

Pless, N. M., & Maak, T. (2004). Building an inclusive diversity culture: Principles, processes and practice. *Journal of Business Ethics, 54,* 129–147.

Pollack, M. (2004). *Colormute: Race talk dilemmas in an American school.* Princeton, NJ: Princeton University Press.

Proudford, K. L., & Smith, K. K. (2003). Group membership salience and the movement of conflict: Reconceptualizing the interaction among race, gender and hierarchy. *Group and Organization Management, 28*(1), 18–44.

Purdie-Vaughns, V., Steele, C. M., Davies, P. G., Ditlmann, R., & Crosby, J. R. (2008). Social identity contingencies: How diversity cues signal threat or safety for African Americans in mainstream institutions. *Journal of Personality and Social Psychology, 94*(4), 615–630.

Pyles, L., & Kim, K. M. (2006). A multilevel approach to cultural competence: A study of the community response to underserved domestic violence victims. *Families in Society, 87*(2), 221–229.

Richeson, J. A., & Nussbaum, R. J. (2004). The impact of multiculturalism versus color-blindness on racial bias. *Journal of Experimental Social Psychology, 40,* 417–423.

Roberson, Q. M. (2006). Disentangling the meanings of diversity and inclusion in organizations. *Group & Organization Management, 31*(2), 212–236.

Roberts, D. (2002). *Shattered bonds: The color of child welfare.* New York: Basic Civitas Books.

Rodenborg, N. A. (2004). Services to African American children in poverty: Institutional discrimination in child welfare? *Journal of Poverty, 8*(3), 109–130.

Ryan, C. S., Hunt, J. S., Weible, J. A., Peterson, C. R., & Casas, J. F. (2007). Multicultural and color blind ideology, stereotypes and ethnocentrism among black and white Americans. *Group Processes & Intergroup Relations, 10,* 617–637.

Simons, T., Friedman, R., Liu, L. A., & McLean Parks, J. (2007). Racial differences in sensitivity to behavioral integrity: Attitudinal consequences, in-group effects, and "trickle down" among Black and non-Black employees. *Journal of Applied Psychology, 92*(3), 650–665.

Spencer, M. E. (1994). Multiculturalism, "political correctness," and the politics of identity. *Sociological Forum, 9*(4), 547–567.

Tomlinson, F., & Egan, S. (2002). Organizational sensemaking in culturally diverse setting: Limits to the "valuing diversity" discourse. *Management Learning, 33*(1), 79–97.

Thomas, D. A. (1989). Mentoring and irrationality: The role of racial taboos. *Human Resource Management, 28*(2), 279–290.

Tsui, A., Egan, T., & Xin, K. (1995). Diversity in organizations: Lessons from demography research. In M. Chemers, S. Okampo, & M. Costanzo (Eds.), *Diversity in organizations: New perspectives from a changing workplace,* Vol. 37 (pp. 191–219). Thousand Oaks, CA: Sage.

Uttal, L. (2006). Organizational cultural competence: Shifting programs for Latino immigrants from a client-centered to a community-based orientation. *American Journal of Community Psychology, 38,* 251–262.

van Dick, R., van Knippenberg, D., Hagele, S., Guillaume, Y. R. F., & Brodbeck, F. C. (2008). Group diversity and group identification: The moderating role of diversity beliefs. *Human Relations, 61,* 1463–1492.

van Knippenberg, D., Haslam, S. A., & Platow, M. J. (2007). Unity through diversity: Value-in-diversity beliefs, work group diversity, and group identification. *Group Dynamics: Theory, Research and Practice, 11*(3), 207–222.

van Knippenberg, D., & Schippers, M. C. (2007). Work group diversity. *Annual Review of Psychology, 58,* 515–541.

Walsh, K. C. (2007). *Talking about race: Community dialogues and the politics of difference.* Chicago, IL: University of Chicago Press.

Wolsko, C., Park, B., & Judd, C. M. (2006). Considering the Tower of Babel: Correlates of assimilation and multiculturalism among ethnic minority and majority groups in the United States. *Social Justice Research, 19*(3), 277–306.

Wolsko, C., Park, B., Judd, C. M., & Wittenbrink, B. (2000). Framing interethnic ideology: Effects of multicultural and color-blind perspectives on judgments of groups and individuals. *Journal of Personality and Social Psychology, 78*(4), 635–664.

Yan, M. C. (2005). How cultural awareness works: An empirical examination of the interaction between social workers and their clients. *Canadian Social Work Review, 22*(1), 5–29.

5

Organizational and Individual Colorblindness Approaches to Past Injustice

Ruth K. Ditlmann, Elena Wright Mayville, and Valerie Purdie-Vaughns

In front of the main library at Yale University visitors find the "women's fountain." Through the water on the surface, carved into marble, they can see a chronology of women admitted to Yale. At the nearby Evergreen Cemetery, the same visitors can marvel at a monument to Dr. Edward Bouchet, the first African American to receive a Ph.D. from an American university in 1874. Such sites are visible reminders that organizations that pride themselves in valuing diversity today often have a history that contradicts these values. Facing a history of exclusion, conflict, and oppression is extremely difficult. To minimize their discomfort or to avoid the challenging topic altogether, individuals and organizations often adopt a colorblindness strategy. But what does the idea that people are universally similar and that group differences should be minimized (Plaut, 2002) mean in the face of past injustice? What colorblind strategies do individuals use to cope with past injustice, and do these strategies extend to organizations? The latter question is especially important considering that colorblind ideologies often perpetuate the power dynamics underlying structural inequalities between groups (Dovidio, Gaertner, & Saguy, 2007; Saguy, Tausch, Dovidio, & Pratto, 2009). Because organizations are generally more powerful than individuals, the inequalities perpetuated by colorblind ideologies are even more pronounced if they are promoted on the organizational rather than the individual level. The goal of the current chapter is twofold. First, we analyze colorblindness strategies that individual White Americans use when reflecting about the history of slavery, and explore the benefits they derive from this strategy. Second, we analyze if similar strategies exist at the level of organizations that deal with their own role in the history of slavery. Drawing on our analysis of individuals' and organizations' colorblindness strategies, we argue that moving the history of racial injustice to the center of an organization—a color conscious strategy—benefits both Whites and Blacks, and thus improves the organization overall.

Our arguments apply more broadly to organizations that adopt a colorblindness ideology to avoid engaging with uncomfortable topics that relate to members of different groups within the organization, and in the current chapter we specifically analyze the topic of slavery. We focus on the history of slavery as opposed to other topics because it is arguably at the root of racial inequality and power dynamics that disadvantage African Americans today (Ogletree, 2002; 2003). Many long-standing organizations in power in the United States have ties to slavery, either through owning slaves themselves or through having founders who made their fortunes in the slave trade; examining how organizations overall acknowledge and discuss slavery can shed light into the costs and benefits of adopting a colorblind ideology. Probably because of its centrality to current day inequality, the history of slavery is one of the most taboo topics in American society (Loewen, 1995; Rothstein, 2011). In other words, if individuals and organizations use a colorblindness approach to slavery, they will take a colorblind approach to anything.

INDIVIDUAL COLORBLINDNESS APPROACH TO THE HISTORY OF SLAVERY

While past research clearly established that members of majority groups prefer colorblind ideologies when considering topics related to race (Apfelbaum, Sommers, & Norton, 2008; Knowles, Lowery, Hogan, & Chow, 2009), psychologists have not yet analyzed how these are reflected in individual beliefs about slavery. How is it possible to ignore or minimize the topic of race when writing about slavery? We conducted a laboratory study to understand how White students manage to adopt a colorblindness strategy when discussing a topic as deeply about race as slavery. We then used the strategies we identified on the level of individual participants as a lens to examine what kinds of strategies organizations use in the same situation.

Methods. Fifty-six White American participants (65.5% female) from a private university in the northeastern United States participated in this study; they each received $18 for their participation. Selection criteria restricted participants to those who identified as White and were American citizens. One participant was excluded because they did not complete the dependent variables of interest, leaving 55 participants in the final sample. Participation in this study took approximately one hour and participants engaged in a number of activities.[1] Most important to the focus of the current chapter, they were instructed to write a letter about "the implications of slavery for intergroup relations today" to an ostensible Black fellow university student. Two independent raters later coded whether the letters adopted a colorblind or multicultural approach to the topic of slavery. After writing the letters, participants completed a large battery of computer-based questionnaires that included a measure of collective guilt.

Based on the colorblindness literature (Bonilla-Silva, 2003; Brown et al., 2003; Carr, 1997; Omi & Winant, 1994; Pollock, 2004), the authors developed a coding manual to code for colorblindness and multiculturalism. In this chapter we focus on the results for colorblindness. Colorblindness was coded when participants (1) adopted a post-racial mindset, (2) shifted their focus away from race, and (3) listed pure facts. These categories are described in more details in the results section. Essays that could be characterized as colorblind but did not fit into any of these subcategories were coded as "colorblindness other." Once these categories were established, two independent coders coded each participant letter for the absence or presence of colorblindness (Cohen's kappa = .86, $p < .01$) and, in a second step, specified which sub-rule best described the letter content (Cohen's kappa = .78, $p < .01$).

Results. We found that 58% or our participants indeed adopted a colorblindness perspective when writing about slavery. Sixteen percent adopted a post-racial mindset, another 16% shifted their focus away from race, while 20% listed pure facts (see Figure 5.1). The absence of race in White participants' essays about slavery has parallels in the remarkable absence of slavery in some mainstream representations of history, for example, when speaking of certain plantation sites (Alderman & Modlin, 2008; Modlin, 2008). In his essay about the Charleston Museum, journalist Edward Rothstein contends that, given the prevalence of the presence of slavery, "it becomes poignantly evident just how major an achievement is reflected by slavery's enduring absence" (Rothstein, 2011, last para.). For

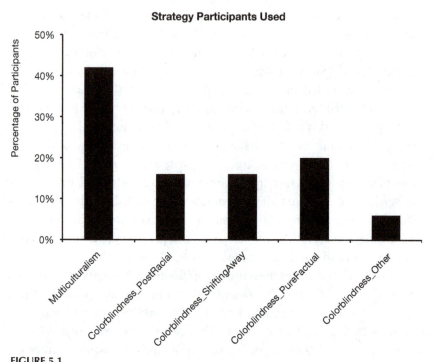

FIGURE 5.1
Colorblindness strategy participants used

example, the centrality of the enslavement of Blacks in the history of the United States, avoiding race in a letter to a Black partner represents a similar "achievement."

COLORBLINDNESS IN INDIVIDUAL LETTERS

To understand how White students manage to adopt a colorblindness strategy when discussing a topic as deeply about race as slavery, we examined their colorblind letters more closely.

Post-racial ideology: "Let's not dwell on it." Post-racial area was coded for letters that suggest that America has moved beyond race. In these essays, participants acknowledge that race in America once mattered and racism did exist, but contend that those issues are no longer prevalent or should no longer matter. For example, one White student described the history of race relations from 1865 onwards, expressed deep regret about what happened and then concluding her letter in the following way[2]:

> It took until the 1960s for you to finally gain full rights and full opportunities, which to the best of my knowledge you maintain in most of the country to this day. I know it must be hard for you to forgive us for our past and you feel as if you are owed in some way. I understand this feeling but I also think the past is the past and there is a need to move on and accept what's been done.

The student expressed regret for the events of the past, yet clearly distanced herself from the past and prompted her Black partner to do the same. Students often focused on the past as a reference point, and concluded that racial equality has been achieved. One asked "Who would have thought that one day the country would go from slavery to having a black president?" Another one claimed, "Those of us born after the Civil Rights Movement finally live in a world where slavery and all the other marks of black oppression such as Jim Crow Laws are taught to us as history, not as what occurs in the present day." Both of these students focused on how far we have come relative to the past. These letters echo the findings of Eibach and Ehrlinger (2006) who suggest that it is because of this focus on the past that Whites perceive more racial progress than Blacks, who instead focus on how far we still have to go.

In addition to using the past as a reference point for judging racial progress, some White participants expressed strong opposition to Blacks "dwelling" on the past. Many seemed aware of how racially polarized constructions of the past are and used their letters to persuade their Black partners whom they presumed to have a different perspective. One particularly strongly worded letter stated unequivocally:

> I think people need to suck it up and get over it. Yes slavery happened and yes it was bad but people focus so much on the past that they forget to look into the future. Times change. We have Obama as the president who is Black and Black people have more rights. Yes it is important to remember what happened but lets not dwell on it. Black people were not the only ones oppressed there were Christians, Jews, Muslims being oppressed right now. Let's not forget about those as well. Black people sometimes use slavery as

an excuse to be racist towards White people or they make it sound like they were slaves. Excuse you but it was your ancestors NOT you. So shut the fuck up.

Another student expressed a similar opinion but in the somewhat softer style of writing that characterized the majority of letters:

America is the land of opportunity, where immigrants from all over the world come to compete for a chance to succeed. It now offers equal opportunities to all. However, the impact of slavery has changed the culture of the United States in that we are unsure what kind of retribution should be given to African Americans. We must all remember what happen, acknowledge it as a mistake, and apologize for it—but at one point we have to move on ALL TOGETHER, as one. One group cannot demand special privileges over another just because of race.

Both of these students are concerned that Blacks will demand special privileges because of their race. This form of colorblindness has a hard edge and asserts that even though injustices have occurred in the distant past, today everybody has the same opportunities and is personally responsible for making the most out of these. Unlike other colorblindness strategies (see below), the post-racial ideology allows an acknowledgment of the existence of present-day complaints about race-based inequality—but does so only to refute them as misdirected. These individuals anticipate the possibility of being accused of racism by calling on Blacks to "move on and accept what's been done," to use the words of one letter writer. The problem becomes not the injustice itself, but rather the attempts for retribution (Bonilla-Silva, 2003). Therefore, Whites are relieved of the burden of blame because they are independent of their forefathers. Blacks, on the other hand, are criticized as either exaggerating problems or dwelling on the past in ways that are unfounded and prevent the rest of the country from advancing.

Strategies such as this could represent defenses that allow Whites to assert themselves as reasonable people who are trying to prevent others from whining or blaming others for self-made problems. At its most intense, this strategy allows Whites to express toward Blacks not anxiety, which would signal uncertainty about the future, but anger, signaling a claim against Blacks for some injustice. Interestingly, here the acknowledg-ment of Black grievances comes with a solution that only requires Blacks to act—specifically, by keeping quiet and accepting blame. By asserting their own post-racial ideology, these people are also demanding Blacks adopt it themselves.

Shifting Focus Away from Race: "[We] all came from Africa." Letters that downplay racial differences in discussing the implications of slavery for the present were coded as "shifting focus away from race." In these letters, participants often emphasized the importance of paying attention to individual characteristics or the commonality of being human over classifying people according to race. For example, one student, after describing how deeply impacted she was by the slavery documentary that left her "speechless," concluded her essay with a commitment to defeat racial inequality:

> It is my goal to continue to the trend we have been able to go to since the illegalization of slavery in believing all are created and treated equally, teaching this to my children so that one day we can all look past skin color, ethnicity, etc. and see one another for the people we truly are.

Another student provided an even stronger comment on innate similarity across races and even species by encouraging her partner and everyone else:

> [to] go have their genome studied to trace their primordial origins. They'll find that they all came from Africa, at some point in the evolutionary trail. Before that, we were all swinging from trees. And before that, we were slithering around in swamps. This truth exposes racism for the filthy lie that it is. Perhaps if children spent more time in school learning about the wonders of human evolution, they'd spend less of their life even entertaining the possibility that someone of a different color is better or worse than they are, or even of a different "race" than he or she is. We're all part of the human race, and we should count our blessings every day that we were lucky enough to be born a human—regardless of color—and not a salamander, or a flea, or some other lowly creature.

Most students who wrote letters in this category began by expressing their horror for the history of slavery. Adopting a colorblind mindset appeared to be their proposed solution for overcoming racial inequality. Many seemed deeply distressed by America's past and see colorblindness as an anti-racist strategy that they both utilize themselves and recommend to others, including their partner.

Another way in which attention was shifted from the specifics of Black and White relations in U.S. history was by making a broader point about the violation of human rights, oppression of minorities, or exploitation in the name of capitalism. One student appropriates the history of slavery to make a point about human rights:

> Europeans were enslaving, beating, and raping each other for hundreds of years before America was discovered; American slavery was important but it is just one of the hurdles the world has jumped on its path to acknowledging human rights.

In an intergroup context, this strategy is full of potential pitfalls. Members of the former victim group often want to commemorate their own specific misfortune rather than reflect about injustice more broadly (Vollhardt, 2013). As a group, the letters that shift focus away from race demonstrate how an ideology stemming from a motivation of true egalitarianism can easily go awry and could send confusing and potentially invalidating signals to an intergroup partner.

Pure Facts. Finally, a substantial portion of White participants exclusively reported historic facts in their letters. They provided no personal opinion and instead simply listed historic facts in a style that would be more appropriate for a textbook than a personal letter to another student. We suspect that this unusual use of colorblindness is related to other studies of interracial dyads demonstrating that Whites often go to great lengths to avoid discussing race even in appropriate contexts (Norton, Sommers, Apfelbaum, Pura, & Ariely, 2006; Pollock, 2004). It is possible that participants used this strategy in order to avoid potential discomfort that might arise from a frank discussion of current and related racial issues.

COLORBLINDNESS AND COLLECTIVE GUILT

To explore why participants might use a colorblindness strategy we conducted a t-test to investigate how the mentioning of colorblindness versus multiculturalism relates to mean differences in participants' collective guilt following the letter writing exercise (Doosje, Branscombe, Spears, & Manstead, 2006). We found that Whites who scored low on collective guilt were more likely to adopt a colorblindness strategy than Whites who scored high on collective guilt, $t(53)=2.33$, $p=.02$. Consistent with the two different usages of colorblindness we identified above, it is possible that students who express colorblindness are the ones who experience less collective guilt to begin with, possibly because they endorse a post-racial mindset and do not see themselves as responsible in any way. It is also possible that colorblindness is an emotion suppression strategy to deal with the anxiety the topic provokes initially.

PSYCHOLOGICAL BENEFITS OF COLORBLINDNESS AT THE LEVEL OF INDIVIDUALS

Interacting with individuals from other groups can be extremely difficult for some Whites, involving high levels of anxiety (Blascovich, Mendes, Hunter, Lickel, & Kowai-Bell, 2001; Ickes, 1984; Mendes, Major, McCoy, & Blascovich, 2008; Shelton & Richeson, 2006). Intergroup anxiety, defined as anxiety experienced during real or imagined interactions with outgroup members, can influence avoidance of intergroup contact as well as stereotyping of outgroup members and assuming greater dissimilarity from them (Stephan & Stephan, 1985). Intergroup anxiety also affects how intergroup contact unfolds. For instance, Trawalter and Richeson (2008) observed that Whites exhibited more nonverbal anxiety in interracial dyads compared with same-race dyads, and within the interracial dyads, they exhibited greater anxiety than their Black partner. Intergroup anxiety is partially influenced by perceptions of being judged by outgroup members (Vorauer, 2006). A wealth of research has shown that Whites in general fear rejection by Blacks (e.g., Shelton & Richeson, 2005) and fear being perceived to be racist (e.g., Frantz, Cuddy, Burnett, Ray, & Hart, 2004). The experience of anxiety experienced by Whites in an interracial context might present an uncomfortable state that must be regulated either by seeking information about how one is being perceived (Vorauer, 2006) or by utilizing strategies that will alleviate the anxiety. Colorblindness strategies might allow for down-regulation of anxiety, thereby relieving Whites of the burden of uncertainty about how they will be perceived.

The colorblind strategies utilized in the current study might have regulated anxiety in a number of different ways. First, using colorblindness might reduce the likelihood of feared negative outcomes, such as being judged to be racist, and by doing so reduce current fear and anxiety. For instance, concern that one will be judged negatively by outgroup members might increase the attractiveness of focusing strictly on facts, as such a strategy is hard to argue because of its objectivity. Focusing on facts also relieves Whites of the burden of entering into an uncomfortable discussion about the lingering problems of racism. Shifting focus away from race does the same thing, but with a twist—Whites are communicating to Blacks that the Blacks should not see them as enemies but rather as a common ally, passively viewing slavery as a terrible human atrocity rather than having anything to do with race. That "horrible time" in human history is long past, and the world is all the better for it. Adopting this mindset frees Whites to feel protected from blame of Blacks because they have distanced themselves from the perpetrators of a historic crime and therefore cannot be held responsible for those misdeeds. This is perhaps an idealistic spin on colorblindness that emphasizes a common, important American value of egalitarianism while simultaneously demanding Blacks to give up their own claims of lingering inequity. Further, avoiding discussions of the effects of race and the negative emotions that can arise might help Whites feel better about their own actions, attitudes, and beliefs and reduce guilt.

In conclusion, subscribing to the colorblindness perspective that dominates engagement with past injustice in the United States, protects Whites from a number of unpleasant psychological consequences. Whites using this strategy are free to feel sad about the past but are protected from intergroup anxiety because their future is defined as being completely separate from and unaffected by slavery. In addition, they protect themselves from feeling attacked for being racist by Blacks, either by relying on irrefutable facts about the past, allying themselves with Blacks when lamenting the past as a broad-based atrocity, or pre-emptively attacking Blacks for holding onto the past too tightly.

COLORBLINDNESS IN ORGANIZATIONS

Like the White participants in the study who endorsed a colorblind ideology when discussing slavery, institutions in U.S. society approach the topic of slavery largely by ignoring it. In recent years, political, media, and educational organizations and even historical sites and tourist organizations have been criticized for omitting important information about the history of slavery or even for misrepresenting facts. For example, many cities across the United States have had policies in place that prohibited their Black residents from physically being present in the city after a certain time in the evening (Loewen, 2005). Even though a large number of towns in the United States are estimated to have been so called "sundown towns" at some point, it is difficult to properly document this history because most towns have not kept records of the ordinances or signs that marked the town's sundown status (Loewen, 2005). Historic representations of slavery in the public space are rare and highly contested (Fredrickson, 2010). A simple online search for slavery museums reveals that few exist and many struggle with funding shortage. Meanwhile, every year, thousands of Americans visit historic plantations in Georgia, Louisiana, North and South Carolina, just to name a few states. They learn about the "master" who owned the plantation, the architecture, furnishings, gardens, and crops but little if anything about the slave experience that was so central to life on most of these sites. Driving home the point that organizations prescribe colorblindness and thus often perpetuate structural inequalities between groups, Alderman and Modlin have suggested that "tourism landscapes are constructed and marketed in selective ways that reaffirm long-standing patterns of social power and inequalities and thus influence whose histories and identities are remembered and forgotten" (Alderman, & Modlin Jr., 2008, p. 266). Thus, there is a pattern of adopting race-blind ideologies within institutions in the United States.

Perhaps even more strikingly than passive avoidance of the topic, some organizations adopt a colorblind position even when forced to confront the topic of the history of slavery. To understand how organizations manage to adopt a colorblindness strategy when engaging with the topic of slavery, which seems to be deeply related to race, we examined how the three types of colorblind ideology identified in the colorblind letters (i.e., post-racial ideology, shifting focus away from race, and pure facts) are used by some organizations. Facing the history of slavery poses different kinds of challenges and also provides different opportunities for organizations based on their specific goals as we will outline below. In particular, whether they teach or sell history, fear facing reparation lawsuits, or have primarily an educational mission seems to be associated with what strategy they use.

Post-Racial Ideology: "Let's Not Dwell on It." In letters from individuals this strategy was characterized by an acknowledgment that although race in America once mattered and racism did exist, those issues are no longer prevalent or should no longer matter. Organizations that teach or "sell" history seem to be particularly prone to using this strategy. In an attempt to move forward, such organizations may be tempted to ignore or even remove evidence of past oppression from the present. A different example is New South Books who published a version of Mark Twain's *Adventures of Tom Sawyer* and *Huckleberry Finn* where they removed the word "nigger" and replaced it with the less offensive word "slave" (Version of *Huckleberry Finn*, 2011). This idea was initiated by Mark Twain scholar Alan Gribben and embraced by New South books with the stated purposes of counteracting the pre-emptive censorship that occurs because teachers worry about offending students and their parents (La Rosa, 2011). According to Twain scholar Dr. Gribben, removing the N-word is adapting Mark Twain's original book to an altered cultural context. In his opinion, this strategy is not an attempt to be colorblind: "Race matters" he asserts "but it is mostly how you express that in the 21st century" (Schultz, 2011, para. 3). Critics disagree, referring to New South Book's efforts as an attempt to "needlessly whitewash a period that deserves no whitewashing" (Petri, 2011, para. 2). They argue that removing the N-word deprives teachers of the opportunity to teach about the complexities of race relations in America. Others contend that facing that history in all its offensiveness is important for transcending it (Fishkin, 2011). Both supporters and critics agree that New South Books is selling a book, which enables adopting a colorblind perspective towards the uncomfortable and potentially divisive topic of slavery – they disagree, however, whether adopting this perspective is desirable.

In addition to adopting a well-intended post-racial mindset, some organizations may express strong opposition to "dwelling" on the past. Organizations that fear monetary or other forms of compensation requests for example in the form of reparation litigations seem to be particularly prone to use this strategy. For example, when the insurance company Aetna Inc. together with several other companies faced a reparation lawsuit for its early ties to the transatlantic slave trade (Ogletree, 2002) their chairman, John W. Rowe, MD, issued the following statement: "We do not believe a court would permit a lawsuit over events which—however regrettable—occurred hundreds of years ago. These issues in no way reflect Aetna today" (Aetna statement, 2002). This statement is an example for the "let's not dwell on the past" colorblindness strategy because it emphasizes that the past is the past and, while regrettable, does not matter today. John W. Rowe did offer an apology for Aetna's "role in an awful period in our country's history" and reasserted their commitment to reducing racial disparities in health care and investing in a broad range of minority programs at the annual shareholders meeting in 2002 (Excerpts of remarks, 2002; ww.aetna-foundation.org).

Taking this strategy one step further, Jeff Jacoboy, *Boston Globe* columnist, criticized Kennedy Thompson, the former chairman of another company, Wachovia bank, for apologizing in the first place because of the implications this apology might have for reparation requests (Jacoby, 2005). His column is an epitome of the "let's not dwell on the past" colorblind ideology. He argues:

> Thompson's apology was for something Wachovia didn't do, in an era when it didn't exist, under laws it didn't break. And as an act of contrition for this wrong it never committed, it can now expect to pay millions of dollars to activists for a wrong they never suffered. (para. 5)

His broader argument is that most Black Americans did not descend from slaves and most White Americans came as immigrants after slavery and would therefore be better off leaving the past alone. He further contends that America already paid its price for slavery with the civil war (Jacoby, 2005).

Shifting Focus Away from Race: "[We] All Came from Africa." In letters from individuals this strategy was characterized by downplaying racial differences in discussing the implications of slavery for the present, emphasizing the importance of paying attention to individual characteristics or the commonality of being human over classifying people according to race and integrating slavery in broader conceptual frameworks such as the violation of human rights, oppression of minorities or exploitation in the name of capitalism. Organizations with a clear mission to educate such as universities and museums should be prone to adopt this strategy. Acquiring and disseminating knowledge is central to such organizations. In this context, coming to terms with an organization's history can become a search for meaning, a process of redefining an organization's tradition and identity (Brown University, 2006). During this process, educators and students, perhaps unwillingly, may shift their focus away from organizations' involvement with the transatlantic slave trade and instead engage in a broader discourse about racism, oppression, and human rights.

This is at least partly what happened at Columbia University when, in 2007, a noose (which is understood to be a symbol with particular reference to Black lynching in the Southern US) was found hanging from a Black professor's office door (Michels, 2007). Similar incidences happened at the University of Maryland, where in 2007 a noose was found hanging in a tree near the Black Cultural Center on campus (Martin, 2007), and at UC San Diego where a noose hung from a campus library bookcase (Gordon, 2010). A noose is a common and very specific symbol of Black lynching in the Southern United States. In response to this incident, Columbia University adopted some strategies that fall into the shifting focus away from race category. For example, according to The New York Times, at a meeting between students and Columbia University president Lee C. Bollinger, "students have used the noose as a point of departure to talk about other issues, including Columbia's plans to expand into adjacent neighborhoods" (Gootman & Baker, 2007, para. 16). Bollinger also issued a statement saying that the incident "is an assault on African-Americans, and therefore is an assault on every one of us" (Michels, 2007, p. 2). In the same vein, when the events sparked a protest, students held signs saying, "Oppression of any is oppression of us all" (Gootman & Baker, 2007). These strategies emphasize the commonality of being human over classifying people according to race and integrate the noose, a specific symbol of Black lynching in the South, with broader conceptual frameworks including the violation of human rights, oppression of minorities, gentrification or exploitation in the name of capitalism. To be sure, there is value in adopting a comparative perspective and the universal principles of human rights are a hard fought achievement of tremendous value. Yet it is important to be mindful that such a comparative perspective can also shift focus away from the specifics of Black–White relations and an organization's own history with regards to racism and slavery.

Brown University is a good example of a university that remembers and commemorates the specifics of the history of slavery at the institution while simultaneously embedding the historical facts in a larger discourse on universal human rights and crimes against humanity. Ruth J. Simmons, the first African American president of an Ivy League school, did not wait for an incendiary racial incident to react to intergroup relations at Brown; instead, she proactively tackled the topic of slavery. In 2003 she founded a Steering Committee on Slavery and Justice to research the University's historical relationship to slavery and the transatlantic slave trade (Brown University, 2006). Her goal was also to set an example, for if universities that are organizations devoted to the discovery and dissemination of knowledge cannot face their past, few organizations probably can (Brown University, 2006). Brown University managed to use this as an opportunity to reflect on their traditions and their identity, acknowledge what happened and how it impacts the present and engage in an open dialogue about this uncomfortable topic. They also used the history of slavery at Brown University as a teachable moment not only about U.S. history but also about the history and development of universal human rights more broadly. The Steering Committee issued a detailed report (Brown University, 2006) outlining how the school benefited from slavery, the involvement of early supporters of what was then called College of Rhode Island, in the transatlantic slave trade. According to this report, Esek Hopkins was both a member of Board of Trustees of College of Rhode Island and also commander of the deadly slave ship Sally. The committee's activities included educational programs, with talks and lectures at Brown University and beyond (Goldschmidt, 2011), as well as a museum exhibition and the commissioning of a memorial commemorating the university's ties to slavery (Baum, 2012).

Pure Facts. In letters from individuals this strategy is characterized by simply listing facts without providing a personal opinion. Simply listing facts is what the so-called slavery disclosure ordinances passed in Chicago in 2002 as the first of its kind demand from companies wanting to do business with the city (Slater, 2002). Revealing such facts does not compromise a company's ability to do business with the city—they simply have to make the information public. In compliance with this ordinance, Wachovia, JP Morgan Chase, ABN AMRO, Lehman Brothers, and US Bank have all disclosed involvement in the slave trade (see City and County of San Francisco, 2007 for summary). Oakland, Milwaukee and San Francisco, Los Angeles, Detroit, Philadelphia, Berkley, New York City, and Philadelphia, Cleveland, and the whole state of California followed suit in subsequent years with similar initiatives to Chicago's ordinance, though with somewhat less fanfare (Benner, 2005; City and County of San Francisco, 2007).

While cities' requirements usually are limited to companies researching and making public their historical involvement in slavery and the slave-trade, companies often accompany these historical findings with an apology and in some cases even restitution efforts in the form of programs that serve Black Americans today (e.g., Excerpts of remarks, 2002; www.aetna-foundation.org). Unfortunately, public information only provides insight into how companies present themselves publicly after publishing the potentially disturbing historic fact. Whether they use the slavery disclosure ordinance as an opportunity to engage in an internal dialogue about these issues remains unknown.

BENEFITS OF COLORBLINDNESS AT THE LEVEL OF ORGANIZATIONS

Given that institutional ideologies are often created and maintained by individuals in an institution (Dacin, Goodstein, & Scott, 2002) and individuals' cognitions are embedded in and shaped by their social reality (Johnson, 1998), it is perhaps not surprising that we were able to map colorblindness strategies we identified in individuals onto the strategies used by a range of organizations. Because institutions are composed of individuals, it is also likely that the benefit companies derive from these strategies is similar to what we argue occurs on an individual level: regulation of collective anxiety.

For educational organizations it seems that adopting a post-racial or shifting focus away from race strategies is anxiety reducing. In the case of New South Books, the explicitly stated purpose of removing the N-word was to reduce teachers' and students' anxiety when reading Mark Twain's *Huckleberry Finn* and thus to make the new edition of the book more marketable. Perhaps less explicitly it seems that Columbia University's response to finding the noose on a Black professor's door also served as an anxiety regulation goal. Shifting focus away from race and the history of lynching in the South with well-meant slogans such as "oppression of any is oppression of all" creates an inclusive climate where all members of campus feel like they belong. Yet, through engaging in a broad based discussion of oppression, crimes against humanity, and hate, individual students and the organization avoid analyzing their own specific privilege and how the history of slavery may have contributed to that.

For companies, listing facts related to their historic ties to the transatlantic slave raises image concerns. Unlike individuals in our study who wrote letters in private and anonymously, organizations are often in the public spotlight and do not get away with listing facts alone. Once they make facts related to their historic involvement in the slave trade public, supporters of slavery-disclosure ordinances hope that the public demand they take a position and some may be reluctant to do business with them (Slater, 2002). In other words, demanding pure facts from companies is a colorblindness strategy as we identified in letters from individuals above, that supporters of the ordinance hope will ultimately lead to a color-conscious strategy.

THE COST OF COLORBLINDNESS

Our analysis of individual letters and our case analyses of organizations showed that many individuals and organizations adopt the predominant colorblindness strategy when they reflected about slavery. In line with previous research suggesting that colorblindness can be construed in different ways by Whites (Knowles et al., 2009; Purdie-Vaughns, Steele, Davies, Ditlmann, & Crosby, 2008), we found that the colorblind strategies Whites as well as organizations adopted in discussing past injustice fell into broader categories that ranged in terms of how overtly aggressive they were toward the outgroup. Some individuals demonstrated colorblindness by denying associations with the past, thus denying their own responsibility and placing the burden on African Americans as a group. On an organizational level, we observed this strategy in arguments against redistribution payments. Other individuals and organizations seemed to use colorblindness to deal with their own anxiety and maintain an egalitarian self-image while addressing the challenging topic of slavery. We argue that from an organizational perspective, regardless of what Whites' motivations are behind it and regardless of some of the short-term benefits that they derive from it, there are serious long-term costs for organizations that use colorblindness as a way of ignoring injustice and inequality or to deal with conflict.

For Whites, ignoring race means that they might never be comfortable talking about racial inequality, since they may associate colorblindness with reduction in distress and thus negatively reinforce avoidance of such topics. Discomfort with discussions of this nature might lead to greater and greater discomfort talking about race owing to a continued fear of being mis-perceived as racist. It may well lead to avoidance of interacting with Blacks altogether. Further, Whites might be less likely to promote social change if they are not willing to confront modern day racism. Overall, when faced with a system or institution that denies their multicultural reality, Blacks are forced to choose whether to fight for change in ways that can be further traumatizing, or whether to passively wait for Whites to change on their own without any incentives or urging. A third option is to disengage from the system entirely. In the context of an organization, adopting a colorblind ideology might be counter to its interests because of the potentially detrimental effects on Black members. Organizations may have an unselfish interest in addressing race openly in order to reduce discrimination, but such openness also has rewards for the interests of the organization. Overall, Blacks and Whites can all thrive in organizations that do not resort to a simple colorblind ideology. In the next section, we discuss how organizations might play a role in creating a validating or invalidating context in which these discussions might be had.

BENEFITS OF ADOPTING A COLOR-CONSCIOUS STRATEGY

Many organizations in the United States shape and reflect individual colorblindness beliefs. This cycle, where organizational and individual colorblind strategies mutually reinforce one another, is difficult to break. Moving the injustice underlying structural inequalities between groups to the center of an organization should break this dynamic. Adopting a color-conscious strategy should benefit both Whites and Blacks and thus improve the organization overall. For instance, a clear position on race might help lessen racial tension in the long run, thereby minimizing long-term conflict that might contribute to an unpleasant atmosphere. In addition, there is evidence that the more Blacks fear unfair treatment, the more they disengage and contribute less to an organization (Purdie-Vaughns et al., 2008). Finally, Whites themselves benefit when organizations are egalitarian, in terms of increased happiness and productivity (Mendes, Gray, Mendoza-Denton, Major, & Epel, 2007).

Because people use social context to decide whether a mental experience is a reasonable belief and good judgment (Mitchell & Johnson, 2009), an organization that explicitly owns up to a history of benefiting from a system that exploited or oppressed specific minority groups (e.g., Black Americans, women) should make it difficult for members in the organization to maintain a colorblind perspective. Denying or ignoring injustice is harder—though not impossible—in an environment with vivid reminders of the injustice. A recent literature review on self-criticism in dominant groups that is inherent in a color-conscious strategy showed that while rare, self-criticism is nevertheless possible and more likely to occur if representations of injustice are vivid, public, and memorable (Leach, Zeinnedine, & Cehajic-Clancy, 2013). Organizations ideally should prevent Whites from relying on coping strategies that help them maintain a colorblind, self-serving ideology by offering them institutional support to bolster their efforts of addressing institutional change in a healthier way. Moving injustice to the center of an organization further reinforces and affirms members of the formerly oppressed group who now find their own perspective represented. This experience should satisfy their need for empowerment (Shnabel, Nadler, Ullrich, Dovidio, & Carmi, 2009) and respect (Bergsieker, Shelton, & Richeson, 2010) and thus may increase their trust in and engagement with the organization. Adopting a color-conscious strategy thus should serve members of both the dominant and subordinate group at least in the long run.

Another positive consequence of adopting a color-conscious strategy is that it allows organizations and communities to learn from the past and accept its present-day implications with greater understanding. This benefit was acknowledged by the Wachovia Corporation's chairman, Ken Thompson, who stated, "We want to promote a better understanding of the African-American experience, including the unique struggles, triumphs and contributions of African-Americans, and their important role in America's past and present" (Benner, 2005, para. 6). When Wachovia was denying an involvement with slavery, the company had no stated intention of promoting understanding about the Black American experience; after accepting, investigating, and publicly acknowledging its involvement in the slave trade, the company was able to move forward in a productive way. Similarly, state and city ordinances asking companies to disclose their involvement with slavery have sometimes included voluntary funds and grants specifically for Black Americans (e.g., the San Francisco ordinance; City and County of San Francisco, 2007); again, these would not be available were it not for the institutions choosing to adopt a more color-conscious strategy of handling race.

BEYOND LIP SERVICE: THE NEED FOR TRUE CHANGE

There are a number of important caveats to consider when exploring ways for organizations to adopt a color-conscious approach to inequality and injustice. First, organizations have to be ready for true change. Because "a society is not just the sum of individual group experiences but rather the result of power struggles and the economic subordination of racial ethnic groups" (Andersen, 1999, p.14), organizations have to be ready to undergo true structural change if they want to effectively change the intergroup dynamics within their institution. Acknowledging past injustice is only convincing if it is accompanied by true structural change. Members of minority groups tend to expose mere lip service for what it is; for example minorities are sometimes dissatisfied with a public apology that comes without financial compensation (Blatz, Schumann, & Ross, 2009). Second, in the beginning dialogues about past injustice may lead to an increase in tension because views are even more polarized (Paluck, 2010) and Whites are extremely uncomfortable with the topic. However, over time as the anxiety decreases, Whites should endorse a more color-conscious view, Blacks' trust should increase, and overall there should be more agreement between Blacks and Whites. Third, both Whites and Blacks have to be exposed to the information about injustice. The representation has to be truly public and both Blacks and Whites need to know that both groups are accessing it. Otherwise, it becomes the problem of one group— and that problem leads to segregation and discontent instead of meaningful dialogue.

PRACTICAL IMPLICATIONS

We would like to conclude by providing a few practical implications that follow from our theoretical reasoning for organizations that wish to address a difficult and challenging topic that involves unequal power dynamics. An example for such a topic could be a sexual harassment case that was unresolved in a company or a history of not admitting Black Americans in an educational institution. First, it is important to create broad-based public representations of the injustice. For example, the organizational leadership could send out an email that informs members of the organization about the injustice, or they could erect a memorial in a public place within the organization. It is important to make clear that all members of the organizations are exposed to the information. The email should obviously be addressed to everybody (rather than, for example, only women in the organization) and the memorial should be situated at a public location that all members of the organization pass by regularly. Furthermore, the information should be specific to the injustice that occurred in a given organization rather than creating a broader, universal message about equality and social justice. In the case of the previous examples, the email should describe the specific sexual harassment case that happened in the company, and the memorial should commemorate the individuals that were unjustly denied admission to the educational organization. The information should *not* attempt to make a broader statement about human compassion, injustice, or other social problems.

In addition, organizations should create venues for dialogue between members of the different groups and encourage a discussion of core issues. Organizations understandably often strive to avoid such potentially divisive dialogues; however, we argue that these dialogues can at times yield positive results. In past research, Blacks were more comfortable when talking about a race-relevant rather than race-neutral topic (Trawalter & Richeson, 2008) while Whites were at least equally anxious in both conditions. For example, an organization can invite members to an event to inform about the injustice. This event should include small group discussions with groups composed of diverse members of the organization. Finally, organizations should encourage individuals to interact as individuals rather than ambassadors for their groups. For example, if they have small group discussions, facilitators of these discussions should encourage individuals to introduce themselves and provide individualizing background information. This facilitates a positive individual experience against the backdrop of public representation of injustice. According to our theorizing, the unique combination of public representation of the specific injustice that happened in an organization together with the opportunity for dialogue with members of diverse groups who engage with the process as individuals rather than ambassadors for their own separate groups can create a climate where diverse members of an organization collaborate with each other to transform their organization from colorblind to color-conscious.

NOTE

1. For a detailed description of the study please refer to Ditlmann, 2012.
2. The authors corrected typographical errors and false spelling in the original quotations.

REFERENCES

Aetna statement regarding slavery reparations lawsuit (2002, March 27). *Aetna.* Retrieved from www.aetna.com/news/2002/pr_20020327.htm

Alderman, D. H., & Modlin Jr., A. E. (2008). (In)visibility of the enslaved within online plantation tourism marketing: A textual analysis of North Carolina websites. *Journal of Travel and Tourism, 25* (3–4), 265–281.

Andersen, M. L. (1999). The fiction of "diversity without oppression": Race, ethnicity, identity and power. In R. H. Tai, & M. L. Kenyatta (Eds.), *Critical ethnicity: Countering the waves of identity politics* (pp. 5–20). Oxford: Rowman & Littlefield.

Apfelbaum, E. P., Sommers, S. R., & Norton, M. I. (2008). Seeing race and seeming racist? Evaluating strategic colorblindness in social interaction. *Journal of Personality and Social Psychology, 95*(4), 918–932.

Baum, D. (2012, February 11). Martin Puryear to design slavery memorial. *Brown University News and Events.* Retrieved from http://news.brown.edu/pressreleases/2012/02/puryear

Bergsieker, H. B., Shelton, J. N., & Richeson, J. A. (2010). To be liked versus respected: Divergent goals in interracial interactions. *Journal of Personality and Social Psychology, 99*(2), 248.

Benner, K. (2005, June 2). Wachovia apologizes for slavery ties: Bank satisfies Chicago ordinance requiring companies with city contracts to disclose slavery ties. *CNN Money.* Retrieved from http://money.cnn.com/2005/06/02/news/fortune500/wachovia_slavery

Black 8th grader's essay comparing education system to slavery ignites outrage. (2012, March 1). Black Youth Project. Retrieved from www.blackyouthproject.com/2012/03/8th-grader-public-education-salvery-analogy/#more-23941

Blascovich, J., Mendes, W. B., Hunter, S. B., Lickel, B., & Kowai-Bell, N. (2001). Perceiver threat in social interactions with stigmatized others. *Journal of Personality and Social Psychology, 80*(2), 253.

Blatz, C. W., Schumann, K., & Ross, M. (2009). Government apologies for historical injustices. *Political Psychology, 30*(2), 219–241.

Bonilla-Silva, E. (2003). *Racism without racists: Colorblind racism and racial inequality in contemporary America*. Lanham, ML: Rowman & Littlefield.

Brown, M. K., Carnoy, M., Currie, E., Duster, T., Oppenheimer, D. B., Shultz, M. M., & Wellman, D. (2003). *Whitewashing race*. Berkeley, CA: University of California Press.

Brown University Steering Committee on Slavery and Justice, Slavery and Justice. (2006). *Report of the Brown University Steering Committee on Slavery and Justice*. Retrieved from http://brown.edu/Research/Slavery_Justice/report/index.html

Carr, L. G. (1997). *Color-blind racism*. Thousand Oaks, CA: Sage.

City and County of San Francisco. (2007). Slavery era disclosure ordinance: Report to the Mayor and Board of Supervisors. Retrieved from www.sfgsa.org/index.aspx?page=4500

Dacin, M. T., Goodstein, J., & Scott, W. R. (2002). Institutional theory and institutional change: Introduction to the special research forum. *The Academy of Management Journal, 45*(1), 43–56.

Ditlmann, R. K. (2012). Voicing the unspeakable: Implicit power motive predicts when and how African Americans frame past racial injustice to White Americans. (Unpublished Doctoral Dissertation). Yale, CT: Yale University.

Doosje, B. E. J., Branscombe, N. R., Spears, R., & Manstead, A. S. R. (2006). Antecedents and consequences of group-based guilt: The effects of ingroup identification. *Group Processes & Intergroup Relations, 9*(3), 325–338.

Dovidio, J. F., Gaertner, S. L., & Saguy, T. (2007). Another view of "we": Majority and minority group perspectives on a common ingroup identity. *European Review of Social Psychology, 18*(1), 296–330.

Eibach, R. P., & Ehrlinger, J. (2006). "Keep your eyes on the prize": Reference points and racial differences in assessing progress toward equality. *Personality and Social Psychology Bulletin, 32*(1), 66–77.

Excerpts of remarks delivered by John W. Rowe, M.D., Chairman, President and CEO, Aetna Inc. (2002, April 26). *Aetna*. Retrieved from www.aetna.com/news/2002/slavery_reparations_issue.html

Fishkin, S. F. (2011, January 5). Take the n-word out of "Huck Finn"? It's an insult to Mark Twain—and to American history. *NYDailyNews*. Retrieved from www.nydailynews.com/opinion/n-word-huck-finn-insult-mark-twain-american-history-article-1.151086#ixzz2GYYonfiw

Frantz, C. M., Cuddy, A. J. C., Burnett, M., Ray, H., & Hart, A. (2004). A threat in the computer: The race implicit association test as a stereotype threat experience. *Personality and Social Psychology Bulletin, 30*(12), 1611–1624.

Fredrickson, G. (2010). Models of American ethnic relations: Hierarchy, assimilation, and pluralism. In H. Markus, & P. M. L. Moya (Eds.), *Doing race: 21 essays for the 21st century* (pp. 23–34). New York: W. W. Norton.

Goldschmidt, D. (2011, May 23). Colleges come to term with slave-owning pasts. *CNN US*. Retrieved from http://articles.cnn.com/2011-05-23/us/university.slavery_1_slave-trade-slave-labor-slavery-and-justice/2?_s=PM:US

Gootman, E., & Baker, A. (2007, October 11). Noose on door at Columbia prompts campus protest. *The New York Times*. Retrieved from www.nytimes.com/2007/10/11/education/11columbia.html?_r=2&www.nytimes.com/2007/10/11/education/11columbia.html?_r=0

Gordon, L. (2010, February 27). Noose ignites more protests at UC San Diego. *The Los Angeles Times*. Retrieved from http://articles.latimes.com/2010/feb/27/local/la-me-uc-protests27-2010feb27

Ickes, W. (1984). Compositions in Black and White: Determinants of interaction in interracial dyads. *Journal of Personality and Social Psychology, 47*(2), 330–341.

Jacoby, J. (2005, June 9). The slavery shakedown. *The Boston Globe*. Retrieved from www.boston.com/news/globe/editorial_opinion/oped/articles/2005/06/09/the_slaver y_shakedown/

Johnson, M. (1998). Individual and cultural reality monitoring. *The Annals of the American Academy of Political and Social Science, 560*(1), 179–193.

Knowles, E. D., Lowery, B. S., Hogan, C. M., & Chow, R. M. (2009). On the malleability of ideology: Motivated construals of color blindness. *Journal of Personality and Social Psychology, 96*(4), 857.

La Rosa, S. (2011, January 4). A word about the New South edition of Markus Twain's *Tom Sawyer* and *Huckleberry Finn*. *NewSouth, Inc.* Retrieved from www.newsouthbooks. com/pages/2011/01/04/a-word-about-the-newsouth-edition-of-mark-twains-tom-sawyer-and-huckleberry-finn/

Leach, C. W., Zeinnedine, F. B., & Cehajic-Clancy, S. (2013). Moral immemorial: The rarity of self-criticism for previous generation's genocide or mass violence. In J. Vollhardt, & M. Bilewicz (Eds.), *Journal of Social Issues, 68*(1), 34–53.

Loewen, J. W. (1995). *Lies my teacher told me: Everything your American history textbook got wrong*. New York: The New Press.

Loewen, J. W. (2005). *Sundown towns: A hidden dimension of American racism*. New York: The New Press.

Martin, M. (2007, September 18). Noose found on Maryland Campus. Retrieved from www.npr.org/templates/story/story.php?storyId=14496865

Mendes, W. B., Gray, H. M., Mendoza-Denton, R., Major, B., & Epel, E. S. (2007). Why egalitarianism might be good for your health: Physiological thriving during stressful intergroup encounters. *Psychological Science, 18*(11), 991–998.

Mendes, W. B., Major, B., McCoy, S., & Blascovich, J. (2008). How attributional ambiguity shapes physiological and emotional responses to social rejection and acceptance. *Journal of Personality and Social Psychology, 94*(2), 278–291.

Michels, S. (2007, October 12). Columbia U. hate crime investigation widens. *ABC News*. Retrieved from http://abcnews.go.com/TheLaw/story?id=3714328&page=2#.UO CRRbam65U

Mitchell, K. J., & Johnson, M. K. (2009). Source monitoring 15 years later: What have we learned from fMRI about the neural mechanisms of source memory? *Psychological Bulletin, 135*(4), 638–677.

Modlin, E. A. (2008). Tales told on the tour: Mythic representations of slavery by docents at North Carolina plantation museums. *Southeastern Geographer, 48*(3), 265–287.

Norton, M. I., Sommers, S. R., Apfelbaum, E. P., Pura, N., & Ariely, D. (2006). Color blindness and interracial interaction. *Psychological Science, 17*(11), 949–953.

Ogletree, C. J. Jr. (2002, March 31). Litigating the legacy of slavery. *The New York Times*. Retrieved from www.nytimes.com/2002/03/31/opinion/litigating-the-legacy-of-slavery.html?pagewanted=all&src=pm

Ogletree, C. J. Jr. (2003). Repairing the past: New efforts in the reparation debate in America. *Harvard Civil Rights–Civil Liberties Review, 38*, 279–320.

Olson, W. (2008, October 31). So long, slavery reparations. *The Los Angeles Times*. Retrieved from http://articles.latimes.com/2008/oct/31/opinion/oe-olson31

Omi, M., & Winant, H. (1994). *Racial formation in the United States: From the 1960s to the 1990s*. New York: Routledge.

Paluck, E. L. (2010). Is it better not to talk? Group polarization, extended contact, and perspective taking in Eastern Democratic Republic of Congo. *Personality and Social Psychology Bulletin, 36*(9), 1170–1185.

Petri, A. (2011, January 4). Why a new edition of *Huckleberry Finn* is wrong to remove the N-word. *The Washington Post*. Retrieved from http://voices.washingtonpost.com/compost/2011/01/why_a_new_edition_of_huckleber.html

Plaut, V. C. (2002). Cultural models of diversity in America: The psychology of difference and inclusion. In R. Shweder, M. Minow, & H. R. Markus (Eds.), *Engaging cultural differences: The multicultural challenge in liberal democracies* (pp. 365–395). New York: Russell Sage.

Pollock, M. (2004). *Colormute: Race talk dilemmas in an American school*. Princeton, NJ: Princeton University Press.

Protest at Columbia (2007, October 11). *New York Times Video*. Retrieved from www.nytimes.com/2007/10/11/education/11columbia.html?_r=2&www.nytimes.com/2007/10/11/education/11columbia.html?_r=0

Purdie-Vaughns, V., Steele, C. M., Davies, P. G., Ditlmann, R., & Crosby, J. R. (2008). Social identity contingencies: How diversity cues signal threat or safety for African Americans in mainstream institutions. *Journal of Personality and Social Psychology*, *94*(4), 615–630.

Rothstein, E. (2011, March 11). Emancipating history. *The New York Times*. Retrieved from www.nytimes.com/2011/03/12/arts/design/charlestons-museums-finally-chronicle-history-of-slavery.html?pagewanted=all

Saguy, T., Tausch, N., Dovidio, J., & Pratto, F. (2009). The irony of harmony. *Psychological Science*, *20*(1), 114–121.

Schultz, M. (2011, January 3). Upcoming NewSouth "Huck Fin" eliminates the "N" word. *Publishers Weekly*. Retrieved from www.publishersweekly.com/pw/by-topic/industry-news/publisher-news/article/45645-upcoming-newsouth-huck-finn-eliminates-the-n-word.html

Shelton, J. N., & Richeson, J. A. (2005). Intergroup contact and pluralistic ignorance. *Journal of Personality and Social Psychology*, *88*(1), 91–107.

Shelton, J. N., & Richeson, J. A. (2006). Interracial interactions: A relational approach. *Advances in Experimental Social Psychology*, *38*, 121–181.

Shnabel, N., Nadler, A., Ullrich, J., Dovidio, J. F., & Carmi, D. (2009). Promoting reconciliation through the satisfaction of the emotional needs of victimized and perpetrating group members: The needs-based model of reconciliation. *Personality and Social Psychology Bulletin*, *35*(8), 1021–1030.

Slater, E. (2002, October 6). Working with Chicago requires a disclosure of slavery. *The Los Angeles Times*. Retrieved from http://articles.latimes.com/2002/oct/06/nation/na-slavery6

Stephan, W. G., & Stephan, C. W. (1985). Intergroup anxiety. *Journal of Social Issues*, *41*(3), 157–175.

Trawalter, S., & Richeson, J. A. (2008). Let's talk about race, baby! When Whites' and Blacks' interracial contact experiences diverge. *Journal of Experimental Social Psychology*, *44*(4), 1214–1217.

Version of "Huckleberry Finn" to remove "N" word. (2011, January 4). *CBSNews*. Retrieved from www.cbsnews.com/2100-207_162-7212343.html

Vollhardt, J. R. (2013). "Crime against humanity" or "Crime against Jews"? The importance of acknowledgment in construals of the Holocaust for intergroup relations. *Journal of Social Issues*, *69*(1), 144–161.

Vorauer, J. D. (2006). An information search model of evaluative concerns in intergroup interaction. *Psychological Review*, *113*(4), 862–886.

6

Occupational Sex Segregation

Disciplinary and Ideological Approaches to Understanding Women's and Men's Employment Patterns[1]

Margaret S. Stockdale and Joel T. Nadler

The promise of a diverse workplace is not merely one that contains diversity but one that values and effectively utilizes its diversity. This promise cannot be met if the labor force remains highly segregated by gender, race, or other important social identity characteristics. Despite legislation against sex discrimination in employment and progressive shifts in attitudes regarding women's employment, a large proportion of the U.S. workforce is employed in occupations that are highly dominated by their own sex. The U.S. Census bureau estimates that approximately 50% of employed women and men would have to change occupations from one dominated by their own sex to a more neutral or gender-incongruent occupation in order to eliminate occupational sex segregation (Hegewisch, Liepmann, Hayes, & Hartmann, 2010). Moreover, male-dominated occupations are characterized by greater compensation, both in terms of salary and benefits, greater independence and control, better advancement opportunities and greater authority than occupations dominated by women (e.g., Baron & Bielby, 1985; Reskin, 1993; Tomaskovic-Devey, 1993). Occupational sex segregation accounts for arguably 40% of the gender wage gap (Hegewisch et al., 2010), estimated in 2010 to be 77%. The median income for men in 2010 was $50,063, whereas for women it was $38,531 (U.S. Census Bureau, 2011).

Although these facts are undisputed, theories of occupational sex segregation vary widely from strong supply-side orientations, such as

Human Capital Theory (e.g. Becker, 1957) and Evolution theory (e.g., Browne, 2006), which posit natural differences between the sexes as the source of differential occupational paths, to strong demand-side orientations, which posit nefarious acts of employer discrimination and other forms of institutional sexism that differentially channel women and men into traditional occupational roles. Mid-range theories examine gender socialization forces, family structures, and gender differences in work and non-work values on occupational decisions. These theories are grounded in ideologies regarding gender and equality. The purpose of this book is to explore the differences in ideologies about diversity and the impact of these ideologies on scientific research and the development of interventions that address diverse communities and the management of diversity in organizations. The purpose of this chapter is to examine the disciplinary ideologies concerning an important signpost of diversity progress, or lack thereof: occupational sex segregation. We review major theories of occupational sex segregation, their ideological underpinnings and their empirical support. We conclude with practical implications for addressing occupational sex segregation.

OCCUPATIONAL SEX SEGREGATION TRENDS IN THE U.S. LABOR ECONOMY

Occupational sex segregation is typically operationally defined as the percentage of women (or men) in the labor market that would need to change occupations to a gender neutral one or one currently dominated by men (women) in order for there to be no gender segregation. The dissimilarity index (*D*) (Duncan & Duncan, 1955) calculates this proportion with the formula

$$D = \frac{1}{2}\sum_{1}^{k}|x_w - x_m|$$

where x_w and x_m are the proportions of women and men, respectively, in any particular occupation (*k*). *D* ranges from 0% (reflecting complete integration) to 100% (reflecting complete segregation). *D* is the most common method of determining the degree of occupational segregation, but has been criticized on a number of grounds;[2] nonetheless it suffices for descriptive purposes. Early quantitative examinations demonstrated that from the 1900s to the 1960s occupational segregation (*D*) was unchanged at 67% (Preston, 1999, citing Gross, 1968), meaning that 67% of women (men) would have to change to a more male- (female-) dominated occupation in order for there to be no occupational sex segregation (although researchers using more sophisticated methods found more fluctuation during this time period, see Weeden, 1998). Scholars agree, however, that segregation began to drop in the 1960s and did so fairly rapidly until the mid 1980s. From the 1980s to the early 2000s, the trend in desegregation decelerated to around 50%. Wells (1999) calculated standardized[3] dissimilarity indices of 477 occupational categories to be 58.6% in 1980 and 54.7% in 1990 using data from the decennial census. Using data from the Current Population Survey (CPS), a national probability sample, standardized dissimilarities indices in 1990 were estimated to be 54.6% and 53.1% by 1997. Also relying on CPS data, Hegewisch et al. (2010) showed that since the late 1990s, *D* has dropped very slowly to about 50% in 2002 and upticked slightly to 51% in 2003, which has remained stable.

Queneau (2010) compared dissimilarity indices in 175 occupations across the years 1983, 1993, and 2002 and also decomposed the indices to evaluate changes owing to shifts in occupational structure (relative size of the occupations) as well as true changes in the relative proportion of men and women within the occupations (sex composition effect). He found that the dissimilarity index decreased from 56.88 in 1983 to 47.60 in 2002 and 73.2% of this reduction was owing to changes in the sex composition effect. Sex segregation decreased at a slower pace from 1993 to 2002 (3.44 points) than it did from 1983 to 1993 (5.84 points). Changes in the sex composition effect were similar in both time periods (accounting for 72.6% of the reduction from 1983 to 1993 and 74.1% of the reduction from 1993 to 2002).

During the 1960s the drop was attributed mostly to men moving into female occupations and in the 1970s and 1980s to women moving into previously male occupations, particularly in the white-collar and service sectors (Blau, Simpson, & Anderson, 1988; Preston, 1999; Watts, 1995). There was a fairly rapid increase in the proportion of women moving into managerial, professional, and technical jobs from the late 1970s to the early 1980s, which began to slow in the mid 1980s (Watts, 1995) and there has been very little change in the occupational segregation of blue-collar jobs. Queneau (2010) found that changes in occupational sex segregation from 1983 to 2002 were due to gender shifts in sales, managerial, service, administrative support, and professional specialty categories, with the largest shift in the sex composition effect occurring from women moving into sales occupations from 1983 to 1993 and into managerial occupations between 1993 and 2002. Another factor accounting for the slowdown after the mid 1980s was re-segregation: occupations that were previously male-dominated were becoming female-dominated, such as real-estate sales. Preston (1999) also attributed the 1980s slowdown to the conservative political climate of the time and backlash toward Affirmative Action.

Estimates of occupational segregation are also affected by the level of abstraction of job categories. The more refined job categories are defined, the higher the level of segregation (Preston, 1999; Tomaskovic-Devey et al., 2006). For example, examining the distribution of women and men in the eight broadest levels of U.S. occupations (e.g., managerial, professional, technical, sales), Gabriel and Schmitz (2007) calculated the dissimilarity index as 31% in 2001, whereas Queneau's calculation on the basis of 175 occupations at roughly the same time was 47.6%; and, as reported above, Hegewisch et al. (2010) estimated this figure to be about 51% on the basis of the U.S. Census Bureau's detailed occupation codes of over 400 occupations for the civilian labor force aged 25 to 64. Also, within firms, sex segregation has been found to be very high at the job-title level. Bielby and Baron (1986) examined the distribution of men and women in 290 Californian firms between 1964 and 1979 that employed both women and men. The sample represented over 40,000 men, 11,000 women, and around 10,000 job titles. They found that while there was often overlap in job attributes and duties, firms created different titles and as such there was a high degree of segregation across job titles. For example, in two different manufacturing departments in the same firm, one job in department A may be labeled "operatives," and staffed almost entirely by men, whereas virtually the same job in department B may be labeled "assemblers" and staffed almost entirely by women. Bielby and Baron also found that for the same job title, the job may have been male dominated in one firm and female dominated in another firm. For example, waiters in restaurant firm A may be exclusively male (e.g., *Joe's Stone Crab*) whereas waiters in restaurant firm B may be exclusively female (e.g., *Hooters*). The theoretical implications of these findings are discussed later in this chapter, but the results suggest that the concept of "occupational" segregation may not adequately reflect the real extent of segregation of women's and men's work experiences.

Occupations requiring four or more years of college have consistently been more desegregated than other occupations and the rate of desegregation in these occupations has been stronger (changing from approximately 64% to approximately 43% in 2009). Comparatively, in occupations requiring less than four years of college, *D* equaled roughly 69% in 1972 and 57% in 2009 (Hegewisch et al., 2010). Finally, occupational segregation has decreased more rapidly in the public sector than in the private sector, which may be owing to more aggressive enforcement of anti-discrimination laws and the relatively higher levels of education of public-sector employees compared with those in the private sector, among other reasons (Barón & Cobb-Clark, 2010).

Research addressing occupational sex segregation (as well as race segregation) has interested scholars and policy makers in several social science disciplines including economics, sociology, psychology, and even geography (e.g., Hanson & Pratt, 1991). Ideologies about the sources and causes of sex segregation range from strong essentialist perspectives (women and men are naturally different and their job choices reflect these differences) to strong feminist perspectives (the patriarchal structure of society is perpetuated by isolating and subordinating women into less desirable jobs so that they cannot compete with men). We provide an overview of disciplinary and ideological perspectives in economics, sociology, and psychology in order to provide a balanced and comprehensive discussion of occupational sex segregation.

ECONOMIC PERSPECTIVES

Economists study the production, distribution, and consumption of goods and services and labor economists in particular examine these dynamics with regard to the market for labor. A dominant perspective of labor economics is the *neoclassical* model, which assumes that labor markets act rationally according to the laws of supply and demand. Prospective workers (or households according to some models) reflect supply whereas prospective employers reflect demand. Many, but not all, economists either dismiss or assume that workers internalize gender-role expectations and socialization practices that may differentially affect women's and men's labor attributes. Accordingly, individuals choose occupations that maximize the balance between preferences for time spent in employment and time spent on other matters (e.g., leisure, household tasks) and employers purchase (employ and pay wages to) labor that maximizes the desired characteristics of workers in comparison to their cost (all else being equal). Much of the attention that economists have paid to the issue of occupational sex segregation (and related issues such as the gender wage gap) has focused on supply side factors: those characteristics of individuals that influence their choice of occupations or that make them attractive to employers.

Within the neoclassical perspective, *human capital* theory (Becker, 1957) has generated hypotheses and research to explain occupational sex segregation, as well as other labor-related phenomena, such as the gender–wage gap. According to human capital theory, "workers seek out the best-paying jobs after taking into consideration their own personal endowments (e.g., education and experience), constraints (e.g., your child to take care of), and preferences (e.g., pleasant work environments)" (Anker, 1997, p. 316). Human capital theory, therefore, contends that it is supply-side factors that result in the different distribution of women and men across occupations. Although women have achieved parity with men and even recently exceeded them in educational attainment, the subjects they study in college impact their human capital (as they do for men). Gender differences in college majors, for example, set the stage for gender differences in occupations. Although her focus was on the gender–wage gap, Morgan (2008) examined gender differences in college majors in the 1993 National Survey of College Graduates (a national probability survey conducted by the Bureau of Census for the National Science Foundation of over 11,000 individuals identified in the 1990 census as having completed a Bachelor's degree in the past five years). Morgan found that sex segregation in college majors accounted for a large portion of the gender differences in entry-level pay differences and suggested that supply-side decisions about what major to pursue were largely responsible for employment-related discrepancies between women and men.

Shauman (2006) looked at choice of college major as well as worker characteristics for a wide variety of occupations. Worker characteristics were derived from a factor analysis of O*Net data (an online database of job descriptions including worker attributes maintained by the U.S. Department of Labor) which determined the extent to which occupations load on need for cognitive abilities, physical abilities, job zone (reflecting amount of job-specific training, part-time availability, and the extent to which career breaks are tolerated), intrinsic rewards, extrinsic rewards, authority, and working with people versus things. In her analysis of the same data set that Morgan (2008) used, Shauman found that choice of college major was less related to career choice for women than it was for men. Women tended to major in liberal arts and humanities, which could lead to many different occupational choices, whereas men tended to major in professionally linked programs, such as engineering and business. Furthermore, there were significant gender differences on the job zone factor such that women were more likely to select jobs for which part-time work was available, which, as we discuss latter, is often tied to childbirth and childrearing demands. In addition, gender differences were found in occupational worker characteristics related to extrinsic and intrinsic rewards, such that women were less likely than men to be in occupations that utilized abilities and creativity, led to a sense of accomplishment, and possessed autonomy, status, and recognition. Finally, women were more likely than men to choose occupations in which they were likely to work with people than with things. Interestingly, women were more likely than men to select occupations requiring verbal ability and job-specific trainings—factors that are associated with increased earnings—but the effect sizes were small.

Other relevant human capital variables include work experience, job-specific training, and career commitment. Using a national sample Gronau (1988) found that two thirds of the pay gap between men and women was explained by differences in training, and gender differences in training experiences and its effects on career paths continue to be substantiated (Munasinghe, Reif, & Henriques, 2008). Escriche (2007) suggested that cultural transmission of gender role expectations accounted for differential levels of job training between men and women and she presented a model of occupational segregation that differentiated the occupational preferences of women into two categories: family priority versus job priority. Women who have a high family priority tend to choose family over work when a conflict between the two is present whereas women with a high job priority favor work over family in similar situations. Although men can also be divided into these categories, research shows men rarely interrupt their career owing to work/family conflicts (Sicherman, 1996). The predominant individual orientation of job priority or family priority stems from the socialization efforts of parents attempting to maintain their own cultural values, expectations, and career attitudes. For example, Lee (2012) found that children are strongly influenced in their career aspirations by the careers and attitudes of their parents. Women's job priority has been increasing, however, which has narrowed the gender gap in experience and training (Olsen & Sexton, 1996). Finally, women are more likely to enter male-dominated fields when they have a higher commitment to the workforce characterizing a job priority orientation (Berryman & Waite, 1987). These preferences in orientation can have long-term impacts on careers.

A standard neoclassical/human capital assumption is that people consider the tradeoffs between the expectations for time spent in work and non-work roles in determining their choice of job or career. Because women's work role conflicts with traditional expectations for non-work roles, especially family roles, they are expected to choose occupations that offer more flexibility and for which they will not be penalized for intermittent work patterns. That is, women are more likely than men to choose occupations that they can return to easily after a few years break for child-rearing. Such jobs are typically low paying and require little skill updating. Polachek (1975) reasoned that women who expect to bear and raise children (e.g., married women) would invest less in human capital (job-related training) and thus accept lower-level positions that pay poorly, have little opportunity for advancement, and as a result are female dominated. England (1982), however, found that women with continuous employment were as likely as women with intermittent employment to be employed in female-dominated occupations and that there was no evidence that women are penalized less for intermittent employment in female-dominated occupations than in other occupations. Anker (1997) also argued against the benefits of intermittent employment as an explanation for sex segregation by pointing out that the amount of hours spent on house and family-related activities has steadily decreased owing to decreased fertility rates, and increases in household aids (e.g., dishwashers and vacuum cleaners). Women's employment commitment has steadily increased in recent decades such that there is no longer an age-based double hump in labor force participation (suggesting that there is not a period in women's adult lives when they tend to leave the workforce and then return). Yet rates of occupational segregation remain high.

Another dynamic in the neoclassic tradition is the influence of marriage on gendered occupational decisions. Although it may seem irrational for women to decrease their chances of high earnings by investing less in marketable human capital, such investments appear more rational when considered as part of a family unit. Women who are or who anticipate being married consider both their market role as well as their family role in making occupational decisions (Mincer & Polachek, 1974). The "marriage market" reflects factors that influence the prospects of being married or the choice of a mate.

Weichselbaumer (cited in Badgett & Folbre, 2003) placed two ads in the personals section of a Massachusetts newspaper, both of which described a White woman in her early thirties who was financially stable, good looking, and physically active. They differed only in occupation: nurse vs. electrician. After five weeks the nurse received 77 responses while the electrician received 39. In their own empirical study of personal ads, vignettes that were composed by the authors to vary gender conformity and occupational status, Badgett and Folbre (2003) found that gender nonconformity of women's careers negatively impacted their selection as potential mates, especially if those careers were considered low status (e.g., electrician vs. surgeon). A woman in a low status, but feminine occupation (e.g., secretary) was rated as desirable as a potential mate as was a woman in a high status feminine occupation (e.g., human resources manager). Men in a masculine high-status job were considered the most attractive, holding other characteristics constant. Along similar lines of logic, Gould (2008) found in his analysis of the National Longitudinal Survey of Youth that young men chose occupations that required more working hours, higher educational attainment, and that were in the white-collar sector largely because of the returns of these factors on the marriage market.

According to economists who espouse the *New Home Economics* approach, the labor market and the marriage market are inextricably connected. Women are advantaged in the marriage market to the extent that they pursue traditionally female occupations that allow them to simultaneously fulfill domestic roles. Although this reduces their economic power compared to their male spouses employed in more traditional masculine occupations, they gain power in the family by securing romantic love, spousal commitment, life satisfaction, and a portion of their spouse's income (Neuman, 1991). Therefore, the forces impinging on women to pursue traditional female occupations are strong and can only be overcome if the value of the rewards of a traditional marriage is outweighed by the economic (or other) benefits of nontraditional employment.

This brief review of the predominant economic perspectives on occupational sex segregation suggests that individuals and family units make rational decisions about their career choices that take into consideration various influences such as their expected non-work role investments and their fitness in the marriage market. Some economists have calculated that the neoclassical models (i.e., those that examine gender differences in human capital variables) account for between 86% and 90% of the occupational sex segregation gap (Gabriel & Schmitz, 2007). Working in a high wage-earning, high skill-updating, and otherwise high-status occupation is consonant with the traditional breadwinner role for men and makes men highly attractive as mates. Working in a low-wage, low skill-updating, non-professional occupation is less likely to conflict with the traditional caregiver role for women and does not hinder women's attractiveness as mates. As such, women and men invest (or fail to invest) in human capital characteristics that maximize the function of these joint contingencies. While there are notable exceptions, economists tend to support supply-side explanations for gender differences in occupational attainment (and its impact on sex segregation) and therefore have been criticized for refusing to consider the influence of bias and discrimination on these outcomes (Bergmann, 2007). Research that has accounted for supply-slide human capital differences still finds significant gender differences in pay (Bayard, Hellerstein, Neumark, & Troske, 2003; Blau & Kahn, 2000). Sociologists, and to a large extent psychologists, tend to favor demand-side explanations for gender differences in occupational outcomes, to which our attention next turns.

SOCIOLOGICAL PERSPECTIVES

Sociologists examine social activity and seek to understand economic and occupational disparities among social groups. To the question of sex discrimination in employment, Ridgeway and England (2007) state that sociologists examine "the extent of gender disparities in employment . . . [and] on finding the causes for inequalities between men's and women's work and especially for the inequalities in rewards reaped from work"

(p. 189). Like economists, sociologists categorize the sources of workplace inequality as deriving from supply or from demand. Sociologists pay particular attention to disparities in power and to hegemonic forces that operate at many levels of analyses to structure social relations that favor powerful entities. Marxist sociologists, for example, critically and empirically examine how capitalist forces, such as the ownership of production, affect labor and worker solidarity and, ultimately, the persistence of social stratification. Feminist sociologists focus on the importance of gender relations and how patriarchy works sometimes independently of profit-maximizing economic forces to maintain men's control over women (Strober, 1984). These forces may operate at interpersonal levels in the form of cultural beliefs, stereotypes, and gender status beliefs (Ridgeway & England, 2007); at group levels in the form of ingroup biases, such as homosocial reproduction—the tendency to favor people like oneself (Kanter, 1977); at institutional levels in the form of firm policies and practices that shape employment dynamics; and even at state and national levels in the form of political actions and labor practices that affect the movement of women and men into various occupations (e.g., Moller & Li, 2009).

Occupational sex segregation is "perhaps the most striking gender disparity in the contemporary world of paid work" (Ridgeway & England, 2007, p. 191), and is largely perpetuated by widespread, implicit beliefs about women and men, their perceived attributes and the roles they are presumed to occupy in relation to one another. Sociologists, therefore, are generally skeptical of supply-side focused explanations that place primary responsibility on gender differences in human capital attainment including free choices about career paths and career breaks. More compelling, they argue, is the allocation process by which men and women are sorted into different job queues such that jobs that presumably require masculine skills and authority (e.g., physical strength, decision making, vigor) go to men and jobs that require feminine skills (e.g., emotional, communicative, or finger dexterity) go to women, as long as such jobs do not gain too much status (Reskin & Roos, 1990). When jobs become identified as female dominated they are downgraded, poorly compensated, and marginalized. In a vicious cycle, such jobs remain female dominated because men tend to stay clear of female-dominated jobs and are more likely to be sorted into higher status, higher paying, and more generally rewarding occupations.

Sewell, Hauser, and Wolf's (1980) 18-year longitudinal study found that men gained more prestige in their occupations while women suffered a reduction in prestige over the same time period. Women who did not experience childbirth and childrearing experienced career advancement patterns similar to men. Similarly, Rindfuss, Cooksey, and Sutterlin (1999) studied a group of high school seniors from 1972 through 1986. Women tended to actually move to less prestigious positions or leave the workforce altogether over the years of the study. Men tended to move to higher prestige positions and become managers over the same period of time.

Demand-side explanations for occupational segregation, therefore, focus on the ways in which employers and the institutional structures they create act on beliefs about gender and status to perpetuate advantages for men. *Expectation states theory* (Berger, Rosenholtz, & Zelditch, 1980; Ridgeway, 1991) explains that status is an organizing principle that shapes people's perceptions and expectations of others. Traits such as competence and authority are attributed to individuals who are presumed to be high status and although task- and other situation-specific characteristics may shape beliefs about status, gender (among other salient demographic characteristics, such as race) serves as a ubiquitous "master status" variable that shapes beliefs about others. Due to widespread cultural beliefs about gender, men are presumed to possess agentic characteristics that are highly valued in most work-related roles, whereas women are presumed to possess seemingly nicer, but less valued communal traits (Ridgeway & England, 2007). These beliefs about gender can either predominate in workplace actors' (e.g., hiring managers) perceptions of the appropriateness of an individual for a particular job or occupation, or they can interact with job-specific information to shape these perceptions. For example, a woman may be perceived as more appropriate than a man for the job of a nurse, but a male nurse may be perceived as more authoritative (because of his status of being male) and thus considered more appropriate than a woman for a managerial job in nursing.

Similar to expectations, states theory is the process of *statistical discrimination* in which workplace actors rely on beliefs about gender differences (even if such beliefs have a basis in fact) to infer whether a given individual has the requisite characteristic(s) for a particular job or occupation. For example, while there is a reliable gender difference in upper body physical strength (Thomas & French, 1985), a hiring manager may presume that a particular male applicant for job requiring such strength is more qualified than a particular female applicant and thus rely on this belief about gender differences in making a hiring decision without having to administer an actual abilities test to these applicants.

Evidence of actual gender comparisons on most job-related traits, however, points to minimal differences (Hyde, 2005), therefore as beliefs about gender differences in traits diminish, it would seem that so too would statistical discrimination. However, a feminist interpretation argues that patriarchal pressures channel beliefs toward other kinds of differences that maintain male superiority in occupational queuing (Strober, 1984). Beliefs about organizational commitment and job stability therefore become salient. Women on average are believed to be less stable employees because they might drop out of the paid labor force for periods of time to raise children. Therefore, the additional status characteristic of "motherhood" further erodes perceptions of women's fitness for many types of careers (Correll, Benard, & Paik, 2007; Crosby, Williams, & Biernat, 2004; Cuddy, Fiske, & Glick, 2004).

Sociologists have also recognized supply side influences that impact occupational segregation. Hough (1987) suggested that occupational segregation results from differences between men and women on the importance of family and levels of family responsibility. Supporting Hough, women faculty members report greater stress and worry regarding family demands in relation to their career advancement compared with men who were more concerned with power and promotion (Dey, 1994; Perna, 2005; Vagg, Spielberger, & Wasala, 2002). Additionally, women faculty reported that becoming a mother had negatively impacted their academic careers (Marshall & Jones, 1990). Kaufman and Uhlenberg (2000) found that mothers were less likely to be employed or were employed for fewer hours than non-mothers. Additionally, greater numbers of children predicted a greater reduction in women's hours worked. By contrast, men with children were more likely to be employed than men without children and men with more children worked more hours than men with fewer children. Additionally, Presser and Hermsen (1996) found men were more willing to travel compared with women in similar occupations. Egalitarian attitudes increased the odds of women traveling regularly as a part of their careers but not men. Baldridge, Eddleston, and Veiga (2006) found gender-role pressures on women resulted in women being less likely to relocate for work. Women expressed significantly less willingness to relocate than did men. Gender differences in willingness to travel and willingness to relocate may impact both occupational segregation and job segregation. Women may be less likely to choose occupations that tend to involve travel and relocation. Additionally, women may be less likely to take a sales job that requires travel and/or relocation compared with a sales job that lacks such demands.

Also, from a supply-side perspective, sociologists have examined gender differences in occupational expectations. Longitudinal analyses of 4,000 white women found family responsibilities affected women's career choices (Drobnic, Blossfeld, & Rohwer, 1999). Married women, with and without children, were more likely to transition from employment to non-employment compared with all other groups of men and women. Presser (1994) found within dual-earning married couples women spent twice the amount of time doing household chores compared with their husbands. Additionally, working women spent more than three times the amount of time on feminized tasks such as cleaning and cooking compared with their working husbands, and, likewise, men spent considerably more time on masculine tasks such as yard work compared with their wives. More recent examinations of gender differences in family roles have found these differences between men and women are reducing, but are still present (Bond, Thompson, Galinsky, & Prottas, 2002).

Returning to the demand side, sociologists distinguish between occupational segregation and job segregation. Occupations are broad classifications and span across firms whereas jobs are within-firm designations that encompass a specific set of tasks and responsibilities. Employers impact decisions about which applicants get chosen for particular jobs within their firms, whereas individuals (applicants) make decisions about which occupations they wish to pursue. If job segregation by gender is merely a matter of gender differences in occupational choices (or gender differences in human capital for various occupations) then the degree of segregation within firms should generally be the same as the degree of occupational sex segregation that is evident across firms; however, if job gender segregation is higher than occupational segregation, then this implies that demand-side influences (e.g., cultural stereotypes) are affecting employers' decisions about job placement. Studies of job gender segregation of firms in California (Bielby & Baron, 1984; 1986) and North Carolina (Tomaskovic-Devey, 1995) show much higher rates of job segregation than occupational segregation in their respective states. Bielby and Baron (1986) found that the discrimination index for jobs in California firms in the mid 1960s and

1970s was 96%. Tomaskovic-Devey (1995) reported that in North Carolina in the late 1980s, men were in jobs that averaged 8.06% female whereas women were in jobs that were 87.93% female—figures that are much higher than national levels of occupational sex segregation at comparable times delineated in the first section of this chapter.

Institutional sociologists argue that structures and processes within firms play a large role in perpetuating or abating job segregation problems. Such structures and practices include internal promotion opportunities, preferential treatment programs, compensation structures, as well as a host of affirmative action and diversity initiatives. Institutional structures that exacerbate job segregation include promotion patterns that privilege jobs that men tend to occupy. Sears Roebuck Company, for example, faced a class-action sex discrimination suit because positions that led to promotions into management were those held primarily by men (e.g., large appliance sales positions), whereas jobs held primarily by women (check-out clerks) rarely led to management positions (EEOC v. Sears, 1988). The plaintiffs alleged that Sears tended to steer female applicants into clerk positions and male applicants into sales positions.[4] Recently, sociologists have argued that unfettered managerial discretion in hiring and promotion practices capitalizes on implicit stereotypes and biases which disadvantage women's placement into positions of authority (Bielby, 2005).

By contrast, institutional practices that curtail job segregation (promote integration) are those that create structures of responsibility for diversifying occupations and promotion ladders. Without clear responsibilities within firms for these initiatives, edicts for diversity are generally ignored as managers tend to more pressing matters such as deadlines and budgets (Kalev, Dobbin, & Kelly, 2006). Kalev et al. (2006) examined the effects of various affirmative action and diversity initiatives on the sex and race desegregation of managerial positions in over 700 private sector firms in the U.S. from 1971 to 2002. Initiatives that created positions of responsibility for affirmative action and EEO oversight, such as an office of diversity with full-time staff that had the responsibility of setting affirmative action goals and monitoring their progress, were the most successful in increasing the percentage of women and African Americans in managerial positions. Initiatives aimed at increasing understanding of bias, stereotyping, and prejudice (i.e., diversity training) had negligible effects on increasing managerial gender diversity and had negative effects on race diversity in management.

The sociological approach to understanding occupational and job sex segregation, therefore, eschews the assumptions that occupationally relevant actors pursue rational, economically maximizing courses of action in job allocation decisions and instead are subject to the forces of power, patriarchy, and social control. These forces act at multiple levels. As individuals in a social world we possess and act on beliefs about women and men and their presumed traits and roles; as groups we privilege those who are most similar to us and isolate those who are different; as institutions we create structures and practices that codify our biases and prejudices. Indeed, interventions to change institutional structures to be more "family friendly" or supportive of gender diversity have shown positive impacts on decreasing occupational segregation in some sectors (e.g., Kalev et al., 2006).

PSYCHOLOGICAL PERSPECTIVES

Psychology is the study of human behavior and as such often focuses at the individual level of analysis. Psychology complements the economic and sociological approaches to occupational sex segregation by examining both demand- and supply-side factors. Psychologists differ from sociologists and economists, however, in how they examine the influence of market and social forces on individual decision making, behaviors, and attitudes. Psychological research on supply-side factors focuses on individual differences in career choices and job preferences, whereas research on demand-side factors includes psychological research on stereotyping, prejudice, and discrimination. Like sociologists, psychologists recognize relevant constructs at multiple levels of analyses that impact the dynamics of occupational segregation, but the central focus is on individual behavior. For example, institutional policies and practices that privilege members of one gender over another may be characterized as "institutional sexism" but it is an individual acting alone or in a group who engages in a sexist act. Similarly, occupational sex segregation is a population-based phenomenon, but it is individuals (again, acting alone or as part of a social unit, such as a family) who select careers, occupations, or jobs. The question psychologists ask, therefore, is what are the internal (e.g., traits, attitudes, beliefs), social (e.g., group norms and roles, cultural expectations), structural (e.g., organizational arrangements), and other higher-level factors that influence individual career or job choices (from the supply perspective) or an individual's discriminatory behavior (from the demand perspective)?

Psychologists' approach to demand-side factors that affect occupational segregation has primarily focused on stereotypes, prejudice, and discriminatory behaviors that may result in women and men being differentially selected for various jobs and occupations. Glick and Fiske (2007) state that psychologists research sex discrimination and occupational sex segregation by considering:

> not only what goes on inside the individual's mind, but how the individual is affected by and adapts to social contexts, ranging from proximal influences (e.g., the norms of one's immediate work group) to more distal influences (e.g., the division of male and female roles in society). (p. 156)

The psychological study of human behavior shows that rational individualistic decision making is rarely driven by only internal attributes and attitudes. Indeed, attitudes are often poor predictors of behavior (Glassman & Albarracin, 2006). Individual behaviors and decision-making processes are strongly affected by the situation and by both conscious and unconscious awareness and endorsement of stereotypes and gender roles. Explicit and implicit stereotyping impacts factors that affect whether an individual will be considered appropriate for various types of occupations or be promoted into higher levels of authority within an occupation. Gender bias and discrimination can result from overt sexism and intentional societal structures aimed at reducing access to women. However, intent or conscious awareness and endorsement of gender role stereotypes is not necessary for bias and discrimination to occur (Greenwald, Poehlman, Uhlmann, & Banaji, 2009). People are influenced by cultural gender stereotypes that they do not consciously endorse (Banaji & Greenwald, 1995) and people are influenced by associations of cultural stereotypes and how they interact with individuals from stereotyped groups (Rudman & Kilianski, 2000).

Psychologists recognize that stereotypes are further divided into descriptive and prescriptive forms (Rudman & Glick, 2001). Descriptive stereotypes are beliefs individuals hold regarding what traits are likely to be found within a particular group. Prescriptive stereotypes are beliefs about how members of particular groups should behave. Thus, a descriptive stereotype regarding women may be that women are generally more emotional and supportive than men. A prescriptive stereotype is that because "Jane" is a woman she should be more emotional and supportive. Research has found that women who violate prescriptive feminine stereotypes by, for example, excelling in a male-dominated field or showing masculine traits such as dominance are seen as less feminine and less likable (Eagly & Karau, 2002; Rudman & Glick, 2001). This backlash explains some of the difficulty women may experience in advancing in male-dominated fields or leadership positions.

In their approach to demand-side influences on occupational sex segregation, psychologists also consider how social systems such as organizational or cultural stereotypes introduce bias into employment-related decision-making processes. Stereotypes of men and women as well as stereotypes of masculine and feminine traits associated with various jobs can lead to bias and discrimination. Stereotypes link traits, attitudes, and abilities with social categories. *Social role theory* (Eagly, 1987) suggests that traditional divisions of labor between men and women have over time shaped stereotypes of both people (men and women) as well as occupations (masculine and feminine typed jobs). Men have traditionally occupied roles outside of the home and have become associated with agentic traits such as competence, aggression, ambition, and independence. In contrast, women have been associated with home and childrearing roles and are associated with communal traits such as compassion, caring, weakness, and interdependence. Additionally, certain careers have become associated with women and communal stereotypes and other careers have become associated with men and agentic stereotypes. For example, Schein (1975; 2001) found that the stereotypical traits associated with successful managers are congruent with the agentic traits that are associated with men in general, but not women. Men are more likely to be seen as a good fit for masculine-typed jobs and are more likely to be hired and promoted in such occupations (Eagly & Carli, 2007, chapter 5; Eagly & Karau, 2002). Likewise, women are more likely to be seen as a good fit for feminine-typed jobs. These perceptions of the fit between individuals and jobs that are based on gender stereotypes of people and occupations perpetuate occupational segregation through biases in hiring, appraising job performance, and promotion decisions.

Women also suffer stereotype-based discrimination through the process of sex-role spillover. Gender-role expectations of women often spill over into work roles resulting in female employees being expected to assume housework type tasks in the workplace regardless of specific job tasks (Eckes, 2002). The tendency for women to be seen as more feminine and therefore more communal often increases when gender is salient. For example, attractive people are seen as more competent in the workplace (Hamermesh & Biddle, 1994); however, attractive women are more strongly associated with feminine stereotypes than less attractive women and may be at a further disadvantage in masculine-typed jobs that are high in prestige (Heilman & Stopek, 1985). Gutek (1985, chapter 8) suggests sexualized work environments can lead to highly discriminatory behaviors, such as sexual harassment. Sexualized work environments are those characterized by a strong imbalance in the ratio of women to men (i.e., sex segregated), and a high degree of sexual banter and other sexual stimuli being present. Thus, the culture of a sex segregated workplace perpetuates occupational segregation by making gender very salient and by facilitating behaviors (i.e., sexual harassment) that reduce the likelihood of the minority gender (women) pursuing or remaining in the sexualized work environment.

Corporate cultures may emphasize masculine or feminine environments, which in turn may heighten gender bias in decision making. Numerous situational variables have been found to hamper women's placement and advancement in masculine careers. Professions that are male-dominated are more likely to result in stereotyping of women and an increased likelihood of women relegated to feminine-typed communal functions within the organization (Gutek, 1985, chapter 8). Such minority status serves to increase the salience of the individual's social category (woman), further heightening stereotyped expectations of behaviors (Taylor, 1981). Further, stereotypes are strongest when individuating information is absent (Tosi & Einbender, 1985) such as when a group has little experience with a social group in a particular setting. Finally, managers with less oversight and more power who are far-removed from observing the day-to-day work behaviors of employees are more likely to fall prey to bias based on stereotypes (Fiske, 1993). All of these situational factors are likely to present barriers to women entering male-dominated fields by presenting barriers to occupational integration, stilted advancement opportunities, and higher rates of attrition for women who attempt to establish careers in male-dominated occupations.

Structural barriers such as discrimination in hiring and biased promotion systems also explain occupational sex segregation (Gutek, 1993). For example, Martell, Lane, and Emrich (1996) demonstrated the devastating effect of a small sexist bias in an organization's hiring and promotion using a computer simulation. A one percent bias favoring men over women at each promotion level of an average multinational company explained the "real world" gender disparity favoring men in upper management. Hostile work environments including sexual harassment are examples of within organizational barriers. For example, hostile work environments (sexual harassment) have been shown to be associated with higher rates of attrition in women workers (Sims, Drasgow, & Fitzgerald, 2005). Women in the face of such structural barriers may re-evaluate or lower their career expectations.

Gender role theory (a specific derivative of social role theory) is also relevant to psychologists' examination of supply-side forces on occupational segregation. Gender role theory (Eagly, 1987) suggests that men and women have different preferences when examining potential jobs and career choices resulting from gendered socialization. In short, men and women are socialized to prefer different job attributes (Konrad, Corrigall, Lieb, & Ritchie, 2000). Boys and men are pressured to become income providers while girls and women are pressured to become homemakers. These pressures are societal and are communicated through parents, teachers, media, and culturally supported stereotypes of male and female types of occupations. These occupational roles are further supported with gender role expectations for women to be nurturing (possessing communal traits) and men to be achievement oriented (possessing agentic traits) (Eagly & Karau, 2002).

Gender role theory predicts that men will desire jobs that provide high earnings, advancement, and prestige, whereas women desire jobs that provide opportunities to help others and flexible hours to accommodate family demands. The more women conform to gendered socialization expectations, the stronger their preferences for feminized job attributes (Konrad, 2003). Additionally, women prefer greater flexibility in occupations, especially early in their careers coinciding with their childbearing years (Konrad, Yang, Goldberg, & Sullivan, 2005). In a meta-analytic review Chapman, Uggerslev, Carroll, Piasentin, and Jones (2005) found women were more likely to attend to job characteristics such as work flexibility and time off when determining the attractiveness of a job position compared with men. Additionally, women were more likely than men to be attracted to jobs that minimized family–role conflicts.

Gender roles establish pathways that guide individual career choices. Children and adolescents develop images of themselves in various career roles and these images are shaped by their gender role socialization (Gottfredson, 1981). Gottfredson's circumscription and compromise theory states that gender guides the development of self-concept and the subsequent desirability of various careers. Additionally, the theory suggests that gender self-concept in vocational choices is robust and that individuals resist violating their vocational gender self-concept. According to Gottfredson, gender is the primary individual difference variable that predicts vocational interests. Gottfredson and Lapan (1997) further suggest that gendered self-concept results in both men and women limiting their vocational choices, often eliminating potentially enjoyable choices at which they might excel.

Gender differences have been found in both vocational interests and self-efficacy with women reporting more interest than men in social occupations (Betz, Harmon, & Borgen, 1996; Holland, 1985). Holland (1985; Holland, Krause, Nixon, & Trembath, 1953) proposed that vocational interests can be divided into six broad categories: realistic, investigative, artistic, social, enterprising, and conventional, and the theory serves as a model for matching individuals with compatible career interests. Lent, Brown, and Hackett (1994) suggested that self-efficacy (i.e., beliefs regarding one's ability with regard to an interest area) in addition to orientation toward Holland's interest types determined vocational choices. Gender roles impact both Holland's interest types and self-efficacy regarding those interests (Betz et al., 1996). Women are more likely to express interest and self-efficacy in Holland's social and realistic areas and men are more likely to express self-efficacy and interest in conventional areas (Betz et al., 1996). Gender-based differences extend to job attributes that define the Holland interest categories as well. A meta-analysis of over 200 studies representing a total sample size of over 600,000 found gender differences corresponding to gender stereotypes and roles in 33 of the 40 job attributes used in Holland's typography (Konrad, Ritchie, Lieb, & Corrigall, 2000). Although these differences were generally small they illustrated gender role differences with women preferring attributes associated with communal occupations and men preferring agentic attributes. Additionally, men were more likely to be drawn to attributes such as wages and responsibility and women were more focused on hours and helping others. These differences were found to be more pronounced in the earlier studies analyzed compared with the more recent articles (Konrad et al., 2000).

Gender roles and perceptions of various career-related stressors, such as work–family conflict, and expectations that one will encounter bias, discrimination, sexual harassment, and other gender-based stressors affect self-selection of career interests (Phillips & Imhoff, 1997). Self-selection, with women opting out of various occupations, occurs at all points within the process from initial career decisions, to education and training and through attrition once on the job. Crocker, Karpinski, Quinn, and Chase (2003) found that women who were pursuing a stereotypically male dominated college major experienced reduced self-esteem and reduced identification with their major compared with men in the same major. Murphy, Steele, and Gross (2007) found that masculine cues reduced women's interest in male-dominated fields such as science and math. Similarly, Cheryan, Plaut, Davies, and Steele (2009) found that stereotypical cues reduced women's interest in computer science. The results indicated that male-stereotypical cues affected women's, but not men's, sense of belonging to groups. Additionally, Cheryan et al. found that women's awareness of the environment (actual ratio of men to women) or stereotype-based knowledge of the ratio reduced their sense of belonging to the group and subsequently reduced their interest in joining the group. Stereotypical cues in a group's environment send persuasive messages to potential members about the type of person that belongs in that group.

The psychological approach to understanding occupational sex segregation suggests that the environment influences individual decision making on both the demand side and supply side. Both conscious and unconscious knowledge of prescriptive and descriptive stereotypes guide career choice from a supply side, and hiring, performance appraisals, and promotions impact career decisions from a demand side. Psychologists find that women are influenced by individual preferences for certain careers and are drawn more than men to flexible family-friendly work. However, these preferences are driven by knowledge of stereotypical expectations within occupations. Likewise, decision makers are motivated to find the optimal employees for job openings, but are influenced by societal stereotypes in their evaluations, especially when their stereotypes of women or men are incongruent with their stereotypes of the occupation under consideration.

CONCLUSIONS

Descriptive studies from national probability samples to full census data research paint a clear picture of the existence of occupational sex segregation (Hegewisch et al., 2010; Queneau, 2010). Women and men occupy different careers and different levels of authority within careers. Additionally, women are more likely to be overrepresented in lower prestige, lower paid, and less skilled careers and underrepresented in higher prestige, higher paid, and higher skilled careers. The question is not whether occupational segregation is occurring but what drives occupational segregation, and whether we can move toward a more egalitarian labor force.

Economics, sociology, and psychology have examined the nature of occupational sex segregation, trends over time, and various potential causes from differing yet sometimes overlapping perspectives. These perspectives differ in their focus on demand or supply side forces and on the level of analysis: societal, organizational, or individual. Economics focuses on macro level (societal and organizational) supply-side issues and presupposes that rational choices based on market realities fuel gendered differences within the workforce. Economists appear to regard gender differences in socialization processes as part of the bag of goods (i.e., supply-side characteristics) that workers bring to the job market, whereas sociologists and psychologists deconstruct that bag of goods using feminist, Marxist, or related lenses to show how differentials in the structure of power in society drive stereotypes, social identities, and other processes that place constraints on choices and preferences. Sociology primarily focuses on issues affecting the demand side and suggests that the power differences inherent in work dominated by men compared with work dominated by women are endemic. Cultural and organizational level structures maintain such inequality. Finally, psychology examines both supply- and demand-side forces on a micro or individual level but shows how macro-level structures and processes interact with individual decision making and career choices. These three perspectives may appear to be competing, but in reality are examining the same phenomenon simply from differing assumptions and levels of analysis. All three perspectives are collaborative and provide vital pieces of the organizational sex segregation puzzle. When researches from these three fields are viewed holistically, a broader understanding of how cultural norms and gender expectations are reinforced and reproduced on multiple levels of analysis is revealed.

Occupational gender segregation can result from pressures at the individual, organizational, and cultural levels; however, the most likely explanation for the outcome of these forces, statistically observable occupational gender segregation, is a combination of all three. It is only through an interdisciplinary approach that all of the causes and antecedents that result in gender disparity in various careers can be fully understood.

Do rational decisions result in gender differences in occupations with little need to invoke bias, prejudice, or issues of power? Do cultural structures maintain and perpetuate gender inequities to perpetuate White men's greater access to wealth, prestige, and power? Do gender role socialization processes impact the development of human capital characteristics of women and men (girls and boys) for the occupations and jobs they expect to attain? Do these same processes shape employers' stereotypes, attitudes, and biases toward their labor markets? Evidence from all three disciplines provides solid and well researched answers to these questions. Rational supply-side perspectives call attention to macro-level forces that influence the ebb and flow of labor markets under conditions of optimization. What we may ultimately learn from the economic view is what to expect when labor market forces are acting rationally so that sociologists and psychologists can illuminate where rationality breaks down and why. The question becomes one of both increasing social justice and optimal utilization of the available workforce.

All three perspectives value an increase in the egalitarian nature of the workforce and society. From an economic viewpoint, factors that reduce the value of labor attributes, no matter their source, degrade the quality and supply of labor. This may increase wage disparity if men's attributes (e.g., perceived steady employment) are perceived as both valuable and scarce in comparison with women's perceived attributes. It is important to understand how these economic principles work in order to design policies and practices to counteract them. From a sociological standpoint, societies that perpetuate injustice are likely to be less politically and financially stable (Engerman, Haber, & Sokoloff, 2000). When a social system contains structural elements that restrict access to jobs based not on ability and skill, but on demographic traits, these systems need to be challenged and changed. From a psychological standpoint, occupational sex segregation results in individual decision making on both the supply and demand sides that results in less than optimal outcomes. Bias in individual decision making within organizations results in less qualified applicants being hired and promoted based on group membership, not ability. Likewise, individuals choose less than optimal careers or opt out to slower advancement paths owing to their own perceptions of their gender roles.

The fields of economics, sociology, and psychology may disagree on the level of analysis that is most important to study and the underlying reasons to change to a more integrated work force. But, all three disciplinary approaches suggest the reduction in occupational segregation can be obtained through changes at the levels of analysis that are their focus. If societal expectations and messages regarding gendered differences in career choices and abilities are reduced and replaced with more egalitarian messages, then occupational sex segregation will decrease. Holding organizational units and individual managers accountable for their biases in decision making will also help reduce occupational segregation. Finally, occupational sex segregation will decline if we do not release the pressure on socializing agents to break open the molds of traditional gender role expectations so that occupational choices are unconstrained.

All three perspectives provide clarity in what needs to be changed and what can be changed to address occupational segregation. Only considered in totality does a multilevel approach become apparent. Occupational sex segregation occurs owing to demand- and supply-side reasons, and on societal, organizational, and individual levels. Escriche (2007) suggests that occupational sex segregation can be addressed on a societal level through interventions at the individual, family, and work levels. Organizations need to optimize policies to acknowledge family obligations, equalize training opportunities, and socialization experiences for both genders. Simultaneously, parents need to educate their children about the realities of gendered work preferences and potential long-term outcomes on career success. Gendered differences in career choices are large and are not supported by ability or motivational differences. All three perspectives provide leverage points to initiate change resulting in a more efficient, more qualified, and a more socially just workforce.

NOTES

1. Portions of the chapter formed the basis of a published commentary: Stockdale, M. S., & Nadler, J. T. (2013), Paradigmatic assumptions of disciplinary research on gender disparities: The case of occupational sex segregation. *Sex Roles, 68*, 207–215.

2. Preston (1999) summarizes these shortcomings as follows: (a) trends documented by the D index are positively affected by growth in occupations even if there is no change in the gender imbalance across occupations; and (b) if used to document changes in occupational segregation over time, the index fails to replace workers who move to other occupations.
3. The standardized D controls for shifts in the distribution of occupations over time.
4. Sears contended that gender differences in initial job placement were based on applicant preferences.

REFERENCES

Anker, R. (1997). Theories of segregation by sex: An overview. *International Labour Review*, *136*, 315–339.

Badgett, M. V. L., & Folbre, N. (2003). Job gendering: Occupational choice and the marriage market. *Industrial Relations, 42*, 270–298.

Baldridge, D. C., Eddleston, K. A., & Veiga, J. F. (2006). Saying no to being uprooted: The impact of family and gender on willingness to relocate. *Journal of Occupational and Organizational Psychology, 79*, 131–149.

Banaji, M. R., & Greenwald, A. G. (1995). Implicit gender stereotyping in judgments of fame. *Journal of Personality and Social Psychology, 68*, 181–198.

Baron, J. N., & Bielby, W. T. (1985). Organizational barriers to gender equality: Sex segregation of jobs and opportunities. In A. Rossi (Ed.), *Gender and the life course* (pp. 233–251). New York: Aldine.

Barón, J. D., & Cobb-Clark, D. A. (2010). Occupational segregation and the gender wag gap in private- and public-sector employment: A distributional analysis. *The Economic Record, 86*, 227–246.

Bayard, K., Hellerstein, J., Neumark, D., & Troske, K. (2003). New evidence on sex segregation and sex differences in wages from matched employee–employer data. *Journal of Labor Economics, 21*, 887–922.

Becker, G. S. (1957). *The economics of discrimination.* Chicago, IL: University of Chicago Press.

Berger, J., Rosenholtz, S. J., & Zelditch, M., Jr. (1980). Status organizing processes. *Annual Review of Sociology, 6*, 479–508.

Bergmann, B. R. (2007). Discrimination through the economist's eye. In F. J. Crosby, M. S. Stockdale, & S. A. Ropp (Eds.), *Sex discrimination in the workplace: Multidisciplinary perspectives* (pp. 213–234). Malden, MA: Blackwell.

Berryman, S. E., & Waite, L. (1987). Young women's choice of nontraditional occupations. In C. E. Bose, & G. D. Spitze (Eds.), *Ingredients for women's employment policy* (pp. 115–136). Albany, NY: State University of New York Press.

Betz, N. E., Harmon, L. W., & Borgen, F. H. (1996). The relationships of self-efficacy for the Holland themes to gender, occupational group membership, and vocational interest. *Journal of Counseling Psychology, 43*, 90–98.

Bielby, W. T. (2005). Applying social research on stereotyping and cognitive bias to employment discrimination litigation: The case of allegations of systematic gender bias at Wal-Mart Stores. In L. B. Nielsen, & R. L. Nelson (Eds.), *Handbook of employment discrimination research: Rights and realities* (pp. 395–408). Dordrecht, Netherlands: Springer.

Bielby, W. T., & Baron, J. N. (1984). A woman's place is with other women: Segregation within organizations. In B. F. Reskin (Ed.), *Sex segregation in the workplace: Trends, explanations, and remedies* (pp. 27–55). Washington, DC: National Academy Press.

Bielby, W. T., & Baron, J. N. (1986). Men and women at work: Sex segregation and statistical discrimination. *American Journal of Sociology, 91*, 759–799.

Blau, F. D., & Kahn, L. M. (2000). Gender differences in pay. Retrieved January 31, 2009, from NBER Working Paper No. W7732 website: http://ssrn.com/abstract=232114.

Blau, F. D., Simpson, P., & Anderson, D. (1988). Continuing progress? Trends in the occupational segregation in the United States over the 1970s and 1980s. *Feminist Economics, 4*, 29–71.

Bond, J. T., Thompson, C., Galinsky, E., & Prottas, D. (2002). *Highlights of the National Study of the Changing Workforce*. New York: Families & Work Institute.

Browne, K. R. (2006). Evolved sex differences and occupational segregation. *Journal of Organizational Behavior, 27*, 143–162.

Chapman, D. S., Uggerslev, K. L., Carroll, S. A., Piasentin, K. A., & Jones, D. A. (2005). Applicant attraction to organizations and job choice: A meta-analytic review of the correlates of recruiting outcomes. *Journal of Applied Psychology, 90*, 928–944.

Cheryan, S., Plaut, V. C., Davies, P. G., & Steele, C. M. (2009). Ambient belonging: How stereotypical cues impact gender participation in computer science. *Journal of Personality and Social Psychology, 97*(6), 1045–1060.

Correll, S. J., Benard, S., & Paik, I. (2007). Getting a job: Is there a motherhood penalty? *American Journal of Sociology, 112*, 1297–1339.

Crocker, J., Karpinski, A., Quinn, D. M., & Chase, S. K. (2003). When grades determine self-worth: Consequences of contingent self-worth for male and female engineering and psychology majors. *Journal of Personality and Social Psychology, 85*, 507–516.

Crosby, F. J., Williams, J. C., & Biernat, M. (2004). The maternal wall. *Journal of Social Issues, 60*, 675–582.

Cuddy, A. J. C., Fiske, S. T., & Glick, P. (2004). When professionals become mothers, warmth doesn't cut the ice. *Journal of Social Issues, 60*, 701–718.

Dey, E. L. (1994). Dimensions of faculty stress: A recent survey. *Review of Higher Education, 17*, 305–322.

Drobnic, S., Blossfeld, H., & Rohwer, G. (1999). Dynamics of women's employment patterns over the family life course: A comparison of the United States and Germany. *Journal of Marriage and the Family, 61*, 133–146.

Duncan, O. D., & Duncan, B. (1955). A methodological analysis of segregation indices. *American Sociological Review, 20*, 200–217.

Eagly, A. H. (1987). *Sex differences in social behavior: A social-role interpretation*. Hillsdale, NJ: Erlbaum.

Eagly, A. H., & Carli, L. L. (2007). *Through the labyrinth: The truth about how women become leaders*. Boston, MA: Harvard Business School Press.

Eagly, A. H., & Karau, S. J. (2002). Role congruity theory of prejudice toward female leaders. *Psychological Review, 109*, 573–598.

Eckes, T. (2002). Paternalistic and envious gender stereotypes: Testing predictions from the stereotype content model. *Sex Roles, 47*, 99–114.

E.E.O.C. v. Sears, Roebuck & Co., 839 F2d 302 (7th Cir. 1988).

Engerman, S. L., Haber, S. H., & Sokoloff, K. L. (2000). Inequality, institutions and differential paths of growth among new world economies. In Claude Ménard (Ed.),

Institutions, contracts and organizations: Perspectives from new institutional economics (pp. 108–134). Northampton, MA: Edward Elgar.

England, P. (1982). The failure of human capital theory to explain occupational sex segregation. *The Journal of Human Resources, 17,* 358–370.

Escriche, L. (2007). Persistence of occupational segregation: The role of the intergenerational transmission of preferences. *The Economic Journal, 117,* 837–857.

Fiske, S. (1993). Controlling other people: The impact of power on stereotyping. *American Psychologist, 48,* 621–628.

Gabriel, P. E., & Schmitz, S. (2007). Gender differences in occupational distributions among workers. *Monthly Labor Review, June,* 19–24.

Glassman, L. R., & Albarracin, D. (2006). Forming attitudes that predict future behavior: A meta-analysis of the attitude-behavior relation. *Psychological Bulletin, 132,* 778–822.

Glick, P., & Fiske, S. T. (2007). Sex discrimination: The psychological approach. In F. J. Crosby, M. S. Stockdale, & S. A. Ropp (Eds.), *Sex discrimination in the workplace* (pp. 155–188). Malden, MA: Blackwell.

Gottfredson, L. S. (1981). Circumscription and compromise: A developmental theory of occupational aspirations. *Journal of Counseling Psychology, 28,* 545–579.

Gottfredson, L. S., & Lapan, R. T. (1997). Assessing gender-based circumscription of occupational aspirations. *Journal of Career Assessment, 5,* 419–441.

Gould, E. D. (2008). Marriage and career: The dynamic decisions of young men. *Journal of Human Capital, 2,* 337–378.

Greenwald, A. G., Poehlman, T. A., Uhlmann, E., & Banaji, M. R. (2009). Understanding and using the Implicit Association Test: III. Meta-analysis of predictive validity. *Journal of Personality and Social Psychology, 97,* 17–41.

Gronau, R. (1988). Sex-related wage differentials and women's interrupted careers: The chicken or the egg? *Journal of Labor Economics, 6*(3), 277–301.

Gross, E. (1968). Plus ça change . . .? The sexual structure of occupations over time. *Social Problems, 16,* 198–208.

Gutek, B. A. (1985). *Sex and the workplace: The impact of sexual behavior and harassment on women, men, and organizations.* San Francisco, CA: Jossey-Bass.

Gutek, B. A. (1993). Changing the status of women in management. *Applied Psychology: An International Review, 42,* 301–311.

Hanson, S., & Pratt, G. (1991). Job search and the occupational segregation of women. *Annals of the Association of American Geographers, 81,* 229–253.

Hamermesh, D., & Biddle, J. (1994). Beauty and the labor market. *The American Economic Review, 84,* 1174–1194.

Hegewisch, A., Liepmann, H., Hayes, J., & Hartmann, H. (2010). Separate and not equal? Gender segregation in the labor market and the gender wage gap. *Institute for Women's Policy Research Briefing Paper, IWPR C377.* Washington, DC: Institute for Women's Policy Research. Retrieved from www.iwpr.org

Heilman, M., & Stopek, M. (1985). Attractiveness and corporate success: different causal attributions for males and females. *Journal of Applied Psychology, 70,* 379–388.

Holland, J. L. (1985). *Making vocational choices* (2nd ed.). Englewood Cliffs, NJ: Prentice Hall.

Holland, J. L., Krause, A. H., Nixon. M. E., & Trembath, M. F. (1953). The classification of occupations by means of Kuder interest profiles: I. the development of interest groups. *Journal of Applied Psychology, 37,* 263–269.

Hough, J. R. (1987). *Education and the national economy.* New York: Croom Helm.

Hyde, J. S. (2005). The gender similarities hypothesis. *American Psychologist, 60*, 581–592.

Kalev, A., Dobin, F., & Kelly, E. (2006). Best practices or best guesses? Assessing the efficacy of corporate affirmative action and diversity policies. *American Sociological Review, 71*, 589–617.

Kanter, R. M. (1977). *Men and women of the corporation.* New York: Basic Books.

Kaufman, G., & Uhlenberg, P. (2000). The influence of parenthood on the work effort of married men and women. *Social Forces, 78*, 931–949.

Konrad, A. M. (2003). Family demands and job attribute preferences: A 4-year longitudinal study of women and men. *Sex Roles, 49*, 35–46.

Konrad, A. M., Corrigall, E., Lieb, P., & Ritchie, J. E., Jr. (2000). Sex differences in job attribute preferences among managers and business students. *Group and Organization Management, 25*, 108–131.

Konrad, A. M., Ritchie, J. E., Lieb, P., & Corrigall, E. (2000). Sex differences and similarities in job attribute preferences: A meta-analysis. *Psychological Bulletin, 126*, 593–641.

Konrad, A. M., Yang, Y., Goldberg, C., & Sullivan, S. E. (2005). Preferences for job attributes associated with work and family: A longitudinal study of career outcomes. *Sex Roles, 53*, 303–315.

Lee, H. (2012). "What do you want to do when you grow up?" Occupational aspirations of Taiwanese preschool children. *Social Behavior and Personality: An International Journal, 40*, 115–127.

Lent, R. W., Brown, S. D., & Hackett, G. (1994). Towards a unifying social cognitive theory of career and academic interest, choice, and performance. *Journal of Vocational Psychology, 45*, 79–122.

Marshall, M. R., & Jones, C. H. (1990). Childbearing sequence and the career development of women administrators in higher education. *Journal of College Student Development, 31*, 531–537.

Martell, R. F., Lane, D. M., & Emrich, C. G. (1996). Male–female differences: A computer simulation. *American Psychologist, 51*, 157–158.

Mincer, J., & Polachek, S. (1974). Family investments in human capital: Earnings of women. *Journal of Political Economy, 82*, S76–S108.

Moller, S., & Li, H. (2009). Parties, unions, policies and occupational sex segregation in the United States. *Social Forces, 87*, 1529–1560.

Morgan, L. A. (2008). Major matters: A comparison of the within-major gender pay gap across college majors for early-career graduates. *Industrial Relations, 47*, 625–650.

Munasinghe, L., Reif, T., & Henriques, A. (2008). Gender gap in wage returns to job tenure and experience. *Labour Economics, 15*, 1296–1316.

Murphy, M. C., Steele, C. M., & Gross, J. J. (2007). Signaling threat: How situational cues affect women in math, science, and engineering settings. *Psychological Science, 18*, 879–885.

Neuman, S. (1991). The marriage market and occupational sex segregation: A "New Home Economics" approach. *Journal of Socio-Economics, 20*(4), 347–358.

Olsen, R. N., & Sexton, E. A. (1996). Gender differences in the returns to and the acquisition of the on-the-job-training. *Industrial Relations, 35*, 59–77.

Perna, L. W. (2005). Sex differences in faculty tenure and promotion: The contribution of family ties. *Research in Higher Education, 46*, 277–307.

Phillips, S. D., & Imhoff, A. R. (1997). Women and career development: A decade of research. *Annual Review of Psychology, 48*, 31–59.

Polachek, S. W. (1975). Differences in expected post-school investment as a determinant of market wage differentials. *International Economic Review, 16*, 451–470.

Preston, J. A. (1999). Occupational gender segregation: Trends and explanations. *The Quarterly Review of Economics and Finance, 39*, 611–624.

Presser, H. B. (1994). Employment schedules among dual-earner spouses and the division of household labor by gender. *American Sociological Review, 59*, 348–364.

Presser, H. B., & Hermsen, J. M. (1996). Gender differences in the determinants of overnight work-related travel among employed Americans. *Work & Occupations, 23*(1), 87–115.

Queneau, H. (2010). Trends in occupational sex segregation in the USA: Evidence from detailed data. *The Empirical Economics Letters, 9*, 1–6.

Reskin, B. F. (1993). Sex segregation in the workplace. *Annual Review of Sociology, 19*, 241–270.

Reskin, B. F., & Roos, P. (1990). *Job queues, gender queues* (2nd ed.). Thousand Oaks, CA: Pine Forge Press.

Ridgeway, C. (1991). The social construction of status value: Gender and other nominal characteristics. *Social Forces, 70*, 367–386.

Ridgeway, C. L., & England, P. (2007). Sociological approaches to sex discrimination in employment. In F. J. Crosby, M. S. Stockdale, & S. A. Ropp (Eds), *Sex discrimination in the workplace: Multidisciplinary perspectives* (pp. 189–211). Malden, MA: Blackwell.

Rindfuss, R. R., Cooksey, E. C., & Sutterlin, R. L. (1999). Young adult occupational achievement: Early expectations versus behavioral reality. *Work and Occupations, 26*, 220–263.

Rudman, L. A., & Glick, P. (2001). Prescriptive gender stereotypes and backlash towards agentic women. *Journal of Social Issues, 57*, 743–762.

Rudman, L. A., & Kilianski, S. E. (2000). Implicit and explicit attitudes toward female authority. *Personality and Social Psychology Bulletin, 26*, 1315–1328.

Schein, V. E. (1975). Relationships between sex role stereotypes and requisite management characteristics among female managers. *Journal of Applied Psychology, 60*, 340–344.

Schein, V. E. (2001). A global look at psychological barriers to women's progress in management. *Journal of Social Issues, 57*, 675–688.

Sewell, W. H., Hauser, R. M., & Wolf, W. C. (1980). Sex, schooling, and occupational status. *American Journal of Sociology, 86*, 551–583.

Shauman, K. A. (2006). Occupational sex segregation and the earnings of occupations: What causes the link among college-educated workers? *Social Science Research, 35*, 577–619.

Sicherman, N. (1996). Gender differences in departures from a large firm. *Industrial and Labor Relations Review, 49*, 484–505.

Sims, C. S., Drasgow, F., & Fitzgerald, L. F. (2005). The effects of sexual harassment in turnover in the military: Time-dependent modeling. *Journal of Applied Psychology, 90*, 1141–1152.

Strober, M. H. (1984). Toward a general theory of occupational sex segregation: The case of public school teaching. In B. R. Reskin (Ed.), *Sex segregation in the workplace: Trends explanations, remedies* (pp. 144–156). Washington DC: National Academy Press.

Taylor, S. E. (1981). A categorization approach to stereotyping. In D. L. Hamilton (Ed.), *Cognitive processes in stereotyping and intergroup behavior* (pp. 83–114). Mahwah, NJ: Erlbaum.

Thomas, J. R., & French, K. E. (1985). Gender differences across age in motor performance: A meta-analysis. *Psychological Bulletin, 98,* 260–282.

Tomaskovic-Devey, D. (1993). *Gender and racial inequality at work: The source and consequences of job segregation.* Ithaca, NY: IRL Press.

Tomaskovic-Devey, D. (1995). Sex composition and gendered earnings inequality: A comparison of job and occupational models. In J. Jacobs (Ed.), *Gender inequality at work* (pp. 23–56). Thousand Oaks, CA: Sage.

Tomaskovic-Devey, D., Zimmer C., Stainback, K., Robinson, C., Taylor, T., & McTague, T. (2006). Documenting desegregation: Segregation in American workplaces by race, ethnicity, and sex, 1966–2003. *American Sociological Review, 71,* 565–588.

Tosi, H. L., & Einbender, S. W. (1985). The effects of the type and amount of information in sex discrimination research: A meta-analysis. *Academy of Management Journal, 28,* 712–723.

U.S. Census Bureau (2011). Historical Income Tables: People. Table P-36. Full-Time, Year-Round All Workers by Median Income and Sex: 1955 to 2010. Retrieved July 12, 2012 from www.census.gov/hhes/www/income/data/historical/people/.

Vagg, P. R., Spielberger, C. D., & Wasala, C. F. (2002). Effects of organizational level and gender on stress in the workplace. *International Journal of Stress Management, 9,* 243–261.

Watts, M. (1995). Divergent trends in gender segregation by occupation in the United States: 1970–1992. *Journal of Post Keynesian Economics, 17,* 357–379.

Weeden, K. A. (1998). Revisiting occupational sex segregation in the United States, 1910–1990: Results from a log-linear approach. *Demography, 35,* 475–487.

Wells, T. (1999). Changes in occupational sex segregation during the 1980s and 1990s. *Social Science Quarterly, 80,* 370–380.

7

To Be or Not to Be; and to See or Not to See

The Benefits of LGBT Identity Consciousness for Organizations and Employees

Michelle R. Hebl, Larry R. Martinez, Jeanine L. Skorinko, Laura G. Barron, and Eden B. King

Employees are greatly influenced by the diversity-related initiatives, management styles, and policies that organizations adopt. These initiatives are often informed by an overarching diversity ideology that top management, and ultimately the organization, holds. For instance, Plaut, Thomas, and Goren (2009) differentiated between two main diversity ideologies, one of assimilation–colorblindness and the other of cultural pluralist–multiculturalism, both of which have tremendous influence on diverse employees' workplace experiences. With assimilation–colorblindness ideologies, or what we refer to as *identity blind ideologies*, people adopt a model of diversity in which they ignore others' diversity (e.g., race) and instead focus on a sense of shared humanity (Park & Judd, 2005). With cultural pluralist–multiculturalism, or what we refer to as *identity conscious ideologies*, people adopt a model of diversity in which they acknowledge and embrace group differences (Norton, Vandello, Biga, & Darley, 2008). Importantly, research suggests that a more inclusive definition of organizational "diversity" is critical to the success of organizational efforts such as diversity training (see Rynes & Rosen, 1995). Unfortunately, most research on the impact of competing diversity ideologies has focused primarily on racial diversity, without full consideration of the implications of these ideologies for other types of diversity, such as diversity in sexual orientation or gender identity or diversity in multiple ways (e.g., sexual orientation and racial diversity).

In considering diversity ideologies for LGBT employees, we break this chapter into five sections. First, we consider the current level of protection for LGBT employees in the workplace. This is important because LGBT individuals, unlike many other stigmatized groups, do not have uniform protection; therefore, our discussion of this major caveat must precede our investigation into diversity ideologies. Second, we describe potential diversity ideologies that could be adopted in organizations. Third, we describe why it is important for organizations to "see" their LGBT diversity and support it; hence, to adopt identity conscious (versus blind) ideologies, particularly when it comes to diversity related to sexual orientation. Fourth, we describe why it is important for LGBT employees to embrace organizations who "see" by following this up (and sometimes preceding it) with the decision to "be." That is, we argue that LGBT employees must individually weigh the pros and cons of "coming out" in their workplaces, but that as a whole, those who "come out" may be best serving larger LGBT initiatives and support within their organizations and communities. Fifth and finally, we discuss how LGBT allies can serve as strong catalysts for promoting and supporting a diversity ideology of identity consciousness.

STATUS OF LGBT EMPLOYEES IN ORGANIZATIONS

Before investigating the different diversity ideologies relevant to LGBT employees, we consider the status of LGBT employees in organizations, as their status differs dramatically from other groups (e.g., race, gender). Until recently, LGBT employees in the workplace suffered from a stark lack of uniform protection from discrimination. While there is still no widespread, ubiquitous protection for LGBT employees, there have been recent changes in some existing federal and state protection. We will also discuss local protection and organizational policies.

Federal Protection

Federal protection is afforded to U.S. employees on the basis of race, color, national origin, sex, religion (Title VII of the Civil Rights Act), age (Age

Discrimination in Employment Act), and disability (Americans with Disabilities Act). Since 1994, there have been efforts to enact legislation that protects employees from discrimination based on sexual orientation, and sometimes also gender identity (Employment Non-Discrimination Act, or ENDA), but each time the bill has failed to become law. And, until recently, the federal protections afforded by the Equal Employment Opportunity Commission (EEOC) and Title VII did not extend to gender identity (specifically, transgender individuals). However, in April of 2012, the EEOC changed its position on gender identity under Title VII as a result of Macy v. Holder (2012). Macy filed an employment discrimination complaint against the Bureau of Alcohol, Tobacco, Firearms, and Explosives on the basis of sex, gender identity, and sex stereotyping. The accusations stemmed from the fact that Macy initially applied for the position as a male. During the background check and after reassurances the position was Macy's, Macy underwent the transformation process from male to female and notified the agency. Shortly after notifying the agency of the gender change, Macy was informed the position had been cut owing to budget issues; however, in reality, the position had been given to another applicant. The EEOC initially denied the complaint arguing that the issues raised (gender identity stereotyping) were not under the EEOC or Title VII jurisdiction. However, the EEOC, in April of 2012, reversed its decision upon appeal and based this decision on Price v. Waterhouse (1989) where the courts decided that gender stereotyping was a form of sex discrimination. Applying this logic to the case of transgender individuals, it is not legal to discriminate against transgender individuals owing to their sex or the stereotypes held about them (see EEOC website for more information).

State Protection

While federal legislation protecting LGBT employment is currently undergoing changes to afford protections to these individuals, several states had previously enacted protection for these employees within their boundaries. Wisconsin was the first state to ban employment discrimination based on sexual orientation in 1982, while Minnesota became the first state to offer protection for both sexual orientation and gender identity in 1993. Currently, eight states offer protection on the basis of sexual orientation and 15 states offer employment protection based on both sexual orientation and gender identity. At the time of this writing, an additional 13 states have executive orders that protect public (but not private) employees from discrimination on the basis of sexual orientation (four states), gender identity (two states), or both (five states). In addition, as of July 1, 2012, House Bill 3810 went into effect in Massachusetts, explicitly prohibiting gender identity discrimination toward employees or applicants. This law will also afford protections for these individuals in terms of hate crimes, harassment, school policies, public accommodations, credit and lending, and other rights. Looking at this from a national perspective, approximately 30 states offer some type of protection based on sexual orientation, gender identity, or both. Thus, while there is certainly a growing trend in offering protections, almost half of the states still lack any form of legal protection for LGBT employees.

Local Protection

At the time of this writing, approximately 137 cities and counties offer local protection to LGBT individuals. However, most of these exist in states that already offer such protection. There are currently 32 cities/counties that offer protection outside of state protection on the basis of sexual orientation and/or gender identity. Thus, as with national and state protection, there is some awareness that these issues need to be addressed; however, the majority of local municipalities have yet to address protection issues for sexual orientation, gender identity, or both.

ORGANIZATIONAL POLICIES

Even in the absence of legal protection of any kind, many large organizations enact policies that protect their own employees. The Human Rights Campaign (HRC) has provided a Corporate Equality Index that serves as a rating of how desirable an organization is on the basis of LGBT equality issues since 2002. The 2011 index reported that 337 large corporations—which employ over 8.3 million individuals—received scores of 100% (the maximum possible).

Organizational support can take several forms. For example, organizations can enact formal policies that offer protection on the basis of diverse employees, including and not limited to sexual orientation and/or gender identity. For LGBT employees specifically, they can extend the same benefits to partners of LGBT employees that the partners of heterosexual employees enjoy and ensure that these partners are welcome at organization-sponsored events. They can foster and support advocacy groups within the organizations that cater to the needs of LGBT employees. And, they can reach out to the larger LGBT community outside of the organization by advertising/ marketing at or sponsoring LGBT events (e.g., pride parades, festivals). All of these things have been shown to be related to less perceived discrimination in the workplace by LGBT employees (see Ragins & Cornwell, 2001). In addition, controlled research on the decisions of human resource managers confirms the positive role of organizational policies in promoting more equitable hiring evaluations of gay employees (Barron, 2010a).

Yet, in comparing the organizations that provide protection to LGBT individuals with those that do not, a clear picture emerges—organizational policies (such as national, state, and local legislation) can be inadequate and inconsistently enforced. While many organizations provide protection to diverse employees including LGBT individuals, many do not. Even for organizations that provide some sort of protection for LGBT employees, the questions of "which policies work and/or are most advantageous?" and "what is the best way to implement them?" remain. One type of policy that many organizations have already enacted is a zero-tolerance policy for transgressions against gender or race (Allen, Dawson, Wheatley, & White, 2004). For instance, Plass (2005) highlights several instances in which employees were fired after single transgressions including sexual harassment and racial slurs, and widely argues for instituting broader zero-tolerance antidiscrimination policies. However, whether these same consequences would be effective for transgressions against LGBT employees is not conclusively known, and no research to date has examined the effects of zero tolerance policies on LGBT employees or doubly stigmatized employees (i.e., Black gay men).

Another form of protection implemented for racial minorities and women is diversity training programs that aim to make diversity a topic of conversation and a factor that the organization explicitly focuses on and cares about (Rynes & Rosen, 1995). Studies examining the effects of diversity training programs show mixed results; sometimes they are effective and sometimes they are met with great resistance and can backfire (Chrobot-Mason, Hays-Thomas, & Wishik, 2008; Day, 1995; Mobley & Payne, 1992, Rynes & Rosen, 1995; Sims & Sims, 1993). Thus, it is especially unclear how effective diversity training with respect to sexual orientation or gender identity may be. One of the key problems with including LGBT under traditional diversity training programs is that sexual orientation and gender identity issues are thematically different from gender and race issues because there is often an underlying notion that non-traditional sexual orientations and gender identities greatly violate moral or religious beliefs. In addition, there may also be difficulties in tailoring diversity policies to specific issues faced by LGBT employees. For example some policies may be more important for LGBT workers than for other diverse employees (e.g., racial minorities). Specifically, Ragins and Cornwell (2001) found that of the various diversity-related initiatives enacted by organizations, gay and lesbian employees rated that having their same-sex significant other accepted at company-sponsored events (e.g., picnics, socials, parties) was the most valued, yet this is less of a concern for other diverse populations.

In conclusion, much more research is needed on the different types of policies that are currently in effect and whether they can be applied to LGBT employees and employees that belong to multiple stigmatized groups, such as LGBT and racial minorities. This need for further research is especially pertinent for diversity training programs in relation to the inclusion of LGBT employees and employees of multiple stigmatized groups. This is particularly important because: individuals can resist diversity training programs and they can consequently backfire, the issues faced by diverse employees are not always similar, and research shows that individuals who belong to multiple stigmatized groups are often seen as "invisible" because they do not fit the prototype of any of the groups to which they belong (Purdie-Vaughns & Eibach, 2008).

Thus, organizations face complex challenges with respect to LGBT inclusiveness and protection that are simply not present with other diverse groups. Given the limited policies that exist and the importance of these policies, we next describe different diversity ideologies that may be enacted with respect to LGBT employees.

DIVERSITY IDEOLOGIES

The extent to which organizations maintain policies supporting and protecting LGBT employees depends in large part on the types of diversity ideologies that managers within those organizations hold. Thus, in this section we describe the different types of ideologies that individuals (and ultimately, organizations) might adopt.

Identity Blind vs. Identity Conscious Policies

Two dominant ideologies concerning group differences have been examined primarily in the context of race relations. In this context, they have been called "colorblind" and "multiculturalism." We extend the basic tenets of these diversity ideologies beyond race relations and argue that they can be applied to other diversity groups as well (e.g., LGBT employees). As such, we use the terms "identity blind" and "identity conscious" to refer to policies that encompass the ideals of colorblindness and multiculturalism, respectively.

Identity blind policies downplay or ignore group differences while identity conscious policies recognize or celebrate group differences. In the context of LGBT protection, organizations that ignore sexual orientation or gender identity would be characterized as identity blind, whereas organizations that actively address these characteristics (e.g., by having advocacy groups or otherwise actively supporting LGBT employees) would be characterized as identity conscious. Although both policies are "diversity policies" and both advocate for equality in some form, their effectiveness in achieving positive organizational climates for minorities is disparate. Specifically, organizations that adopt identity blind policies (i.e., which reflect the legal minimum with regard to race, gender) may have more bias within their organizations than organizations that adopt identity conscious policies (which are typically legally voluntary; Apfelbaum, Sommers, & Norton, 2008; Neville, Lilly, Duran, Lee, & Browne, 2000; Plaut et al., 2009; Richeson & Nussbaum, 2004; Saguy, Dovidio, & Pratto, 2008; Verkuyten, 2005; Wolsko, Park, & Judd, 2006). However, organizations that adopt voluntary organizational identity blind policies (i.e., non-discrimination on the basis of sexual orientation or gender identity, when their localities do not afford such legal protection) have less bias or discrimination based on sexual orientation than organizations that do not adopt such organizational policies (see Button, 2001; Griffith & Hebl, 2002; Ragins & Cornwell, 2001; also Barron, 2010a).

In addition, the diversity ideologies adopted by individual employees can affect the work lives of minority employees within the organization.

For instance, White employees' adherence to identity conscious organizational ideals (e.g., "organizational policies should support racial and ethnic diversity") was positively related to minority employees' psychological engagement on the job. Contrarily, Whites' adherence to identity blind organizational ideals (e.g., "the organization should encourage racial and ethnic minorities to adapt to mainstream ways") was negatively related to minorities' psychological engagement (Plaut et al., 2009).

Don't Ask, Don't Tell as a Diversity Ideology

The U.S. military's Don't Ask, Don't Tell (DADT) policy represents a third type of diversity ideology and given the current political and public attention on the Senate's recent repeal of the United States Military's DADT policy, the time is particularly ripe for considering ideologies (O'Keefe, 2010). The DADT policy is characterized as a special kind of identity blindness in which gay and lesbian individuals are allowed to serve as long as they do not make their sexual orientations known. Hence, DADT resembles an assimilation-colorblindness, or identity blind, policy by the assertions of ignoring one's sexual orientation by not asking about it. In fact, we conclude that the DADT policy was not identity blind at all (though it may have been presented as such to servicemembers). That is, the DADT policy fails to protect the rights and interests of LGBT employees because the policy dictates that if one's non-heterosexual sexual orientation becomes evident, then the military can and will discriminate based on this information. That is, LGBT servicemembers potentially could face discharge if someone were to find out they were involved in a (monogamous, consensual) romantic relationship; yet, heterosexual servicemembers would not have faced discharge if someone were to find out that they were involved in a romantic relationship. Thus, if one's non-heterosexual sexual orientation is made known, the blindness is revoked and the individual is subject to expulsion on its basis. Thus, what may have reflected a desire for identity blindness, soon transforms into open discrimination. In effect, the DADT policy sends mixed signals to servicemembers by stating that they are not inherently unfit to serve, but that the revelation of their sexual orientation to others disqualifies them because of the claimed potential disruption of unit cohesion and morale that would ensue. Thus, the DADT policy discourages the acceptance of openly gay and lesbian servicemembers into the ranks by inherently assuming that doing so would be detrimental.

This notion can foster negative assumptions such that military members may expect that having an openly gay or lesbian service member would be more disruptive than if this idea was never communicated.

Over the last 17 years, the DADT policy cost the U.S. military 13,000 discharges and over $363 million (University of California Blue Ribbon Report, 2006). Thus, the negative ramifications of the DADT policy extended not just to those soldiers whose sexual orientations became public, but also to the overall military infrastructure. Public controversy over the DADT policy has risen, the senate recently repealed the policy, and the military has begun training personnel on the application of the new policy. The effectiveness of the application of a different diversity ideology within the U.S. military still awaits testing; however, the DADT policy shows organizational detriments that can result from the application of LGBT diversity ideologies presented as identity blind.

TO SEE OR NOT TO SEE: HOW ORGANIZATIONS CAN MAKE A DIFFERENCE

Up until the recent changes to the EEOC, there was absolutely no federal protection for LGBT employees. However, the changes in the EEOC only extend to gender identity and not to all LGBT employees (i.e., does not have bearing on sexual orientation issues). Therefore, the impetus to establish policies that protect all LGBT employees is on the organizations themselves. Regardless of the changes in federal legislation, organizational leaders may feel a moral obligation to treat all of their employees equally, including LGBT employees. Moreover, the codes of corporate social responsibility emphasize that organizations are responsible for both the well-being of their immediate stakeholders and the communities in which they operate. Indeed, King and Cortina (2010) argued that LGBT employees are, in fact, important stakeholders in the organization.

And, there are many reasons to maintain an organizational climate that is aware, inclusive, and supportive of LGBT employees. One such reason is that diversity policies that include sexual orientation and gender identity can improve the workplace experiences of LGBT and multiply diverse employees. First, LGBT employees face discrimination. For example, several studies show a wage gap based on sexual orientation. This effect is particularly robust for gay men, as findings show that gay men earn between 10% and 32% less than comparable heterosexual men (Badgett, Lau, Sears, & Ho, 2007; Tebaldi & Elmslie, 2006). This statistic contradicts the stereotype that gay men are the wealthy urbanites often popularized by the media. When comparing the wages of lesbian women with those of heterosexual women, the differences tend to not be as severe, and, at times, lesbians may earn more than heterosexual women. However, these results do not indicate that discrimination does not exist for lesbians; rather, the gaps are smaller owing to the already lower wages that women earn (Valian, 2000). In addition, the research shows that compared with heterosexual women, lesbian women are more likely to participate in occupations in more male-dominated (and consequently higher paying) fields (Blandford, 2003). Lesbians are also less likely to have children and this may also predict why lesbian women are more likely to participate in male-dominated jobs that typically give less incentives (e.g., time off) for child-rearing responsibilities (Blandford, 2003). In addition, the wage numbers are based on those who openly disclose their sexual orientations in the workplace and their income; therefore, the numbers reported will not include those who are not comfortable "outing" themselves in their workplaces and are less likely to include those in lower income brackets because they are less willing to report their incomes (Weichselbaumer, 2003). Transgender employees who transition genders on the job have been particularly targeted with termination and other forms of discrimination (Gagne, Tewksbury, & McGaughey, 1997), although these experiences may subside in response to the recent legal changes with respect to gender identity protection. There is evidence to suggest, however, that transsexual individuals who transitioned from a male to a female persona experienced a reduction in salary of approximately 32%, whereas those who transitioned from a female to a male persona experienced a slight increase in salary (1.5%). Additionally, those who underwent female-to-male transitions experienced an increase in authority and respect, while those who underwent male-to-female transitions experienced increased harassment and discrimination (Schilt & Wiswall, 2008). These results highlight the interactive nature that gender plays in discussions of sexual orientation and gender identity in the workplace. More research is needed to examine the interactive nature that race plays with sexual orientation and gender identity.

In addition to these formal types of discrimination, LGBT employees also experience subtle and interpersonal types of discrimination. In several field studies, job applicants who were presumed to be gay consistently were treated with more hostility and less positivity than those who were presumed to be heterosexual in geographic areas lacking legal protection based on sexual orientation (Hebl, Foster, Mannix, & Dovidio, 2002; Singletary & Hebl, 2009). Importantly, interpersonal discrimination on the basis of sexual orientation was found to be substantially lower in areas with legal protection than in matched areas without legal protection (Barron, 2010a).

While discrimination against LGBT individuals exists in several forms (formal and subtle), research shows that when a formal policy is in place to protect LGBT employees, then these individuals report lower amounts of discrimination in the organization (Ragins & Cornwell, 2001), and human resource managers themselves report more favorable attitudes toward gay and lesbian employees (Barron, 2010b). In addition, there is an increased disclosure of sexual orientation in the workplace when these formal policies exist, which typically leads to greater comfort and feeling less discriminated against in the workplace (Button, 2001; Griffith & Hebl, 2002; Ragins & Cornwell, 2001). The benefits of formal policies extend beyond less discrimination and greater comfort among LGBT employees in the workplace. The presence of these policies is related to increased job satisfaction and organizational commitment among LGBT workers (Day & Schoenrade, 2000). These positive job attitudes and the subsequent productivity (i.e., Griffith & Hebl, 2002; Ragins & Cornwell, 2001) from employees highlight an important reason why companies may want to extend formal protection to their LGBT employees, especially in the absence of federal protection.

In addition to the workplace-related outcomes associated with lower discrimination, there are several negative health-related outcomes from which organizations can help protect their LGBT employees. For instance, discrimination based on sexual orientation can be related to mental health difficulties (Mays & Cochran, 2001) including psychological distress and depression (Smith & Ingram, 2004; Szymanski, 2009; Waldo, 1999). Although no studies link sexual orientation discrimination to physical health symptoms, previous research consistently shows relations between racial discrimination and heart disease, stroke, high blood pressure, and other serious health problems (e.g., Clark, Anderson, Clark, & Williams, 1999; Krieger, Sydney, & Coakely, 1998). Based on these findings, it is likely that LGBT employees who experience discrimination are similarly at risk for these negative physical health outcomes. Moreover, this research also suggests that individuals who are diverse in multiple ways (e.g., LGBT and race) may be especially susceptible to health issues. Thus, organizations that adopt formal policies can effectively improve the lives of their LGBT and multiply diverse employees in and out of the workplace in several ways.

While we have argued why organizations should *want to* promote inclusion, how they do so is another issue. One common mechanism is through formulating and promoting formal diversity policies. While organizations may try to promote inclusion through different diversity ideologies, not every policy works the same way and some are more effective than others. As discussed previously, there are two main types of ideologies: identity blind and identity conscious.

Identity blind ideologies *downplay* differences. While this may seem like an effective strategy to take, research shows that this kind of strategy typically fails. One reason why identity blind policies tend to fail may lie in research concerning thought suppression. This literature illustrates that when instructed to repress a thought, the thought, ironically, seems completely irrepressible and dominates one's consciousness. In a classic example, participants who were told not to think about a white bear were unable to do anything but picture a white bear (Wegner, Schneider, Carter, & White, 1987). This robust phenomenon has been replicated across several domains, including stereotyping and discrimination (Macrae, Bodenhousen, Milne, & Wheeler, 1996). Relating this to identity blind ideologies, instructing employees to ignore group differences may only heighten their awareness and make the differences more salient. For instance, research shows that individuals who have an overt stigma (e.g., a disability) should discuss their stigma and do so early on in an interview setting (Hebl & Skorinko, 2005). One possible explanation for this finding is that discussing one's stigma, especially early on, reduces the amount of suppression that an individual needs to encounter. More directly related to identity blind policies, participants in one study evaluated several old and young applicants for either a stereotype consistent, inconsistent, or neutral job. Prior to making the evaluations, half the participants viewed an identity blind anti-discrimination policy, whereas the remaining half saw no policy. Results show that those who saw the identity blind policy and evaluated a candidate for a stereotype-consistent job showed evidence of stereotype suppression and rebound. In other words, these individuals, who were instructed to ignore differences, actually showed heightened implicit stereotype activation (Eliezer & Skorinko, 2011).

Similarly, a recent study conducted by Madera, Hebl, and Beal (2011) also showed the impact of thought suppression on identity blind policies. In a laboratory experiment, participants were asked to play the role of interviewer, either were given identity blind or identity conscious hiring guidelines, and asked to interview two candidates sequentially. In between the two candidates, the interviewer was asked to switch rooms and place stacked chairs in a seating arrangement for the second interview. While the guidelines did not influence reactions to the first candidate, those interviewers using identity blind guidelines showed evidence of a stereotype rebound by setting up chairs that had a significantly greater distance from each other than those using identity conscious guidelines. In a second, follow-up study, Madera et al. (2011) found that organizations that held identity conscious (versus identity blind) guidelines were actually more likely to make a published list of "top-rated companies to work for." In sum, the act of trying to enforce identity blind ideologies can ironically create environments in which group differences are even more salient.

In contrast to identity blind policies, identity conscious policies recognize group differences. By openly recognizing differences, identity conscious policies release the tension created from trying to suppress unwanted thoughts by allowing these thoughts to exist. Thus, individuals are freed from the cycle of trying to repress thoughts, having these thoughts come to mind, and subsequently trying to repress them even more. From this basic cognitive perspective, all employees (minority and majority alike) are freed from these distractions and can devote their cognitive energy to work or interpersonal relationships with co-workers. Thus, organizations with identity conscious ideologies, which by definition value and support group differences, foster organizational climates in which LGBT employees and their co-workers can navigate sexual orientation and gender identity differences in the open without fear of negative consequences. The type of open environment that is possible in organizations with identity conscious diversity policies is especially necessary in cases that would require slight accommodations, such as transgender employees being allowed to use the bathrooms that align with their gender identities. Moreover, research shows that identity conscious policies are better at reducing bias than identity blind policies (Bielby, 2000; Konrad & Linnehan, 1995). For instance, one study compared and contrasted the two types of policies through a survey of 138 employers in the Philadelphia area, and the results showed that there was much less bias and fewer disparities in career outcomes for diverse employees (e.g., gender and race) when the employer adopted an identity conscious policy (Konrad & Linnehan, 1995).

However, individual-level characteristics of employees may impact the efficacy of diversity policies. For instance, Gurin, Dey, Hurtado, and Gurin (2002) argue that multicultural environments provide opportunities for individuals to learn about other cultures and help form one's own self-concept. Relatedly, some researchers (Dovidio, Kawakami, & Gaertner, 2000; Gaertner, Mann, Murrell, & Dovidio, 1989; Huo, Smith, Tyler, & Lind, 1996) advocate that minorities who adopt "dual-identity" self-concepts can benefit from participating in privileges that are traditionally withheld for majority group members, without completely discarding important cultural ideals.

However, identity conscious policies are not without limitations. First, on an individual level, the effectiveness of different diversity ideologies depends on the extent to which minority individuals identify with their minority groups (see Chrobot-Mason & Thomas, 2002). Second, studies show individuals will, at times, resist diversity training programs that are meant to make identity a conscious part of the work environment, and this resistance can cause the diversity training to backfire (Chrobot-Mason et al., 2008; Day, 1995; Mobley & Payne, 1992; Rynes & Rosen, 1995; Sims & Sims, 1993). Third, identity conscious policies can be viewed in a negative light because they appear to give preferences to certain groups over others, as can be seen in the backlash toward Affirmative Action (see Crenshaw, 2007).

Thus, in comparing the two different types of ideologies, we favor identity conscious or cultural pluralist-multiculturalism ideologies. More specifically, the conglomerate of research shows acknowledging, embracing, and supporting LGBT employees is critical for the good of employees and organizations. If organizations are identity conscious, they may also engage in other diversity-related initiatives, management styles, and have policies that promote LGBT individuals. For example, organizations can engage in and sponsor events that support the LGBT community outside of the organization, provide safe spaces and encourage advocacy groups within the organization, provide ally training to employees, extend partner benefits to LGBT employees' partners, and make a point to welcome these partners to company-sponsored social events. In sum, we argue that it is imperative for organizations to "see" and that they should do so by formally adopting diversity-related initiatives, management styles, and policies.

TO BE OR NOT TO BE: HOW LGBT EMPLOYEES CAN MAKE A DIFFERENCE

In addition to organizations deciding to "see," we also believe that there is an opportunity for LGBT individuals and allies to act responsibly to ensure successful multicultural ideologies thrive in organizations. Because sexual orientation and gender identity are generally concealable identities, identity management is a critical issue for LGBT employees (Button, 2001). Unlike many other diverse groups, LGBT individuals often engage in techniques that limit the awareness of their sexual orientations. For instance, some LGBT individuals try to "pass" or are able to conceal their identities (Yoshino, 2002). Other LGBT individuals try to "cover" or downplay their sexual orientations (Robinson, 2007; Yoshino, 2002). In other words, "covering" occurs when an individual presents themselves as LGBT, but the individual tries to restrain from behaviors that are considered "gay," such as displays of same-sex affection in public.

However, we propose that it is imperative for LGBT individuals to "be" in the workplace, meaning that they should feel able to "come out" and take advantage of the initiatives offered to them. These are clearly personal and individual decisions that are influenced by a number of factors; we respect those who decide the costs are too great or who prefer to remain closeted for any reasons. Nevertheless, we argue that as a whole, the opportunity for change may be facilitated by a critical mass of LGBT individuals who "come out" in the workplace. To show the complexity of this issue (and decision), we first discuss cons and then the pros of coming out in the workplace.

Cons

Deciding to come out in the workplace raises a number of issues and can result in negative consequences. One issue that needs to be considered is the belief that one's sexual orientation may be seen as a private matter that has no place in a work setting. Another issue is that homosexuality is still condemned by others in certain contexts, especially by some religious doctrines and political orientations. Thus, the very act of disclosing one's sexual orientation or gender identity may draw negative attention and may increase the chances of encountering some form of discrimination (formal or interpersonal) that may have otherwise been avoided (see King, Reilly, & Hebl, 2008).

Another factor to be considered is that LGBT individuals may be hesitant to disclose their true sexual orientations or gender identities until they are confident that they have firmly established their workplace identities. To avoid disclosure, LGBT individuals engage in practices that help avoid detections, such as avoiding conversations that may force them to lie about their true identities, actually lying about their identities, and/or inventing opposite gender romantic partners (see Button, 2004). These attempts can often be quite successful and LGBT employees who are hiding can establish fake personas that are well-liked and respected within their organizations. However, disclosing one's true identity after carefully hiding it can interfere with and disrupt relationships that have been fostered at work. For instance, after disclosing, fellow co-workers need to learn to think about the LGBT individual in a different way, and deal with the realization that the person differs from their previous conceptions (King et al., 2008). Moreover, research concerning disclosures of sexual orientation (Griffith & Hebl, 2002) and gender identity (Law, Martinez, Ruggs, Hebl, & Akers, 2011) at work has found that disclosure is related to positive workplace outcomes when co-workers are supportive and positive about the disclosure. Thus, disclosure can be an intimidating obstacle for LGBT employees and some organizational climates may not be conducive to such disclosures, resulting in negative consequences.

Pros

While there are potential negative consequences to disclosing one's sexual orientation and/or gender identity in the workplace, there are also a number of positive consequences related to disclosure. First, for those who feel that being LGBT is a central part of their self-concepts, disclosing at work can be a liberating and validating experience. In fact, often the decision to disclose is informed by how important being LGBT is to one's self-concept, the level of personal acceptance one feels about being LGBT, and the degree to which one has disclosed to individuals outside of the organization (Griffith & Hebl, 2002; Law et al., 2011). Second, managing a hidden identity is another form of thought suppression, and may result in the employee spending more time worrying about inadvertently "outing" him or herself than is necessary (or may impact other workplace outcomes, such as productivity). Third, disclosing hidden LGBT identities in the workplace is related to more positive workplace outcomes (Day & Schoenrade, 2000; Griffith & Hebl, 2002; Law et al., 2011) and employees are more likely to disclose in organizations that are supportive (Ragins & Cornwell, 2001). In addition, LGBT employees who disclose report better mental and physical health as a result of lower stress on the job (Herek, 1996). Finally, research has found that hypothetical individuals who concealed their sexual orientations were rated more negatively than those who did not conceal their sexual orientation (Oswald, 2007).

Coming out in the workplace may be a necessary first step in demonstrating that LGBT employees do exist in organizations and in creating support networks. As Creed and Scully (2000) contend, such "claiming encounters are perhaps the first step in staking a claim to legitimate social standing" (p. 397). Indeed, one common response to efforts to establish LGBT inclusive policies is that they are not needed because "we don't have any of those kinds of people working here." That is, organizations are unaware of the LGBT employees that they already employ. Disclosing at work makes it clear that LGBT employees are a part of the workforce and they should thus be protected from discrimination based on their sexual orientations or gender identities. Similarly, disclosing can signal to other LGBT employees that they are not alone (as they likely previously thought), which can lead to the formation of informal and formal support networks.

It is important to note that there are many exceptional reasons why LGBT employees keep their sexual orientations and/or gender identities hidden in the workplace, not the least of which is that disclosing often results in increased stigmatization and discrimination. Hence, it is imperative for each LGBT employee to carefully weigh the costs and benefits of coming out in the workplace. Furthermore, we believe it is important to state that those individuals who decide to keep their identities hidden are also an extremely important contingent in the workforce—they may serve in ally capacities and there are undoubtedly a set of LGBT individuals who might function very well without organizational support and favorable climates. Yet, we propose that, in most cases, such individuals ultimately will be better served and have more supportive workplace environments if there is a presence of visible LGBT employees and accommodating organizational policies and support.

PARTIALLY "BEING"

Sometimes LGBT employees decide to disclose to some and not others. Within organizations this can represent a tumultuous state of affairs because those trusted confidants may inadvertently or intentionally reveal the secret to others before the LGBT employee is ready. Furthermore, those with partially disclosed secret identities may be even more susceptible to cognitive intrusions than those who are completely hidden at work because each interaction can be painstakingly evaluated for evidence that the co-worker knows, suspects, or has heard a rumor.

Those who are "out" in their personal lives but not at work similarly face the ever-present possibility that these two life spheres will collide and force disclosure in the workplace (Ragins, 2008). For instance, an LGBT individual risks being seen by co-workers outside of work with their partners doing normal activities (e.g., going to dinner, movies). This possible "sighting" will induce increased stress in the employee because it can jeopardize the gay employee's heterosexual at-work persona. Disclosing at work, however, can theoretically reduce these disconnects and align their inner and home self with their work self (see Ragins, 2008).

THE ROLE OF ALLIES IN REINFORCING DIVERSITY IDEOLOGIES

Finally, the opportunity should not fall solely on the shoulders of the LGBT employees in promoting supportive ideologies and climates. Rather, we argue that it is also imperative for LGBT co-workers to serve as allies and support LGBT individuals and the diversity-related ideologies that support them. Clearly, the culture and climate of an organization depends upon those that work there. Organizations may take the first step in developing policies that promote diversity. In addition, the organizations have a responsibility to enforce the policies, especially when transgressions occur.

While organizations certainly need to take the first step to implement the policies, these policies must be embraced by individual employees within the organization in order for them to be effective and salient throughout the organization (see Monteith, Deneen, & Tooman, 1996). That is, employees, like organizations, should also feel responsibility in promoting diversity and enforcing diversity initiatives. In addition, individual non-LGBT employees can work to foster an inclusive environment outside of this formal organizational protection. In most cases, discrimination occurs at the level of the individual; and thus it can be remediated there as well. Diversity-minded employees can act as role models of inclusion and acceptance within the organization. For instance, an employee who addresses discrimination in the workplace as it occurs sends a clear message that that sort of behavior is wrong and will not be tolerated. This is especially effective if non-minority individuals or otherwise respected individuals stand up on behalf of minority individuals (Czopp & Monteith, 2003; Zitek & Hebl, 2007).

Finally, ally co-workers can improve the workplace climate for LGBT employees by joining and supporting advocacy groups sponsored by the organization or in the larger community. For example, allies who actively participate in advocacy groups show support by volunteering time and effort on behalf of LGBT employees. In addition, they could participate as organizational representatives in festivals, parades, or other LGBT-focused events outside of the organization. These acts are profound displays of support that will no doubt show all employees (not just LGBT ones) that diversity is valued and respected in the organization at the ground level.

CONCLUSION

In light of the current state of affairs for LGBT employees, we argue in favor of an identity conscious organizational ideology, or cultural pluralist-multiculturalism. The main crux for this argument is research that demonstrates that it is critical for the well-being of employees and organizations as a whole to acknowledge, embrace, and support their LGBT employees. Moreover, we argued in this chapter that it is imperative for organizations

TABLE 7.1

Possible Practices that Organizations Can Adopt to Establish Identity Consciousness

Policy/Practice	Potential Benefits	Potential Negatives	Mitigation Strategies
Including SO and GI in company non-discrimination policies and having formal consequences in place for infractions	Represents a clear message that diversity is valued and harassment will not be tolerated; legitimizes SO and GI as protected classes	Employees who are punished for harassment may see policy as overly restrictive	Emphasize principles of egalitarianism and justice to avoid perceptions of "special treatment"; highlight importance of respectful behaviors without trying to influence private attitudes
Inviting partners of LGBT employees to company events	Creates a welcoming and accepting environment for LGBT employees and their families; provides a sense of equality	Some employees may feel uncomfortable bringing their partners	Make clear that all families, partners, and friends are welcome and emphasize inclusiveness and camaraderie
Sponsoring and supporting LGBT events and organizations in the organization and the community (e.g., participating in parades)	Communicates that the organization values diversity and the well-being of the employees beyond bottom-line consequences; increases morale/commitment	Can represent an increased cost to the organization	Utility analyses can determine what monetary benefits may be incurred by attracting and retaining highly qualified employees. Highlight the importance of social responsibility and treating employees well
Encouraging disclosure of SO or GI in the workplace	Disclosure can improve work attitudes and decrease negative	Disclosure makes employees more vulnerable to potential	Establish and enforce diversity-related consequences for when

	consequences for LGBT employees; allows for open discussion among diverse employees	discrimination than if identity had remained hidden	harassment or discrimination occur (e.g., no-tolerance policies)
Establish identity conscious recruitment and selection practices	Will reach more LGBT applicants and communicate that they are sought by the organization; communicates acceptance	May be perceived as "special treatment" by others	Maintain same standards of selection as with other employees; emphasize qualifications of LGBT applicants to avoid accusations of "reverse discrimination"
Offer diversity training that includes SO and GI	Legitimizes SO and GI as protected classes within the organization. Provides practical knowledge of how to handle diversity	Diversity training often seen as ineffective or a waste of resources	Establish objective indicators of success and measure whether skills taught in training are transferred to the job. Provide reminders of concepts learned in training that employees can reference quickly
Train managers to be inclusive of LGBT diversity	Managers can model acceptable behavior and monitor the behavior of their subordinates directly; address problems immediately	Increased organizational cost. Some managers may be resistant to training	Establish diversity-related goals as part of larger organizational mission; reward accomplishing and punish failing in these goals; select and promote individuals who are successful at managing diversity

to "see" and that they should do so by formally adopting diversity-related initiatives, management styles, and policies. We have outlined a summary of the particular policies that we have discussed in Table 7.1. Additionally, we argued that there are effective ways that LGBT individuals and allies should responsibly act to ensure successful multicultural ideologies thrive in organizations. Namely, we believe it is imperative for a critical mass of LGBT individuals to "be" in the workplace, meaning that they should feel able to "come out" and take advantage of the initiatives offered to them. We argue that it is also imperative for LGBT co-workers to serve as allies and support LGBT employees and the diversity-related ideologies that support them. Only from the perspective of recognizing and valuing diverse identities will LGBT employees be fully embraced by organizations.

We also call for future empirical research to continue to examine the antecedents and consequences of disclosing, and the efficacy of different diversity ideologies and policies (not just identity conscious and identity blind) at both the individual and organizational levels with respect to sexual orientation and gender identity. For instance, future research should examine the different diversity policies that are currently being practiced at different organizations and explore whether they can be applied or modified to meet the needs of LGBT and multiply diverse employees. More specifically, there is a dire need to investigate whether zero tolerance policies are effective for reducing discrimination toward LGBT and/or multiply diverse employees (i.e., Black gay men). Likewise, future research needs to investigate how effective diversity training programs are for LGBT employees and employees of multiple stigmatized groups. LGBT and multiply diverse employees would also benefit if the work on the health consequences of being part of a stigmatized group extended to their groups. In addition, research that illuminates the best ways for allies to be supportive of LGBT employees is needed to inform future diversity management efforts.

REFERENCES

Allen, R., Dawson, G., Wheatley, K., & White, C. S. (2004). Diversity practices: Learning responses for modern organizations. *Development and Learning in Organizations, 18*, 13–15.

Apfelbaum, E. P., Sommers, S. R., & Norton, M. I. (2008). Seeing race and seeming racist? Evaluating strategic colorblindness in social interaction. *Journal of Personality and Social Psychology, 95*, 918–932.

Badgett, M. V., Lau, H., Sears, B., & Ho, D. (2007). *Bias in the workplace: Consistent evidence of sexual orientation and gender identity discrimination.* Los Angeles, CA: The Williams Institute, University of California. Retrieved from http://williamsinstitute. law.ucla.edu/headlines/research-on-lgbt-workplace-protections/

Barron, L. G. (2010a). Promoting the underlying principle of acceptance: The effectiveness of sexual orientation antidiscrimination legislation. *Journal of Workplace Rights, 14*, 251–268. Retrieved from http://connection.ebscohost.com/c/articles/52339584/ promoting-underlying-principle-acceptance-effectiveness-sexual-orientation-employment-antidiscrimination-legislation

Barron, L. G. (2010b). *The force of law: Effects of legislation on formal and interpersonal discrimination towards gay and lesbian job applicants* (Doctoral dissertation). Available from Dissertations and Theses Database (UMI No. 3421213).

Bielby, W. T. (2000). Minimizing workplace gender and racial bias. *Contemporary Sociology, 29*, 120–129. Retrieved from www.jstor.org/stable/2654937

Blandford, J. (2003). The nexus of sexual orientation and gender in the determination of earnings. *Industrial & Labor Relations Review, 56*, 622–642. Retrieved from http://digitalcommons.ilr.cornell.edu/ilrreview/vol56/iss4/4

Button, S. B. (2001). Organizational efforts to affirm sexual diversity: A cross-level examination. *Journal of Applied Psychology, 86*, 17–28.

Button, S. B. (2004). Identity management strategies utilized by lesbian and gay employees: A quantitative investigation. *Group & Organization Management, 29*, 470–494.

Chrobot-Mason, D., Hays-Thomas, R., & Wishik, H. (2008). Understanding and defusing resistance to diversity training and learning. In K. M. Thomas (Ed.), *Diversity resistance in organizations. Series in applied psychology* (pp. 23–54). New York: Taylor & Francis Group.

Chrobot-Mason, D., & Thomas, K. M. (2002). Minority employees in majority organizations: The intersection of individual and organizational racial identity in the workplace. *Human Resource Development, 1*, 323–244.

Clark, R., Anderson, N. B., Clark, V. R., & Williams, D. R. (1999). Racism as a stressor for African Americans: A biopsychosocial model. *American Psychologist, 54*, 805–816.

Creed, W. E., & Scully, M. A. (2000). Songs of ourselves: Employees' deployment of social identities in workplace encounters. *Journal of Management Inquiry, 9*, 391–412.

Crenshaw, K. W. (2007). Framing Affirmative Action. *Michigan Law Review, First Impressions, 105*. Retrieved from www.michiganlawreview.org.ezproxy.wpi.edu/ articles/framing-affirmative-action

Czopp, A. M., & Monteith, M. J. (2003). Confronting prejudice (literally): Reactions to confrontations of race and gender bias. *Personality and Social Psychology Bulletin, 29*, 532–544.

Day, L. E. (1995). The pitfalls of diversity training. *Training and Development, 49*, 25–29.

Day, N. E., & Schoenrade, P. (2000). The relationship among reported disclosure of sexual orientation, anti-discrimination policies, top management support, and work attitudes of gay and lesbian employees. *Personnel Review, 29*, 346–366.

Dovidio, J. F., Kawakami, K., & Gaertner, S. L. (2000). Reducing prejudice and discrimination. In S. Oskamp (Ed.), *The Claremont symposium on applied social psychology* (pp. 137–163). Mahwah, NJ: Lawrence Erlbaum Associates.

Eliezer, D., & Skorinko, J. L. (2011). When non-discrimination policies fail: Stereotype suppression and discrimination against elderly workers. Unpublished manuscript.

Gaertner, S. L., Mann, J., Murrell, A., & Dovidio, J. F. (1989). Reducing intergroup bias: The benefits of recategorization. *Journal of Personality and Social Psychology, 57*(2), 239–249.

Gagne, P., Tewksbury, R., & McGaughey, D. (1997). Coming out and crossing over: Identity formation and proclamation in a transgender community. *Gender & Society, 11*(4), 478–508.

Griffith, K. H., & Hebl, M. R. (2002). The disclosure dilemma for gay men and lesbians: "Coming out" at work. *Journal of Applied Psychology, 87,* 1191–1199.

Gurin, P., Dey, E. L., Hurtado, S., & Gurin, G. (2002). Diversity and higher education: Theory and impact on educational outcomes. *Harvard Educational Review, 72*(3), 330–367.

Hebl, M. R., Foster, J. M., Mannix, L. M., & Dovidio, J. F. (2002). Formal and interpersonal discrimination: A field study examination of bias toward homosexual applicants. *Personality and Social Psychology Bulletin, 28,* 815–825.

Hebl, M. R., & Skorinko, J. L. (2005). Acknowledging one's physical disability in the interview: Does "when" make a difference? *Journal of Applied Social Psychology, 35,* 2437–2492.

Herek, G. M. (1996). Why tell if you're not asked? Self-disclosure, intergroup contact, and heterosexuals' attitudes toward lesbians and gay men. In G. M. Herek, J. Jobe, & R. Carney (Eds.), *Out in force: Sexual orientation and the military* (pp. 197–225). Chicago, IL: University of Chicago Press.

Huo, Y. J., Smith, H. J., Tyler, T. R., & Lind, E. A. (1996). *Psychological Science, 7*(1), 40–45.

King, E. B., & Cortina, J. M. (2010). The social and economic imperative of lesbian, gay, bisexual, and transgendered supportive organizational policies. *Industrial and Organizational Psychology, 3,* 69–78.

King, E. B., Reilly, C., & Hebl, M. R. (2008). The best of times, the worst of times: Exploring dual perspectives of "coming out" in the workplace. *Group & Organization Management, 33,* 566–601.

Konrad A. M., & Linnehan, F. (1995). Formalized HRM structures: Coordinating equal employment opportunities or concealing organizational practices? *Academy of Management Journal, 38,* 787–820.

Krieger, N., Sidney, S., & Coakely, E. (1998). Racial discrimination and skin color in the CARDIA study: Implications for public health research. Coronary artery risk development in young adults. *American Journal of Public Health, 88,* 1308–1313. Retrieved from http://ajph.aphapublications.org/doi/pdf/10.2105/AJPH.88.9.1308

Law, C. L., Martinez, L. R., Ruggs, E. N., Hebl, M. R., & Akers, E. (2011). Trans-parency in the workplace: How the experiences of transsexual employees can be improved. *Journal of Vocational Behavior, 79,* 710–723.

MacRae, N., Bodenhousen, G. V., Milne, A. B., & Wheeler, V. (1996). On resisting temptation for simplification: Counterintentional effect of stereotype suppression on social memory. *Social Cognition, 14,* 1–20.

Madera, J., Hebl, M. R., & Beal, D. (2011). Staffing policies and interview structure: How they relate to diversity and discrimination. Rice University. Unpublished manuscript.

Mays, V. M., & Cochran, S. D. (2001). Mental health correlates of perceived discrimination among lesbian, gay, and bisexual adults in the United States. *American Journal of Public Health, 91,* 1869–1876. Retrieved from http://core.ecu.edu/soci/vanwilligenm/mays.pdf

Mobley, M., & Payne, T. (1992). Backlash! The challenge to diversity training. *Training and Development, 46,* 45–52.

Monteith, M. J., Deneen, N. E., & Tooman, G. D. (1996). The effect of social norm activation on the expression of opinions concerning gay men and blacks. *Basic and Applied Social Psychology, 18,* 267–288.

Neville, H. A., Lilly, R. L., Duran, G., Lee, R. M., & Browne, L. (2000). Construction and initial validation of the Color-Blind Racial Attitudes Scale (CoBRAS). *Journal of Counseling Psychology, 47,* 59–70.

Norton, M. I., Vandello, J. A., Biga, A., & Darley, J. M. (2008). Colorblindness and diversity: Conflicting goals in decisions influenced by race. *Social Cognition, 26,* 102–111.

O'Keefe, E. (2010, December 19). "Don't ask, don't tell" is repealed by Senate; bill awaits Obama's signing. *Washington Post.* Retrieved from www.washingtonpost.com/wp-dyn/content/article/2010/12/18/AR2010121801729.html

Oswald, D. L. (2007). "Don't ask, don't tell": The influence of stigma concealing and perceived threat on perceivers' reactions to a gay target. *Journal of Applied Social Psychology, 37,* 928–947.

Park, B., & Judd, C. M. (2005). Rethinking the link between categorization and prejudice within the social cognition perspective. *Personality and Social Psychology Review, 9,* 108–130.

Plass, S. (2005). Reinforcing Title VII with zero tolerance rules. *Suffolk University Law Review, 125,* 127–157. Retrieved from http://heinonline.org/HOL/LandingPage?collection=journals&handle=hein.journals/sufflr39&div=11&id=&page=

Plaut, V. C., Thomas, K. M., & Goren, M. J. (2009). Is multiculturalism or color blindness better for minorities? *Psychological Science, 20,* 444–446.

Purdie-Vaughns, V., & Eibach, R. P. (2008). Intersectional invisibility: The distinctive advantages and disadvantages of multiple subordinate-group identities. *Sex Roles, 59,* 377–391.

Ragins, B. R. (2008). Disclosure disconnects: Antecedents and consequences of disclosing invisible stigmas across life domains. *Academy of Management Review, 33,* 194–215.

Ragins, B. R., & Cornwell, J. M. (2001). Pink triangles: Antecedents and consequences of perceived workplace discrimination against gay and lesbian employees. *Journal of Applied Psychology, 86,* 1244–1261.

Richeson, J. A., & Nussbaum, R. J. (2004). The impact of multiculturalism versus color-blindness on racial bias. *Journal of Experimental Social Psychology, 40,* 417–423.

Robinson, R. K. (2007). Uncovering Covering. *Northwestern University Law Review, 101,* 1809–1850.

Rynes, S., & Rosen, B. (1995). A field survey of factors affecting the perceived success of diversity training. *Personnel Psychology, 48,* 247–270.

Saguy, T., Dovidio, J. F., & Pratto, F. (2008). Beyond contact: Intergroup contact in the context of power relations. *Personality and Social Psychology Bulletin, 34,* 432–445.

Schilt, K., & Wiswall, M. (2008). Before and after: Gender transitions, human capital, and workplace experiences. *The Berkeley Electronic Journal of Economic Analysis & Policy, 8*(1) (Contributions), Article 39. Retrieved from www.bepress.com/bejeap/vol8/iss1/art39

Sims, S. J., & Sims, R. R. (1993). Diversity and difference training in the United States. In R. R. Sims, & R. F. Dennehy (Eds.), *Diversity and differences in organizations: An agenda for answers and questions* (pp. 73–92). Westport, CT: Quorum.

Singletary, S. L., & Hebl, M. R. (2009). Compensatory strategies for reducing interpersonal discrimination: The effectiveness of acknowledgments, increased positivity, and individuating information. *Journal of Applied Psychology, 94,* 797–805.

Smith, N. S., & Ingram, K. M. (2004). Workplace heterosexism and adjustment among lesbian, gay, and bisexual individuals: The role of unsupportive social interactions. *Journal of Counseling Psychology, 31,* 57–67.

Szymanski, D. M. (2009). Examining potential moderators of the link between heterosexist events and gay and bisexual men's psychological distress. *Journal of Counseling Psychology, 56,* 142–151.

Tebaldi, E., & Elmslie, B. (2006). Sexual orientation and labour supply. *Applied Economics, 38,* 549–562.

University of California Blue Ribbon Report (2006). *Financial analysis of "don't ask, don't tell": How much does the gay ban cost?* Santa Barbara, CA: University of California.

Valian, V. (2000). *Why so slow? The advancement of women.* Cambridge, MA: MIT Press.

Verkuyten, M. (2005). Ethnic group identification and group evaluation among minority and majority groups: Testing the multiculturalism hypothesis. *Journal of Applied Psychology, 87,* 220–229.

Waldo, C. R. (1999). Working in a majority context: A structural model of heterosexism as minority stress in the workplace. *Journal of Counseling Psychology, 46,* 218–232.

Wegner, D. M., Schneider, D. J., Carter, S. R. III, & White, T. L. (1987). Paradoxical effects of thought suppression. *Journal or Personality and Social Psychology, 53,* 5–13.

Weichselbaumer, D. (2003). Sexual orientation discrimination in hiring. *Labour Economics, 10,* 629–642.

Wolsko, C., Park, B., & Judd, C. M. (2006). Considering the tower of Babel: Correlates of assimilation and multiculturalism among ethnic minority and majority groups in the United States. *Social Justice Research, 19,* 277–306.

Yoshino, K. (2002). Covering. *The Yale Law Journal, 111,* 769–939.

Zitek, E. M., & Hebl, M. R. (2007). The role of social norm clarity in the influenced expression of prejudice over time. *Journal of Experimental Social Psychology, 43,* 867–876.

8

Diversity Ideologies in the U.S. Military

Christina Stevens Carbone, Kizzy M. Parks,
and Daniel P. McDonald

> In this age, I don't care how tactically or operationally brilliant you are,
> if you cannot create harmony—even vicious harmony—on the
> battlefield based on trust across service lines, across coalition and
> national lines, and across civilian/military lines, you really need to go
> home, because your leadership in today's age is obsolete.
> (General James Mattis, Commander of the U.S. Joint Forces, 2010)

In many ways, the United States Armed Forces is like any other
organization that must adapt to meet the challenges and realities of today's
world, including changing demographic trends, evolving technology, and
America's increasing involvement in the global community. Also, like
other organizations, the U.S. military continues to struggle with issues of
diversity—how to define it, how to measure it, and how to foster and
manage it. The policies and practices adopted by the military over its history
reflect shifting diversity ideologies, or ways of understanding how to
manage people with different backgrounds, including segregation,
assimilation, and various forms of multiculturalism. Unlike the civilian
sector, however, the military stands uniquely positioned as an institution
in terms of its culture, its structure, and the types of demands and missions
it is called upon to fulfill. This institutional uniqueness has helped shape
the military's approach to diversity in many ways. For example, while
leading the country in terms of formal desegregation, the military has
retained policies that limit the service of women and, until very recently,
excluded openly gay and lesbian individuals from serving. Within the last
decade, the military has focused around a new vision of diversity as
inclusion that is seen as critically important to the institution's success in
the 21st century.

This chapter looks at the U.S. military as a case study of how diversity approaches and policies play out within a particular organizational setting—a setting that in many ways represents the extreme in terms of the stakes involved in proper management of diversity. After examining the factors motivating the military's most recent approach to diversity policy, we analyze how current conceptions of diversity map onto the different ideologies articulated within the scholarly literature on the topic. Finally, we provide some examples of the specific initiatives and strategies proposed and utilized by the Services (Army, Navy, Marine Corps, Air Force, Coast Guard, and National Guard) to implement their contemporary vision of diversity.

A BRIEF HISTORY OF INTERGROUP RELATIONS IN THE U.S. MILITARY

In 1948, two landmark actions profoundly affected the United States military: President Truman signed Executive Order 9981, which called for "equality of treatment for all persons in the Armed Services without regard to race, color, religion, or national origin," and Congress passed the Women's Armed Services Act that established permanent status for women in the military (Dansby & Landis, 2001). Despite being legal milestones, these actions failed to fully integrate minority personnel or elevate service women to a status equivalent to their male counterparts. Indeed, following the efforts of two commissioned bodies to assess and make recommendations to improve military practices related to intergroup relations—the Fahy Committee in 1949 and the Gesell Committee in 1962—the persistence of inequality within the military organization violently erupted during the Vietnam Era (Dansby & Landis, 2001).

Racial tensions during the Vietnam Era jeopardized combat readiness, with race riots and other violent disturbances breaking out state-side and in Germany, Korea, and Vietnam as minority members vocalized equal opportunity concerns (Dansby, Stewart, & Webb, 2001). The lack of demographic diversity within the officer corps, coupled with discrimination, created a situation where "racial strife in the ranks was entirely commonplace" and the military was "on the verge of self-destruction" (Gratz v. Bollinger, 2003; Grutter v. Bollinger, 2003). In response, the military took aggressive action (Dansby & Landis, 2001). The Services established equal opportunity officers and human relations councils as well as removed leaders who failed to end discrimination. To supplement the policy changes of the 1940s, the Department of Defense issued Directive 1322.11 in 1971 to established race relations education and Directive 1350.2 in 1988 to call for greater compliance with standards and policies of equity and fairness (Dansby & Landis, 2001). Additionally, Directive 1350.3 provided instruction on Affirmative Action plans and assessments that fell under the responsibility of equal opportunity professionals. All of these directives drew upon Equal Employment Opportunity (EEO) laws and regulations applicable in the civilian sector to establish the Armed Forces' own Military Equal Opportunity (MEO or EO) program. Despite these many efforts, subtle or covert discrimination continues to exist in the Services, thus decreasing the opportunity for career enhancement and promotion (Dansby & Landis, 2001; Parks, Knouse, Crepeau, & McDonald, 2008; Smith, 2010). Certain social groups continue to be or, until recently, have been conspicuously marginalized (e.g., women and homosexuals) and issues of equity are something with which the military still struggles. For example, despite progress in repealing the Don't Ask Don't Tell policy which allowed for the discharge of openly gay and lesbian servicemembers, the Navy recently rescinded their decision to allow gay marriages in Navy chapels because of pressure from political conservatives (Eckholm, 2011).

Most recently, the military has dedicated an enormous amount of resources and attention to an agenda of fostering and managing diversity— a way of addressing intergroup relations explicitly separate and distinct from equal opportunity policy. While equal opportunity policies center on legal obligations to achieve fairness and equity, diversity policies view an inclusive, engaging environment as necessary to organizational functioning and goal attainment (i.e., mission readiness and capability) (U.S. Office of Personnel Management Office of Diversity and Inclusion, 2011). In theory, these distinct policy goals also represent differing foci on which groups are targeted by the policies: equal opportunity policies focus on protected and historically marginalized groups whereas diversity policies target individuals with certain competencies—beyond group identity—that are consistent with the military's competitive success as both an employer and defender of national security. In practice, with some notable exceptions, diversity initiatives are still largely focused on the demographic representation and outcomes of members from particular social groups (MLDC, 2011a).

THE MILITARY: JUST ANOTHER JOB?

Before examining approaches to diversity within the military organization, it is appropriate to note the ways in which the military is similar to and unique from other types of organizations. Given the size[1] and importance of the U.S. military as an institution, issues of diversity within this context are significant in their own right. Nonetheless, being mindful of certain distinguishing characteristics of the military is important before making generalizations to other organizational contexts.

As elaborated further below, the military shares with other organizations many of the motivating factors that lead it to continually attend to and evaluate its diversity policies and programs. For example, some of the Services emphasize that increased diversity coupled with proper management has the potential to enhance certain institutional goals, such as operating with optimal productivity, efficiency, and innovation—the so-called "business-case" arguments for diversity (MLDC, 2011a). In this sense, the military is like any other organization called to perform certain jobs and meet set targets, and diversity can be instrumental in fulfilling these demands. As another example, just as the use of work teams is a growing trend in virtually every industry (Ilgen & Pulakos, 1999; Wisner & Feist, 2001), the military has a long tradition of relying on teams to carry out missions. Successful teams require that its members trust one another, communicate effectively, maintain a positive and cohesive climate, and encourage each member to fully contribute to the project. Managing diversity proves important in this context because of the frequency and closeness of interactions among team members.

A number of factors make the military stand out as a unique institution and arguably impact the manner and extent to which diversity is addressed. First, it is somewhat misleading to conceive of "the military" as a single entity or organization. While at some level the military is unified under the ultimate control of the U.S. President as Commander-in-Chief, the day-to-day functioning might be more aptly described as several loosely connected organizations. The Army, Navy, Air Force, Marine Corp, and National Guard all fall under the auspices of the Department of Defense, headed by the Secretary of Defense, though they each have their own separate leadership structure. The Coast Guard falls under the domain of the Department of Homeland Security. While members of each service branch must often collaborate together on missions and are unified by a common military identity, each branch has its own unique history, traditions, training, and core values. As shown in more detail below, each branch has taken on responsibility for developing and implementing branch-specific diversity policies and programming in addition to diversity efforts occurring at the level of the Departments of Defense and Homeland Security.

Second, while many organizations have a distinct climate or culture, the military culture is particularly robust and pervasive. Though each service branch emphasizes its own set of core values, military tradition has cultivated a culture in which every service member becomes indoctrinated upon joining. As one military scholar notes:

> It is a community of values, in which duty, patriotism, and loyalty to the group are paramount . . . Its emphasis on the group rather than the individual makes the military an anomaly in contemporary America. Rules and regulations that seem absurd or intolerable to civilians often make sense in the context of the best interests of the community.
>
> (Baker, 2008, pp. xiii–xiv)

Military culture can further be described as placing a higher value on hierarchy and obedience, maintaining clearly defined roles, and demanding strict conformity with common standards (Baker, 2008). Moreover, this organizational culture bridges over into the personal lives of service-members more so than in the civilian sector, such that military service seems less of an occupation than a way of life. For example, military personnel must meet certain standards even when off-duty and family life is continually shaped by the military service. This strong organizational culture undoubtedly affects the ways in which individual servicemembers think of themselves and interact with others in the military. The inherent hierarchical leadership structure of the military may facilitate crucial operational adaptability (Soeter, van Fenema, & Beeres, 2010). To the extent military culture is receptive to change, its pervasiveness within everyday activities may make the pursuit of certain diversity ideologies more impactful and successful than is possible in other organizations.

A third major distinguishing characteristic of the military is that personnel are often called upon to perform their duties under high-stress conditions. With long-term operations continuing in Afghanistan and Iraq, military resources and capabilities have been pushed to the limit, with personnel working longer hours than ever before (Baker, 2008). Many servicemembers are deployed for as many as 180 days per year and the Reserve and National Guard units are mobilized repeatedly, placing heavy strains on individuals, families, and civilian employers (Baker, 2008). Those stationed in combat zones must also face the psychological and physical stress inherent in any war-time situation. The high-stress conditions often encountered by military personnel could potentially impact issues of diversity in different ways. On the one hand, stressful conditions might arguably magnify any existing tensions, causing more interpersonal conflict and compromising mission performance. On the other hand, one can imagine these types of situations necessitating greater reliance among team members to cope with the stress, resulting in greater group cohesion. Additionally, conflict situations present group members with a common enemy or goal to unify around, which could potentially de-emphasize intra-group differences (see Gaertner & Dovidio, 2005).

Another characteristic that has shaped discussions of diversity within the military is the fact that the military has a closed personnel system, meaning that it takes 20–30 years to develop leaders at the senior levels. While there is greater personnel movement between organizations in the civilian sector, there is no such thing as a lateral hire in the military. Given the time it takes to develop senior leaders, the rapidly changing demographics of the general population in the United States is likely to increase the degree of underrepresentation of certain groups among the top leadership. Thus, much of the current focus within the military is on recruiting large numbers of underrepresented groups up front and (perhaps more importantly) coming up with strategies to retain those numbers as military personnel progress through the career pipeline (MLDC, 2011b).

While issues of diversity and managing interpersonal conflict are important to every organization, the stakes are enormously higher within the military context. People's lives and national security are potentially at stake when it comes to being able to successfully perform one's military duties in collaboration with others. The perceived importance of diversity in this regard likely accounts for the impressive amount of attention given to diversity policy, strategy, education, and training over the last two decades, both at the Department of Defense and within each of the Services.

DIVERSITY AS A MILITARY NECESSITY

The current focus on issues of diversity has been motivated by several interrelated factors, each of which will be elaborated below: (1) mission readiness and performance, (2) competition for talent, and (3) legitimacy. Not only have these factors been politically important in terms of bringing attention and resources to the issue of diversity, but they have also helped shape the military's current understanding of diversity and how to manage it.

Mission Readiness and Performance

Understandings about diversity in the military have been directly influenced by research and experiences found in the private sector. With diversity programs proliferating throughout the private sector (Edelman, Fuller, & Mara-Drita, 2001), the business case supporting diversity policies is built upon the belief that increased workforce diversity will increase an organization's effectiveness, performance, and innovation (MLDC, 2011a). The existing evidence in this regard suggests that the effects of workforce diversity may differ depending on the level of analysis (e.g., individual, work-group, or organization) and whether certain conditions are in place (e.g., proper management tools and senior leadership commitment) (MLDC, 2011a). In developing its current vision of diversity, the military has looked to models and discourses prevalent among top civilian-sector companies, such as Disney, Lockheed Martin, Walmart, and General Electric (MLDC, 2009). Like these other organizations, the military has chosen to invest and support diversity policies and initiatives in the hopes of realizing some of the performance benefits suggested by business-case arguments, though there is relatively little articulation of the mechanisms behind the relationship between diversity and mission readiness.

Unlike other organizations, however, identifying and measuring performance benefits are more difficult in the military context because of the shifting nature of the "work product." While companies such as Walmart or Lockheed Martin can assess their performance by looking at sales figures, market share, or number of clients, military success rests on the completion of missions, the ability to meet outside challenges, and maintenance of the nation's security. Starting in the early 1990s, it was becoming clear that terrorist groups, organized crime, and failing states posed the newest threats to the United States, requiring in response a transformation of the military into a highly trained, flexible, and professional force (Baker, 2008). The U.S. is currently engaged in two sustained wars in Afghanistan and Iraq and maintains roughly 1,000 military installations in 135 nations (Bilchik, 2011; Department of Defense, 2009). Unlike so-called "traditional" warfare, the U.S. Armed Forces are increasingly confronted with situations that blur the line between combat and non-combat action as well as changing technology that makes maintaining national security more difficult and complex (MLDC, 2011b). In addition to combat action, military forces are called upon to fulfill a broad range of tasks requiring different skill sets, including domestic emergencies, counterdrug efforts, managing populations, providing humanitarian aid, intelligence gathering, peacekeeping, restructuring, and training. Developing and managing a diverse military force with a broad set of backgrounds, talents, and knowledge is seen as critical to effectively meeting these modern-day challenges. In particular, as part of their diversity initiatives, many Services have directed their efforts toward recruiting individuals from STEM (Science, Technology, Engineering, and Math) fields. For example, the Navy changed its policies in 2010 to begin incorporating women onto submarines in order to better leverage those graduating with technically based degrees, a growing number of them held by women (Submarine Forces Public Affairs, 2010). Some Services (e.g., Army and Air Force) have also put an explicit focus on recruiting individuals with cultural competency and foreign language skills who can add value to the military's increasingly global presence and need to interface with different cultures during missions (MLDC, 2011a). Together, these two efforts represent the most direct link between particular skills sets and mission capability.

The military's decision to support and expand diversity policies and programs also stems from its own experiences of the costs involved when there is a failure to properly manage intergroup dynamics. For example, while racial tensions during the Vietnam Era made clear the need for the development of formal equity policies (e.g., military equal opportunity regulations), these historical events are referenced today in support of current diversity initiatives, specifically for the proposition that diversity is a key element to mission readiness and, in turn, national security (Brief for Becton et al., 2003). These lessons from history, still salient in the collective memory of military leadership, continue to reinforce the belief that diversity is a military necessity.

Competition for Talent

Since becoming an all-volunteer force after the Vietnam Era, the military is in a "Battle for Talent" with private sector organizations for recruiting the top talent from the eligible and available workforce (Department of Defense, 2012). The military spends millions of dollars on advertising and recruiting campaigns each year to sell itself as one of the best organizations to work for (Baker, 2008). Emphasizing the military's commitment to diversity and inclusion is itself a strategy to situate the military in a competitive position relative to private industry vying for the same talent pool.

Recruiting individuals from diverse backgrounds into the military personnel pipeline is becoming increasingly challenging. Because of the many entry requirements related to education, test scores, citizenship, health status, and criminal record, three out of four people aged 17–24 are not eligible to enlist in the military (MLDC, 2011b). For example, a 2010 report released by Mission: Readiness, a nonprofit group of 130 retired military leaders, characterized the rise in obesity rates as a matter of national security, with over 9 million young adults weighing too much to join the military (Considine, 2010). The number of eligible racial/ethnic minorities is even less because of the correlations between eligibility factors and race. For example, high school drop-out rates are four times higher for Hispanics (21.4%) than Whites (5.3%) and three times higher than Blacks (8.4%) (National Center for Education Statistics, 2009). A recent study "Shut Out of the Military" reported that minorities earned the lowest scores on the entrance test for military enlistment (Theokas, 2010). Similarly, the differential rates of youth (ages 16–25) incarceration across racial groups means that more minorities are ineligible for military service than are Whites (Blacks = 6.5%; Hispanics = 2.7%; and Whites = 1.2%) (Pew Hispanic Center, 2009). As military jobs become more sophisticated, the military must compete for well-educated, highly skilled recruits who also have a wide range of attractive opportunities available to them in the private sector (Baker, 2008). Additionally, because of prolonged military engagement in Iraq and Afghanistan, public support for military service is not particularly strong, so parents, teachers, and other key influencers are less likely to encourage today's youth to join (Baker, 2008).

Fostering diversity within the military organization and demonstrating this commitment to the public are seen as important to recruiting success. Putting together a competent and flexible workforce requires recruiting and retaining individuals of all different backgrounds and experiences. Youth are more likely to become interested in military service if they see others like them succeeding and being valued by the institution (MLDC, 2011b). In addition to a role-modeling function, demonstrating a commitment to diversity presumably provides insight into the type of workplace climate one is likely to encounter. Similarly, individuals once recruited are more likely to stay with the organization if they perceive they work in an inclusive environment that provides them the tools to advance and succeed.

Legitimacy

In supporting diversity initiatives, some military leaders stress that "the military has to reflect the nation it serves" (John-Hall, 2009). Given the mission of the military—protecting the Nation and upholding democratic values core to the American identity—it only seems appropriate that people from all backgrounds be included in this endeavor. Exclusion of some groups or overrepresentation by others can undermine the perceived legitimacy of the organization. Such was the case during the Vietnam Era when many sectors of the public perceived that minorities were serving as "cannon fodder" for White military leaders (MLDC, 2011b). Because the military draws its strength from the support of the general public, it is important people see the organization as operating as an extension of themselves.

It is equally important that servicemembers within the organization see it as legitimate, too, in part, by having opportunities for advancement open to all and having group representation at all levels of the organization. Again, past experiences from the Vietnam Era are instructive here: with only a small fraction of African Americans holding command positions, African American servicemen "lost confidence in the military as an institution" and "concluded that the command structure had no regard for whether African-Americans would succeed in military careers" (Brief for Becton et al., 2003, p. 16). In line with this concern, recent discussions in the military have focused especially around demographic diversity among the more senior levels of leadership.

It is often the case military personnel are the first or main contact that people around the world have with the United States, representing our country to the rest of the international community. Fostering diversity and inclusiveness within the military serves the additional function of signaling to other countries that we stand behind our Nation's core values of equality and freedom of opportunity in a concrete way (Lim, Cho, & Curry, 2008).

DIVERSITY IDEOLOGIES WITHIN THE MILITARY

What model or ideology of diversity characterizes the military's approach? Where does this model of diversity derive from or, in other words, what social, political, or cultural systems have shaped this conception of diversity? A model or ideology of diversity refers to the "shared understandings and practices of how groups come together or should come together, relate to one another, and include and accommodate" one another in light of the differences associated with group identity" (Plaut, 2002, p. 368). In other words, it represents "certain theories about how intergroup relations function—what difference is and what difference it makes" (Plaut, 2010, p. 85).

Several models of diversity have been described (Plaut, 2002; Fredrickson, 2010), most prominently those of color blindness (i.e., the idea that racial categories should be ignored or avoided) and multiculturalism (i.e., the belief that differences among groups should be explicitly acknowledged and valued). Models of diversity need not be mutually exclusive and the boundaries between them can become blurred (Plaut, 2002). We argue that the ideas and practices of the military contain elements of the Common Ingroup Identity model, the Value-added model, and the All-inclusive Multiculturalism model of diversity.

The Common Ingroup Identity (CII) Model

The Common Ingroup Identity (CII) model developed by Gaertner and Dovidio (2000, 2005) begins with the premise that the process of social categorization can lead to intergroup bias through either indifference toward outgroup members and/or favoritism toward ingroup members. Categorizing people along group lines, e.g., race, gender, or rank, can lead to an "us" versus "them" mentality, such that intergroup interactions and positive affect toward outgroup members are less likely. To counteract this bias, the CII model argues that the salience of social categorizations and group differences can be diminished by recategorizing oneself and others under a common, superordinate identity. The effect of this common identity is to increase perceptions of connectedness between people across group lines and transfer egocentric biases favoring the self to other ingroup members. The process of recategorization can be facilitated by inducing intergroup cooperation, drawing attention to common group member-ships, or introducing factors (e.g., common goals) that are shared by everyone. The CII model suggests that, distinct from a full assimilationist approach, less inclusive identities based on social categories need not be completely abandoned during the development of a common group identity, leaving open the possibility for multiple identities to coexist within a single context.

The military is able to facilitate the perception of a common group identity like no other institution. Prior to entering the military, most recruits are embedded in a sociocultural context that privileges and values the American ideal of liberal individualism—the tendency to see people as individuals rather than as members of a group and the encouragement of individual thought, nonconformity, and uniqueness (see Plaut, 2002). From the first day of basic training, however, recruits undergo a process of indoctrination to embrace a military culture centered around commu-nitarian values and to know one's place within the military group (Baker, 2008). The extremely rigorous and highly regimented features of basic training are designed in part to train members to subordinate their own individual preferences and tendencies to the needs of the group. This process is necessary to organizational functioning since "[t]he only way soldiers will have any hope of surviving the chaos of battle is to act together as a team, unquestioningly obeying the commands of a leader exactly as received" (Baker, 2008, p. 25). A focus on a common military group identity is further reinforced by inculcating recruits with the core values held by their Service (e.g., "Honor, Courage, Commitment" in the Navy and Marine Corps), enforcing common practices (e.g., saluting, standard operating procedures, common vocabulary), and having visible markers of group membership (e.g., uniforms). Evidence of the military's focus on a larger overarching identity is found in the short-lived life of the Army's campaign slogan of "Army of One," which ran for only five years and was critiqued from the beginning as focusing too much on the individual ("Army launching," 2006).

Not only are the training and more general institutional practices effective at increasing the salience of the military group as a key identity source, but the very nature of military functioning requires its members to unite behind a shared mission and to rely on one another to accomplish this mission. Moreover, the importance of teamwork to accomplish a common purpose is intensified in the military context given the high stakes often involved. All of these factors facilitate a recategorization process such that military group membership predominates over perceived differences between social groups.

At the same time, some of the military's diversity initiatives specifically target and support less inclusive social identities of servicemembers, thus facilitating the coexistence of multiple identities within the organizational context. For example, some of the Services have established affinity groups to provide support and resources for minority groups as well as mentorship programs. Awards honoring and special events directed at members from certain social groups (e.g., the Navy's Black Engineer of the Year Award and hosting of the 2011 Women's Surface Force Waterfront Symposium) likewise signal to members that their social category identities are acknowledged and valued within the larger military identity.

The Value-added Model

The Value-added (VA) model and the All-inclusive Multiculturalism (AIM) model are both derivatives of the more general multiculturalism framework. A multiculturalism approach to diversity "explicitly acknowledges differences among groups and promotes the notion that differences associated with social identities should be valued and even celebrated" (Plaut, 2010, p. 85). A VA model recognizes that differences among groups of people are substantial and should be utilized because and to the extent they add value to the organization (Plaut, 2002). This kind of acknowledgment and appreciation of difference is clearly present in the understandings of diversity found among all the Services. Moreover, the military emphasizes a direct link between having a diverse workforce and enhancing organizational outcomes.

This Value-added approach to diversity is evident in how the Department of Defense (DoD) and some of the Services define diversity (see Table 8.1). For the DoD, diversity encompasses those characteristics and attributes that are "integral to overall readiness and mission accomplishment" (Army Regulation 600-13), i.e., those that contribute or add value to overall better organizational functioning. Similarly, the Navy emphasizes characteristics "which enhance the mission readiness of the Navy." Diversity thus plays a very instrumental role within the military, with definitions directly tied to specific end-goals of the particular service branch. Implicit in these definitions is the belief that diversity creates certain performance advantages, though exactly how differences are thought to contribute to the military and how differences are to be utilized are things not highly elaborated or analyzed (Plaut, 2002). In part, this value-added perspective reflects an attempt to distinguish diversity policy from equal opportunity policy, which had been the focus since 1948. Whereas equal opportunity policies are centered on complying with laws that make it illegal to discriminate against an individual on the basis of race, religion, gender, or other protected categories, diversity policies are centered on actively fostering and utilizing the diversity of the military workforce to achieve particular goals. While consistent with one another, the focus of diversity goes beyond eliminating discrimination to leveraging differences *"because they are critical to the new approaches and practices needed for a successful fighting force"* (MLDC, 2011b, p. 14, emphasis in the original).

Several historical and contemporary examples illustrate this value-added approach, with some key aspects of group membership being utilized in a particular way to advance mission capability. During World War I, Native Americans from the Choctaw Nation served in the U.S. Army as the first "code talkers" by transmitting secure messages in their native language, effectively changing the tide of battles during the Mousse–Argonne campaign (Allen, n.d.). Similarly, during World War II, Navajo code talkers were utilized in the U.S. Marine Corps during every major engagement of the Pacific theater to bypass Japanese intelligence deciphers (Naval History & Heritage Command, n.d.).

A recent example comes from some service branches' explicit emphasis on recruiting and valuing members with skill sets relevant to communicating and interacting with foreign military personnel and civilians. Given the evolving geopolitical environment and the U.S. military's global presence, individuals with foreign language or cultural competency skills are valued because their specific talents can enhance the

TABLE 8.1

Definitions of Diversity within the U.S. Military

Department of Defense[a]	Diversity is all the different characteristics and attributes of the DoD's Total Force, which are consistent with our core values, integral to overall readiness and mission accomplishment, and reflective of the nation we serve
National Guard[b]	Diversity is a cultural climate which allows people to maximize their potential by embracing and promoting each other's holistic characteristics
Army[c]	The different attributes, experiences, and backgrounds of our Soldiers, Civilians, and Family Members that further enhance our global capabilities and contribute to an adaptive, culturally astute Army
Navy[d]	All the different characteristics and attributes of individual Sailors and civilians which enhance the mission readiness of the Navy
Marine Corps[e]	[No formal definition per se.] Diversity in the background and experience of those who join the Marine Corps is not only a reflection of American society but also a key element to maintaining the strength and flexibility required to meet today's national security challenges
Air Force[f]	A composite of individual characteristics, experiences and abilities consistent with the Air Force Core Values and the Air Force Mission. Air Force Diversity includes but is not limited to: personal life experiences, geographic background, socioeconomic background, cultural knowledge, educational background, work background, language abilities, physical abilities, philosophical/spiritual perspectives, age, race, ethnicity, and gender
Coast Guard[g]	Diversity is variety. It includes all the characteristics, experiences, and differences of each individual. Diversity can be identified as physical characteristics such as skin color and gender, or it may be differences in culture, skills, education, personality type, or upbringing

[a] DoD Diversity and Inclusion Strategic Plan (2012); [b] National Guard Joint Diversity Executive Council (2011); [c] Department of the Army (2009); [d] Secretary of the Navy (2007); [e] Conway (2008); [f] Donley, M. B. (2010); [g] U.S. Coast Guard Office of Diversity (n.d.).

success of military engagements and partnership building. The Army's definition of diversity directly reflects this instrumental perspective by valuing those backgrounds that "further enhance our global capabilities and contribute to an adaptive, culturally astute Army."

Another contemporary example is the formation of Female Engagement Teams (FET) to conduct counterintelligence operations in Iraq and Afghanistan. Since cultural norms and laws in Muslim nations restrict interactions between Muslim women and adult men, FETs are able to interface with women in places where men are unable to go, including into their homes. Servicewomen have been trained over the last decade with FET counterinsurgency units to understand Afghan communities, specifically their need for medical services, the gathering of intelligence, and the opening/reconstruction of schools (Female Engagement Teams, 2011). Given this access, commanders are able to receive a more comprehensive perspective with the intelligence gathered by FETs, thus providing a unique contribution to the military campaign in that region.

This last example also raises a cautionary note for this model of diversity, which is, if not implemented carefully, group members can become pigeonholed into certain positions in ways that marginalize them or fail to integrate them fully into the organization (Thomas & Ely, 1996). Thus, while women in the military can certainly add to mission effectiveness by fulfilling gender-relevant roles, it is important that they not be restricted to them. At the same time that women are serving a unique role on FETs, they are still restricted from participating in the full spectrum of field assignments. At the time of this writing, military policies generally prohibit women from serving in infantry, tank, armor, Special Forces units, as well as other combat roles (Bumiller, 2010). For example, the Army Policy for the Assignment of Female Soldiers, consistent with the 1994 Department of Defense Combat Exclusion Policy, reads:

> The Army's assignment policy for female soldiers allows women to serve in any officer or enlisted specialty or position except in those specialties, positions, or units (battalion size or smaller) which are assigned a routine mission to engage in direct combat or which collocate routinely with units assigned a direct combat mission.

The impact of these exclusion policies ranges in severity across the different Services. While the Army and Marine Corps maintain the worst statistics with 30% and 35% of positions closed to women, an excess of 90% of Air Force positions and all career fields in the Coast Guard are open to women (Bacon, 2011). One major consequence of these exclusion policies is that they impede the ability for women to move up in the officer ranks since advancement is often tied to serving in a tactical career. For example, in 2008, 65% of flag/general officers came from tactical career fields (MLDC, 2010, p. 4). Unfortunately, tactical fields are restricted for women because of the combat exclusion policy. Critics have noted that these policies act more to preserve the all-male characteristics of combat units than to protect women from exposure to enemy combat (Putko, 2008). Though repealing combat exclusion policies has been recommended by the recent Congressionally chartered Military Leadership Diversity Commission (MLDC, 2011b), it remains a controversial topic. However, the roles of women in the military have necessarily expanded de facto given the war tactics employed by insurgents in Iraq and Afghanistan, which tend to expose all servicemembers, regardless of sex, to hostile fire.

All-Inclusive Multiculturalism

While policies and initiatives stemming from a multiculturalism approach are often perceived as associated with or targeted only to minority group members (Plaut, Stevens, Buffardi, & Sanchez-Burks, 2011; Unzueta & Binning, 2010), the AIM model suggests that organizations can frame diversity in a way that is inclusive of all employees—both minorities and non-minorities alike (Stevens, Plaut, & Sanchez-Burks, 2008). This approach emphasizes the contributions that all groups can make to the organization and affirms the identity and belonging of each person. The AIM model suggests building an inclusive environment in part by communicating to employees that non-minorities are included in the concept of diversity, avoiding exclusive language in messaging and activities, framing policies in ways that demonstrate the benefit to everyone—either directly or indirectly, and promoting both minority and non-minority involvement and leadership on diversity-related initiatives.

The military's approach to diversity contains the core element of the AIM model, specifically the idea that all servicemembers can potentially contribute something valuable to the organization's diversity. While the proponents of the AIM model developed their approach with demographic or social identity groups in mind (Stevens et al., 2008), the military has attempted to create the same all-inclusive environment by broadening the concept of diversity to include all relevant dimensions of difference. This all-inclusiveness is explicitly recognized by military leaders. The Marine Corps, for example, has stated that "[d]iversity issues concern women, minorities, *and* the majority" (U.S. Marine Corps, 2010, emphasis in the original). Other Services have noted that every servicemember is considered a stakeholder in the military's diversity (Makell, 2010). By framing diversity as critical to mission readiness and success, the military also ties the well-being of every service member to its diversity project. This broadened conception of diversity, which extends beyond just minority groups is also directly captured by many of the service branches' definition of diversity (see Table 8.1). While some service branches refer to protected group characteristics such as race or gender, these are only one component of a larger vision of diversity that includes a wide range of characteristics, attributes, skills, and experiences along which individuals can differ. The Air Force, for example, defines diversity as "a composite of individual characteristics, experiences and abilities . . . includ[ing] but [] not limited to: personal life experiences, geographic background, socioeconomic background, cultural knowledge, educational background, work background, language abilities, physical abilities, philosophical/spiritual perspectives, age, race, ethnicity, and gender."[2] Similarly, the Coast Guard's definition notes that diversity can be "identified as physical characteristics such as skin color and gender, or it may be differences in culture, skills, education, personality type, or upbringing."

A couple of the Services describe diversity as something more than just a collection of differing characteristics of people; rather, diversity is an "inclusive culture" or, as referred to elsewhere by the Coast Guard, a "state of being" (MLDC, 2009). Similarly, the National Guard explicitly aims to achieve inclusion, which it has defined as "organizational strength when all people foster a positive work environment that promotes and respects our differences and similarities—both seen and unseen" (National Guard Joint Diversity Executive Council, 2011). This conception of diversity reflects a goal of maintaining a certain kind of diversity climate within the organization and an acknowledgement of the need to manage diversity properly. Additionally, it references the type of attitude that ought to be taken toward diversity: differences among people ought to be recognized, appreciated, respected, and utilized to achieve the greatest potential for both the individual and the organization (MLDC, 2009). Discussions within the military emphasize the need to institutionalize diversity as a core value. In addition to adjusting policies and practices to become more inclusive, a cultural change needs to take place such that respect for diversity permeates all levels of the organization. A focus on diversity climate and culture facilitates a move away from an "illusion of inclusion" (MLDC, 2011b) or purely symbolic systems (Edelman, 1992) of diversity. Much of the discussion within the military recognizes that in order to develop an inclusive climate, visible and robust commitment must come from the top leadership and be reinforced through systematic monitoring, accountability, and enforcement (MLDC, 2011b). For example, Lieutenant General William E. Ingram Jr., the director of the Army National Guard, recently was quoted as saying, "growing leaders should be done regardless of race or sex or anything else." "If we are doing that across the board and mentoring our subordinates to understand that as well, then it permeates the organization. That's the way we have to do business" (Salazar, 2012).

Consistent with a focus on engendering an inclusive environment, the service branches have at their disposal a few tools to measure organizational climate and servicemembers' attitudes about diversity. Over one million passwords are issued annually to administer the Defense Equal Opportunity Management Institute Organizational Climate Survey (DEOCS), a commander-requested management survey that focuses on military equal opportunity, civilian equal employment opportunity, sexual assault prevention and response, and organizational effectiveness, with an option for commanders to add locally developed and short answer questions (DEOMI, 2012). As part of the organizational effectiveness component, commanders can get unit-level feedback on organizational commitment, trust in the organization, work group effectiveness, work group cohesion, leadership cohesion, and job satisfaction. More specific to diversity issues, roughly 80,000 military personnel have completed the Diversity Management Climate Survey (DDMCS). This 50-item survey measures nine factors focused on perceptions of diversity and diversity management, including workplace inclusion, benefits, justice, mentoring, work group effectiveness, work group cohesion, personal accountability, training and development, and leadership (DEOMI, 2011). Other similar unit climate assessment tools are available at the request of commanders. A couple of the service branches (e.g., Navy and Air Force) have policies in place that require the use of a climate survey under particular circumstances (e.g., within 90 days of assuming command with annual follow-up assessments or on units with more than 50 personnel assigned every two years) (Buckley Air Force Base, n.d.; Department of the Navy, 2007). However, the degree of adherence to these policies or the extent to which commanders utilize these surveys (and their results) is sometimes low.

Given its broad conception of diversity and its focus on incorporating an appreciation for diversity into the organizational climate, the military's approach arguably encourages all servicemembers to feel included and valued in a way that will "foster[] organizational commitment and trust, internal motivation, and satisfaction for both minorities and non-minorities alike" (Stevens et al., 2008). Yet, some scholars have been critical of conceptions of diversity that move too far away from a focus on historically disadvantaged and underrepresented groups because doing so obscures issues of intergroup inequality (Linnehan & Konrad, 1999). A broadened conception of diversity may "reinforce . . . a view of racial diversity simply as distinctive viewpoints and cultural practices" (Plaut, 2010, p. 89), thus failing to appreciate that race and gender are categories imbued with social meanings and connected to practices of group conflict and subordination (Haney-Lopez, 2005). In response to these types of critiques, a recent Congressionally chartered commission reviewing military policy argued that "understanding diversity more broadly can help to build the representation of these [underrepresented] populations in the military leadership because these populations have always offered the skills and talents that military leadership requires" (MLDC, 2011b, p. 13). Though sentiments of equity or "because it's the right thing to do" linger in the background of diversity initiatives to a small degree, the rhetoric justifying and defining diversity is dominated by the more instrumental, goal-oriented view described earlier. Group inequality is largely left to be addressed within the domain of equal opportunity policy. Yet, equal opportunity policies, grounded in legal norms and anti-discrimination law, are arguably insufficient on their own to fully address the structural and historical barriers that contribute to intergroup inequalities.

A divergence between diversity rhetoric and actual practice, however, must be acknowledged. When it comes to assessing and tracking progress on the diversity front, much of the focus remains on the extent to which demographic diversity (i.e., protected classes of minorities and women) is being achieved. Apart from the climate surveys mentioned previously, few tools currently exist to evaluate whether diversity goals are being met other than to simply count and keep track of group representation at different levels of leadership and across field or assignment types. Because it takes 20–30 years to develop the leaders of tomorrow, the military is particularly sensitive to the United States' rapidly changing demographics (MLDC, 2011b). Current population projections show that the percentage of racial/ethnic minorities is increasing and, conversely, the percentage of non-Hispanic Whites is decreasing. Indeed, estimates show that non-Hispanic Whites will become the numeric minority sometime between 2040 and 2050 (Ortman & Guarneri, 2009). Data on the demographic makeup of active duty personnel shows that while in general the enlisted ranks reflect levels of demographic diversity fairly comparable to population demographics, this is less the case at the officer level (DoD Open Government, 2010). The gap widens even further if one looks at more senior levels within the officer ranks. Reviews of recent accessions to the Reserve Officers' Training Corps and the Officer Candidate School/Officer Training School programs showed that at least one racial/ethnic minority group was underrepresented in each service, and women were underrepresented across the board (MLDC, 2011b). The focus on demographic diversity has helped shape the strategies adopted by the military, including recruitment efforts targeted at underrepresented populations and the presence of affinity groups and mentoring programs within some of the Services.

Growing out of a particular concern over the lack of women and minorities represented among senior leadership, Congress chartered the Military Leadership Diversity Commission (MLDC) in 2009. The MLDC was tasked to "conduct a comprehensive evaluation and assessment of policies that provide opportunities for the promotion and advancement of minority members of the Armed Forces, including minority members who are senior officers" (The Duncan Hunter National Defense Authorization Act, 2009). The Commission was composed of active-duty and retired officers, senior enlisted personnel, executives from major corporations and civil servants. In the spring of 2011, the MLDC released their final report which outlined several recommendations addressing various aspects of diversity and diversity policy, including: 1) a broad, mission-relevant definition of diversity, 2) the importance of the military leadership to be trained and committed to diversity, 3) improvement and expansion of current recruitment strategies, 4) set up of accountability processes/reviews to ensure diversity goals are being met, 5) policy changes aimed at more equity in promotion processes (e.g., greater transparency and elimination of combat exclusion policies for women), 6) tracking demographic gaps for women and minorities within the most senior leadership ranks, 7) the implementation of robust diversity strategic plans and making these efforts part of the organizational climate, 8) increasing servicemembers' knowledge of career development and resource opportunities, and 9) requiring a standardized metrics system, annual diversity reports, and annual meetings among senior leaders to forward diversity goals. These recommendations reflect the dual aspect of the military's understanding of diversity: commitment to a broadened conception of diversity (mostly through formal definitions and policy) but strategies (mostly) centered around historically underrepresented groups. An intended focus on leadership involvement and accountability moving forward is evident, though what accountability might look like in practice is unclear.

In spite of concerns stemming from the military's broad conception of diversity, substantial policy changes have been made recently that directly target issues of group inequality, including the Navy's opening up of assignments for women on submarines and greater attention to family-friendly policies. Most notable among them is the repeal of the Don't Ask Don't Tell (DADT) policy which prohibited military officials from asking about or mandating servicemembers to reveal their sexual orientation (Herek & Belkin, 2006; see also Hebl et al., Chapter 7, this volume). Under this policy, those who did openly identify as homosexuals were discharged from service, a consequence that affected over 12,000 servicemembers since the inception of the policy through 2007. The sustained criticism directed at the DADT policy culminated in its repeal, which President Obama signed into law on December 22, 2010.[3]

The new policy states that sexual orientation is a personal issue, has no bearing on the individual's service and is no basis for military discharge. To successfully implement the repeal of DADT, a program of rigorous training sessions was developed and executed with the objective of informing servicemembers about the repeal of DADT, the content of the new policy, and how it is enforced. The information presented focuses on policy and emphasizes that gays and lesbians are allowed to openly serve in the military and all servicemembers must be treated with respect and dignity.

The seeming disconnect between diversity rhetoric and the emphasis on demographic representation could stem from several factors. First, examining outcomes for different social groups is one way to evaluate whether equal opportunity is really available, or whether discrimination—either interpersonal and/or structural—is present in policies and practices. Therefore, despite efforts to conceptually distinguish diversity from equal opportunity policy, slippage between the two may exist since one may be a type of indicator for the success of the other. Relatedly, the face of the military informs perceptions of legitimacy, which, as described above, carries important value to the military as an institution. Others have suggested that this disconnect may exist because a broader definition of diversity is difficult to act on, that a focus on protected categories may be a logical starting point and other attributes will be incorporated over time, or that other dimensions of diversity will be adequately represented, assuming they are uniformly distributed across different social groups (Lim et al., 2008). One concern stemming from this mismatch between rhetoric and practice is that, to the extent that it is perceived by servicemembers, diversity efforts will be seen as "code" or a disguise for equal opportunity policies targeted at traditional minority groups, thus undermining the benefits of the AIM model. A challenge for the military moving forward will be to develop tools that close the gap between policy and practice.

CONCLUSION

An analysis of military rhetoric, policy, and practice reveals, on the one hand, an endorsement of a broad conception of diversity that is inclusive of all servicemembers and values those competencies that further mission readiness and military success in the 21st century. On the other hand, there remains a focus on diversity as demographic representation, one particularly concerned with minority and women within the senior levels of military leadership. Understandings of difference, including what differences matter and in what ways, are neither natural nor static. Rather, they are shaped by one's positioning in the world and sociocultural context (Plaut, 2010). Throughout this chapter we have identified several factors that in combination have shaped the military's approach to diversity, including its own historical experiences with intergroup dynamics, the development of a strong military culture imbued with core values, exposure to certain dominant discourses spreading among organizational actors in the private sector, pressures to remain a competitive employer, and changes to the nature of the tasks and situations military personnel face across the globe. One of the challenges facing the military moving forward is translating the ideals of diversity expressed through formal policy into effective change on the ground that maintains a truly inclusive environment. The serious and systematic way in which the military has embraced its diversity project is laudable; however, more work needs to be done to strike a balance between the goals of intergroup fairness and mission capability and between a focus on minority groups and inclusion for all.

NOTES

1. As of 2009, the military had roughly 1.44 million active duty forces in the five service branches, with an additional over 0.8 million reserve forces (Coast Guard, 2010; The Air Force in facts and figures, 2009).
2. The Air Force has delineated four dimensions or types of diversity that it seeks: (1) demographic diversity, (2) behavioral/cognitive diversity—differences in personality type and styles of thinking and working, (3) structural diversity—leveraging other service branches, components, and occupations, and (4) global diversity—foreign language and cultural skills (MLDC, 2009).
3. Though, even here, the basic principle of equality was placed in check by an overriding focus on organizational functioning and mission success because the repeal could not take effect until "60 days after the President, the Secretary of Defense, and the Chairman of the Joint Chiefs of Staff attest to Congress that implementation of policies and regulations are consistent with standards of military readiness, effectiveness, unit cohesion, and recruiting and retention" (Donley, 2011).

REFERENCES

Allen, P. (n.d.). Choctaw Indian code talkers of World War I. Retrieved August 29, 2012, from www.choctawnation.com/history/people/code-talkers/code-talkers-of-wwi/

Army Launching. (2006, October 9). Army launching "army strong" ad campaign. *USA Today.* Retrieved from www.usatoday.com/news/washington/2006–10–09-army-slogan_x.htm

Army Regulation 600–13, *Army Policy for the Assignment of Female Soldiers.*

Bacon, L. M. (2011). Rules limiting female GIs' careers could change. *ArmyTimes.* Retrieved from www.armytimes.com/news/2011/04/army-women-in-combat-041711w/

Baker, A. P. (2008). *Life in the Armed Forces: (Not) just another job.* Westport, CT: Praeger Security International.

Bilchik, G. S. (2011). Military mystery: How many bases does the US have, anyway? *Occasional Planet.* Retrieved from www.occasionalplanet.org/2011/01/24/military-mystery-how-many-bases-does-the-us-have-anyway/

Brief for Becton, J. W. Jr., et al. as Amici Curiae supporting respondents, Gratz v. Bollinger, 539 U.S. 244 (2003) (no. 02-241); and Grutter v. Bollinger, 539 U.S. 306 (2003) (no. 02-516), 2003 WL 1787554.

Buckley Air Force Base (n.d.). Unit climate assessments (UCA). Retrieved August 30, 2012, from www.buckley.af.mil/library/equalopportunityprogram/unitclimateassessments.asp

Bumiller, E. (2010, October 2). For female marines, tea comes with bullets. *New York Times,* p. A1. Retrieved August 30, 2012 from www.nytimes.com/2010/10/03/world/asia/03marines.html?pagewanted=all&_r=0

Coast Guard (2010). Coast Guard 2010 Snapshot. Retrieved from www.uscg.mil/top/about/doc/uscg_snapshot.pdf

Considine, B. (2010). U.S. military: Obesity is a matter of national security. *NJ.com.* Retrieved from www.nj.com/news/index.ssf/2010/04/us_military_obesity_a_matter_o.html

Conway, J. T. (2008). Commandant of the Marine Corps diversity policy. Retrieved August 28, 2012, from www.marines.mil/unit/29palms/CI/EEO/Documents/CMC/diversiity%20letter.pdf

Dansby, M. R., & Landis, D. (2001). Intercultural training in the United States military. In M. R. Dansby, & J. B. Stewart (Eds.), *Managing diversity in the military: Research perspectives from the Defense Equal Opportunity Management Institute* (pp. 513–540). Brunswick, NJ: Transaction Publishers.

Dansby, M. R., Stewart, J. B., & Webb, S. C. (2001). Introduction. In *Managing diversity in the military: Research perspectives from the Defense Equal Opportunity Management Institute,* edited by Authors. New Jersey: Transaction Publishers.

DEOMI (Defense Equal Opportunity Management Institute) (2011). Talking paper on DEOMI diversity management climate survey (DDMCS). Retrieved August 30, 2012, from www.deocs.net/ddmcs/DocDownloads/Talker_DDMCS.pdf

DEOMI (2012). The defense equal opportunity management institute (DEOMI) organizational climate survey (DEOCS) version 3.35. Retrieved August 30, 2012, from www.deocs.net/DocDownloads/GeneralDescriptionwithSA.pdf

DoD (Department of Defense) (2009). Active duty military personnel strengths by regional area and by country (309A). Retrieved from www.globalsecurity.org/military/library/report/2009/hst0906.pdf

DoD (2012). Department of Defense Diversity and Inclusion Strategic Plan 2012–2017. Retrieved August 28, 2012, from http://diversity.defense.gov/docs/DoD_Diversity_Strategic_Plan_%20final_as%20of%2019%20Apr%2012[1].pdf

Department of the Army (2009). Army policy on diversity. Retrieved August 28, 2012, from http://usarmy.vo.llnwd.net/e2/-images/2009/04/08/34756/index.html

Department of the Navy (2007). OPNAV instruction 5354.1F. Retrieved August 30, 2012, from www.cnic.navy.mil/navycni/groups/public/@pub/@hq/documents/document/cnicc_068590.pdf

DoD Open Government. (2010). Distribution of active duty services by service, rank, sex, and race-with hispanic indicator. Retrieved from http://open.dodlive.mil/data-gov/demographics/

Donley, M. B. (2010). Air Force policy directive 36–70. Retrieved August 28, 2012, from www.e-publishing.af.mil/shared/media/epubs/AFPD36–70.pdf

Donley, M. B. (2011). Policy, education and training implementation guidance for DADT repeal. Retrieved August 30, 2012 from http://adam.curry.com/2011/03/04/afPolicy educationtrainingImplementationGuidanceForDadtRepealsecafSigned7Feb11.pdf

Eckholm, E. (2011, May 12). Navy rescinds guidelines for same-sex marriages. *New York Times*, p. A20.

Edelman, L. B. (1992). Legal ambiguity and symbolic structures: Organizational mediation of civil rights law. *American Journal of Sociology, 97*, 1531–1576.

Edelman, L. B., Fuller, S. R., & Mara-Drita, I. (2001). Diversity rhetoric and the managerialization of law. *The American Journal of Sociology, 106*, 1589–1641.

Female engagement teams work with Parwan women (2011). *ISAF Releases.* Retrieved from www.isaf.nato.int/article/isaf-releases/female-engagement-teams-work-with-parwan-women.html

Fredrickson, G. M. (2010). Models of American ethnic relations: Hierarchy, assimilation, and pluralism. In H. R. Markus, & P. M. L. Moya (Eds.), *Doing race: 21 essays for the 21st century* (pp. 23–34). New York: W. W. Norton.

Gaertner, S., & Dovidio, J. (2000). *The common ingroup identity model.* Philadelphia, PA: Psychology Press.

Gaertner, S. L., & Dovidio, J. F. (2005). Understanding and addressing contemporary racism: From aversive racism to the common ingroup identity model. *Journal of Social Issues, 61*, 615–639.

Haney-Lopez, I. (2005). Race and colorblindness after Hernandez and Brown. *Chicano-Latino Law Review, 25*, 61–76.

Herek, G. M., & Belkin, A. (2006). Sexual orientation and military service: Organizational and individual change in the United States. In T. W. Britt, A. B. Adler, & C. A. Castro (Eds.), *Military life: The psychology of serving in peace and combat* (Vol. 4: Military Culture, pp. 119–142). Westport, CT: Praeger Security International.

Ilgen, D. R., & Pulakos, E. D. (1999). *The changing nature of performance: Implications for staffing, motivation, and development.* San Francisco, CA: Jossey-Bass.

John-Hall, A. (2009). Admiral wants hands of all colors on bridge—not just on deck. *Naval Leadership: Learn to Lead!* Retrieved from http://navaleadership.blogspot.com/2009/07/annette-john-hall-admiral-wants-hands.html

Lim, N., Cho, M., & Curry, K. (2008). *Planning for diversity: Options and recommendations for DoD leaders* [MG-743-OSD]. Santa Monica, CA: RAND Corporation.

Linnehan, F., & Konrad, A. M. (1999). Diluting diversity: Implications for intergroup inequality in organizations. *Journal of Management Inquiry, 8*, 399–414.

Makell, W. J. (2010). Championing diversity leadership: A program and initiatives overview. Military Leadership Diversity Commission Briefing. Retrieved from http://mldc.whs.mil/download/documents/meetings/201003/CG_CDR_Makell_MLDC_Accountability_Brief_Feb2010.pdf

Military Leadership Diversity Commission. (2009). Examples of diversity definitions (Issue paper #3). Retrieved from http://mldc.whs.mil/download/documents/Issue%20Papers/3_Diversity_Definitions.pdf

Military Leadership Diversity Commission. (2010). Women in combat: Legislation and policy, perceptions, and the current operational environment (Issue paper #56). Retrieved from http://mldc.whs.mil/download/documents/Issue%20Papers/56_Women_in_Combat.pdf

Military Leadership Diversity Commission. (2011a). Decision paper #5: Defining diversity. Retrieved August 28, 2012, from http://diversity.defense.gov/Resources/Commission/docs/Decision%20Papers/Paper%205%20-%20Defining%20Diversity.pdf

Military Leadership Diversity Commission. (2011b). From representation to inclusion: Diversity leadership for the 21st-century military. Retrieved from http://mldc.whs.mil/index.php/final-report

National Center for Education Statistics. (2009). The condition of education 2009 (NCES 2009-081, Table A-20-2). Washington, DC: Author.

National Guard Joint Diversity Executive Council (2011). A leader's guide to diversity: The decade of diversity (1st edition). Retrieved August 28, 2012, from www.nationalguard.mil/features/vdc//Diversity.pdf

Naval History & Heritage Command. (n.d.). Navajo code talkers: World War II fact sheet. Retrieved August 29, 2012, from www.history.navy.mil/faqs/faq61-2.htm

Ortman, J. M., & Guarneri, C. E. (2009). United States population projections: 2000 to 2050. Retrieved from www.census.gov/population/www/projections/analyticaldocument09.pdf

Parks, K. M., Knouse, S., Crepeau, L., & McDonald, D. P. (2008). Latina perceptions of diversity climate in the military. *Business Journal of Hispanic Research, 2*, 48–61.

Pew Hispanic Center. (2009). Between two worlds: How young Latinos come of age in America. Washington, DC: Author. Retrieved from http://pewhispanic.org/files/reports/117.pdf

Plaut, V. C. (2002). Cultural models of diversity in America: The psychology of difference and inclusion. In Richard A. Shweder, Martha Minow, & Hazel Rose Markus (Eds.), *Engaging cultural differences: The multicultural challenge in liberal democracies* (pp. 365–395). New York: Russell Sage.

Plaut, V. C. (2010). Diversity science: Why and how difference makes a difference. *Psychological Inquiry, 21*, 77–99.

Plaut, V. C., Stevens, F. G., Buffardi, L., & Sanchez-Burks, J. (2011). What about me?: Perceptions of exclusion and non-minority reactions to multiculturalism. *Journal of Personality and Social Psychology, 101*, 337–353.

Putko, M. M. (2008). The combat exclusion policy in the modern security environment. In M. M. Putko, & D. V. Johnson, II (Eds.), *Women in combat compendium*. Strategic Studies Institute. Retrieved from www.strategicstudiesinstitute.army.mil/pubs/display.cfm?pubID=830

Salazar, D. (June 28, 2012). *National Guard to host virtual diversity update.* Retrieved September 14, 2012, from www.af.mil/news/story.asp?id=123307937

Secretary of the Navy (2007). Department of the Navy diversity policy statement. Retrieved from www.public.navy.mil/bupers-npc/support/diversity/Documents/DONPolicy.pdf

Smith, I. III (2010). Why black officers still fail. *Parameters, Autumn 2010*, 1–16.

Stevens, F. G., Plaut, V. C., & Sanchez-Burks, J. (2008). Unlocking the benefits of diversity: All-inclusive multiculturalism and positive organizational change. *Journal of Applied Behavioral Science, 44*, 166–133.

Soeter, J., van Fenema, P., & Beeres, R. (2010). *Managing military organizations: Theory and practice.* Cass Military Studies. Abingdon: Routledge.

Submarine Forces Public Affairs (2010, April 29). Navy policy will allow women to serve aboard submarines. Retrieved from www.navy.mil/submit/display.asp?story_id=52954

The Air Force in Facts and Figures. (2009). *Air Force Magazine*. Retrieved from www. airforcemagazine.com/MagazineArchive/Magazine%20Documents/2009/May%2020 09/0509facts_fig.pdf

Theokas, C. (2010). *Shut out of the military: Today's high school education doesn't mean you're ready for today's Army.* Retrieved from www.edtrust.org/sites/edtrust.org/files/ publications/files/ASVAB_4.pdf

Thomas, D. A., & Ely, R. J. (1996). Making differences matter: A new paradigm for managing diversity. *Harvard Business Review, 74,* 79–90.

Unzueta, M. M., & Binning, K. R. (2010). Which racial groups are associated with diversity? *Cultural Diversity and Ethnic Minority Psychology, 16,* 443–446.

U.S. Coast Guard Office of Diversity (n. d.). Diversity 101: What is diversity? Retrieved August 28, 2012, from www.uscg.mil/diversity/Diversity101.asp

U.S. Marine Corps (2010). Implementation and accountability information for MLDC. Retrieved from http://mldc.whs.mil/download/documents/meetings/201003/USMC _March.pdf

U.S. Office of Personnel Management Office of Diversity and Inclusion (2011). Government-wide diversity and inclusion strategic plan. Retrieved from www. opm.gov/diversityandinclusion/reports/GovernmentwideDIStrategicPlan.pdf

Wisner, P. S., & Feist, H. A. (2001). Does teaming pay off? *Strategic Finance, 82,* 58–64.

9

The Intersection of Organizational and Individual Diversity Ideology on Diverse Employees' Perceptions of Inclusion and Organizational Justice

Ny Mia Tran, Kecia M. Thomas, and
Kerrin E. George

> This emerging generation is more predisposed to a world of diversity
> and inclusion, and we better be ready to work with them.
> (Henry G. "Hank" Jackson, CPA, President and CEO,
> Society for Human Resource Management (SHRM))

> Many of us struggle with this tension and attempt to maintain and
> promote our cultural and ethnic identities in a society that is often
> ambivalent about how to deal with its differences.
> (Supreme Court Justice Sonia Sotomayor)

These quotes accentuate the expressed social uncertainty brought from the demographic change and the increasing presence of diverse groups in society. How should society respond to group differences? Should we embrace or de-emphasize these group differences? These ideological questions pose more than a social dilemma. Similar sentiments are echoed in the workplace as more and more diverse individuals enter the workforce. In the workplace, this social issue is rebranded as diversity ideology. Those in favor of minimizing differences between groups are proponents of colorblindness, whereas appreciation for group differences represents a multicultural perspective. These ideologies of diversity have sparked an ongoing debate around which of the two drives the best outcomes for a given company. On one hand proponents of colorblindness have argued that people are the same and we should break down social group categories to minimize disunification (see Jones, 1998; Verkuyten, 2005; Wolsko, Park, Judd, & Wittenbrink, 2000). On the other, those in favor of multiculturalism suggest the importance of recognizing diverse categories and valuing the differences in order to achieve inclusivity (for reviews see Plaut, 2010; Rattan & Ambady, 2013). Regardless of which ideology is adopted, each has been advocated as the ideal to attaining equality and fairness over the other.

Literature on diversity ideology is still in its developing stage (Embrick, 2011; Rattan & Ambrady, 2013; Wolsko et al., 2000). From an organizational standpoint, diversity ideology was reflected in the company's diversity efforts as either multicultural or colorblind. A multicultural organization has been described as one that has policies and practices that support and value diverse organizational members (Cox, 1991). Organizations that espouse colorblindness stress that employees strive for a unified organizational identity and ignore racial categories (Cox, 1991; Thomas & Ely, 1996). Organization-level diversity ideology has been used to describe workplace cultures and climate (Purdue-Vaughns, Steele, Davis, Ditlmann, & Crosby, 2008). Recently, research included the prominence of endorsed multicultural and colorblind ideologies from the people that make up the organization. These ideologies have been explored from both majority and minority group perspectives. Some studies have investigated how majority group members' diversity beliefs affect minorities' outcomes (Holoien & Shelton, 2012; Plaut, Thomas, & Goren, 2009). Others have evaluated the degree to which majority and minority group members endorse a given diversity ideology (Arends-Tóth & van de Vijver, 2003; Morrison & Chung, 2011; Ryan, Hunt, Weible, Peterson, & Casas 2007; Verkuyten, 2005).

Although these works have provided invaluable information at the organizational and individual level of diversity ideology, separately, there is, however, a lack of insight on how diversity ideologies at different levels of analysis interact, given that the organization and its constituents are interconnected and always shaping and influencing one another. The aim of this chapter is to propose an interactive model of how organizational-level and individual-level diversity ideology impact diverse employees' perceptions of inclusion and organizational justice. Specifically, we are interested in how a lack of congruence between these two levels of diversity ideologies may impact minority and majority employees. The model suggests both ideologies independently and interdependently foster positive and negative worker outcomes. Here, we focused on inclusion and organizational justice as consequences of ideological interactions. As a preface to the chapter propositions, we find it appropriate to provide a general review of the origin and history of each diversity ideology, in order to understand its role in an organizational context.

A REVIEW OF DIVERSITY IDEOLOGY

Within social, cross-cultural, ethnic-minority, and organizational psychology domains, diversity ideologies represent attitudes, beliefs, and practices regarding how to respond to diversity and how groups should interact with one another (Plaut, 2002; Plaut, Garnett, Buffardi, & Sanchez-Burks, 2011; Rattan & Ambady, 2013). Two prominent but distinct diversity ideologies emerged from the literature: colorblindness and multicultural-ism. Both colorblindness and multiculturalism are well regarded within research and practice as effective diversity ideologies to mitigate diversity conflict and inequities (e.g., Ryan et al., 2007), although neither is exempt from the criticism of endorsing aversive discrimination to generating separatism (e.g., Gutiérrez & Unzueta, 2010; Richeson & Naussbaum, 2004; Wolsko et al., 2000).

Colorblindness surfaced as an attempt to dismantle the system of social inequalities (Knowles, Lowery, Hogan, & Chow, 2009). The doctrine of colorblindness originated from the Plessy v. Ferguson Supreme Court case resting on Justice Harlan's argument, in the "view of the Constitution, in the eyes of the law, there is in this country no superior, dominant, ruling class of citizens. There is no caste here. Our constitution is color-blind, and neither knows nor tolerates classes among citizens" (1896). The colorblind ideology has also been associated with the assimilation acculturation process, in which the person abandons his/her donor cultural identity and adopts the host-dominant cultural identity (Berry, 1984; Plaut et al., 2009; see also Jones, 1998). The concept of assimilating into a harmonious homogeneous culture was also referred to as the "melting pot" metaphor during the eighteenth and nineteenth century. However, recently the notion of assimilation and colorblindness as a similar entity has been questioned within the social psychology field. Both colorblind and assimilation focus on de-emphasizing group differences; although the assimilationist approach focuses less on valuing all group members regardless of differences and more on devaluing outgroup members (i.e., minority groups) (Hahn, Judd, & Park, 2010). Hahn et al. further elaborate and suggest that assimilation beliefs are the mere "sister ideology [to colorblind ideology] that manifest similar beliefs about group differences but that are based on much more negative evaluations of the outgroup members" (p. 121). Others suggest colorblind and assimilation as two separate ideologies (Levin et al., 2012). Levin et al. noted that assimilation operates differently from colorblindness; assimilation was shown to be a hierarchy-enhancing ideology as opposed to colorblindness. Given the recent attention on the differences in the degree of outgroup appreciation between colorblind and assimilation (Hahn et al., 2010), hereforth we will refer to the colorblind ideological framework separately from the assimilation ideological framework. The initial goal of adopting a colorblind society was to inhibit group categorizations in order to diffuse intergroup conflict, bias, prejudice, and discrimination. Early social and cognitive psychology suggests that social categorization, grouping individuals as ingroups or outgroups based on salient characteristics, fosters stereotyping and prejudice (Park & Judd, 2005). Specifically, one can minimize dependency on existing categorization structures (Dovidio, Gaertner, & Saguy, 2009; Gaertner, Dovidio, Banker, Houlette, Johnson, & McGlynn, 2000) by ignoring group differences (see Park & Judd, 2005). The cognitive explanation of social intergroup conflicts provided the forum for promotion of the colorblind perspective to attenuate bias and prejudice.

Contrary to the initial proposition of achieving equality, the ideology of colorblindness received several criticisms by others as more divisive than unifying. Some argued that reducing intergroup prejudice and bias might be possible without proposing a monocultural society, grounded in the colorblind ideology, but rather to pursue cultural pluralism. Cultural pluralism, coined by Horace Kallen in the early twentieth century, was introduced as an ideological challenge to the melting-pot vision and that no one's group or culture should dominate (Ratner, 1984). The theory posited for a coexisting society consisted of self-identity preservation and coinciding acceptance of other cultural identities. Fredrickson discussed the cultural pluralism model as "the best hope for a just and cohesive society . . . that is fully inclusive" (1999, p. 33). Cultural pluralism is parallel to the multicultural ideology that is most commonly discussed in social and organizational psychology. Multiculturalism surfaced as an alternative ideology and encourages appreciation and celebration of group differences and multiple group identification (Banks, 2004; Zirkel, 2008; see also Rattan & Ambady, 2013). As noted by Verkuyten, "as an ideology, multiculturalism offers a positive view of cultural maintenance by ethnic minority groups and, as such, as a concomitant need to accommodate diversity in an equitable way" (2005, p. 121).

Given the history of multiculturalism and colorblindness, the ideological debate on the ideal perspective has permeated discussions on group relations across academic research, educational reforms, and social policies (Bennett, 1995; Hirschfeld, 1996; Plaut, 2010; Schlesinger, 1992). Proponents of multiculturalism suggest that minimizing group differences and not appreciating multiple identities devalues other social identity groups (Markus, Steele, & Steele, 2000). Drawing from social identity theory, a person possesses and identifies with more than one identity and each identity serves a unique and pertinent role in the human identity development and self-conception (Tajfel & Turner, 1979, 1986). Multiculturalism suggests, "that divisions between individuals must be acknowledged and valued as meaningful sources of identity and culture, and attempts to minimize such distinctions are viewed as critical shortcomings of the colorblind perspective" (Rattan & Ambady, 2013, p. 13). Instead, the colorblind ideology perpetuates the exact social status hierarchy, superordinate and subordinate groups that it was propositioned to break down (Park & Judd, 2005). Colorblindness proponents would propose otherwise: multiculturalism promotes separatism and inequality (Wolsko et al., 2000) by heightening racial fault lines and reifying cultural boundaries (Brewer, 1997; Gutiérrez & Unzueta, 2010; Prentice & Miller, 1999). Moreover, not only does it perpetuate racial divisions but it threatens American ideas of individualism and meritocracy on which it was built to form social unity and cohesion (Verkuyten, 2005). This ongoing debate has also emerged in the corporate world. An organization's diversity ideology is reflected in their diversity efforts and management. Some have argued that colorblind diversity ideology has "enabled many organizations to curtail deeper investigations into the gender and racial inequalities that continue to persist in the workplace" (Embrick, 2011, p. 542).

Empirical works were carried out in response to the tension between the two diversity ideologies. However, an organization's diversity ideology may not be indicative of its employee's diversity ideology. Organizational members may have diversity beliefs different from or similar to their organization. How does the diversity ideology congruence or incongruence between the organization and its employees influence work related outcomes? First, the chapter will separately highlight existing literature and works on diversity ideology[1] at the organizational and individual level, followed by introducing the diversity ideology interactive model and the impact on diverse employees' perceptions of inclusion and organizational justice.

Organizational Diversity Ideology

Many corporations have come to adopt a diversity is good for business mindset by portraying themselves as advocates of equality in their policies and practices. These diversity efforts reflect and cultivate the organization's diversity ideology. The organizational diversity ideology is depicted through their corporate procedures, human resource policies, websites, mission statement, and employee demographics (Embrick, 2011). The term organizational diversity ideology can be conceptually comparable to "diversity paradigms and models" found under the diversity management umbrella in the organizational psychology literature (Cox, 1991; Cox & Finley-Nickelson, 1991; Thomas & Ely, 1996). A colorblind organization ideology is parallel to a monolithic and assimilating organization (Cox, 1991; Cox & Finley-Nickelson, 1991) operating within the discrimination and fairness paradigm (Thomas & Ely, 1996). The discrimination and fairness paradigm emphasizes organizational members to view each other as the same. A multicultural organization ideology can be described as an organization that values and embraces diversity and works under the learning and effectiveness paradigm (Thomas & Ely, 1996)—"differences and similarities as dual aspects of diversity" (Kim, 2006, p. 81).

A multicultural organization has a higher tendency to view "diversity as more than minority representation and understand the need to modify its processes and structures to reflect an environment that truly values differences" (Chrobot-Mason & Thomas, 2002, p. 330). Cox (1991) further describes a multicultural organization as one that encourages employees to embrace group differences in order to foster a low group conflict and cultural bias work environment for all group members. A colorblind organization encourages employees to "judge others as individuals and not on the basis of their social group membership" (Wolsko et al., 2000, p. 637). Therefore this diversity strategy de-emphasizes social categories as an important factor in employment decision makings. Colorblind organizational practices may have positive reactions by employees from marginalized groups who would prefer to not be judged on the basis of a category but would neither want their identity ignored or minimized.

Individual Diversity Ideology

Organizational members that comprise the company also bring their individual diversity beliefs into the workplace. Individual diversity ideology plays a role in how the employee responds to diversity within their company and how it influences their perception of the workplace climate and decision makings. An employee's endorsed diversity ideology may differ depending on the individual's social group membership, so we will discuss it from the minority and majority group's endorsement of diversity ideologies and its impact on intergroup relations and work outcomes.

Several studies have explored the potential benefits or downsides of either embracing or minimizing group differences across group memberships. Accumulated findings suggest no clear affirmation of either ideological framework as more effective than the other in leading to positive outcomes, as both have been found linked to positive and negative effects of intergroup relations (Hahn et al., 2010). Richeson and Nussbaum (2004) found endorsing a multicultural ideology among White American undergraduates generated less racial attitude bias. Plaut et al. (2009) found White's endorsement of a colorblind ideology was negatively related to psychological engagement and positively related to perception of bias for minorities. On the other hand, colorblind ideology has been found to reduce stereotyping and bias in intergroup relations (Wolsko et al., 2000). Wolsko et al. (2000) conducted a series of studies examining White undergraduate diversity ideologies' impact on intergroup judgments. Their findings implied that both ideologies led to more positive evaluations of Blacks, while simultaneously those who were asked to adopt a multicultural perspective recognized greater racial group differences. Despite the increased awareness of differences between their own race and Blacks, Whites were more accurate in their perceptions of actual group differences and maintained positive evaluations of their racial group and Blacks. Additionally, Vorauer, Gagnon, and Sasaki (2009) found minorities' endorsement of colorblind ideology led to decreased anxiety. Importantly these studies denote the mixed findings for the two ideologies despite their distinct conceptual differences. Both ideologies share similar end-goal intentions of equality and cohesion yet both are related to positive and negative outcomes.

Studies also indicated group differences in diversity ideology preferences. Colorblindness was more endorsed and positively accepted by dominant group members than minorities and vice versa (Ryan, Casas, & Thompson, 2010; Ryan et al., 2007). This may be owing to Whites viewing multiculturalism as an unfair advantage to minorities and as an attempt at exclusion (Verkuyten, 2005; Plaut et al., 2011). In further support, previous research suggests that Whites and/or men may hold different perspectives on diversity ideology and perceive the implications of diversity management in modern organizations differently compared with racial–ethnic minorities and women (e.g., Mor Barak, Cherin, & Berkman, 1998; Stevens, Plaut, & Sanchez-Burks, 2008).

The current state of the diversity ideology research highlights the need to continue investigations, not only independently at the organizational or individual level but interdependently. The chapter proposes an interacting relationship between the organizational and individual diversity ideology that we will further discuss in the proceeding section.

INTERACTIVE MODEL OF ORGANIZATIONAL AND INDIVIDUAL DIVERSITY IDEOLOGY

As previously mentioned, diversity ideology has been discussed and explored at the organizational and individual level. According to Thompson, Falls, and Berrian (1997) an organization's diversity beliefs and strategy play a role in affirming and transmitting culture, promoting development, and shaping identity values within the organization. Therefore, we do not assume that individual or organizational ideology operates in isolation; rather, it is likely that the congruence or incongruence between employees' diversity beliefs and the organization's approach to diversity management relate to each another. As an effort to fill this research gap in the diversity ideology literature, our chapter presents an interactive diversity ideology model that incorporates the intersection of the two diversity ideology levels (individual and organizational) and the two ideological frameworks (colorblind and multiculturalism).

Similar to Chrobat-Mason and Thomas' (2002) racial identity interactive model, we proposed a model of individual and organizational diversity ideology relationships. Despite the framework adapted, our model presented here is distinctive from the racial identity interactive model. Chrobot-Mason and Thomas' model focuses on individuals' progress through a series of one's own racial identity group development in relation to the organization's approach to managing diversity. In comparison, the diversity ideology interactive model focuses on the congruency between both organizations' and employees' *beliefs on how to respond to diversity* in the workplace. The second distinction between the two models is that the racial identity interactive model focuses exclusively on racial group differences and development; whereas, the diversity ideology interactive model incorporates more than just race within the component of diversity. Diversity here encompasses also gender, sexual orientation, age, religion, disability, or other sources of historic and socially significant difference that may shape diversity ideology in the workplace. Individuals that may represent the dominant group in terms of race may still feel marginalized on the basis of other aspects of their identity and, moreover, evidence suggests that demographic characteristics of individuals may interact to shape their experience in the workplace (c.f., Berdahl & Moore, 2006).

We propose an interactive model that crosses the two ideologies at the individual and organizational level resulting in a fourfold typology: multiculturalism parallel, colorblindness parallel, incongruent minority group, and incongruent majority group. We will discuss the model from a majority and minority employee assessment and how it may serve as a work-related advantage or disadvantage along the intersecting ideology relationships. The incongruent typology is presented in alignment with previous research on group differences in diversity ideology preferences (e.g., Verkuyten, 2005). Studies have shown that majority group members tend to endorse a colorblind ideology to a greater degree than minority group members (Ryan et al., 2007, 2010; Schofield, 1986, 2007; see also Rattan & Ambady, 2013); whereas, minority group members were found to more likely endorse multiculturalism than are majority group members (Arends-Tóth & van de Vijver, 2003; Verkuyten, 2005). In essence, incongruent minority group employee typology is a minority employee holding multiculturalism beliefs in a colorblind organization. Incongruent majority group employee typology is an employee belonging in the majority group with a colorblind ideology in a multicultural organization.

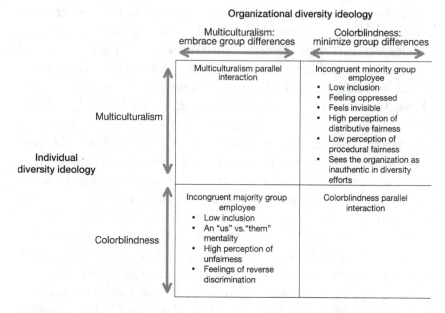

FIGURE 9.1
Interactive model of individual and organizational diversity ideology on diverse employees' outcomes

Our interactive model also integrates Hahn et al.'s (2010) proposition of these two ideological approaches on diversity to be organized along two different dimensions rather than just one. As shown in our figure, an arrow represents a separate valence dimension for each ideology. A person can vary along the multiculturalism dimension to the extent of positively embracing group differences; the colorblindness dimension is the degree of the person's diversity beliefs in minimizing group differences. In concurrence with Hahn and colleagues' contention, we suggest that these ideological frameworks are to be cautiously discussed when they are examined along the same continuum. As mentioned earlier, the end goals of both ideologies are analogous to achieving equality and positive group relations. However, it is their different approach to attaining these outcomes that leads to mixed findings of relatively favorable to unfavorable responses among different group memberships. Thus, our model is more representative of the true nature and related outcomes of each diversity ideology when evaluated along two dimensions as opposed to one.

We propose that organizations and employees will receive the greatest benefits when there is a fit or match of diversity attitudes, beliefs, and values between the organization and its members (i.e., multiculturalism parallel and colorblindness parallel relationships). Both ideologies have been linked to positive consequences (e.g., Wolsko et al., 2000) and a common egalitarian orientation (Levin et al., 2012). Therefore, the greater degree of alignment between the ideology levels along either the multiculturalism or colorblindness dimension, the greater the probability of producing positive outcomes. We also draw this assertion from the person–organization (P–O) fit literature—organizational members associate positive affect when there is congruence between organizational values and individual values (Chatman, 1989; Kristof, 1996; Ng & Burke, 2005). Kristof (1996) provided a holistic conceptual definition of P–O fit as the level of compatibility between people and organizations that results in satisfying the needs of at least one of the entities and/or possesses similar fundamental character- istics. An organization that satisfies the needs, desires, and preferences of its employees generates a greater perception of P–O fit. The fundamental characteristics consist of culture, values, goals, and attitudes that the organization or person possesses. Based on the P–O fit, these shared fundamental characteristics are related to employees' work attitude and behavior (Elfenbein & O'Reilly, 2007; Resick, Baltes, & Shantz, 2007). A high level of P–O fit has been found related to greater employee job satisfaction (Ambrose, Arnaud, & Schminke, 2008; Liu, Liu, & Hu, 2010) and fewer turnover intentions (Chatman, 1991; Vancouver, Millsap, & Peters, 1994). Parallel to the P–O fit research, diversity attitudes, values, and beliefs possessed by the organization and people would be categorized in the fundamental characteristics description. In this case, the overlapping shared beliefs and attitudes on how to respond to diversity in the workplace between the employee and the organization may lead to more positive work-related outcomes that meet the needs of the organization and/or employees.

On the other hand, the incongruence between the organization and its members makes the interactive diversity ideology model more complex and dynamic. The discrepancy between the organization and its employees' ideology may result in either diversity resistance or acceptance within the workplace. Employees who believe that group differences should be ignored in the workplace may express resistance to the organization's diversity pressure and encouragement to acknowledge group differences. It's this discrepancy between organization and individual ideology levels that may pin one ideological diversity approach as having negative affects over the other. Under the proposition of diversity ideology as multidimensional, the incongruent typologies may be the least fruitful and developmental relationships for either the organization or employees since the ideologies are grounded in two different dimensions. Again using the P–O fit theory to support our interactive model proposed consequences. This notion of P–O fit or lack of has been found related to employees' tendency to act counterproductively (e.g., aggression and hostility among people, deviant behavior by employees) (Sharkawi, Rahim, & AzuraDahalan, 2013). Similarly, we project that a poor fit of diversity values and attitudes between the organization and employees may result in negative affective outcomes. As mentioned, the incongruent typologies may be more likely associated to negative outcomes than the parallel typologies but the discrepancy may operate differently by group membership.

An incongruent colorblind organization level and multicultural individual level relationship may more likely pose as a challenge for minority group employees, referred to here as the incongruent minority group employee typology. Minority employees who endorse multiculturalism in the workplace may feel marginalized and oppressed by their organization's colorblind diversity efforts. Ironically, the minimization of social categories and differences may likely foster aversive effects for minority groups who believe that differences do matter and should be recognized. For instance, Plaut et al. (2009) found that Whites' colorblindness negatively affected minorities' psychological engagement. Although the study did not evaluate diversity ideology at the organizational level, other research argues that the dominant group's beliefs are strongly instilled in the organization's own culture and attitudes as a result of their dominant numeric representation and access to power in most American corporations and industries (see Plaut et al., 2011 discussion). In essence, we speculate similar affects within this typology for minority group employees.

In a situation of an incongruent majority group employee relationship, the organization's multicultural practices and policies that construe attitudes toward recognizing group differences within the workplace may foster an initial "us" versus "them" mentality among majority group members who endorse a colorblind ideology. Majority group employees that fit this typology may likely misinterpret their organization's diversity efforts as a system of heightening social categories, and challenge the status and preservation of their dominant group identity. However, it is possible that how the organization delivers the multicultural orientation in their policies and structure and the length of exposure to these policies may result in positive outcomes for majority group members who originally held a colorblind ideology. Within this intersecting relationship, the discrepancy of ideologies between the two levels may exert temporary resistance by the dominant group, which could in turn evolve into a developmental process for employees over time.

Worker Outcomes

How do the interactive diversity ideology relationships affect diverse employees' outcomes? We recommend the importance for future research to examine the interaction between individuals' and organizations' diversity ideologies congruence and whether it presents as a negative, beneficial, or developmental process for employees. More specifically, we propose that the intersecting ideology across levels may have different impacts on minority and majority employees' perception of inclusion and organizational justice (see Figure 9.1). Employees that endorse multiculturalism may view a colorblind organization as threatening to the valuing of employees' unique backgrounds, which may hamper their perceived inclusion and whether they believe the organization appropriately considers differences in decision making. By contrast, employees that endorse colorblindness may feel uncomfortable in a multicultural organization and may view organizations that emphasize differences as violating values of individualism and meritocracy (see Verkuyten, 2005), ultimately undermining perceptions of fairness.

Inclusion. It would be presumptuous to insinuate that merely increasing diversity in the organization equates to an inclusive work environment. More often than not, organizations assume that employment of diverse groups is sufficient to satisfy diversity goals. However, diversity and inclusion conceptually should not be used interchangeably or exclusively discussed as a part of a causal relationship. Mor Barak and Cherin (1998) conceptualized perception of inclusion as a degree to which the employee feels integrated into critical organizational processes such as access to resources and information, voice and influence in decision making, having the opportunity to engage in social and professional networking, and being valued by other employees. Roberson (2006) also highlighted the difference between diversity and inclusion. Diversity of itself places a greater emphasis on the demographic composition of the organization (i.e., the numbers), whereas inclusion focuses on organizational members' degree of involvement and integration into organizational processes. Diversity without inclusion is just a numbers game that maintains and supports the status quo, thus limiting and excluding minorities from career advancements and networks.

How important is inclusion in the workplace? Thomas and Ely (1996) indicated that the ability of diversity to hamper or improve work performance depends on the level of perceived inclusion. Perception of inclusion has been found to be positively associated with organizational commitment (Cho & Mor Barak, 2008; Mor Barak, Findler, & Wind, 2001) and employees express a greater degree of job satisfaction in relation to their feelings of being accepted and included in their organization (Lawler, 1994). Inclusion has also been found to directly influence employees' perceptions of psychological well-being and lowered stress (Findler, Wind, & Mor Barak, 2007; Greenhaus, Parasuraman, & Wormly, 1990; Mor Barak et al., 1998).

The core of diversity ideology is rooted in social group dynamics that is likewise found in inclusion. The overarching conceptual frameworks for diversity ideology and inclusion are theoretically linked to the psychological process of group identification, classification, and attachment (i.e., social identity theory) (Cho & Mor Barak, 2008; Findler et al., 2007), in essence implying a potential relationship between the two variables. To our knowledge, one study to date evaluated the association of diversity ideology and inclusion. Plaut et al. (2011) used an implicit test of Whites' cognitive association of inclusion and exclusion to multicultural and colorblind ideologies. In Study 1, they found Whites implicitly associated multicultural ideology with words denoting exclusion. Their second study incorporated an all-inclusive multicultural ideology that framed Whites as part of multiculturalism and found no implicit association between multiculturalism and exclusion. Their study provided preliminary grounds for examining the relationship between perceived inclusion and diversity ideologies. Proponents of colorblindness profess that by creating a unifying organizational identity while curtailing the salience of differences, organizations will promote an inclusive work environment where treatment of employees is not contingent on their race or biases that may be elicited from group categorizations are minimized (Stevens et al., 2008; Thomas & Chrobot-Mason, 2005). By contrast, multiculturalism is said to foster the recognition and valuing of differences, leading to unification and inclusion without needing to suppress unique aspects of its members to achieve those goals (Stevens et al., 2008; Thomas & Chrobot-Mason, 2005).

Our model proposes that a parallel ideology relationship is more likely to induce an inclusive work environment. A positive climate for inclusion depends on the diversity values and beliefs held by those composing the workforce and the diversity practices implemented within the organization; although, we suspect that a parallel multicultural ideology is the ideal relationship in facilitating greater inclusion by both group memberships. Employees who believe that group differences should be valued and groups should be treated equally regardless of differences may feel more included within a multicultural organization that practices equal treatment, but yet recognize the value of employees' unique identities (Stevens et al., 2008).

Opposite to the previous proposition, incongruent diversity ideology typology may foster the least inclusive corporate environment for the majority and minority organizational members. Majority group employees who espouse colorblindness in a multicultural organization may express sentiments of division and alienation that thus foster exclusion. In this case, we argue that the majority group employee may see the organization's emphasis on unique groups as building an "us" versus "them" workplace climate. Consequently, these employees feel less belonging to the company because they may perceive the organization as operating not as one unit. In contrast, minority group employees with a multiculturalism ideology in an organization that minimizes group distinctions (i.e., incongruent minority group employee) may report feelings of oppression and invisibility, thus generating perceptions of lower inclusion. Under this typology, minority group employees may feel rejected and undervalued by the organization's efforts to downplay group differences. Minority group employees who believe that their unique identities contribute to the organization's effectiveness and success may feel less belonging to the organization that chooses to ignore employees' unique identities.

Organizational Justice. Organizational justice is referred to as an employee's perception of equity and fairness on outcomes offered by their organization (Beugré, 1998; Cropanzano & Greenberg, 1997; Greenberg, 1987). Fairness perceptions have been commonly explored to understand workplace attitudes and behaviors (Ambrose, Hess, & Ganesan, 2007;

Cropanzano & Rupp, 2003). Employees' perceptions of fairness are positively associated with career satisfaction, supervisory trust, and commitment (Bakhshi, Kumar, & Rani, 2009; Colquitt, Conlon, Wesson, Porter, & Ng, 2001; Cohen-Charash & Spector, 2001; Kumar, Bakhshi, & Rani, 2009; McFarlin & Sweeney, 1992; Martin & Bennett, 1996; Thomas & Nagalingappa, 2012). Pay satisfaction has also been associated with perceived fairness in decision making (Folger & Konovsky, 1989; McFarlin & Sweeney, 1992; Xiaoyi & Wang, 2008). Employees' reactions to perceived unfairness can result in retaliation (Skarlicki & Folger, 1997) and turnover intentions (Dailey & Kirk, 1992; Fatt, Khin, & Heng, 2010; Harr & Spell, 2009; Kim & Leung, 2007; Kim, Solomon, & Jang, 2012).

The range of organizational justice research is neither under developed nor limited in organizational psychology. In spite of this notion, no known work has explicitly explored the relationship between organizational justice and diversity ideology. Research on justice perceptions and diversity in the workplace has not been exhausted (Richard & Kirby, 1999; Roberson & Stevens, 2006). We draw most of our theoretical support from diversity management and organizational justice literature. One study by Knowles et al. (2009) evaluated the relationship between Whites' endorsement of colorblindness and organizational justice dimensions (i.e., procedural and distributive). The dimensionality of organizational justice consists of mainly distributive and procedural fairness (Chen, Lin, Tung, & Ko, 2008). *Distributive justice* refers to the perceived fairness of the decision and outcomes for the organizational member. *Procedural justice* refers to the perceived fairness of the process used to influence these organizational decisions and outcomes (Folger & Konovsky, 1989). According to Knowles et al.'s findings, colorblindness may be associated with different justice principles—colorblindness as a procedural justice principle is associated with supporting equal treatment in a way that reasserts the status quo; whereas, colorblindness as a distributive justice principle is associated with decreasing inequalities between groups. Richard and Kirby (1999) evaluated the role of justice perceptions on attitudes toward organizations' diversity programs. Additionally, Roberson and Stevens (2006) explored how perceptions of justice influenced employees' accounts of diversity-related incidents as negative or positive. Both studies support fairness as being fundamental to diversity management (Ely & Thomas, 2001; Mor Barak et al., 1998). Recently, Fujimoto, Hartel, and Azmat (2013) proposed a diversity justice management model that integrated organizational justice principles into diversity management literature. Their conceptual framework entails diversity-oriented work events to predict organizational justice, which, in turn influences employees' affective, behavioral, cognitive outcomes (i.e., diversity-reference outcomes). All organizational justice and diversity references have framed diversity around organizations' diversity practices and policies. Thus, the research question posed is, does the intersecting diversity ideology influence employees' degree of perceived organizational justice?

Since diversity ideology is rooted with the intention to promote fairness, we would suspect a relationship between organizational justice and diversity ideology. We propose a positive relationship between parallel ideology interactions and perception of organizational justice. Previous research has shown that both ideologies are effective in garnering the intended benefits of diversity in its own way (e.g., Wolsko et al., 2000). However, we encourage a multicultural ideology match between the organization and employees to foster a higher perception of fairness. We based our contention for this typology on the notion that individuals that support multiculturalism have a greater understanding of racial discrimination (Verkuyten & Martinovic, 2006) and more positive perceptions of diversity practices as a mechanism for reducing inequalities (e.g., Simmons, Wittig, & Grant, 2010; Verkuyten, 2005; Wolsko, Park, & Judd, 2006). Hence, they may have a more keen understanding of initiatives used by their organization to create a level playing field for all groups and view those practices as more fair. Because multiculturalism can foster appreciating all backgrounds when effectively framed, it has the potential to enhance the perception that all are included in and benefit from the organization's diversity management, which may then in turn create more positive evaluations of the outcomes of those efforts.

Organizational justice is expected to be lower in the incongruent majority group employee typology. Majority group employees who endorse colorblindness may perceive unfairness with the company's multicultural decision-making process (procedural justice) and outcomes (distributive justice). The perceived unfairness from organizations' multicultural diversity practices may result from majority group employees' belief that group differences are irrelevant to how work-related decisions are made. Most importantly, the acknowledgment of group differences breaks down the system of inequality that has been historically used in most organizations' process of employment decisions that simultaneously supports the dominant group power structure and status quo. Colorblind endorsed majority group employees may regard distributive justice using a multicultural approach as a form of reverse discrimination, thus inducing perceptions of unfairness. These majority group employees may mistakenly perceive the organization's acknowledgment of group differences as an effort to meet diversity quotas across corporate ranks in advancement decisions. Thus, this perception elicits unfairness that a minority group employee received a promotion ahead of a qualified majority group employee.

We suspect opposite directions of perceived fairness in the incongruent minority group employees' typology across the justice dimensions. We based these propositions on Knowles et al.'s (2009) research findings on the relationship between colorblindness and justice dimensions. Minority group employees with multicultural ideology may feel that the organization's colorblind procedural justice may be entrenched in prejudice, stereotyping, and bias. These implicit inequities help maintain the norm and position minority groups at a disadvantage by perpetuating existing inequalities and, in turn, heighten their perception of unfair procedures. On the other hand, organizations that use the colorblind approach in their distributive justice (i.e., outcomes, allocations) may contribute to higher perceptions of fairness by minority group employees. Despite minority employees endorsing multicultural beliefs, they may support the belief that organizations should not focus on social categories and group differences (i.e., colorblind perspective) in determining employment outcomes such as advancement or compensation, but focus more on the merit, skills, and competence of the employee under evaluation. Our argument is supported by the distributive justice concept of outcomes being allocated based on talent, effort, and hard work.

CONCLUSION

Although diversity ideology has garnered recent attention in the debate over the best approach for organizational diversity management and promoting inclusion (Stevens et al., 2008; Thomas & Chrobot-Mason, 2005), limited research has examined the interacting role between organizational and employees' own diversity beliefs in work-related outcomes. Previous research has explored how the endorsement of particular ideologies, colorblindness or multiculturalism, is related to racial bias and behavioral prejudice (Holoien & Shelton, 2012; Richeson & Nussbaum, 2004; Vorauer et al., 2009; Wolsko et al., 2000), support for diversity friendly practices (Simmons et al., 2010; Verkuyten, 2005; Wolsko et al., 2006), and the concept of inclusion (Plaut et al., 2011). The present chapter had two primary purposes. One was to present a model that extended these findings by proposing that both the individual and organizational espoused diversity ideologies and their interaction impact employees' perception of inclusiveness at work and organizational justice. A second was to acknowledge that a person's group membership (majority or minority group status) might determine their individual diversity beliefs and how they interact with their organization's diversity beliefs, thus leading to positive or negative work-related outcomes.

The proposed interactive model provides an important practical tool for managers and executives to establish a more inclusive and just organization. In order to understand the role of diversity ideology in the workplace, practitioners must first assess diversity ideology dimensions at the employee level as well as the organizational level. Consequently, based on the assessed typology, the organization's management team can recognize the potential associated outcomes of the congruent or incongruent diversity ideology relationships. Acknowledging the interdependent diversity ideology relationships may provide insights for practitioners in various work domains (e.g., educational institutions, business corporations, military sector) on how to respond to majority or minority group employees' resistance to diversity initiatives of multiculturalism or colorblindness.

In terms of achieving organizational fairness, as noted by Fujimoto et al. (2013), "the realization of actual and perceived fairness depends upon the extent to which a justice-based decision-making process is present or absent in the organization, and relies heavily on the presence of justice responsive managers" (p. 159; see also Fortin & Fellenz, 2008). The organization's level of influence on molding the individual diversity ideology can ameliorate potential negative consequences (e.g., unjust procedures or outcomes) of incongruent diversity ideology relationships. Based on our proposed model, organizational inclusiveness consists of a work environment that endorses similar diversity beliefs among the company and its members. Therefore, organizations can consistently motivate employees to adopt a diversity ideological framework that is parallel to the diversity values that are embedded in the company's policies and practices.

We believe that our model may also provide diversity effectiveness strategies for training and development. In line with Chrobat-Mason and Thomas' (2002) suggested implications, our interactive model can provide insights on how to improve diversity training effectiveness. Diversity trainers and administrators would be more aware and equipped to develop diversity training programs that integrate relevant and beneficial diversity tools and content in conjunction with the needs of the different interactive diversity ideology relationships. Assessments of the diversity ideology at each level will facilitate the development of the diversity training approach. The training format can highlight and address employees' possible misconceptions and resistance toward the organization's diversity ideology (see Chrobot-Mason, Hays-Thomas, & Wishik, 2008). For instance, given there is an incongruent majority group employee typology, the diversity training can accentuate how both groups may benefit from celebrating group differences rather than ignoring them.

Our model is not entirely exhaustive and should be regarded as a general interactive model to facilitate our understanding of the role of diversity ideology in the workplace. More importantly, depending on contextual and individual factors, diversity ideology at both levels is subjected to change. Therefore, we suggest a few additional areas for future development that were not discussed in this chapter but yet may have significant influence on work-related outcomes. Purdie-Vaughns et al. (2008) found that organizational ideologies may be differentially related to the psychological outcomes of employees, depending on the demographic composition of the organization, suggesting that ideology may be malleable, as they found minorities respond more favorably to a colorblind, diverse organization than to a colorblind, White organization. Similarly, Knowles and colleagues (2009) also propose the dynamic nature of ideologies and that "rather than pulling static ideologies 'off the shelf', individuals are able to mold ideologies—even ones with which they usually disagree—into a form that suits their goals in the moment" (p. 866). It will be necessary to examine the implications of diversity ideology across organizations with different demographic compositions (e.g., predominantly male or female and White or minority). Moreover, reactions to endorsed ideology by the organization may depend on the degree of employee diversity within the company (Apfelbaum, Norton, & Sommers, 2012).

The second area for future research is the inclusion of other potential individual factors, as the research has provided support of personality (e.g., Gutiérrez & Unzueta, 2010; Plaut et al., 2011) and cultural factors (Gutiérrez & Unzueta, 2010) influencing diversity ideology preference. A person's diversity ideology may modify depending on their tenure with the organization. The longer the person is employed and strongly identified with their organization, the greater the probability of their individual ideology becoming aligned with the organizational diversity ideology. Interestingly, it has been suggested that employees that value colorblindness may benefit from exposure to multicultural ideals that prepare them to adapt and perform in increasingly diverse organizations (Chrobot-Mason & Thomas, 2002). Another consideration is the person's level of diversity competence over time. An organizational member's increased exposure to diversity and intergroup relations may subsequently affect their diversity ideology.

The third area that future research should explore is whether the interactive model typologies have the same effect on other types of work-related outcomes across group memberships. Would the incongruent typologies have the same result for job satisfaction, commitment, turnover intentions, or citizenship behavior outcomes? Moreover, would these outcomes impact majority and minority group employees similarly or differently? This only further suggests the complexity of the proposed interactive model and the need for future research on intersecting ideologies that exist at multiple levels of organizations, and the subsequent outcomes for both individual worker and organizations.

NOTE

1. We acknowledge that there are several ideological frameworks on group relations existing within the literature (e.g., assimilation, multiculturalism, colorblindness). Multiculturalism and colorblindness were found to be hierarchy attenuating in nature when operated with an egalitarian orientation as opposed to assimilation (Levin et al., 2012). Aligned with the purpose of our chapter, we will frame our propositions around the two dominant ideologies, colorblindness and multiculturalism.

REFERENCES

Ambrose, M., Arnaud, A., & Schminke, M. (2008). Individual moral development and ethical climate: The influence of person–organization fit on job attitudes. *Journal of Business Ethics, 77*(3), 323–333.

Ambrose, M., Hess, R. L., & Ganesan, S. (2007). The relationship between justice and attitudes: An examination of justice effects on event and system-related attitudes. *Organizational Behavior and Human Decision Processes, 103,* 21–36.

Apfelbaum, E. P., Norton, M. I., & Sommers, S. R. (2012). Racial colorblindness: Emergence, practice, and implications. *Current Directions in Psychological Science, 21,* 205–209.

Arends-Tóth, J., & van de Vijver, F. J. R. (2003). Multiculturalism and acculturation: Views of Dutch and Turkish–Dutch. *European Journal of Social Psychology, 33,* 249–266.

Bakhshi, A., Kumar, K., & Rani, E. (2009). Organizational justice perceptions as predictor of job satisfaction and organization commitment. *Journal of Business and Management, 4,* 145–154.

Banks, J. A. (2004). Multicultural education: Historical developments, dimensions, and practice. In J. A. Banks, & C. A. M. Banks (Eds.), *Handbook of research in multicultural education.* (pp. 3–30). San Francisco, CA: Jossey Bass.

Bennett, C. I. (1995). *Comprehensive multicultural education: Theory and practice* (3rd ed.). Boston, MA: Allyn & Bacon.

Berdahl, J. L., & Moore, C. (2006). Workplace harassment: Double jeopardy for minority women. *Journal of Applied Psychology, 91,* 426–436.

Berry, J. W. (1984). Cultural relations in plural societies: Alternatives to segregation and their socio-psychological implications. In M. B. Brewer & N. Miller (Eds.), *Groups in contact* (pp. 11–27). New York: Academic Press.

Beugré, C. (1998). Implementing business process reengineering: the role of organizational justice. *The Journal of Applied Behavioral Science, 34,* 347–360.

Brewer, M. B. (1997). The social psychology of intergroup relations: Can research inform practice. *Journal of Social Issues, 53,* 197–211.

Chatman J. (1989). Improving interactional organizational research: A model of person–organization fit. *Academy of Management, 14,* 333–349.

Chatman J. (1991). Matching people and organizations: Selection and socialization in public accounting firms. *Administrative Science Quarterly, 36,* 459–484.

Chen, Y., Lin, C., Tung, Y., & Ko, Y. (2008). Associations of organization justice and ingratiation with organizational citizenship behavior: The beneficiary perspective. *Social Behavior and Personality, 36,* 289—302.

Cho, S., & Mor Barak, M. E. (2008). Understanding of diversity and inclusion in a perceived homogeneous culture: A study of organizational commitment and job performance among Korean employees. *Administration in Social Work, 32(4),* 100–126.

Chrobot-Mason, D., Hays-Thomas, R., & Wishik, H. (2008). Understanding and defusing resistance to diversity training and learning. In K. M. Thomas (Ed.), *Diversity resistance in organizations* (pp. 23–54). Mahwah, NJ: Erlbaum.

Chrobot-Mason, D., & Thomas, K.M. (2002). Minority employees in majority organizations: The intersection of individual and organizational racial identity in the workplace. *Human Resource Development Review, 1,* 323–344.

Cohen-Charash, Y., & Spector, P. E. (2001). The role of justice in organizations: A meta-analysis. *Organizational Behavior and Human Decision Processes, 86,* 278—321.

Colquitt, J. A., Conlon, D. E., Wesson, M. J., Porter, C. O. L. H., & Ng, K. Y. (2001). Justice at the millennium: A meta-analytic review of 25 years of organizational justice research. *Journal of Applied Psychology, 86*, 425–445.

Cox, T., Jr. (1991). The multicultural organization. *Academy of Management Executive, 5*, 35–47.

Cox, T., & Finley-Nickelson, J. (1991). Models of acculturation for intra-organizational cultural diversity. *Canadian Journal of Administrative Sciences, 8*, 90–99.

Cropanzano, R., & Greenberg, J. (1997). Progress in organizational justice: Tunneling through maze. In C. L. Cooper, & I. T. Robertson (Eds.), *International review of industrial and organizational psychology*, Vol. 12 (pp. 317–372). Chichester: John Wiley & Sons.

Cropanzano, R., & Rupp, D. E. (2003). An overview of organizational justice: Implication for work motivation. In L. W. Porter, G. A. Bigley, & R. M. Steers (Eds.), *Motivation and Work Behavior* (pp. 82–95). Burr Ridge, IL: McGraw-Hill Irwin.

Dailey, R. C., & Kirk, D. J. (1992). Distributive and procedural justice as antecedents of job dissatisfaction and intent to turnover. *Human Relations, 45*(3), 305–317.

Dovidio, J. F., Gaertner, S. L., & Saguy, T. (2009). Commonality and the complexity of "we": Social attitudes and social change. *Personality and Social Psychology Review, 13*, 3–20.

Elfenbein, H. A., & O'Reilly, C. A. III. (2007). Fitting in: The effects of relational demography and person–culture fit on group process and performance. *Group Organizational Management, 32*, 109–142.

Ely, R. J., & Thomas, D. A. (2001). Cultural diversity at work: The effects of diversity perspectives on work group processes and outcomes. *Administrative Science Quarterly, 46*, 229–273.

Embrick, D. G. (2011). The diversity ideology in the business world: A new oppression for a new age. *Critical Sociology, 37*, 541–556.

Fatt, C. K., Khin, E. W. S., & Heng. T. N. (2010). The impact of organizational justice on employee's job satisfaction: The Malaysian companies' perspective. *American Journal of Economic and Business Administration, 2*(1), 56–63.

Findler, L., Wind, L. H., & Mor Barak, M. E. (2007). The challenge of workforce management in a global society: Modeling the relationship between diversity, inclusion, organizational culture, and employee well-being, job satisfaction, and organizational commitment. *Administration in Social Work, 31*(3), 63–94.

Folger, R., & Konovsky, M. A. (1989). Effects of procedural and distributive justice on reactions to pay raise decisions. *The Academy of Management Journal, 32*(1), 115–130.

Fredrickson, G. M. (1999). Models of American ethnic relations: A historical perspective. In D. A. Prentice, & D. T. Miller (Eds.), *Cultural divides: Understanding and overcoming group conflict* (pp. 23–34). New York: Russell Sage.

Fortin, M., & Fellenz, M. (2008). Hypocrisies of fairness: Towards a more reflexive ethical base in organizational justice research and practice. *Journal of Business Ethics, 78*, 415–433.

Fujimoto, Y., Hartel, C. E. J., & Azmat, F. (2013). Towards a diversity justice management model: Integrating organizational justice and diversity management. *Social Responsibility Journal, 9*, 148–166.

Gaertner, S. L., Dovidio, J. F., Banker, B. S., Houlette, M., Johnson, K., & McGlynn, E. (2000). Reducing intergroup conflict: From superordinate goals to decategorization, recategorization and mutual differentiation. *Group Dynamics, 4*, 98–114.

Greenberg, J. (1987). A taxonomy of organizational justice theories. *Academy of Management Review, 12*, 9–22.

Greenhaus, J. H., Parasuraman, S., & Wormley, W. M. (1990). Effects of race on organizational experiences, job performance evaluations, and career outcomes. *Academy of Management Journal, 33*, 64–86.

Gutiérrez, A. S., & Unzueta, M. M. (2010). The effect of interethnic ideologies of the likability of stereotypic vs. counterstereotypic minority targets. *Journal of Experimental Social Psychology, 46*, 775–784.

Hahn, A., Judd, C. M., & Park, B. (2010). Thinking about group differences: Ideologies and national identities. *Psychological Inquiry, 21*,120–126.

Harr, M. J., & Spell, S. C. (2009). How does distributive justice affect work attitudes? The moderating effects of autonomy. *The International Journal of Human Resource Management, 20*,1827–1842.

Hirschfeld, L. A. (1996). *Race in the making.* Cambridge, MA: MIT Press.

Holoien, D. S., & Shelton, J. N. (2012). You deplete me: The cognitive costs of colorblindness on ethnic minorities. *Journal of Experimental Social Psychology, 48*(2), 562–565.

Jones, J. M. (1998). Psychological knowledge and the new American dilemma of race. *Journal of Social Issues, 54*, 641–662.

Kim, B. Y. (2006). Managing a workforce diversity: Developing a learning organization. *Journal of Human Resources in Hospitality & Tourism, 5*, 69–90.

Kim, T. K., Solomon, P., & Jang, C. (2012). Organizational justice and social workers' intentions to leave agency positions. *Social Work Research, 36*, 31–39.

Kim, Tae-Yeol, & Leung, K. (2007). Forming and reacting to overall fairness: A cross-cultural comparison. *Organizational Behavior & Human Decision Processes, 104*, 83–95.

Knowles, E. D., Lowery, B. S., Hogan, C. M., & Chow, R. M. (2009). On the malleability of ideology: Motivated construals of colorblindness. *Journal of Personality and Social Psychology, 96*, 857–869.

Kristof, A. L. (1996). Person–organization fit: An integrative review of its conceptualizations, measurement, and implications. *Personnel Psychology, 49*, 1–49.

Kumar, K., Bakhshi, A., & Rani, E. (2009). Organizational justice perceptions as predictor of job satisfaction and organizational commitment. *IUP Journal of Management Research, 8*, 24–37.

Lawler, E. III (1994). Creating the high involvement organization. In J. Galbraith, & E. Lawler III (Eds.), *Organizing for the future* (pp. 172–193). San Francisco, CA: Jossey-Bass.

Levin, S., Matthews, M., Guimond, S., Sidanius, J., Pratto, F., Kteily, N., & Pitpitan, E. V. (2012). Assimilation, multiculturalism, and colorblindness: Mediated and moderated relationships between social dominance orientation and prejudice. *Journal of Experimental Social Psychology, 48*, 207–212.

Liu, B., Liu, J., & Hu, J. (2010). Person–organization fit, job satisfaction and turnover intention: An empirical study in the Chinese Public Sector. *Social Behavior and Personality, 38*(8), 615–626.

McFarlin, D. B., & Sweeney, P. D. (1992). Distributive and procedural justice as predictors of satisfaction with personal and organizational outcomes. *Academy of Management Journal, 35*, 626–637.

Markus, H. R., Steele, C. M., & Steele, D. M. (2000). Colorblindness as a barrier to inclusion: Assimilation and non-immigrant minorities. *Daedalus, 129*, 233–259.

Martin, C. L., & Bennett, N. (1996). The role of justice judgments in explaining the relationship between job satisfaction and organizational commitment. *Group & Organizational Management, 21*(1), 84–104.

Mor Barak, M. E., & Cherin, D. A. (1998). A tool to expand organizational understanding of workforce diversity: Exploring a measure of inclusion–exclusion. *Administration in Social Work, 22*(1), 47–64.

Mor Barak, M. E., Cherin, D. A., & Berkman, S. (1998). Organizational and personal dimensions in diversity climate: Ethnic and gender differences in employee diversity perceptions. *Journal of Applied Behavioral Sciences, 34*, 82–104.

Mor Barak, M. E., Findler, L., & Wind, L. H. (2001). Diversity, inclusion, and commitment to organizations: International empirical explorations. *Journal of Behavioral and Applied Management, 2*, 70–91.

Morrison, K., & Chung, A. H. (2011). "White" or "European American"? Self-identifying labels influence majority group members' interethnic attitudes. *Journal of Experimental Social Psychology, 47*, 165–170.

Ng, E. S. W., & Burke, R. J. (2005). Person–organization fit and the war for talent: Does diversity management make a difference? *International Journal of Human Resource Management, 16*, 1195–1210.

Park, B., & Judd, C. M. (2005). Rethinking the link between categorization and prejudice within the social cognition perspective. *Personality and Social Psychology Review, 9*, 108–130.

Plaut, V. C. (2002). Cultural models of diversity: The psychology of difference and inclusion. In R. Shweder, M. Minow, & H. R. Markus (Eds.), *Engaging cultural differences: The multicultural challenge in a liberal democracy* (pp. 365–395). New York: Russell Sage.

Plaut, V. C. (2010). Diversity science: Why and how difference makes a difference. *Psychological Inquiry, 21*, 77–99.

Plaut, V. C., Garnett, F. G., Buffardi, L. E., & Sanchez-Burks, J. (2011). "What about me?" Perceptions of exclusion and Whites' reactions to multiculturalism. *Journal of Personality and Social Psychology, 101*, 337–353.

Plaut, V. C., Thomas, K. M., & Goren, M. J. (2009). Is multiculturalism or color blindness better for minorities? *Psychological Science, 20*, 444–446.

Plessy v. Ferguson, 163 U.S. 537, 559 (1896) (Harlan, J., dissenting).

Prentice, D. A., & Miller, D. T. (1999). The psychology of cultural contact. In D. A. Prentice, & D. T. Miller (Eds.), *Cultural divides: Understanding and overcoming group conflict* (pp. 1–19). New York: Russell Sage.

Purdie-Vaughns, V., Steele, C. M., Davies, P. G., Ditlmann, R., & Crosby, J. R. (2008). Social identity contingencies: How diversity cues signal threat or safety for African Americans in mainstream institutions. *Journal of Personality and Social Psychology, 94*(4), 615–630.

Ratner, S. (1984). Horace M. Kallen and cultural pluralism. *Modern Judaism, 4*, 185–200.

Rattan, A., & Ambady, N. (2013). Diversity ideologies and intergroup relations: An examination of colorblindness and multiculturalism. *European Journal of Social Psychology, 43*, 12–21.

Resick, C. J., Baltes, B. B., & Shantz, C. A. (2007). Person–organization fit and work-related attitudes and decisions: Examining interactive effects with job fit and conscientiousness. *Journal of Applied Psychology, 92*, 1446–1455.

Richard, O., & Kirby, S. (1999), Organizational justice and the justification of workforce diversity programs. *Journal of Business and Psychology, 14*, 109–118.

Richeson, J. A., & Nussbaum, R. J. (2004). The impact of multiculturalism versus color-blindness on racial bias. *Journal of Experimental Social Psychology, 40*(3), 417–423.

Roberson, Q. M. (2006). Disentangling the meanings of diversity and inclusion in organizations. *Group and Organization Management, 31*, 212–236.

Roberson, Q. M., & Stevens, C. K. (2006). Making sense of diversity in the workplace: Organizational justice and language abstraction in employees? Accounts of diversity-related incidents. *Journal of Applied Psychology, 9*, 379–91.

Ryan, C. S., Casas, J. F., & Thompson, B. K. (2010). Interethnic ideology, intergroup perceptions, and cultural orientation. *Journal of Social Issues, 66*, 29–44.

Ryan, C. S., Hunt, J. S., Weible, J. A., Peterson, C. R., & Casas, J. F. (2007). Multicultural and colorblind ideology, stereotypes, and ethnocentrism among Black and White Americans. *Group Processes and Intergroup Relations, 10*, 617–637.

Schlesinger, A. M., Jr. (1992). *The disuniting of America: Reflections on a multicultural society* (2nd ed.). New York: W.W. Norton.

Schofield, J. W. (1986). Causes and consequences of the colorblind perspective. In J. F. Dovidio, & S. L. Gaertner (Eds.), *Prejudice, discrimination, and racism* (pp. 231–254). New York: Academic Press.

Schofield, J. W. (2007). The colorblind perspective in school: Causes and consequences. In J. A. Banks, & C. A. McGee Banks (Eds.), *Multicultural education: Issues and perspectives* (pp. 271–295). New York: Wiley.

Sharkawi, S., Rahim, A. R. A., & AzuraDahalan, N. (2013). Relationship between person organization fit, psychological contract violation on counterproductive work behaviour. *International Journal of Business and Social Science, 4*, 173–183.

Simmons, S. J., Wittig, M. A., & Grant, S. K. (2010). A mutual acculturation model of multicultural campus climate and acceptance of diversity. *Cultural Diversity and Ethnic Minority Psychology, 16*(4), 468–475.

Skarlicki, D. P., & Folger, R. (1997). Retaliation in the workplace: The roles of distributive, procedural, and interactional justice. *Journal of Applied Psychology, 82*(3), 434–443.

Stevens, F. G., Plaut, V. C., & Sanchez-Burks, J. (2008). Unlocking the benefits of diversity all-inclusive multiculturalism and positive organizational change. *The Journal of Applied Behavioral Science, 44*(1), 116–133.

Tajfel, H., & Turner, J. C. (1979). An integrative theory of intergroup conflict. In Austin, W. G., & Worchel, S. (Eds.), *The social psychology of intergroup relations* (pp. 94–109). Monterey, CA: Brooks-Cole.

Tajfel, H., & Turner, J. C. (1986). The social identity theory of intergroup behavior. In S. Worchel, & W. G. Austin (Eds.), *The psychology of intergroup relations* (pp. 7–24). Chicago, IL: Nelson-Hall.

Thomas, D. A., & Ely, R. J. (1996). Making differences matter: A new paradigm for managing diversity. *Harvard Business Review, 74*(5), 79–90.

Thomas, K. M., & Chrobot-Mason, D. (2005). Demographic group based discrimination: Theories and conclusions. In R. Diboye, & A. Colella (Eds.), *Discrimination at work: The psychological and organizational bases* (pp. 63–88). Mahwah, NJ: Laurence Erlbaum Associates.

Thomas, P., & Nagalingappa, G. (2012). Consequences of perceived organizational justice: An empirical study of white-collar employees. *Journal of Arts, Science, & Commerce, 3*, 54–63.

Thompson, C. E., Falls, C., & Berrian, A. (1997). It takes a whole village to raise a child. In C. E. Thompson, & R. T. Carter (Eds.), *Racial identity theory* (pp. 201–217). Mahwah, NJ: Lawrence Erlbaum Associates.

Vancouver, J. B., Millsap, R. E., & Peters, P. A. (1994). Multilevel analysis of organizational goal congruence. *Journal of Applied Psychology, 79*, 666–679.

Verkuyten, M. (2005). Ethnic minority identification and group evaluation among minority and majority groups: Testing the multiculturalism hypothesis. *Journal of Personality and Social Psychology, 88*, 121–138.

Verkuyten, M., & Martinovic, B. (2006). Understanding multicultural attitudes: The role of group status, identification, friendships, and justifying ideologies. *International Journal of Intercultural Relations, 30*(1), 1–18.

Vorauer, J. D., Gagnon, A., & Sasaki, S. J. (2009). Salient intergroup ideology and intergroup interaction. *Psychological Science, 20*(7), 838–845.

Wolsko, C., Park, B., & Judd, C. M. (2006). Considering the Tower of Babel: Correlates of assimilation and multiculturalism among ethnic minority and majority groups in the United States. *Social Justice Research, 19*(3), 277–306.

Wolsko, C., Park, B., Judd, C. M., & Wittenbrink, B. (2000). Framing interethnic ideology: Effects of multicultural and color-blind perspectives on judgments of groups and individuals. *Journal of personality and social psychology, 78*(4), 635–654.

Xiaoyi, W., & Wang, C. (2008). The impact of organizational justice on employees' pay satisfaction, work attitudes and performance in Chinese hotels. *Journal of Human Resources in Hospitality & Tourism, 7*, 181–195.

Zirkel, S. (2008). The influence of multicultural educational practices on student outcomes and intergroup relations. *Teachers College Record, 110*(6), 1147–1181.

10

Diverse and United at the Same Time

Social Psychological Recommendations for a Diverse Workplace

Adam Hahn, Ana P. Nunes, Bernadette Park, and Charles M. Judd

As exemplified in this volume, many social scientists, and especially social psychologists, have recently shown interest in the respective merits of a multicultural as opposed to a colorblind ideology of diversity. Much of the work conducted in organizational settings in this field defines these ideologies in the following way. Multiculturalism is often broadly defined as being sensitive towards cultural differences and the cultural particularities of racial and ethnic minorities, or people of different genders (Stockdale & Nadler, Chapter 6, this volume), or even people of different sexual orientations (Hebl, Martinez, Skorinko, Barron, & King, Chapter 7, this volume). In order to describe an opposite ideology, the concept of "colorblindness" is used to broadly refer to the lack of such sensitivity, either through the ignorance of particular needs of social outgroups, through expecting minorities to assimilate to majority norms (e.g., Plaut, Thomas, & Goren, 2009; Tran, Thomas, & George, Chapter 9, this volume; among others), or even through the simple denial that group membership can have disadvantages and that discrimination of any form still exists (e.g., Neville, Spanierman, & Doan, 2006). Unsurprisingly, most of these analyses find that companies that endorse an attitude toward minorities that has the intention of being sensitive toward their needs (i.e., a multicultural perspective) show better adaptation of minority workers, whereas an oblivious or assimilationist perspective (often called "colorblindness" in these studies as described above) leads to poor adjustment (e.g., Plaut et al., 2009).

The purpose of the current chapter is to examine what social-psychological research has to say about ideologies on diversity, and how it can inform our understanding of models of diversity. Specifically, one aim is to simply introduce the reader to other theories on diversity that have been developed by so-called "basic researchers"—social psychologists who simulate real-world scenarios with social–cognitive methods in the laboratory. Our aim is to introduce the reader to three theories specifically that, at first glance, appear to make somewhat different recommendations. As a second aim we will try to integrate these different perspectives and see whether one common recommendation that satisfies all models can be made. Specifically, we will try to see whether a review of these models might lead to an understanding of interethnic ideologies that goes beyond simply being sensitive toward differences or not. Does social–cognitive laboratory research inform us such that we can make more nuanced and refined recommendations for a diverse work environment that leads to satisfaction among all workers? In the final portion of this chapter we will attempt to make such a recommendation for an organizational setting based on all three models reviewed.

PREVIOUS SOCIAL–COGNITIVE RECOMMENDATIONS

The theories we review in the current chapter specifically concern the social–cognitive literature on diversity that stems from a social-identity perspective. Social identity theory (Tajfel & Turner, 1986) starts from the basic premise that people categorize others in their social world much in the same way as they categorize non-social objects such as furniture into chairs, tables, etc. Importantly, however, people belong to some categories and not others and thus have so-called "social identities" that result from these categorization processes. And these identities have consequences for how people relate to each other. Specifically, much research has shown that people tend to evaluate groups to which they belong ("ingroups") more positively than groups with which they do not identify ("outgroups"; Turner, Brown, & Tajfel, 1979). This tendency can be seen as a product of a primary human motivation, specifically, the need to belong, to feel that one is an accepted, valued, and included member of the social world (Baumeister &

Leary, 1995). In seeking to fulfill this need, individuals navigate a variety of social identities (Correll & Park, 2005; Tajfel & Turner, 1986; Turner, Oakes, Haslam, & McGarty, 1994). At the same time, social beings experience an opposing need, that of viewing the self as a unique and individual member of society (c.f., Optimal Distinctiveness Theory, Brewer, 1991). These opposing needs play out in many aspects of social life, including the culture of organizations that strive to find the right balance between respecting diversity among employees from different ethnic backgrounds, while at the same time wanting all workers to feel included in the larger organizational identity. On the one hand, people have a need to see their group as different from other groups, since this makes their group more meaningful and satisfies a need for uniqueness. On the other hand, seeing other groups as especially different from one's own also strengthens perceived group boundaries, increasing the likelihood that ingroup members will be evaluated more positively than outgroup members.

The question then becomes, how can people be brought to interact positively with individuals even if these people are members of so-called "outgroups," or how can people be brought to appreciate outgroups as a whole? And what amount of perceived differences between groups is the right amount? In the intergroup relations literature, three strategies of how to treat differences between social groups have been proposed (Brewer & Gaertner, 2004; Gaertner et al., 2000; Hornsey & Hogg, 2000a, 2000b). Specifically, *decategorization* describes the idea of tearing down all social categories and reminding people of their common humanity and individuality. The core idea behind this strategy is that the very existence of social categories is, in and of itself, the problem, and people, societies, and companies, should thus strive to abolish them and relate to each other independent of social categories (cf. Brewer & Miller, 1984, 1988; Miller, Brewer, & Edwards, 1985). Thus Barack Obama is not an African American, but rather a successful politician with a law degree from Harvard Law School. *Recategorization* describes a strategy that focuses on emphasizing alternative social dimensions of categorization under which former outgroup members become ingroup members (cf. Gaertner, Dovidio, Anastasio, Bachman, & Rust, 1993; Gaertner, Dovidio, Nier, Ward, & Banker, 1999a). Thus Barack Obama is not an African American but rather simply an American. Lastly, *mutual differentiation and appreciation despite differences* describes a strategy according to which one might leave group boundaries intact and even celebrate them, and emphasize qualities of both ingroups and outgroups (Hewstone, 1996; Hewstone & Brown, 1986; for a review, see Brewer & Gaertner, 2004; Gaertner et al., 2000; Hornsey & Hogg, 2000a, 2000b). Here, we recognize that Barack Obama is an African American and see this as a potential enrichment and advancement for the United States. Blacks and Whites are viewed as different groups that nevertheless share some larger goals with respect to the fate of our country, and humanity more generally.

These strategies form the basis of models for how best to reduce intergroup conflict. We will focus on three models that have been proposed, and examine specifically how each makes use of one or more of the above strategies. The core ideas behind each model, example studies, and the strategies they use, are summarized in Table 10.1. We review Gaertner and Dovidio's (2005; Gaertner et al., 2000) Common Ingroup Identity model (CIIM) as an example of a *recategorization* strategy, and work on colorblind and multicultural ideologies from our own lab (Park & Judd, 2005) as examples of *decategorization* and *mutual differentiation* strategies (although we define these ideologies somewhat differently from the descriptions presented at the beginning of this chapter). We also review Mummendey and Wenzel's (1999) Ingroup Projection Model (IPM) because, although it does not recommend a specific prejudice-reduction strategy that maps directly onto any of the three strategies described above, it is very informative in terms of thinking about the process dynamics responsible for group hostility and prejudice.

All of these models, despite generally sharing a positive intention with regard to intergroup harmony, make quite different recommendations as to how to achieve this goal, at least at first glance. In the following we will describe each of these models in turn, and attempt to analyze what recommendations for diversity in the workplace each model would make. In the final section of this paper we will try to integrate these models and see whether, despite their different emphases, one common set of recommendations that satisfies all three models can be made.

GAERTNER AND DOVIDIO'S COMMON INGROUP IDENTITY MODEL (CIIM)

The main idea behind Gaertner and Dovidio's Common Ingroup identity model (CIIM, Gaertner et al., 2000) is that in order for two groups to engage

TABLE 10.1

Three Models for Intergroup Relations

Model	Idea	Prominent Example	Intergroup Strategy	Potential Initial Recommendation
The Common Ingroup Identity Model (CIIM) (Gaertner & Dovidio, 2005; Gaertner et al., 2000)	Different groups should focus on a category to which they both belong	White college students answer requests of Black students from their own college more willingly than requests of a Black student from a different college (Nier et al., 2001)	*Recategorization*	Emphasize common identity (to which both ingroup and outgroup members belong)
The Ingroup Projection Model (IPM) (Mummendey & Wenzel, 1999)	Each group projects its own characteristics onto the next (more superordinate) level of categorization. Other subgroups within the same superordinate group are seen as not matching this prototype	Germans evaluate other Europeans more negatively to the extent that they perceive a typical European to be typically German (Waldzus, Mummendey, & Wenzel, 2005; Waldzus, Mummendey, Wenzel, & Weber, 2003; Weber, Mummendey, & Waldzus, 2002; Wenzel, Mummendey, Weber, & Waldzus, 2003)	N/A	De-emphasize superordinate identity Do not overemphasize differences between groups
Multiculturalism (MC) & Colorblindness (CB) (Wolsko, Park, Judd, & Wittenbrink, 2000; Park & Judd, 2005)	One can either appreciate or de-emphasize the meaning of race and other social categories, and this will have differential consequences for intergroup perception and interaction	White Americans primed with a multicultural or a colorblind message evaluate American ethnic minorities more positively than participants not primed with such a message (e.g., Wolsko et al., 2000)	*Decategorization* (CB) *Mutual Differentiation* (MC)	Emphasize and respect differences between groups

in positive contact and interaction, it is helpful to remind them of a common ingroup of which they are both part. As can be seen in Table 10.1, this model thus emphasizes *recategorizing* individuals who belong to separate groups into an overarching social category based on some shared commonality. Many studies, both in the laboratory with artificially created groups (Dovidio, Gaertner, Validzic, & Matoka, 1997; Gaertner et al., 2000, Nier et al., Study 1, 2001), as well as in real-world settings (Nier et al., Study 2, 2001), have demonstrated that creating or reminding people of a common group identity that they share with former outgroup members reduces outgroup bias and creates more positive attitudes toward the outgroup as a whole. For instance, in one study, Gaertner et al. (1999b) created 32 groups of three participants each and let them work together and discuss a topic for a while to establish group cohesion. In a next step each of these groups got together with one other group to discuss the same topic again in this new constellation of six people. Importantly, the two groups either created a new common group label and intermixed at a table (the common-ingroup recategorization condition), or remained separate and maintained their previous group names (did not recategorize themselves but maintained their distinct group identities). When asked to evaluate each other afterwards, participants who had created a new common identity rated members of the former outgroup much more positively than participants who had not created such a common identity. Importantly, this effect could be explained by the fact that participants in the recategorization condition indeed felt more connected as "one group" with the previous outgroup. That is, the effect was statistically mediated by the group members' perception that all six members "felt like one group" during the intergroup interaction.

In a direct application to a racial domain, Nier et al. (2001, Study 2) showed that White spectators at a football game were much more likely to comply with an interview request from a Black interviewer when that interviewer shared their university affiliation than when they did not share that affiliation. However, university affiliation had no effect when the interviewer was White (and thus already shared a salient group membership of being a White college student). Taken together, the CIIM thus recommends reminding members of different groups of an identity that they share. Applied to diversity in organizations, this model would suggest creating a strong corporate identity and emphasizing to all workers that they are part of that one bigger group. This re-orientation of attention to a common identity that is distinct from other identities should create more positive attitudes between different groups within a company.

Examples of prominent organizations that have adopted such an emphasis on corporate identity are the U.S. Army and the Ford Motor Company. The U.S. Army has taken such an approach with its current diversity policy, the "United States Army Diversity Roadmap," where diversity is acknowledged and its attributes revered, but membership in the superordinate group (e.g., U.S. Army) is emphasized. The Ford Motor Company's set of "ONE" objectives: ONE Team, ONE Plan, and ONE Goal, encourages members of its international workforce to all identify as members of the Ford Team and therefore work toward the same goals regardless of the employee's specific race, ethnicity, gender, or specific market. These programs reflect the CIIM, and also incorporate a self-promotional component that integrates sociological research that suggests an employee's strong identification with an organization is related to a positively construed external image of that organization (Riketta, 2005). Ensuring a positive image of an organization fosters greater corporate or group identity that results in positive attitudes toward all members of the group regardless of race, ethnicity, or gender.

MUMMENDEY AND WENZEL'S (1999) INGROUP PROJECTION MODEL (IPM)

Mummendey and Wenzel's (1999, see also Wenzel, Mummendey, & Waldzus, 2007) ingroup projection model (IPM, see also Table 10.1) claims that intergroup hostility happens because people project qualities of their ingroup onto the next level of categorization that encompasses both their ingroup and a relevant outgroup (i.e., the superordinate group). Because this norm is based on ingroup qualities, outgroups will deviate from it and consequently be evaluated relatively more negatively. Support for this model has been found with all sorts of groups (e.g., Waldzus, Mummendey, Wenzel, & Boettcher, 2004; Waldzus et al., 2003; Weber et al., 2002; Wenzel et al., 2003; for an overview see Wenzel, Mummendey, & Waldzus, 2007). For instance, Waldzus et al. (2004) found that elementary school teachers and high-school teachers evaluate each other relatively more negatively to the extent that they believe a "true" teacher should possess the typical qualities of their own group, but not the other group. That is, elementary school teachers saw a "true" teacher as resembling their idea of an elementary school teacher (caring, warm), whereas high-school teachers thought of a good teacher possessing qualities of a good high-school teacher (advanced and knowledgeable in the subject that they teach), respectively. Because the respective other group was perceived to deviate from this norm (e.g. high-school teachers saw elementary school teachers as not necessarily experts in a field that they teach) they evaluated them relatively more negatively. Similarly, German participants evaluated other Europeans—such as Poles (Waldzus et al., 2003; Weber et al., 2002; Wenzel et al., 2003) or Italians and the English (Waldzus et al., 2005)—more negatively the stronger they projected characteristics that they perceived to be typically German onto the category of what constitutes a "typical European." Since Poles, the English, or Italians then deviated from this European norm that was based on characteristics that participants perceived to be German, they were rated less likable. Applied to a corporate setting, Finkelstein, Burke, and Raju (1995) found that young persons with authority to hire tended to rate young job applicants—i.e., applicants similar to their ingroup—more favorably than older ones.

For a corporate context this would mean that the extent to which one group of workers in a company projects the qualities of their ingroup onto the next level of the company as a whole (say White workers believe that the Protestant work ethic and individualism are the most important qualities a worker can contribute to a company), the more they will believe that other cultural groups will deviate from that projected norm, since it is based on ingroup qualities. Intergroup harmony will thus inevitably suffer because all ethnic minority groups will be seen as deviating from that norm (e.g., they have a different cultural background and, for instance, hold a different work ethic). One lesson from Mummendey and Wenzel's (1999) model thus seems to be a warning not to overemphasize the differences between different ethnic groups. The more certain dominant ethnic groups feel that other ethnic groups show different cultural practices, and thus also a different work ethic and behavior, the less such groups will be liked, and intergroup harmony will thus suffer.

The harm of overemphasizing differences has been exemplified by corporate attempts to mitigate tensions between groups. Broadly, diversity programs have been found to result in minority groups feeling even more victimized and vulnerable after attending diversity training than before, and White males report feeling frustrated at being made to feel guilty (Hemphill & Haines, 1997). A specific example of the potential harm that may result from overemphasizing differences is that of the merger of the Union Bank of Finland (UBF) and the Kansallis Banking Group. UBF had a strong Finnish identity whereas Kansallis's identity was Swedish, though bilingual, but particularly tailoring to Swedish speaking Finns. As part of the merger, employees from both groups were required to first articulate perceptions of the ingroup, the outgroup, and finally "The Future"—what the new Finnish Merita Bank would represent. This exercise tended to reinforce the differences between the groups rather than place a greater focus on the characteristics of the merged banks, and therefore, merged workforces. The result was reinforcement of the stereotypes held by each group about the other (Vaara, Tienari, & Santti, 2003).

MULTICULTURALISM AND COLORBLINDNESS

As a last social-psychological model on diversity, we would like to introduce our own conception of work on multiculturalism and colorblindness (Park & Judd, 2005; Wolsko, Park, & Judd, 2006; Wolsko et al., 2000). Work on multiculturalism and colorblindness in social-psychological laboratory research is concerned with how much weight should be given to social category information. That is, much early work in social psychology seemed to suggest that the fact that group boundaries exist is the main problem of intergroup conflict (see Park & Judd, 2005). Accordingly, much research, as well as the traditional American color-blind approach, seemed to suggest that in order to halt intergroup conflict these social category boundaries needed to be deconstructed and ignored. Support for this assumption comes from minimal group studies that show that categorizing people into arbitrary groups is enough to create ingroup preference and outgroup bias (Turner et al., 1979). The conclusion drawn from these findings and the U.S.'s experience with racism and segregation (Plaut, 2010) was that maintaining strong category boundaries was the problem. Colorblindness defined this way has the intention of ending discrimination by discouraging people from paying attention to the categories on the basis of which the discrimination happens (a *decategorization* strategy, see Table 10.1). A traditionally colorblind approach, then, is less concerned with being insensitive to diversity than with being protective of equality. As Chief Justice Roberts argued in Parents Involved v. Seattle Schools (2007, cited in Plaut, 2010): "the way to stop discrimination on the basis of race is to stop discriminating on the basis of race."

The opposing ideology of multiculturalism suggests that group categories are inevitable and their deconstruction not necessary or desirable. Belonging to different social categories is seen as creating legitimately different perspectives on the world, and thus exchanging these can potentially be enriching. Multiculturalism hence suggests that people should appreciate each other's differences and indeed celebrate them (a *mutual differentiation* strategy, see Table 10.1).

Work on the comparative effects of a multicultural as opposed to a colorblind ideology confirms that a colorblind ideology focused on decategorization leads to less stereotyping of ethnic outgroups (i.e., less perception of group differences). However, it also confirms that—in line with the idea of appreciating differences—the higher levels of stereotyping that result from a multicultural ideology do *not* go along with higher levels of ingroup favoritism or outgroup bias. That is, participants that read either colorblind or multicultural messages (are "primed" with the ideology) both show more outgroup acceptance and less bias compared with participants who read control messages (Wolsko et al., 2000; for an overview, see Park & Judd, 2005). Additionally, however, the stereotyping that results from a multicultural ideology is mixed in valence. That is, participants primed with a multicultural message stereotype ethnic outgroups more both on negative dimensions (e.g., they might see Latinos as more uneducated), but also on positive dimensions (e.g., they might also see Latinos as more family-oriented and warm). And importantly, these multicultural stereotypes are actually more accurate when compared with available census data than the weaker stereotyping that follows neutral or colorblind messages (Wolsko et al., 2000).

A lot of laboratory research subsequently followed up on these initial conceptualizations, and started documenting the specific consequences of each ideology opposed to the other for intergroup conflict and harmony. That is, in addition to the positive effects of both ideologies on outgroup evaluation described above, much research has documented the specific ironic negative effects each ideology can have despite its positive intentions.

Considering a colorblind ideology, researchers have documented the possibility for ironic negative effects of suppressing social category information and ignoring this information's potential importance for harmonious interactions. For instance, studies have shown that in high-conflict situations the positive attitudes of White participants that are primed with a colorblind approach tend to backfire. That is, in a study by Correll, Park, and Smith (2008), participants who were primed with a colorblind message to ignore racial categories and treat everyone equally, and were then confronted with a situation in which there is a direct racial conflict (i.e., a direct competition where one racial group will end up having an advantage over the other), tended to initially be more positive toward ethnic outgroup students than participants primed with a multi-cultural approach or participants not primed. However, after a delay, these participants' positive attitudes backfired and turned more negative than the attitudes of participants primed with a multicultural approach. It appears that a colorblind message pressures participants to "play nice" initially, despite stark competition and potential disadvantages, and ignore all thoughts about race. However, the suppression of these thoughts eventually led to even more negative attitudes than the multicultural message that encouraged paying attention to racial differences.

Research has also found that colorblind instructions can lead to a greater prevention focus in interracial interactions compared to multicultural instructions, which lead to a more promotion-oriented conversational style (Vorauer, Gagnon, & Sasaki, 2009). That is, this research showed that participants prompted with a multicultural message before an interracial interaction tended to be more other-focused and ask more questions in the interactions than participants primed with other messages. The colorblind message, on the other hand, led participants to be more careful (out of a fear of appearing "racist" by making reference to their interaction partner's different race and cultural background). And hence, they also appeared less interested. Research in educational settings showed that teachers who endorse an egalitarian-colorblind perspective tend to be less willing to adapt their teaching to diverse classrooms (Hachfeld, Hahn, Schroeder, Anders, & Kunter, 2013). That is, teachers with high colorblind beliefs thought that their teaching should be independent of their students' racial and ethnic backgrounds, and thus also showed less willingness to change and adapt their teaching in especially diverse multicultural situations, such as classes with high percentages of immigrant students

(Hachfeld et al., 2013). In the same domain, Apfelbaum and colleagues have found that elementary-school students primed with a colorblind message were less likely to detect and report instances of overt racial discrimination and prejudice than students primed with other messages (Apfelbaum, Pauker, Sommers, & Ambady, 2010).

In sum, an egalitarian–colorblind attitude that has the intention of motivating people to relate to each other independent of race and ethnicity initially leads to positive intentions among its recipients. Ironically, this positive message can backfire in high-conflict competitive situations: it can lead to more careful and thus less beneficial interactions; it may prevent people from adequately preparing for culturally diverse situations; and it can make people less sensitive to instances of discrimination.

Paying increased attention to group differences in the spirit of multiculturalism, on the other hand, can also have ironic negative effects. For instance, Gutiérrez and Unzueta (2010) have found that multi-culturalism can create the expectation that ethnic group members will fit into the dominant stereotype for their group. In these studies, participants primed with a multicultural message evaluated Black targets who said they liked country music and surfing more negatively than Black targets who liked hip hop. It appears that the emphasis on appreciation of differences that a multicultural ideology proclaims and the higher levels of stereotyping that result from this appreciation (Wolsko et al., 2000) also leads people to expect other group members to conform to these stereotypes. When they do not conform, such as when a Black target claims to like music that is considered "White," they are evaluated more negatively. Plaut, Garnett, Buffardi, and Sanchez-Burks (2011) have found that White participants who have a dispositionally high need to belong tended to prefer a colorblind ideology over a multicultural ideology owing to its emphasis on unity. That is, White American participants appear to often feel excluded and less appreciated when emphasis is put on the merits of cultural diversity (Plaut et al., 2011). In sum, multiculturalism generally leads to greater acceptance of differences and diversity, but can have the ironic negative effects of expecting outgroup members to meet dominant stereotypes, and make majority group members feel unappreciated for their alleged "lack" of an exotic cultural contribution.

Generally, majority groups seem to prefer a colorblind approach (e.g., Plaut et al., 2011), while minorities often prefer a multicultural approach (Dovidio, Gluszek, John, Ditlmann, & Lagunes, 2010; Wolsko et al., 2006) although there appears to be considerable variation (e.g., Guerra et al., 2010; Purdie-Vaughns & Ditlmann, 2010). In sum, much research has documented factors such as personality (e.g., Plaut et al., 2011; Vorauer & Sasaki, 2010;), situational factors (e.g., Gutiérrez & Unzueta, 2010; Plaut et al., 2011), or cultural factors (e.g., Guerra et al., 2010; Hahn, Judd, & Park, 2010), to name only a few, that lead people to prefer one ideology over the other, and make one or the other ideology be more effective in producing intergroup harmony.

Most research conducted in organizational settings, however, possibly as a reaction to the dominant colorblind approach in the U.S., has mainly interpreted these findings as indicating the superiority of a multicultural as opposed to a colorblind approach, and has often defined the colorblind ideal differently from its original formulation as a mostly assimilationist or oblivious ideology (see beginning of this chapter). This specific definition then also unsurprisingly led many researchers to see more positive potential in a multicultural as opposed to a colorblind ideology. While we will return to problems with the definition of colorblindness later, we note for now that most organizational research stemming from the multiculturalism–colorblindness tradition appears to advocate a multicultural approach in organizational settings (Plaut, 2010; Plaut et al., 2009; many contributions in this volume). The direct recommendation for a work environment is for a company to explicitly endorse a multicultural ideology that cherishes diversity. That is, in order for minority workers to feel welcome in a company, that company should explicitly state that their differences are appreciated and recognized by the company. And indeed, research has confirmed that the more White employees in a department endorse a multicultural ideology, the more engagement minority workers in that department report (Plaut et al., 2009).

DIFFERENT RECOMMENDATIONS?

At first glance these three models seem to advocate largely different strategies for intergroup conflict that might appear incompatible. While the CIIM seems to advocate emphasizing the belonging of all people to a superordinate identity, according to the IPM the presence of and emphasis on a superordinate identity may be the source of the problem in the first place (see Table 10.1). The IPM also sees the differences between cultural groups under a superordinate identity as the main source of tension (because all groups see other groups as deviating from the "best" norm, which is a result of projecting their own group's characteristics onto the superordinate category), whereas work in organizational settings on multiculturalism encourages companies to specifically appreciate diversity and emphasize the different contributions ethnic and cultural minorities can contribute to a company. Lastly, the CIIM encourages a company to create one common identity that fits all, while research in organizational settings on multiculturalism–colorblindness lauds the superiority of a multicultural approach that emphasizes separable contributions of each group as opposed to a colorblind approach that emphasizes common ground. How, then, can one reconcile these different models?

Within the IPM framework, Mummendey and Wenzel (1999) have argued and found that the degree to which a person projects ingroup qualities on the superordinate category, and thus also the extent to which this projection then leads to outgroup derogation, depends crucially on the definition of the superordinate identity as diverse and heterogeneous (and thus by definition including other diverse subgroups) or not. In empirical tests of this hypothesis, Waldzus et al. (2003, 2005) found that Germans evaluated other Europeans more positively when they were primed to think about the diversity of Europe as opposed to its unity. It appears that one can inhibit the ingroup projection process of concern to the IPM simply by emphasizing that the superordinate identity is diverse and that such diversity is an asset. Interestingly, this would then also be compatible with the other two models. A common superordinate identity that is defined as gaining strength from diversity would largely fit the tenets of the CIIM that feeling as though members of different groups belong together on a higher level of categorization increases intergroup harmony. In fact, recent developments in the CIIM have tested this assumption (Dovidio, Gaertner, & Saguy, 2009; Guerra et al., 2010). Dovidio et al. (2009) have argued that there are two different ways in which one can construe a superordinate common identity: Either as a "single identity" or as a "dual identity." A dual-identity model advocates not giving up subgroup identities when emphasizing a superordinate common identity. Instead of recategorizing members of former outgroups into only one common identity, the dual-identity version of the CIIM advocates leaving subgroup identities intact while emphasizing that all groups belong together on a larger level in addition to their subgroup membership. As this would automatically define the superordinate level as diverse (since it consists of several subgroups whose identities are maintained), it would largely satisfy the tenets of the IPM that a superordinate identity needs to be construed as diverse to forestall ingroup projection (Waldzus et al., 2003, 2005). This solution also seems to be compatible with theories advocating a multicultural approach, albeit with caveats.

That is, much research on multiculturalism–colorblindness appears to stress that emphasizing differences between different groups is a good thing and leads to good results for intergroup harmony, especially when contrasted with an ideology that demands that minority groups assimilate to majority norms (e.g., Plaut et al., 2009) or is insensitive toward differences and denies the existence of disadvantages (Neville et al., 2006). However, what we learn from reviewing the IPM and the dual-identity conceptualization of the CIIM is that blindly emphasizing differences between different ethnic groups will likely not lead to harmony—first, owing to the resulting salience of the lack of fit of these other ethnic groups with superordinate norms as predicted by the IPM; and second, because emphasizing differences alone would lead to a lack of a sense of shared identity that is crucial for intergroup harmony as predicted by the CIIM. In order to make everyone appreciate group differences as something positive, then, one needs to emphasize that all ethnic groups do belong to the same superordinate category, and importantly, that this superordinate category gains strength from its diversity; i.e., it needs to be defined as diverse in the first place.

To account for these dangers of a too-loose definition of multiculturalism and the ambiguity in the definition of colorblindness, we suggest conceptualizing intergroup ideology as aligning along two dimensions rather than one (see also, Hahn et al., 2010). One dimension, the focus of this chapter thus far, is the appreciation and willingness to use group category information (multiculturalism falls high on this dimension while colorblindness falls low). Another dimension is the explicit evaluation of outgroups. That is, this dimension describes whether or not a person feels positively toward members of outgroups and shows a great deal of respect toward them, or instead feels animosity toward outgroup members and evaluates them negatively. All four ideologies are graphically represented in Table 10.2 (Hahn et al., 2010). In this conceptualization an ideology that demands minority groups to assimilate to majority norms is not called colorblindness, but assimilation or hegemony. In contrast, the term "colorblindness" is used uniquely to describe an ideology that wants to see beyond "color" in the spirit of egalitarianism. That is, we believe overlooking cultural differences simply out of oblivion or to advance the dominant group's interests differs from an egalitarian–colorblind perspective in how much respect is shown toward the minority group. Similarly, appreciating differences can happen out of respect for other groups and viewing diversity as an asset for the greater good of all, as much research has described. This should be called multiculturalism. Appreciating differences without this positive emphasis, however, will likely lead to less harmony and could more fittingly be called "separatism" or "segregation"—since overemphasizing differences can easily bring a person to conclude that other groups are disruptive (i.e., not fitting with the superordinate prototype as predicted by the IPM, and lacking common ground, which is seen as necessary by the CIIM, producing for example anti-immigration sentiments).

To exemplify the four ideologies, consider the following simple scenario (Hahn, Banchefsky, Park, & Judd, 2012). Imagine a young Mexican immigrant, José, who has recently moved to the United States to work in a factory. José has problems integrating and feels alien in his new home and wonders what to do. An assimilationist–hegemonic strategy would say that José needs to learn English, pay better attention to how to be a "real American," try to speak as little Spanish as possible, and surround himself with other non-Latinos to foster his "change" and development into a true American (note that this perspective is often called colorblindness despite its stark contrast to the following ideas). An egalitarian–colorblind perspective, on the other hand, would say that it doesn't matter what language José speaks, what color his skin is, or where he is from. Instead,

TABLE 10.2

The Fourfold Table of Interethnic and Racial Ideology

		Emphasis on Group Differences	
		Low—differences should be overcome	High—differences should be emphasized
Evaluation of	**Positive**	Colorblindness	Multiculturalism
the Outgroup	**Negative**	Assimilation/Hegemony	Separatism/Segregation

an egalitarian–colorblind perspective would say that José should focus on the qualities that have made him succeed in life previously. Whether Mexican or American, according to the colorblind ideal, José's success will depend crucially on these individual qualities and the quality of his work in his factory. In line with other American ideals, José can be whomever he chooses to be at any point in time. Note that both ideologies thus share the belief that social categories need to be overcome for harmonious intercultural interactions, but in one perspective José needs to "change" and his background and personality are not appreciated, whereas in the second version his personality and uniqueness are especially valued.

Similarly, paying attention to José's different background can result in two different recommendations. A multicultural perspective would encourage José to see his challenging cultural experience as enriching. José should try to pay close attention to the differences between his expectations and the expectations of his non-Latino co-workers. In return, he should try to become aware and explain his own unique perspective to his co-workers as much as possible. In a multicultural world, José's experience is an opportunity to make his life and his company more colorful and productive. From a separatist/segregationist perspective, on the other hand, José needs to consider whether he can really get along with other Americans, since he is clearly not American, and whether the economic advantages of living in the United States are worth the personal costs. From this perspective, José might consider moving back to Mexico where he feels more at home, or find a company that uniquely hires Latinos in the US so he doesn't have to interact with non-Latino Americans. José's differences are problematic from a separatist–segregationist perspective, and his legitimately different perspective might make integration into American life difficult if not impossible. Note again that both ideologies, separatism/segregation and multiculturalism, see José's cultural background as legitimately creating different perceptions and experiences. However, in one perspective this legitimately different experience is seen as enriching, whereas in the other perspective it is seen as disruptive.

These ideologies can also be applied to other dimensions than race/ethnicity. For instance, Koenig and Richeson (2010) applied Wolsko et al.'s (2000) work on ethnic ideologies to the domain of gender. Specifically, they developed a unidimensional scale to measure individual differences in endorsement of what they term a sexaware perspective on one end versus a sexblind perspective on the other. Koenig and Richeson hypothesized that mean endorsement of scale items would depend on the context in which the questions were considered. Specifically, in a social context where some relationships are necessarily defined along gender lines (e.g., in a romantic interaction), they hypothesized mean endorsement would be nearer the sexaware end of the scale. In contrast, in a work context where both social and legal norms bar gender bias, mean endorsement was predicted to be nearer the sexblind end of the scale. Consistent with the researchers' expectations, mean ratings to the 12 items were nearer to the sexaware endpoint when asked to rate agreement while thinking about a social than work context. Moreover, the mean rating was significantly lower than the scale midpoint in the social context, indicating a sexaware perspective. However, the mean rating in the work context was not different from neutral, providing only partial support for the notion that a sexblind perspective would be favored in a work setting. Hahn et al. (2012) have further developed these ideas, constructing and validating a scale to measure the four cells parallel to Table 10.2 but with respect to gender. There are both important similarities, and intriguing differences, in the ideologies as they apply to the ethnicity and gender domains.

The conceptualization we are offering may help explain differences between the results of much of the laboratory research, which tend to show more positive intergroup attitudes in response to either a colorblind or multicultural ideology compared with a neutral control, and recent research from organizational settings that appears overwhelmingly supportive of the superiority of a multicultural as opposed to a colorblind approach. Recall from the beginning of this chapter that much of the organizational work on multiculturalism and colorblindness defines colorblindness broadly as being insensitive to the particular needs of minority outgroups and asking them to assimilate to majority norms. As said, in our fourfold table (Table 10.2) this ideology would be called assimilation/hegemony, not colorblindness.

Finally, it is important not to forget that people are individuals and should have the right to choose the identities they prefer for themselves. That is, the greater stereotyping that results from a multicultural perspective, despite its partly positive valence and higher accuracy, has its downsides and differential negative effects as well. Recall, for instance, the stereotypic expectations that follow from a multicultural perspective reported earlier (Gutiérrez & Unzueta, 2010). Bearing these in mind, one might consider that not all individuals who happen to be attracted to the same gender might want to be hired for being supposedly "enrichingly gay." Similarly, some women might not want to be employed uniquely for their allegedly "female" qualities. In sum, despite all the possible negative effects a colorblind ideology can have (e.g., Correll et al., 2008; Vorauer et al., 2009), one should not forget the American historical context that led to the development of the colorblind ideal in the first place (personalization or individuation of others; Bettencourt, Brewer, Croak, & Miller, 1992; Plaut, 2010; Park & Judd, 2005), and one should not prematurely reject the colorblind ideal by confusing it with assimilationist and hegemonic practices. In line with models presented earlier, it remains important to emphasize the belonging of all members of a company to the same superordinate group, regardless of their background, but appreciative of that background and the different perspective it creates at the same time.

In sum, ideologies aligned along the dimensions outlined in Table 10.2 can lead to somewhat different conclusions than a uniformly negative effect of being colorblind and a uniformly positive effect of appreciating differences as legitimate. To the contrary, although admittedly challenging, balancing the right amount of respect for differences on the one hand, along with the need for commonality and respect for individuality on the other, seems to be the most promising strategy for achieving harmony in intergroup relations.

CONCLUSION

In synthesizing research on the CIIM, multiculturalism–colorblindness, and the IPM, one could conclude that the conditions for successful intergroup interaction include emphasizing that all groups are part of a larger category (CIIM); that the superordinate prototype comprises characteristics seen among all different subgroups, and thus each subgroup represents some aspect of the larger category (IPM); and that all subgroups make important and separable contributions to this superordinate identity (multiculturalism and IPM). Importantly, we believe a crucial insight that can be gained from looking at research in social psychology is that emphasizing differences of different ethnic and cultural groups alone has its perils. In order for this emphasis to lead to a true harmonious form of multiculturalism, one needs to also emphasize that all groups belong to the same superordinate group and that each is important in its own way to the larger entity; that is, a unified corporate identity remains important. But in order to forestall ingroup projection by one dominant group (i.e., in order to prevent one dominant group from telling all other groups how to define this superordinate identity), this superordinate identity specifically needs to be defined as gaining strength from its diversity.

Interestingly, consistent with this idea of the "best" superordinate identity, researchers have found that the most effective approach to diversity training is to encourage diversity as a method to advance an organization's primary operational goals (Richard & Johnson, 1999; Williams & O'Reilly, 1998). In other words, by stressing the commonly held organizational goals and therefore the common group identity, diversity becomes a common goal for both majority and minority group members rather than a divisive policy.

We live in an increasingly globalized world. In order to use this diversity to its maximal potential, and to minimize conflict among groups, we need to walk the fine line between emphasizing our unity and individuality while respecting and embracing our cultural differences and diversity. Walking this fine line with ease might be the true challenge for nations and corporations competing to remain effective in our globalized and diverse markets.

REFERENCES

Apfelbaum, E. P., Pauker, K., Sommers, S. R., & Ambady, N. (2010). In blind pursuit of racial equality? *Psychological Science*, *21*, 1587–1592.

Baumeister, R. F., & Leary, M. R. (1995). The need to belong: Desire for interpersonal attachments as a fundamental human motivation. *Psychological Bulletin*, *117*, 497–529.

Bettencourt, B. A., Brewer, M. B., Croak, M. R., & Miller, N. (1992). Cooperation and the reduction of intergroup bias: The role of reward structure and social orientation. *Journal of Experimental Social Psychology*, *28*, 301–319.

Brewer, M. B. (1991). The social self: On being the same and different at the same time. *Personality and Social Psychology Bulletin*, *17*, 475–482.

Brewer, M. B., & Gaertner, S. L. (2004). Toward reduction of prejudice: Intergroup contact and social categorization. In M. B. Brewer, & M. Hewstone (Eds.), *Self and social identity* (pp. 298–318). Malden, MA: Blackwell.

Brewer, M. B., & Miller, N. (1984). Beyond the contact hypothesis: Theoretical perspectives on desegregation. In N. Miller, & M. Brewer (Eds.), *Groups in contact: The psychology of desegregation* (pp. 281–302). Orlando, FL: Academic Press.

Brewer, M. B., & Miller, D. T. (1988). Contact and cooperation: When do they work? In P. A. Katz, & D. A. Taylor (Eds.), *Eliminating racism: Profiles in controversy* (pp. 315–326). New York: Plenum Press.

Correll, J., & Park, B. (2005). A model of the ingroup as a social resource. *Personality and Social Psychology Review, 9*, 341–359.

Correll, J., Park, B., & Smith, J. A. (2008). Colorblind and multicultural prejudice reduction strategies in high-conflict situations. *Group Processes & Intergroup Relations, 11*(4), 471–491.

Dovidio, J. F., Gaertner, S. L., & Saguy, T. (2009). Commonality and the complexity of "we": Social attitudes and social change. *Personality and Social Psychology Review, 13*(1), 3–20.

Dovidio, J. F., Gaertner, S. L., Validzic, A., & Matoka, K. (1997). Extending the benefits of recategorization: Evaluations, self-disclosure, and helping. *Journal of Experimental Social Psychology, 33*(4), 401–420.

Dovidio, J. F., Gluszek, A., John, M.-S., Ditlmann, R., & Lagunes, P. (2010). Understanding bias toward Latinos: Discrimination, dimensions of difference, and experience of exclusion. *The Journal of Social Issues, 66*(1), 59–78.

Finkelstein, L. M., Burke, M. J., & Raju, N. S. (1995). Age discrimination in simulated employment contexts: An integrative analysis. *Journal of Applied Psychology, 80*(6), 652–663.

Gaertner, S. M., & Dovidio, J. F. (2005). Understanding and addressing contemporary racism: From aversive racism to the common ingroup identity model. *Journal of Social Issues, 61*, 615–639.

Gaertner, S. L., Dovidio, J. F., Anastasio, P. A., Bachman, B. A., & Rust, M. C. (1993). The common ingroup identity model: Recategorization and the reduction of intergroup bias. In W. Stroebe, & M. Hewstone (Eds.), *European review of social psychology* (pp. 1–26). London: John Wiley & Sons.

Gaertner, S. L., Dovidio, J. F., Banker, B. S., Houlette, M., Johnson, K. M., & McGlynn, E. A. (2000). Reducing intergroup conflict: From superordinate goals to decategorization, recategorization, and mutual differentiation. *Group Dynamics: Theory, Research, and Practice. Special Issue: One hundred years of group research, 4*(1), 98–114.

Gaertner, S. L., Dovidio, J. F., Nier, J. A., Ward, C. M., & Banker, B. S. (1999a). Across cultural divides: The value of a superordinate identity. In D. A. Prentice, & D. T. Miller (Eds.), *Cultural divides: Understanding and overcoming group conflict* (pp. 173–212). New York: Russell Sage.

Gaertner, S. L., Dovidio, J. F., Rust, M. C., Nier, J. A., Banker, B. S., Ward, C. M., Mottola, G. R., & Houlette, M. (1999b). Reducing intergroup bias: Elements of intergroup cooperation. *Journal of Personality and Social Psychology, 76*(3), 388–402.

Guerra, R., Rebelo, M., Monteiro, M. B., Riek, B. M., Mania, E. W., Gaertner, S. L., & Dovidio, J. F. (2010). How should intergroup contact be structured to reduce bias among majority and minority group children? *Group Processes & Intergroup Relations, 13*(4), 445–460.

Gutiérrez, A. S., & Unzueta, M. M. (2010). The effect of interethnic ideologies on the likability of stereotypic vs. counterstereotypic minority targets. *Journal of Experimental Social Psychology, 46*(5), 775–784.

Hachfeld, A., Hahn, A., Schroeder, S., Anders, Y., & Kunter, M. (2013). Should teachers be colorblind? How multicultural and egalitarian beliefs differentially relate to aspects of teachers' professional competence for teaching in diverse classrooms. Manuscript under review.

Hahn, A., Banchefsky, S. M., Park, B., & Judd, C. M. (2012). *Measuring interethnic ideology.* Manuscript in preparation. Boulder, CO: University of Colorado.

Hahn, A., Judd, C. M., & Park, B. (2010). Thinking about group differences: Ideologies and national identities. *Psychological Inquiry, 21,* 120–126.

Hemphill, H., & Haines, R. (1997). *Discrimination, harassment, and the failure of diversity training: What to do now.* Westport. CT: Greenwood Press.

Hewstone, M. (1996). Contact and categorization: Social psychological interventions to change intergroup relations. In C. N. Macrae, C. Stangor, & M. Hewstone (Eds.), *Stereotypes and stereotyping* (pp. 323–368). London: Guilford.

Hewstone, M., & Brown, R. (1986). Contact is not enough: An intergroup perspective on the "contact hypothesis." In M. Hewstone, & R. Brown (Eds.), *Contact and conflict in intergroup encounters* (pp. 1–44). Oxford: Basil Blackwell.

Hornsey, M. J., & Hogg, M. A. (2000a). Assimilation and diversity: An integrative model of subgroup relations. *Personality and Social Psychology Review, 4*(2), 143–156. School of Psychology, University of Queensland, Brisbane, Australia.

Hornsey, M. J., & Hogg, M. A. (2000b). Intergroup similarity and subgroup relations: Some implications for assimilation. *Personality and Social Psychology Bulletin, 26*(8), 948–958.

Koenig, A. M., & Richeson, J. A. (2010). The contextual endorsement of sexblind versus sexaware ideologies. *Social Psychology (Gottingen), 41*(3), 186–191.

Miller, N., Brewer, M. B., & Edwards, K. (1985). Cooperative interaction in desegregated settings: A laboratory analogue. *The Journal of Social Issues, 41*(3), 63–79.

Mummendey, A., & Wenzel, M. (1999). Social discrimination and tolerance in intergroup relations: Reactions to intergroup difference. *Personality and Social Psychology Review, 3*(2), 158–174.

Neville, H., Spanierman, L., & Doan, B. (2006). Exploring the association between color-blind racial ideology and multicultural counseling competencies. *Cultural Diversity and Ethnic Minority Psychology, 12*(2), 275–290.

Nier, J. A., Gaertner, S. L., Dovidio, J. F., Banker, B. S., Ward, C. M., & Rust, M. C. (2001). Changing interracial evaluations and behavior: The effects of a common group identity. *Group Processes & Intergroup Relations, 4*(4), 299–316.

Park, B., & Judd, C. M. (2005). Rethinking the link between categorization and prejudice within the social cognition perspective. *Personality and Social Psychology Review, 9*(2), 108–130.

Plaut, V. C. (2010). Diversity science: Why and how difference makes a difference. *Psychological Inquiry, 21*(2), 77–99.

Plaut, V. C., Garnett, F. G., Buffardi, L. E., & Sanchez-Burks, J. (2011). "What about me?" perceptions of exclusion and whites' reactions to multiculturalism. *Journal of Personality and Social Psychology, 101*(2), 337–353.

Plaut, V. C., Thomas, K. M., & Goren, M. J. (2009). Is multiculturalism or color blindness better for minorities? *Psychological Science, 20*(4), 444–446.

Purdie-Vaughns, V., & Ditlmann, R. (2010). Reflection on diversity science in social psychology. *Psychological Inquiry, 21*(2), 153–159.

Richard, O., & Johnson, N. (1999). Making the connection between formal human resource diversity practices and organizational effectiveness. *Performance Improvement Quarterly, 12,* 77–93

Riketta, M. (2005). Organizational identification: A meta-analysis. *Journal of Vocational Behavior, 66,* 358–384.

Tajfel, H., & Turner, J. C. (1986). The social identity theory of intergroup behavior. In S. Worchel, & W. G. Austin (Eds.), *The psychology of intergroup relations* (pp. 7–24). Chicago, IL: Nelson Hall.

Turner, J. C., Brown, R. J., & Tajfel, H. (1979). Social comparison and group interest in ingroup favouritism. *European Journal of Social Psychology, 9*(2), 187–204.

Turner, J. C., Oakes, P. J., Haslam, S. A., & McGarty, C. (1994). Self and collective: Cognition and social context. *Personality and Social Psychology Bulletin. Special Issue: The Self and the Collective, 20,* 454–463.

Vaara, E., Tienari, J., & Santti, R. (2003). The international match: Metaphors as vehicles of social identity-building in cross-border mergers. *Human Relations, 56*(4), 419–451.

Vorauer, J. D., Gagnon, A., & Sasaki, S. J. (2009). Salient intergroup ideology and intergroup interaction. *Psychological Science, 20*(7), 838–845.

Vorauer, J. D., & Sasaki, S. J. (2010). In need of liberation or constraint? How intergroup attitudes moderate the behavioral implications of intergroup ideologies. *Journal of Experimental Social Psychology, 46*(1), 133–138.

Waldzus, S., Mummendey, A., & Wenzel, M. (2005). When "different" means "worse": In-group prototypicality in changing intergroup contexts. *Journal of Experimental Social Psychology, 41,* 76–83.

Waldzus, S., Mummendey, A., Wenzel, M., & Boettcher, F. (2004). Of bikers, teachers and Germans: Groups' diverging views about their prototypicality. *British Journal of Social Psychology, 43*(3), 385–400.

Waldzus, S., Mummendey, A., Wenzel, M., & Weber, U. (2003). Towards tolerance: Representations of superordinate categories and perceived ingroup prototypicality. *Journal of Experimental Social Psychology, 39,* 31–47.

Weber, U., Mummendey, A., & Waldzus, S. (2002). Perceived legitimacy of the intergroup status differences: Its prediction by relative ingroup prototypicality. *European Journal of Social Psychology, 32,* 449–470.

Wenzel, M., Mummendey, A., Weber, U., & Waldzus, S. (2003). The ingroup as pars pro toto: Projection from the ingroup onto the inclusive category as a precursor to social discrimination. *Personality and Social Psychology Bulletin, 29*(4), 461–473.

Wenzel, M., Mummendey, A., & Waldzus, S. (2007). Superordinate identities and intergroup conflict: The ingroup projection model. *European Review of Social Psychology, 18,* 331–372.

Williams, K., & O'Reilly, C. (1998). Demography and diversity in organizations: A review of 40 years of research. In B. Staw, & R. Sutton (Eds.), *Research in organizational behavior* (pp. 77–140). Greenwich, CT: JAI Press.

Wolsko, C., Park, B., & Judd, C. M. (2006). Considering the Tower of Babel: Correlates of assimilation and multiculturalism among ethnic minority and majority groups in the United States. *Social Justice Research, 19*(3), 277–306.

Wolsko, C., Park, B., Judd, C. M., & Wittenbrink, B. (2000). Framing interethnic ideology: Effects of multicultural and color-blind perspectives on judgments of groups and individuals. *Journal of Personality and Social Psychology, 78*(4), 635–654.

11

The "Business Case" for Diversity May Not by Itself Make the Strongest Case for Diversity

What a Profit-Maximizing Rationale for Affirmative Action Ignores and Why It Matters

Miguel M. Unzueta and Eric D. Knowles

The "business case" for diversity is a common rationale offered by organizations attempting to create and maintain diverse workforces. In this essay we argue that the business case for diversity, which justifies diversity-prompting efforts in terms of their ability to increase corporate profits, is not in and of itself the most effective way for organizations to foster support for policies that promote meaningful diversity. We highlight problematic aspects of profit-based arguments and suggest ways in which appeals for racial diversity[1] in organizations can be expanded and improved.

THE "BUSINESS CASE" FOR DIVERSITY

The business case for diversity argues that creating and maintaining a racially diverse workforce has the power to make organizations more profitable (Robinson & Dechant, 1997; Thomas Jr., 2001). This rationale identifies various avenues through which racial representation helps the bottom line. First, by casting a wider net when hiring, organizations that pursue racial diversity can expand the talent pool from which they are selecting, thus leading to more talented recruits. Second, by communicating to employees that all aspects of the self are welcomed in the workplace, a diverse workplace environment might allow minority employees to do their best work. Third, employment of racial minorities can provide organizations with specialized knowledge and access to previously untapped consumer bases.

The purpose of this essay is not to question the validity of the business case for diversity in organizations. In fact, there is some research suggesting that diverse companies may be more profitable than homogeneous companies (Herring, 2009; Kochan et al., 2003). Rather, we suggest that the business case for diversity may not by itself represent the most effective way to foster support for race-based diversity policies, such as affirmative action. Although the argument that diversity leads to increased profitability might motivate some people to support redistributive social policies, we suggest that the business case lacks a crucial line of argumentation that would further increase support for affirmative action—namely, acknowledgment of, and grounding in, a sociocultural framework.

THE ABSENCE OF A "SOCIOCULTURAL" FRAMEWORK

The United States continues to be a society characterized by racial inequality (see Plaut, 2010, for a review). For example, compared with Blacks, Whites are half as likely to be unemployed, three times less likely to live in poverty, and six times less likely to be imprisoned ("Report sees 'sobering statistics' on racial inequality," 2009). And, even though some gaps between Blacks and Whites shrank in the 1990s (Bigg, 2008), new evidence suggests that the recent economic recession affected Blacks more than Whites, effectively wiping out Black gains that occurred in the 1990s. Specifically, over the past 4 years, Whites' net worth decreased by 24% whereas Blacks' net worth decreased by 83% (Washington, 2011). In addition, since 2009 the White unemployment rate has *decreased* from 9.4% to 9.1%, whereas the Black unemployment rate has actually *increased* from 14.7% to 16.2%. In all, these numbers suggest that the United States continues to be a racially unequal society.

The business case for diversity carefully avoids any reference to such sociocultural facts and the issues of social justice and fairness that they raise. The presumption, it seems, is that people will be "turned off" by references to societal inequalities and swayed by a profit-maximization argument. In fact, some proponents of the business case for diversity go as far as to argue that "only business reasons will supply the necessary long-term motivation" for diversity efforts to succeed (Thomas Jr., 2001, p. 13). We suggest that social psychological research tells a different story, and that grounding diversity efforts in a sociocultural framework may actually *increase* support for redistributive policies among those reluctant to embrace them (i.e., Whites). Such a framework provides two things that the business case for diversity does not: 1) a clear definition of what constitutes "diversity" in organizations and 2) a psychological motivation to redress societal inequality.

What Constitutes Diversity?

The concept of diversity originally referred to race and other protected categories (e.g., gender) explicitly recognized by law (Edelman, Fuller, & Mara-Drita, 2001). These legal protections, in turn, were responses to specific sociocultural realities affecting protected groups (e.g., the legacy of slavery, Jim Crow, and ongoing patterns of exclusion and discrimination). Through the managerialization of law, or "the process by which conceptions of law may become progressively infused with managerial values as legal ideas move into managerial and organizational arenas" (Edelman et al., 2001, p. 1592), the concept of diversity became an all-inclusive label that now encompasses many demographic dimensions lacking any history of discrimination. Edelman et al. (2001) identify business schools and management consultants as the chief agents of the managerialization of diversity.

From this managerialization process arose the business case for diversity. By focusing on bottom-line benefits, the business case for diversity shifted the focus of diversity efforts from social justice and inclusion to the identification of dimensions of difference that are likely to impact organizationally relevant outcomes, such as efficiency and profitability (see Kelly & Dobbin, 1998). An outcome of the managerialization of diversity can be seen in present-day management research. In this literature, diversity is commonly defined as "*the distribution of differences among the members of a unit with respect to a common attribute X, such as tenure, ethnicity, conscientiousness, task attitude, or pay"* (Harrison & Klein, 2007, p. 1200; italics in the original) or, more simply, as heterogeneity in "personality attributes, personal values, work attitudes, education, and lifestyle" (Laio, Chuang, & Joshi, 2008, p. 112). Moreover, various kinds of diversity (e.g., organizational tenure, cognitive differences, personality) are studied in the academic management literature in order to assess how variance on these dimensions impacts group performance and other outcomes that are organizationally relevant (see Jackson & Joshi, 2011 for a review). In sum, and consistent with the assumptions inherent in the business case for diversity, the concept of diversity in the present-day is a broad term that encapsulates a wide range of dimensions that may impact efficiency and profitability. Long gone are the days in which diversity referred specifically to discriminated against identities such as race (see also Linnehan & Konrad, 1999).

A relatively fixed and well-defined notion of diversity may be a prerequisite for fostering support for efforts to promote socially—as opposed to merely managerially—meaningful diversity (Banks, 2009; Peterson, 1999). The reliance of the business case on a wide-ranging (even nebulous) notion of diversity does nothing to focus the public's already unclear and contradictory understanding of the concept. Indeed, recent work suggests that when asked to define diversity, lay people mention a wide range of demographic dimensions (e.g., race, religion, parenting style, age, or education; Bell & Hartmann, 2007)—an unsurprising finding, perhaps, considering that diversity is operationalized in management research in similarly broad ways.

Other research suggests that even when people are asked to think about diversity specifically in racial terms, they disagree about which particular groups are most associated with diversity. Specifically, Unzueta and Binning (2010) found that minority-group members (i.e., Asian-, Latino/a, and African Americans) perceive diversity as primarily entailing the representation of their ingroup, followed by minority outgroups. In other words, Blacks think of diversity as first and foremost entailing Blacks, Asians perceive diversity as primarily entailing Asians, and Latinos see Latinos as the group most associated with this concept. It appears that even when people are forced to think about diversity along a specific demographic dimension (race), there still exists disagreement regarding what constitutes diversity.

The fact that little agreement exists regarding which groups are associated with diversity does not mean that people think about diversity in haphazard ways. To the contrary, recent research suggests that racial minority and majority group members define diversity in systematically different ways (Unzueta & Binning, 2012). Specifically, Asian and African Americans tend to see an organization as being diverse when the organization is composed of a relatively large number of minority employees (i.e., numerical representation) and also has minority employees represented in the managerial ranks of the organization (i.e., hierarchical representation). Whites, on the other hand, seem to have a less specific and more easily satisfied conception of diversity. More specifically, Unzueta and Binning (2012) found that Whites consider an organization to be diverse if the organization is composed of a relatively large number of minority employees, has minority employees in the managerial ranks of the organization, or has both numerical and hierarchical representation. Such differences in diversity construal suggest that minorities might perceive Whites' diversification goals as incomplete, whereas Whites might see minority demands for increased diversity as overreaching. This may occur because the concept of diversity means systematically different things to members of minority and majority racial groups.

Other research provides additional evidence that diversity is a highly subjective concept. Specifically, Chen (2012) examined the role that social acceptance—the extent to which racial minorities feel comfortable and welcomed in a work setting—plays in individuals' definitions of diversity. In this study, both numerical representation and social acceptance positively predicted Latinos' and Whites' perceptions of diversity. However, Latinos' perceptions of diversity were more heavily influenced by social acceptance than were Whites', whereas Whites' diversity perceptions had more to do with numerical representation than did Latinos'. To a greater extent than Whites, then, Latinos required that "true" diversity succeed in conferring a sense of acceptance and belonging at work.

The research reviewed so far suggests that diversity does, in fact, mean different things to different people. But why? Recent research suggests that people strategically define diversity in order to satisfy underlying social goals. Recent work by Unzueta, Knowles, and Ho (2012) found that majority-group members choose meanings of diversity to match their levels of social egalitarianism. Specifically, anti-egalitarian individuals broadened their construal of diversity to include a societally irrelevant dimension of demographic heterogeneity—specifically, occupational, or work-role, heterogeneity—when an organization's racial heterogeneity was low. In so doing, these individuals felt justified in deeming this racially homogeneous organization "diverse" as a function of the range of work roles (e.g., managers, engineers, and marketers) it employs. For their part, egalitarian individuals broadened their construal of diversity to include occupational diversity when the organization's racial heterogeneity was *high*. These individuals reported that the organization lacked "diversity" because it included relatively few different occupational roles—despite the organization's success in employing a racially diverse workforce.

Unzueta et al. (2012) argue that anti-egalitarian individuals attempted to leverage any available information to justify labeling an organization as "diverse," whereas egalitarians leveraged the same information to legitimize calling the organization "*un*diverse." The results suggest a reason why people do this. Across the spectrum of egalitarianism, the extent to which the organization was perceived as diverse predicted individuals' support for race-based affirmative action in that organization—despite the fact that those perceptions were driven in large part by non-racial demographic dimensions. As such, it appears that for individuals both low and high in egalitarian sentiment, diversity can mean whatever they want it to mean in order to legitimize their attitudes toward equality-promoting policies such as affirmative action.

We suspect that the profit-maximizing rationale, by steadily broadening the meaning of diversity, has contributed to the fact that diversity lacks a clear and specific definition. This ambiguous definition of the concept, in turn, likely contributes to the malleability of diversity and therefore its utility to both increase and decrease social inequality. In order to fix the definition of diversity such that diversity initiatives focus consistently on societally relevant demographic dimensions, such as race and gender, the profit-rationale should be supplemented with an explicitly sociocultural focus on reducing persistent social inequalities. The end result may be that this fuller case for diversity lessens the extent to which intergroup inequality replicates itself within organizations.

A Psychological Motivation to Redress Societal Inequality

As argued above, the business case for diversity carefully avoids justifying diversity policies in terms of sociocultural factors. Ironically, recent research suggests that it is precisely when diversity policies are given the right kind of sociocultural grounding that Whites are most supportive of strong redistributive policies. Several researchers (Lowery, Chow, Knowles, & Unzueta, 2012; Powell, Branscombe, & Schmitt, 2005) contend that inequality can be framed in two ways: as dominant-group privilege or subordinate-group disadvantage. Although formally equivalent, these "inequity frames" have different effects on dominant-group members' support for affirmative action policies. Specifically, when inequity is framed as dominant-group privilege, Whites are especially likely to embrace strong affirmative action policies that require the dominant group to give something up (e.g., disproportionate access to jobs). Lowery et al. (2012) argue that such support helps Whites maintain a positive image of the ingroup—an image threatened by awareness of unearned privileges.

Convincing Whites that they enjoy unearned privileges may well increase their support for strong redistributive policies; nonetheless, research also suggests that Whites go out of their way to avoid reaching this conclusion on their own. For example, discussions of inequity tend to be framed in terms of the disadvantaged rather than the advantaged. One is more likely to hear that "Blacks have less than they deserve" than "Whites have *more* than they deserve." Lowery, Knowles, and Unzueta (2007) argue that this tendency may persist, in part, because dominant group members prefer interpretations of racial inequity that focus attention on the disadvantages of minority groups as opposed to the privileges of the dominant racial group. Because the latter interpretation forces dominant group members to see themselves as less responsible for their successes and more culpable for their failures, framing inequity in terms of the advantages of the dominant group may threaten Whites' desired perceptions of self. Consistent with this idea, these authors found that exposing White participants to a self-image threat resulted in lowered perceptions of White privilege; however, exposure to a self-image threat had no impact on Whites' perceptions of anti-Black discrimination. Moreover, increased perceptions of White privilege were found to increase support for race-based affirmative action policies.

These results are consistent with the idea that an inequity frame that highlights the advantages of the dominant group is threatening to White Americans' desired self-perceptions in a way that an inequity frame that highlights the disadvantages of the minority is not. However, it is this White advantage frame that is most likely to get Whites to support affirmative action policies that may attenuate their unearned privileges. To more directly test this idea, Lowery et al. (2012) manipulated the manner in which a company's affirmative action policy was framed (i.e., helps Blacks vs. hurts Whites). Importantly, an additional manipulation was introduced in which pre-existing inequity at the firm was described either as Black disadvantage or White privilege. In the Black disadvantage condition, Whites were less supportive of an affirmative action policy that hurts the ingroup relative to one that has no discernible impact on fellow Whites. The pattern was reversed, however, in the White privilege condition—when privilege was salient, Whites were especially supportive of a policy described as hurting their ingroup. Thus, in order to dispel the threat of privilege, Whites seem to embrace policies that would dismantle their race-based privilege.

Given these findings, it is unfortunate that the business case for diversity, with its purported impact on efficiency and profits, does not broach issues of fairness and privilege that may need to be considered if majority group members are to understand why redistributive social policies are needed in the first place. As such, the business case for diversity may very well be a psychologically "safe" rationale for Whites because the business case for diversity emphasizes benefits to profit and not issues of justice, fairness, or privilege. The problem with not thinking about issues of fairness and advantage is that without such issues on the table, support may not be garnered for social policies that specifically target advantages that propagate inequality in the present-day.

CONCLUSION

In this essay we argued that a profit-oriented case for diversity might be an incomplete rationale for motivating people (specifically Whites) to support race-conscious diversity policies. Specially, we identified two problems with the business case for diversity. First, even though diversity is a concept commonly talked about within organizations, diversity is a term that is rarely clearly defined (Bell & Hartmann, 2007). And, when attempts at defining diversity are made, the business case for diversity tends to include many different types of demographic categories (e.g., race, gender, sexuality, age, nationality, personality, technical expertise, organizational tenure, etc.). Given that diversity has become the normative (and perhaps euphemistic) way for people to talk about race-related issues in the present day, a lack of clarity regarding the meaning of diversity may ironically undermine progress toward racial equality in organizations by allowing people to consider organizations as being diverse so long as they have heterogeneity within non-racial categories (Unzueta et al., 2012; see also Linnehan & Konrad, 1999).

Second, profit-maximizing arguments for diversity may fail to provide a sociocultural framework that allows individuals to understand why race-based diversity policies are needed in the first place (Plaut, 2010). More specifically, profit-maximizing rationales, because they make no reference to existing patterns of group-based inequality in society at large, do not capitalize on the fact that awareness of such inequality (when framed in terms of unearned privileges enjoyed by dominant groups) may increase support for certain kinds of race-based diversity policies (Lowery et al., 2012).

The purpose of this essay is not to take issue with the possibility that diversity can lead to better organizational performance. As stated above, there is research suggesting that diverse companies do, in fact, outperform homogeneous companies (Herring, 2009; Kochan et al., 2003). However, a complete reliance on business reasons for diversity may not be the most effective rationale to foster support for policies such as affirmative action. Instead, organizations may be able to maximize support for racial equity within their ranks if they make both a business and a sociocultural argument for why diversity policies are still needed today.

NOTE

1. Because our own research has focused on race and racial diversity, this essay emphasizes reactions to race-based diversity policies. Nonetheless, many of the arguments we make may well generalize to other underrepresented identities, such as gender.

REFERENCES

Banks, K. H. (2009). A qualitative investigation of White students' perceptions of diversity. *Journal of Diversity in Higher Education, 2,* 149–155.

Bell, J. M., & Hartmann, D. (2007). Diversity in everyday discourse: The cultural ambiguities and consequences of "happy talk." *American Sociological Review, 72,* 895—914.

Bigg, M. (2008). Racial inequality persists in U.S. *Reuters.com*. Retrieved from www.reuters.com/article/2008/03/05/us-usa-inequality-idUSN0561390420080305

Chen, J. M. (2012). Understanding diversity: From representations to perceptions. Doctoral dissertation, University of California, Santa Barbara.

Edelman, L. B., Fuller, S. R., & Mara-Drita, I. (2001). Diversity rhetoric and the managerialization of law. *American Journal of Sociology, 106,* 1589–1640.

Harrison, D. A., & Klein, K. J. (2007). What's the difference? Diversity constructs as separation, variety, or disparity in organizations. *Academy of Management Review, 32,* 1199–1228.

Herring, C. (2009). Does diversity pay?: Race, gender, and the business case for diversity. *American Sociological Review, 74,* 208–224.

Jackson, S. E., & Joshi, A. (2011). Work team diversity. In S. Zedeck (Ed.), *APA handbook of industrial and organizational psychology* (Vol. 1, pp. 651–686). Washington, DC: American Psychological Association.

Kelly, E., & Dobbin, F. (1998). How affirmative action became diversity management: Employer response to antidiscrimination law, 1961 to 1996. *American Behavioral Scientist, 47,* 960–984.

Kochan, T., Bezrukova, K., Ely, R., Jackson, S., Joshi, A., Jehn, A., et al. (2003). The effects of diversity on business performance: Report of the diversity research network. *Human Resource Management, 42,* 3—21.

Laio, H., Chuang, A., & Joshi, A. (2008). Perceived deep-level dissimilarity: Personality antecedents and impact on overall job attitudes, helping, work withdrawal, and turnover. *Organizational Behavior and Human Decision Processes, 106,* 106–124.

Linnehan, F., & Konrad, A. M. (1999). Diluting diversity implications for intergroup inequality in organizations. *Journal of Management Inquiry, 8,* 399–415.

Lowery, B. S., Chow, R. M., Knowles, E. D., & Unzueta, M. M. (2012). Paying for positive group-esteem: How inequity frames affect dominant group members' responses to redistributive policies. *Journal of Personality and Social Psychology, 102,* 323–336.

Lowery, B. S., Knowles, E. D., & Unzueta, M. M. (2007). Framing inequity safely: Whites' motivated perceptions of racial privilege. *Personality and Social Psychology Bulletin, 33,* 1237–1250.

Peterson, L. (1999). The definition of diversity: Two views: A more specific definition. *Journal of Library Administration, 27,* 17–26.

Plaut, V. C. (2010). Diversity science: Why and how difference makes a difference. *Psychological Inquiry, 21,* 77–99.

Powell, A. A., Branscombe, N. R., & Schmitt, M. T. (2005). Inequality as ingroup privilege or outgroup disadvantage: The impact of group focus on collective guilt and interracial attitudes. *Personality and Social Psychology Bulletin, 31,* 508–521.

Report sees "sobering statistics" on racial inequality. (2009). *CNN.com*. Retrieved from http://articles.cnn.com/2009-03-25/us/black.america.report_1_whites-blacks-urban-league?_s=PM:US

Robinson, G., & Dechant, K. (1997). Building a business case for diversity. *The Academy of Management Executive, 11,* 21–31.

Thomas, R. R., Jr. (2001). From affirmative action to affirming diversity. *Harvard Business Review on Managing Diversity* (pp. 1–31). Boston, MA: Harvard Business Press.

Unzueta, M. M., & Binning, K. R. (2010). Which racial groups are associated with diversity? *Cultural Diversity and Ethnic Minority Psychology, 16,* 443–446.

Unzueta, M. M., & Binning, K. R. (2012). Diversity is in the eye of the beholder: How concern for the in-group affects perceptions of racial diversity. *Personality and Social Psychology Bulletin, 38,* 26–38.

Unzueta, M. M., Knowles, E. D., & Ho, G. C. (2012). Diversity is what you want it to be: How social dominance motives affect construals of diversity. *Psychological Science, 23,* 303–309.

Washington, J. (2011). Blacks' economic gains wiped out in downturn. *Associated Press.* Retrieved from www.msnbc.msn.com/id/43645168

12

Multiculturalism at Work

Examples from the UK and Germany

Joana Vassilopoulou, Karsten Jonsen,
Mustafa Özbilgin, and Ahu Tatli

In this chapter, we explain the notion of multiculturalism as it manifests in social and business studies. Drawing on examples from the UK and Germany, we elaborate why there is a need to reframe multiculturalism, liberating it from its limiting macro-political conceptualisation. Multiculturalism is a concept that has been widely used in social policy in response to ethnic diversity in the UK. Although multiculturalism has not been used as a social policy term in Germany, present political and public debates suggest its failure. We examine multiculturalism in the context of work in Britain and Germany, two countries with distinctly different approaches to social policy to address ethnic differences. In the main, multiculturalism is a macro-political concept. However, multiculturalism acts as a frame of reference in the formation of the equality legislation, public sentiment and organisational responses toward ethnic diversity. Using the example of the UK and Germany, we demonstrate why we need an expanded conception of multiculturalism if this concept is to survive as a successful social policy and management term.

FRAMING CULTURE AND MULTICULTURALISM AT WORK

Since the origin of anthropological studies in the late nineteenth century, culture has served as yardstick for distance among human beliefs and

269

practices. In the early days, the term culture was used to express espoused distinctions between the civilised versus the primitive peoples (Tylor, 1871), a language that has wisely softened over time. But have we really come much further? In the last four decades, culture has been used in management literature as an independent variable or mediator/moderator in the quest for outcome variables such as effectiveness and performance. In other words, the transition from anthropology to management has been fuelled by the hope and anticipation of increasing performance at work by mobilising various forms of organisational and national culture (Sackmann, 2011). This approach informed major streams of cultural research: organisational and national (e.g. Ashkanasy, Neal, Wilderom, & Peterson, 2011; Stahl, Maznevski, Voigt, & Jonsen, 2010).

As a logical consequence of globalisation and an increasingly pluralistic world (Lane, Maznevski, DiStefano, & Dietz, 2009), managers are often asking the question, how can we manage people from different backgrounds? So studies that assumed cultural similarity in single organisational and national contexts have been supplemented with research that explores how multiple cultural norms and practices may exist in the same contexts or across a range of organisations and countries. Dimensions and numbers that are easily available at your fingertips, noticeably from Hofstede (2001), have been used as easy ways to quantify, for example, how the French are different from the British, neglecting the more complex historical and contextual aspects of such manifestations of difference – setting aside the fact that the underlying data collection may stem from supranational institutions and conglomerates that coexist with the state system, yet attempting to override national cultures. Managers are thus pushed to think of multiculturalism as a dichotomy that serves to hinder effectiveness and performance. To achieve the latter objective, they are provided with thoughtful guidelines, to-do-lists, coping strategies and behaviours, and models for acculturation and interventions (e.g. Berry, Denison et al., 1998; 2012; Schein, 1992; Schneider & Barsoux, 2003). The problem is, however, that most often cultural differences are presented in simplistic, inaccurate and ill-informed quick fixes that misrepresent and dishonour local cultures, meanings and contexts. Tipton (2008) accounts for numerous examples where 'sloppy research' leads to universal myths and anecdotes about culture and blunders (perhaps the most widely printed is the Chrysler Nova story which presumably originates from a *Wall Street Journal* article in 1977). The author concludes that business textbooks are infected with multilevel weaknesses, such as errors of facts, interpretation and application of culture-theories.

Values have been linked to the study of people and are embedded in the very definition of *culture* (Geertz, 1973; Hofstede, 2001; Kluckhohn & Strodtbeck, 1961). This relates to the high interest in culture, owing to the presumed relationship between culture (operationalised by values) and effectiveness/performance (O'Reilly & Chatman, 1996), grounded in a lust for causal relationships and the ability to manipulate certain outcomes (Alvesson, 2002). Especially in the 1980s, numerous culture studies and books gained popularity (Deal & Kennedy, 1982; Ouchi, 1981; Peters & Waterman, 1982), prescriptively claiming that companies in which people live one set of (the right) values perform better. The focus on values has been continued in best-selling practitioner literature since then (e.g. Blanchard, O'Connor, & Ballard, 1997; Collins, 2001; Collins & Porras, 1994; George, 2003; George, Sims, & Gergen, 2007). In this regard, the management literature has been less successful penetrating knowledge about national cultures, integration of immigrants and equal opportunities. Although many authors have introduced conditional or critical approaches over time, practitioners' literature has, largely, kept the favourable perspective of cultural manipulation, yet based on inadequate and deceiving methodology (Rosenzweig, 2007).

What has not been lost in translation from the first steps of early anthropology to management is the superiority-based notion of good cultures and bad cultures. Good cultures are defined as strong cultures that do not suffer from ambiguity or heterogeneity around key values (Deal & Kennedy, 1982; Denison, 1990). In a way, management ideology thus becomes intertwined with (organisational) culture, powerfully impregnating cultural patterns (Alvesson, 1995). Instead of guiding managers to systematic, reflective ways of seeing how people live their lives in organisations, i.e. interpreting practices and meanings (the way anthropology has developed throughout most of the twentieth century), culture in mainstream management literature has become a prescription; an aspiration; a symbolic hedge fund of people in which there are few restrictions and expectations of abnormal returns. The deep hope for multiculturalism remains a recognition that cultural difference is not a threat but an opportunity that can help inform organisations and countries to reshape their social and economic policies in a way that reflects the diversity of needs inherent in the diversity of cultures that people subscribe to.

THE CHANGING GOVERNMENT POSITION ON MANAGEMENT OF ETHNIC DIVERSITY IN THE UK: FROM MULTICULTURALISM AND FAIRNESS TO NATIONAL UNITY AND INTEGRATION

Partly owing to its colonial past, British society is characterised by a vibrant ethnic diversity with ethnic minority groups making up a third of the population. Until recently, multiculturalism had been the dominant paradigm in management of ethnic diversity in the UK (Özbilgin & Tatli, 2011). Since 2010, however, a considerable change is taking place in the UK policy landscape with significant consequences for diversity. This section will unpack the changing governmental rhetoric in terms of management of ethnic diversity in the UK. Between 1997 and 2010, multiculturalism was actively promoted by the consecutive Labour Governments at levels of both policy making and government rhetoric. Labour Government's vision of multiculturalism had two elements: (1) fairness and tackling inequality, and (2) emphasis on the business benefits of a multicultural society. Although this vision was criticised for its emphasis on business interests (e.g. Dickens & Hall, 2006), the business case rhetoric had indeed helped construct a positive framing of ethnic minorities with a focus on their contribution to society and on the advantages of a multicultural workforce instead of the deficit model used in countries such as Germany. Consequently, there was popular support for and pride in the multicultural nature of British society and the concept of multiculturalism has been relatively less controversial in Britain compared with continental European counties (Wrench, 2004). Since the Conservative led coalition government came to power in 2010, there has been a shift in the rhetoric and the policy commitment regarding multiculturalism. In 2011, Prime Minister David Cameron declared that multiculturalism has failed in Britain. Furthermore, unlike the Labour Government's targeted policy approach to improve the service delivery to and employment opportunities for the ethnic minority groups, the current Coalition Government's Equality Strategy emphasises universalism, moving away from 'treating people as groups and instead recognises that we are a nation of 62 million individuals' (HM Government, 2010, p. 9). Consequently, rhetoric around 'national unity', 'Britishness' and integration is replacing the previously endorsed lexicon of multiculturalism and fairness. This rhetorical and policy shift takes place in an environment characterised by economic stagnation, high levels of unemployment, and increasingly popular anti-EU and anti-migration public sentiment. The potential consequences of the current governmental approach for the management of ethnic diversity remain to be seen.

In the organisational setting, when diversity management discourse and practices arrived from North America to the UK, it was relatively easy for practitioners to embed diversity management in the multicultural discourse of the national social policy. As an organisational policy, diversity management offered a discourse that recognised the communitarian and individual level differences at work. The congruence between multi-culturalism at the macro level and diversity management at the meso level presented a happy marriage, and can partly explain how and why diversity management discourse was welcomed relatively fast by the UK industry. Therefore, the recent political turn against multiculturalism in the UK presents a setback for continued adoption and progress in the field of diversity management.

HAS THE MULTICULTURAL SOCIETY UTTERLY FAILED IN GERMANY, OR HAS THE PROMOTION OF MULTICULTURALISM BEEN OVERLOOKED?

Germany's majority population started only recently accepting the reality that Germany has become an immigration country during the last 50 years. As a result, Germany has today the third largest number of international immigrants in the world (International Organization for Migration, 2010). A large influx of immigrants can be accredited to the guest worker recruitment in post-war Germany in the 1960s. The majority population received the arrival and settlement of the so-called guest workers very critically. Along with this, the strong belief (or maybe wish) prevailed that the guest workers would return to their home countries. It took the German government 50 years to acknowledge the permanent settlement of its former so-called guest workers. As the German Chancellor, Angela Merkel recently said, 'the beginning of the 60s our country called the foreign workers to come to Germany and now they live in our country.' She later added: 'We kidded ourselves a while, we said: "They won't stay, sometime they will be gone", but this isn't reality' (BBC News Europe, 2010). Mrs Merkel's statement and in particular the fact that she referred to only a 'while', which sadly summarises an era of nearly 50 years of denial, must be viewed as a rather ironical instance and doesn't pay any justice to the influence this denial has had not only on immigration policies, but also on the large number of immigrants who settled down in Germany.

However, Guenter Piening, Germany's Integration Commissioner since 2003 who resigned only recently, provides a rather critical assessment of the integration policy in Germany. In his farewell speech he argued that Germany is still far away from a real recognition of the fact that it is an immigration country. Moreover, he argued that there is no recognition of the need for racial equality in the German context (MIGAZIN, 2012). In particular, the long prevailing disinterest in policies regarding race discrimination and race equality has led to an absence of measures targeting such issues in the organisational context.

Along with this ongoing denial, German studies on immigrants have been and are still dominated by an assimilative notion of integration (Geißler & Pöttker, 2005). The assimilation of immigrants as well as the 'preservation' of the assumed monocultural society is at the core of the study of integration and migration in Germany. This attempt at preserving the reality of a monocultural society that doesn't exist is underlined by a notion of integration that is racially biased and ethnocentric. For instance, Thilo Sarrazin, politician and former executive of the Deutsche Bundesbank, wrote in his 2010 book *Deutschland schafft sich ab* [German does away with itself] that Arab and Turkish immigrants are unwilling and unable to integrate (Jacoby, 2011), implying that particular ethnic groups are less able (and willing) to integrate than others, such as for example Italians or Greeks. Unfortunately, he is not alone in such views in Germany, since the majority population as well as politicians and a number of academics share and constantly reproduce such views. Such negative characterisation of particular ethnic groups shows clearly the underlying racism of the notion of integration, which we call integracism, in the German context (Al Ariss, Vassilopoulou, Özbilgin, & Game, 2013).

Consequently, the idea of cultural diversity and the promotion of multiculturalism and race equality have been ignored in the German context. Considering these insights it is rather astonishing that Mrs Angela Merkel said recently: 'the approach [to build] a multicultural [society] and to live side-by-side and to enjoy each other . . . has failed, utterly failed'

(BBC, 2010). It is surprising, since the German government never declared a multicultural society. The assimilation of immigrants into the dominant culture has always been in the focus of the national agenda (see Berlin-Institute für Bevölkerung und Entwicklung, 2009; Esser, 2001, 2003, 2006).

Breaking all this down to the organisational context, it does not come as a surprise that the notion of multiculturalism does not get much attention in organisations. For example, race equality measures are scarce and hard to find in organisations (Köppel, Yan, & Lüdicke, 2007). Apparently, the racially biased and ethnocentric notion of integration undermines the need to manage ethnic diversity in organisations in the German context (Tatli, Vassilopoulou, Ariss, & Özbilgin, 2013).

CONCLUSION: REFRAMING MULTICULTURALISM

This chapter addresses the vital issue of multiculturalism that is once more gaining attention in the light of the current economic turmoil. Looking at the two examples of Germany and the UK, we found two major issues that need to be considered when attempting to reframe multiculturalism. First, we showed that the notion of multiculturalism is framed differently in different contexts, using the examples of the UK and Germany. While multiculturalism has never been accepted as a notion for dealing with ethnic diversity in the German context, in the UK multiculturalism has been the dominant paradigm in the management of ethnic diversity. The notion of multiculturalism recently changed in the UK; terms such as integration and 'Britishness' are replacing the language of multiculturalism and fairness. Interestingly, we can now observe a convergence of the previously very different notions of multiculturalism in the context of the UK and Germany. What this development shows is not only the dynamic nature of cultural change, but also that notions such as multiculturalism can vary depending on, for example, geography as well as time. In order to liberate the notion of multiculturalism from its limiting macro-political conceptualisation, we need to explore further the meanings and practices attributed to multiculturalism in its local setting. Reframing multiculturalism in this way requires us to develop emic (emerging) rather than etic (predetermined) understandings for multiculturalism, if we are to produce policies and academic work on multiculturalism that are historically and locally sound.

Second, mainstream framing of multiculturalism as a macro-political discourse disallows a fine-grained, contemporary and multilevel conception of multiculturalism, as such multiculturalism is founded on essentialist notions of culture, where cultures exist side by side, not in transition owing to contact with other cultures. Moreover, there is an increasing need to look at how each *individual* is expected to think and behave in comparison with groups of peoples, often with similar thinking styles and practices. This is crucial for cultural developments based on integration and transitions, because individuals are at the forefront of cultural change, yet we described in this chapter how strong culture is treated equally to homogeneity and unified values. An outcome of framing multiculturalism only as a macro-level construct is segregation of ethnic groups in society and at work. As a result we have a society or an organisation that might accept different cultures but that does not learn and evolve as a consequence of such cultural diversity. Macro-conceptualisation of multiculturalism is also imbued with the traps of instrumentalisation and over-financialisation, by which multiculturalism is only considered if it contributes to the organisational bottom line. In order to avoid these traps, we need to explore the human aspects of multiculturalism in terms of its pleasures, pains and tensions. In this way, we may free multiculturalism from the clasp of instrumental logics and consider it in line with its original spirit, a recognition and a reconciliation of cultural differences at national, organisational, group and individual levels.

In this short piece, we also problematise the treatment of culture as part of the multiculturalism discourse. A static notion of culture, which dominates the current understanding of multiculturalism, has a number of negative outcomes for promoting cultural diversity and multiculturalism. First, it locks individuals in different ethnic groups to limited repertoires of cultural choices and expressions. Second, it fails to capture the dynamic nature of cultural change, which happens in time and across all communities of culture and influences notions such as, for example, multiculturalism, culture and cultural diversity. Third, it creates an illusion of welcoming different cultures, when in fact it leaves the hierarchy between dominant and minority cultures intact. Fourth, static conception of multiculturalism is susceptible to reproduction of cultural and ethnic stereotypes, enforcing and entrenching them. The danger in this framing is that cultures, in fact, are more heterogeneous and ethnocentric than they are presented in mainstream literature. Therefore, not only are plans to tap into such cultural resources likely to fail but also they limit recognition of talent among individuals who are culturally different from the mainstream. Finally, compartmentalised and static conception of culture leads to misconception and misjudgement between individuals who supposedly belong to different cultures. The presence of the variety of cultures that exist side by side is the reflection of the multicultural political project in social and organisational life. However, sometimes these multiple cultures yet fail to communicate, which can lead to the separation of individuals rather than to the encouragement of openness and respect for diversity and willingness to learn from differences. Treating cultural diversity as an asset could be one way to not only encourage learning from differences, but also to break the racial bias and ethnocentricism in discourses of integration, a discourse that now competes with more egalitarian social policy notions such as multiculturalism. Lastly, by treating culture as a dynamic multilevel construct or phenomena, cultural diversity becomes an asset, a resource that can be tapped into, manipulated, cherished, mobilised and conjured if and when an organisation or society needs its presumed contribution.

REFERENCES

Al Ariss, A., Vassilopoulou, J., Özbilgin, M., & Game, A. (forthcoming). Understanding career experiences of skilled minority ethnic workers in France and Germany. *The International Journal of Human Resource Management.*

Alvesson, M. (1995). *Management of knowledge-intensive companies.* Berlin: Walter de Gruyter.

Alvesson, M. (2002). *Understanding organizational culture.* Thousand Oaks, CA: Sage.

Ashkanasy, N. M., Neal, M., Wilderom, C., & Peterson, M. (2011). *The handbook of organizational culture and climate* (2nd ed.). Thousand Oaks, CA: Sage.

BBC News Europe (2010). Merkel says German multicultural society has failed. Retrieved December 12, 2010 from www.bbc.co.uk/news/world-europe-11559451

Berlin-Institute für Bevölkerung und Entwicklung (Hrsg.) (2009) *Ungenutzte Potenziale. Zur Lage der Integration in Deutschland.* Berlin: Berlin-Institute für Bevölkerung und Entwicklung.

Berry, J. W. (1998). Intercultural relations in plural societies. *Canadian Psychology, 40,* 12–21.

Blanchard, K. H., O'Connor, M. J., & Ballard, J. (1997). *Managing by values.* San Francisco, CA: Berrett-Koehler.

Collins, J. C. (2001). *Good to great: Why some companies make the leap—and others don't* (1st ed.). New York: HarperBusiness.

Collins, J. C., & Porras, J. I. (1994). *Built to last: Successful habits of visionary companies* (1st ed.). New York: HarperBusiness.

Deal, T. E., & Kennedy, A. A. (1982). *Corporate cultures: The rites and rituals of corporate life.* Reading, MA: Addison-Wesley.

Denison, D. R. (1990). *Corporate culture and organizational effectiveness.* New York: John Wiley & Sons.

Denison, D. R., Hooijberg, R., Lane, N., & Lief, C. (2012). *Leading culture change in global organizations: Aligning culture and strategy.* Hoboken, NJ: Jossey-Bass.

Dickens, L., & Hall, M. (2006). Fairness—up to a point: Assessing the impact of New Labour's employment legislation. *Human Resource Management Journal, 16,* 338–356.

Esser, H. (2001). Kulturelle Pluralisierung und strukturelle Assimilation. Das Proble der ethnischen Schichtung. *Schweizerische Zeitschrift für Politikwissenschaft, 7*(2), 97–108.

Esser, H. (2003). Ist das Konzept der Assimilation überholt? *Geographische Revue, 5,* 5–22.

Esser, H. (2006). Migration, language and integration. AKI Research Review 4 Arbeitsstelle Interkulturelle Konflikte und gesellschaftliche Integration (AKI) Wissenschaftszentrum Berlin für Sozialforschung (WZB).

Geertz, C. (1973). *The interpretation of cultures: Selected essays.* New York: Basic Books.

Geißler, R., & Pöttker, H. (Hrsg.) (2005). *Massenmedien und die Integration ethnischer Minderheiten in Deutschland.* Bielefeld: Problemaufriss—Forschungsstand—Bibliographie.

George, B. (2003). *Authentic leadership: Rediscovering the secrets to creating lasting value.* San Francisco, CA: Jossey-Bass.

George, B., Sims, P., & Gergen, D. (2007). *True north: Discover your authentic leadership.* San Francisco, CA: Jossey-Bass.

HM Government (2010). *The equality strategy: Building a fairer Britain.* London: Government Equalities Office. Retrieved June 25, 2012 from www.homeoffice. gov.uk/publications/equalities/equality-strategy-publications/equality-strategy/

Hofstede, G. H. (2001). *Culture's consequences: Comparing values, behaviors, institutions, and organizations across nations* (2nd ed.). Thousand Oaks, CA: Sage.

International Organization for Migration (2010). Regional and country figures. Retrieved June 14, 2010 from www.iom.int/jahia/Jahia/about-migration/facts-and-figures/regional-and-country-figures

Jacoby, T. (2011). Germany's immigration dilemma: How can Germany attract the workers it needs? *Foreign Affairs, 90*(2), 8–14.

Kluckhohn, F. R., & Strodtbeck, F. L. (1961). *Variations in value orientations.* Evanston, IL: Row, Peterson.

Köppel, P., Yan, J., & Lüdicke, J. (2007). Cultural diversity management in Deutschland hinkt hinterher. Retrieved August 8, 2008 from www.bertelsmann-stiftung.de/cps/rde/xbcr/SID-0A000F14-5385B43A/bst/xcms_bst_Diversitymanagements_21374_2.pdf

Lane, H. W., Maznevski, M. L., DiStefano, J., & Dietz, J. (2009). *International management behavior: Leading with a global mindset* (6th ed.). Oxford: Blackwell.

MIGAZIN (2012). Deutschland ist von einer Anerkennung der Einwanderungsgesellschaft noch weit entfernt, Retrieved June 27, 2012 from www.migazin.de/2012/06/27/deutschland-ist-von-einer-anerkennung-der-einwanderungsgesellschaft-noch-weit-entfernt/?utm_source=feedburnerandutm_medium=feedandutm_campaign=Feed%3A+migazin+%28MiGAZIN%29

O'Reilly, C. A., & Chatman, J. A. (1996). Culture as social control: Corporations, cults, and commitment. In B. M. Staw, & L. L. Cummings (Eds.), *Research in Organizational Behaviour, 18*, 157–200.

Ouchi, W. (1981). *Theory Z: How American business can meet the Japanese challenge.* Reading, MA: Addison-Wesley.

Özbilgin, M., & Tatli, A. (2011). Mapping out the field of equality and diversity: Rise of individualism and voluntarism. *Human Relations, 64*, 1229—1258.

Peters, T. J., & Waterman, R. H. (1982). *In search of excellence: Lessons from America's best-run companies* (1st ed.). New York: Harper & Row.

Rosenzweig, P. (2007). *The halo effect . . . and the eight other business delusions that deceive managers.* New York: Free Press.

Sackmann, S. A. (2011). Culture and performance. In N. M. Ashkanasy, M. Neal, C. Wilderom, & M. Peterson (Eds.), *The handbook of organizational culture and climate* (2nd ed.) (pp. 188–224). Thousand Oaks, CA: Sage.

Schein, E. H. (1992). *Organizational culture and leadership* (2nd ed.). San Francisco, CA: Jossey-Bass.

Schneider, S. C., & Barsoux, J.-L. (2003). *Managing across cultures.* London: Prentice Hall.

Stahl, G. K., Maznevski, M. L., Voigt, A., & Jonsen, K. (2010). Unraveling the effects of cultural diversity in teams: A meta-analysis of research on multicultural work groups. *Journal of International Business Studies, 41*(4), 690–709.

Tatli, A., Vassilopoulou, J., Ariss, A., & Özbilgin, M. (2013, forthcoming). The role of regulatory and temporal context in the construction of diversity discourses: The case of the UK, France and Germany. *European Journal of Industrial Relations.*

Tipton, F. B. (2008). 'Thumbs-up is a rude gesture in Australia': The presentation of culture in international business textbooks. *Critical Perspectives on International Business, 4*(1), 7–24.

Tylor, E. (1871). *Primitive culture.* New York: J. P. Putnam's Sons.

Wrench, J. (2004). Trade union responses to immigrants and ethnic inequality in Denmark and the UK: The context of consensus and conflict. *European Journal of Industrial Relations, 10*, 7–30.

13

Diversity Ideologies

The Case of South Africa

Stella M. Nkomo

The purpose of this chapter is to provide a perspective on diversity ideologies from a different part of the world as the authors of the volume realize that much of the extant diversity management knowledge emanates from the United States and perhaps more recently Western Europe (Klarsfield, 2010). Research inputs from other continents, particularly those in the South are less prominent. Furthermore, much of the literature on multiculturalism has been confined to Western contexts (Bekker & Leildé, 2003; Plaut, 2010). Multiculturalism is a liberal ideology that has been used in different ways across time and context (Stinson, 2009). Countries differ in how they conceive and practise multiculturalism and therefore how they aim to incorporate ethnic diversity into the structures of society including the workplace (Stinson, 2009). More substantially, however, there is a rather unique divide between conceptualizations of multiculturalism in Western and post-colonial societies.

Rex and Singh (2003, p. 106) argue that any examination of multi-culturalism requires the integration of separate fields of research. That is, studies on multiculturalism have mainly been concerned with how to include migrant or minority populations into a more or less culturally homogeneous nation-state. On the other hand, according to Rex and Singh (2003), research on post-colonial societies has focused on conditions of social integration or cohesion in profoundly heterogeneous societies – that is nation building. South Africa presents an interesting case of the latter.[1] Indeed, South Africa provides a particularly relevant context for exploring diversity ideology because most scholars conclude it is a deeply segmented society owing to its racial and cultural heterogeneity, complexity and history (Bekker, 1999; Booysen, 2007; Finchilescu & Tredoux, 2010). It is also a society that has embarked on a course of nation building during its post-apartheid transition. The chapter begins with a description of the historical and current South African context. This is followed by an overview of the current diversity ideology debates and the empirical research associated therewith. The chapter concludes with some implications for our general understanding of how diversity ideologies inform and shape approaches to diversity in South African organizations.

SOUTH AFRICAN CONTEXT

The importance of context to understanding conceptualizations and approaches to the management of diversity in organizations has been increasingly recognized in the last few years (e.g., Janssens & Zanoni, 2005; Nishii & Özbilgin, 2007; Prasad, Pringle, & Konrad, 2006; Risberg & Søderberg, 2008; Zanoni, Janssens, Benschop, & Nkomo, 2010). Thus, it is important to begin a discussion of diversity ideologies in South Africa with an overview of the context that has shaped and continues to shape current debates in the country about how to change social, economic and political relationships among different racial and ethnic groups. South Africa is burdened with the legacy of centuries of racial discrimination and repression of ethnic groups originating in its colonization by two European powers, the British and the Dutch. While many people erroneously believe racial discrimination began with the official introduction of apartheid in 1948, discrimination and repression against the native population can be traced back as far as the arrival of the colonists. However, it was under the system of apartheid that racial separation of races was categorically institutionalized in every sphere of society through hundreds of laws. These oppressive laws and their brutal enforcement kept Whites dominant over Blacks. A racial hierarchy was entrenched, with Whites at the apex followed by Asians, coloureds, and Blacks at the very bottom. Socioeconomic status and access to resources were commensurate with one's race thus ensuring Blacks, coloureds and Asians were relegated to the lowest positions in organizations as well as being excluded from certain professions (Booysen & Nkomo, 2010). Apartheid ensured the White minority population enjoyed a privileged economic and political status. But it also effectively embedded an ideology of racialism – a belief in essentialized differences between races and ethnic groups (Mare, 2005). Racial division was accompanied by patriarchy, with women of all races subordinate to males (Booysen & Nkomo, 2010).

In 1994, after a long protracted struggle, apartheid ended with the election of a democratic government led by Nelson Mandela. The formation of a new united national identity in contradistinction to the former doctrine of racial separateness was clearly articulated in the preamble of the constitution adopted on May 8, 1996:

> We, the people of South Africa, recognise the injustices of the past; honour those who have worked for justice and freedom in our land; respect those who have worked to build and develop our country, *and believe that South Africa belongs to all who live in it, united in our diversity.*
>
> (Constitution of South Africa, 1996,
> Preamble, emphasis added)

Non-racialism and non-sexism are explicitly referred to in Chapter 1. A number of laws have been passed since 1996 in an effort to achieve the ideals established in the constitution. Most relevant to the present discussion are the Employment Equity Act of 1998 and a series of laws pertaining to Black economic empowerment.

The goal of the Employment Equity Act is to achieve employment equity by (a) promoting equal opportunity and fair treatment in employment through the elimination of unfair discrimination; and (b) implementing affirmative action to redress the disadvantages in employment experienced by designated groups (Africans, coloureds, Indians, persons with disabilities and women), in order to ensure their equitable representation in all occupational categories and levels in the workplace (Employment Equity Act, 1998). Achieving the latter remains a challenge for a majority of organizations in South Africa. Recent employment data from the Employment Equity Commission suggest slow transformation of the workplace (Department of Labour, 2012). The Black Economic Empowerment Act of 2003 (BEE) and subsequent amendments in 2004, 2007 and 2011 are aimed at increasing Black ownership of businesses and control over the economy. Yet, Black Economic Empowerment has been heavily criticized for its failure to substantively increase Black ownership of economic wealth (Booysen & Nkomo, 2010).

On a relative basis, South Africa has a greater relative degree of demographic diversity in terms of ethnic, cultural and linguistic pluralism compared to the United States. According to the latest census figures, South Africa has a population of just under 52 million people. Blacks comprise 79.7% of the population while Whites represent 8.9%, followed by coloureds at 8.9% and Asians representing 2.5% (Statistics, South Africa, 2011). Although the country is composed of 31 different cultures, the government recognizes only 11 official languages. The national anthem comprises three different languages and also symbolizes South Africa's intent to embrace its cultural diversity. Although the majority population groups are defined as Blacks, Whites, coloureds and Asians/Indians within each group, there are also ethnic classifications. For example, among Blacks the government officially recognizes nine major languages (ethnic groups): Sepedi, Sesotho, Setwana, siSwati, Tshivenda, Xitsonga, isiNedebele, isiXhosa and isiZulu. Whites are not a homogeneous group. There are the Afrikaans speaking Whites (descendants of the original Dutch settlers) and English speaking Whites (the descendants of the British colonists). In fact, there is a long-standing animosity between the two groups emanating from the Boer War and political ideology differences. Included within the Asian category are Indians who are descendants of Indian indentured servants brought to South Africa in the mid-nineteenth century as well as those who came as what is known as 'passenger Indians' and a small population of Chinese immigrants. Consequently, even though the government has collapsed the South African ethnic groups into four major groups, the finer distinctions among the groups still affect intergroup relations in the workplace (Bornman, 2010).

DIVERSITY IDEOLOGY DEBATE

The diversity ideology debate in South Africa has revolved around two major unresolved tensions since the end of apartheid. First, there is tension between the goal of achieving non-racialism as expressed in the constitution and the need to specifically acknowledge race in order to redress the inequalities and injustices of the past. The effort to achieve non-racialism has been complicated by one of the most striking differences between the South African and United States as well as other Western contexts in respect to issues of difference. In the latter contexts, the goal is the inclusion of a minority both in terms of demographic representation and access to economic and political power (Finchilescu & Tredoux, 2010). The situation is quite different in South Africa. The emphasis is on ensuring the majority of the population gains access to jobs and other economic opportunities (Dupper, 2004) or what scholars refer to as substantive equality – taking cognisance of structural inequality in South African society and attempting to remedy this inequality (Coetzer, 2009). No doubt some progress has been made in restructuring South African society and its major institutions. However, despite the fact that Blacks in South Africa have gained political power, they still experience inequality in the workplace and other aspects of economic opportunity (Booysen, 2007). Recent figures from the annual Commission on Employment Equity Report suggest the legacy of apartheid continues to be reflected in the representation of different racial groups in middle and top management levels (Department of Labour, 2012). Consequently, multiculturalism and colorblindness are less prominent in diversity debates. Instead, transformation and redress dominate the discourse of diversity. Transformation and redress focus on the attainment of equity and equality – changing the workplace representation of the historically disadvantaged.

The main mechanism for redress in the South African workplace has been the Employment Equity Act of 1998. As previously noted, the Act called for affirmative action as a tool to achieve equity in the workplace. Since its inception, affirmative action in South Africa has been contested primarily by the white minority as unfair and as being in conflict with the goals of a non-racial society (Dupper & Garbers, 2009). Many of the arguments against affirmative action evoked in the United States are echoed in the research findings in South Africa. A number of studies have shown that White South African attitudes toward affirmative action and preferential treatment are largely negative (e.g., Oosthuizen & Naidoo, 2010; Wambugu, 2005). Whites generally believe affirmative action is a form of reverse discrimination and that qualified Whites are being disadvantaged to make way for less competent Blacks (Coetzee & Bezuidenhout, 2011; Steyn & Foster, 2008). Some research also indicates that Whites view themselves as victims of affirmative action policies (e.g. Heinecken, 2009). Cumulatively, the research suggests the White minority believes affirmative action contradicts the principles of individual merit and reward for hard work. On the other hand, research suggests Blacks do not question the need for affirmative action but express negativity in respect to its poor implementation and slow results (Hoog, Siebers, & Linde, 2011; Janse van Rensburg & Roodt, 2005; Motileng, Wagner, & Cassimjee, 2006; Zulu & Parumasur, 2009). Blacks also express concern about the unwanted effects of affirmative action that include stigmatization and constantly having to prove themselves (Hoog et al., 2011).

In sum, the doctrine of non-racialism expressed in the Constitution remains a difficult ideology to achieve in practice. The use of racial and ethnic identification continues to be an everyday feature of the South African workplace. For example, companies are required to develop annual equity plans (as required by the Employment Equity Act) and to prepare Black Economic Empowerment Scorecards that indicate the degree to which Blacks and other previously disadvantaged groups have been incorporated as equity partners and suppliers. The slow progress of workplace transformation has become a major concern with calls from Black labour unions and government for even stronger measures to achieve redress (Habib & Bentley, 2008).

The second tension that exists between the goals of entrenching a superordinate South African national identity emphasizes unity among South Africa's diverse people and versus particularism, where cultural differences are acknowledged. The latter goal was aptly referred to by Bishop Desmond Tutu as a 'Rainbow Nation' and can be viewed as South Africa's notion of multiculturalism. As noted by Bornman (2010), this goal was the natural response to the fragmented society created doing apartheid where the population was separated by race and culture. Some scholars argue the notion of a South African superordinate identity is at best tenuous because of the deep scars inflicted by apartheid (Mare, 2005, p. 502). They suggest that the glaring inequities between socioeconomic status of Blacks and Whites impede the quest for an umbrella national identity that all race and ethnics groups can accept (Erasmus, 2010; Mare, 2005). Still others such as Horowitz (1991) contend that a sense of shared national identity within diverse societies might be better achieved by accommodating rather than neglecting or excluding various cultural groups.

A number of recent social psychological studies point to how social identification among the various race and ethnic groups has changed over time. Bornman (2010) compared ethnic group views in 1994, 1998 and 2001. Her 2001 results suggest that despite the overall high levels of pride in being South African, subnational group identities remain important. The initial embracement of a harmonious multicultural 'Rainbow Nation' has waned among Afrikaans-speaking Whites compared with other groups (Bornman, 2010). Bornman (2010, p. 251) attributed this change to their loss of political power. Identification with their racial and ethnic group, and the notion of the South African 'Rainbow Nation' remained important to Blacks according to her research. She found, however, identification with African culture has also become a primary identity. For Blacks, reaffirmation of their African cultural roots has emerged as a powerful source of identity. This is probably explained by the emphasis placed on ideas such as the African Renaissance and Africanism expounded by former President Thabo Mbeki who succeeded Nelson Mandela's presidency (Bornman, 2010). On the one hand, according to Bornman (2010), Blacks identify strongly with both their ethnic and racial group as well as having high pride in being South African, while coloureds, on the other hand, did not identify particularly strongly with any subgroup identity and instead strongly embraced a South African national identity. Bornman (2010) concluded fostering an ideology of a national identity remains important but the existence of diverse subnational identities should not be ignored.

Gibson and Claassen (2010) found in their research that the Black majority has become less reconciled with Whites over the period from 2001 to 2004 although improvement in racial attitudes was observed among the other three groups (i.e. Whites, Indians and coloureds). They concluded that their results offer a mixed view of the extent to which multiculturalism has been embraced within South Africa. Durheim and Dixon (2010) examined attitudes toward racial integration and found White hostility toward other groups has decreased but at the same time there is resistance to policies aimed at achieving equity.

CONCLUSION

In 1994, the African National Congress adopted a 'unity through diversity' approach to its cultural diversity. The ANC reasoned that 'we must seek to provide people with the space to express their multiple identities in ways that foster the evolution of a broader South Africanism as their primary identity' (African National Congress (ANC), 1997). Within South Africa, government discourse has generally refrained from using the term 'multiculturalism' (Stinson, 2009). Indeed, South Africa's approach has been dubbed 'rainbow nation multiculturalism' accompanied by the hope of a unified national identity (Stinson, 2009, p. 22). South Africa's particular brand of multiculturalism might better be described as interculturalism – the aim to balance the recognition and protection of cultural diversity with the functional need for strong shared national values and identity (Stinson, 2009). The situation in South Africa is also complicated by the constitution's recognition of customary or traditional laws of different cultural/ethnic and religious groups. For example, Muslim Personal Law is legally recognized (Domingo, 2011).

Scholars have noted that the challenges South Africa faces in its post-apartheid period are similar to a general problem of other post-independent countries in Africa of how to balance the recognition of ethnic groups with the imperatives of an envisaged nationhood (Dersso, 2008; Ramutsindela, 2001, p. 70; Stinson, 2009). According to Dersso (2008, p. 567), 'what makes this problem particularly formidable is that almost all African states, as products of colonial adventurism in state making, are made of numerous and unequal communities with their own separate culture, language and history'. Nation building became the top agenda of most post-colonial African states as a countermeasure to fragmentation and the need for economic growth and stability (Dersso, 2008).

Despite the emphasis on building a South African national identity, recent social psychology research suggests ethno-cultural ties continue to be a major source of identity for many people in South Africa. In other words, the delicate balance the new government attempted to achieve between 'rainbow multiculturalism' and erasing historical status disparities among South Africans remains a challenge. Most societies that embrace the concept of multiculturalism rely upon the principle of equality of opportunity. South Africa, while establishing equality and protection of individual rights in its constitution, had to also tackle redress to over-come the inequities of the past. South Africa remains one of the most unequal societies in the world; and these continuing social and economic inequalities create faultlines that often reflect the historical divisions between Blacks and Whites during apartheid (Erasmus, 2010; Mare, 2005). Race and ethnicity remain powerful in the lives of everyday South Africans despite a desire for a non-racialized state (Seekings, 2008). Some social psychologists argue that non-racialism and unity can only move from a dream to a reality when redress has been achieved (Erasmus, 2010). Clearly, within the present South African context, colorblindness is not an option as long as there is wide-scale inequality among racioethnic groups (Booysen & Nkomo, 2010).

The current tensions described in this chapter are also reflected in how organizations in South Africa have addressed diversity and transformation. In a recent study of private and public organizations in South Africa Steyn and Kelly (2010) found minimal understanding of the importance of valuing diversity in organizations. Instead, the dominant approach was a compliance motivated response to the Employment Equity Act. Management, for the most part, focused on achieving numerical targets or what Thomas and Ely (1996) described as the discrimination and fairness paradigm. The research also found what might be called cultural awareness interventions including artefacts of different ethnic groups and cultural diversity days where employees sample the food and customs of other cultures (Steyn & Kelly, 2010). Generally, few organizations in South Africa have evolved to the learning and effectiveness paradigm espoused by Thomas and Ely (1996).

As Mare (2005) has noted on the surface, symbolically South Africans have on occasion rallied around a common national identity (e.g. the 2010 World Cup) and have shown interest in the diversity of cultures within the country. But these moments do not appear to have been sustained as the tensions between redress and national unity regularly re-merge. Both ideologies and social identities are not stagnant but evolve and change over time. Thus, whether South African society and its workplace will be able to fashion a diversity ideology that embodies 'rainbow multiculturalism' remains to be seen.

NOTE

1. South Africa's form of colonialism has been described as settler colonialism because the Dutch colonizers became settlers in the country, unlike other forms of colonialism (Loomba, 2005).

REFERENCES

African National Congress. (1997). ANC 50th National Conference Resolution on the National Question. *ANC 50th National Congress, Mafeking, 1997*. Retrieved from www.anc.org/za/ancdocs/ubs/umrabulo/8/umrabulo8d.html

Bekker, S. (1999). Introduction: Recent development in identity studies. In S. Bekker, & R. Prinsloo (Eds.), *Identity? Theory, politics, history* (pp. 1–9). Pretoria, South Africa: Human Sciences Research Council.

Bekker, S., & Leildé, A. (2003). Is multiculturalism a workable policy in South Africa? *International Journal of Multicultural Societies, 5*(2), 199–134.

Booysen, L. (2007). Societal power shifts and changing social identities in South Africa: Workplace implications. *South African Journal of Economic and Management Science, 10*(1), 1–20.

Booysen, A. E., & Nkomo, S. M. (2010). Employment equity and diversity management in South Africa. In Klarsfeld, A. (Ed.). *International handbook of diversity management at work: Country perspectives on diversity and equal treatment* (pp. 218–243). Cheltenham: Edward Elgar.

Bornman, E. (2010). Emerging patterns of social identification in post-apartheid South Africa. *Journal of Social Issues, 66*(2), 237–254.

Coetzee, B., & Bezuidenhout, M. (2011). The fairness of affirmative action: In the eye of the beholder. *Southern Africa Business Review, 15*(2), 75–95.

Coetzer, N. (2009). Affirmative action: The sword versus the shield debate continues. *South African Mercantile Law Journal, 21*, 92–101.

Constitution of South Africa. (1996). Pretoria: South Africa.

Department of Labour. (2012). *11th CEE Annual Report 2010–2011*. Johannesburg, South Africa.

Domingo, W. (2011). Muslim personal law in South Africa: Until two legal systems do us part or meet? *Obiter*, 378–392.

Dersso, S. A. (2008). Constitutional accommodation of ethno-cultural diversity in the post-colonial African state. *South African Journal of Human Rights, 24*(3), 656–592.

Dupper, O. (2004). In defence of affirmative action. *South African Law Journal, 121*, 187–215.

Dupper, O., & Garbers, C. (Eds.). (2009). *Equality in the workplace: Reflections from South Africa and beyond*. Cape Town: Juta.

Durheim, K., & Dixon, J. A. (2010). Racial contact and change in South Africa. *Journal of Social Issues, 66*, 389–402.

Employment Equity Act 55 of 1998. Pretoria: Government Printer.

Erasmus, A. (2010). Contact theory: Too timid for 'race' and racism. *Journal of Social Issues, 66*(2), 387–400.

Finchilescu G., & Tredoux, C. (2010). The changing landscape of intergroup relations in South Africa. *Journal of Social Issues, 66*(2), 223–236.

Gibson, J. L., & Claassen, C. (2010). Racial reconciliation in South Africa: Interracial contact and changes over time. *Journal of Social Issues, 66*(2), 255–272.

Habib, A., & Bentley, K. (2008). *Racial redress and citizenship in South Africa*. Pretoria: HRSC Press.

Heinecken, L. (2009). A diverse society, a representative military? The complexity of managing diversity in the South African armed forces. *Scientia Militaria: SA Journal of Military Studies, 37*(1), 25–49.

Hoog, C. O., Siebers, H., & Linde, B. (2011). Affirmed identities? The experience of black middle managers dealing with affirmative action and equal opportunity policies at a South African mine. *South African Journal of Labour Relations, 34*(2), 60–82.

Horowitz, D. L. (1991). *A democratic South Africa? Constitutional engineering in a divided society.* Berkeley, CA: University of California Press.

Janse van Rensburg, K., & Roodt, G. (2005). Perceptions of employment equity and black economic empowerment as predictors of organisation related commitment. *South African Journal of Human Resource Management, 3*(3), 49–60.

Janssens, M., & Zanoni, P. (2005) 'Many diversities for many services': Theorizing diversity (management) in service companies, *Human Relations, 58*(3), 311–40.

Klarsfield, A. (Ed.). (2010). *International handbook of diversity management at work: Country perspectives on diversity and equal treatment.* Cheltenham: Edward Elgar.

Loomba, A. (2005). *Colonialism/postcolonialism.* London: Palgrave.

Mare, G. (2005). Race, nation, democracy: Questioning patriotism in the new South Africa. *Social Research, 72*(3), 501–530.

Motileng, B. B., Wagner, C., & Cassimjee, N. (2006). Black middle managers' experience of affirmative action in a media company. *South African Journal of Industrial Psychology, 32*(1), 11–16.

Nishii, L. H., & Özbilgin, M. F. (2007). Global diversity management: Towards a conceptual framework. *International Journal of Human Resource Management, 18*(11), 1883–1894.

Oosthuizen, R. M., & Naidoo, V. (2010). Attitudes towards and experience of employment equity. *SA Journal of Industrial Psychology/SA, 36*(1), 836–844.

Plaut, V. C. (2010). Diversity in science: Why and how difference makes a difference. *Psychological Inquiry, 21,* 77–99.

Prasad, P., Pringle, J. K., & Konrad, A. M. (2006). Examining the contours of workplace diversity: Concepts, contexts and challenges. In A. M. Konrad, P. Prasad, & J. K. Pringle (Eds.), *Handbook of workplace diversity.* London: Sage.

Ramutsindela, M. (2001). Down the post-colonial road: Reconstructing the post-apartheid state in South Africa. *Political Geography, 20,* 57–84.

Rex, J., & Singh, G. (2003). Pluralism and multiculturalism in colonial and post-colonial society—thematic introduction. In M. Koenig (Ed.), *Pluralism and multiculturalism in colonial and post-colonial societies. International Journal on Multicultural Societies, 5*(2), 106–118.

Risberg, A., & Søderberg, A.-M. (2008). Translating a management concept: Diversity management in Denmark. *Gender in Management, 23*(6), 426–441.

Seekings, J. (2008). The continuing salience of race: Discrimination and diversity in South Africa. *Journal of Contemporary African Studies, 26*(1), 1–25.

Statistics South Africa (2011). Statistical release (revised) PO 301.4. Pretoria: Statistics South Africa.

Steyn, M., & Foster, D. (2008). Repertoires of talking white: Resistant whiteness in post-apartheid South Africa. *Ethnic and racial studies, 31*(1), 25–51.

Steyn, M., & Kelly, C. (2010). *Widening circles: Case studies of transformation: Consolidated report of DEISA case studies.* Cape Town: Incudisa.

Stinson, A. T. (2009). National identity and nation building in post-apartheid South Africa. Unpublished thesis, Rhodes University.

Thomas, D. A., & Ely, R. D. (1996). Making differences matter: A new paradigm for managing diversity. *Harvard Business Review,* Sept–Oct, 79–90.

Wambugu, J. N. (2005). When tables turn: Discursive constructions of whites as victims of affirmative action in a post-apartheid South Africa. *Psychology in Society, 31*, 57–70.

Zanoni, P., Janssens, M., Benschop, Y., & Nkomo, S. M. (2010). Unpacking diversity, grasping inequality: Rethinking difference through critical perspectives. *Organization: The Critical Journal of Organization, Theory and Society, 17*(1), 9–29.

Zulu, P. S., & Parumasur, S. B. (2009). Employee perceptions of the management of cultural diversity in the workplace transformation. *SA Journal of Industrial Psychology, 35*(1), 1–9.

Author Index

Subject Index